DEVELOPMENT OF PERCEPTION

VOLUME 2
THE VISUAL SYSTEM

BEHAVIORAL BIOLOGY

AN INTERNATIONAL SERIES

Series editors

James L. McGaugh

Department of Psychobiology
University of California
Irvine, California

John C. Fentress

Department of Psychology
Dalhousie University
Halifax, Canada

Joseph P. Hegmann

Department of Zoology
The University of Iowa
Iowa City, Iowa

Holger Ursin, Eivind Baade, and Seymour Levine (Editors), Psychobiology of Stress: A Study of Coping Men

William W. Grings and Michael E. Dawson, Emotions and Bodily Responses: A Psychophysiological Approach

Enoch Callaway, Patricia Tueting, and Stephen H. Koslow (Editors), Event Related Brain Potentials in Man

Larry L. Butcher (Editor), Cholinergic–Monoaminergic Interactions in the Brain

Aryeh Routtenberg (Editor), Biology of Reinforcement: Facets of Brain-Stimulation Reward

Richard N. Aslin, Jeffrey R. Alberts, and Michael R. Petersen (Editors), Development of Perception: Psychobiological Perspectives. Vol. 1: Audition, Somatic Perception, and the Chemical Senses; Vol. 2: The Visual System

In Preparation

J. L. Martinez, Jr., R. A. Jensen, R. B. Messing, H. Rigter, and J. L. McGaugh (Editors), Endogenous Peptides and Learning and Memory Processes

DEVELOPMENT
OF PERCEPTION

Psychobiological Perspectives
VOLUME 2
The Visual System

Edited by

RICHARD N. ASLIN
JEFFREY R. ALBERTS
MICHAEL R. PETERSEN
Department of Psychology
Indiana University
Bloomington, Indiana

ACADEMIC PRESS
A Subsidiary of Harcourt Brace Jovanovich, Publishers
New York   London   Toronto   Sydney   San Francisco   1981

ACADEMIC PRESS, INC.
111 Fifth Avenue, New York, New York 10003

United Kingdom Edition published by
ACADEMIC PRESS, INC. (LONDON) LTD.
24/28 Oval Road, London NW1   7DX

Library of Congress Cataloging in Publication Data
Main entry under title:

Development of perception.

    (Behavioral biology)
    Includes bibliographies and index.
    Contents: v. 2. The visual system.
    1. Visual perception. 2. Neuropsychology. 3. Devel-
opmental psychobiology. I. Aslin, Richard N. II. Alberts,
Jeffrey R. III. Petersen, Michael R. IV. Series:
Behavioral biology (New York, N. Y. : 1978) [DNLM:
1. Visual perception. Wl 705 D489]
QP491.D47   152.1'4   81-7946
ISBN 0-12-065302-8   AACR2

PRINTED IN THE UNITED STATES OF AMERICA

81 82 83 84   9 8 7 6 5 4 3 2 1

Contents

PART B   ANIMAL STUDIES OF VISUAL DEVELOPMENT, 111

4   Development of the Visual System
    and Visually Guided Behavior
    THOMAS T. NORTON

    I. Introduction, 113
    II. Onset of Visually Guided Behaviors, 118
    III. Improvement of Visually Guided Behaviors, 122
    IV. The State of the Visual System at Eye Opening, 124
    V. Sequence of Receptive-Field Development in the Visual System, 137
    VI. Correlation of Receptive-Field Development
            with Behavioral Development, 147
        References, 152

5   Maturation of the Superior Colliculus
    BARRY E. STEIN AND BARBARA GORDON

6   Animal Models of Visual Development: Behavioral Evaluation of
    Some Physiological Findings in Cat Visual Development
    MARK A. BERKLEY

Contributors

Numbers in parentheses indicate the pages on which the authors' contributions begin.

RICHARD N. ASLIN (45), Department of Psychology, Indiana University, Bloomington, Indiana 47405

JANETTE ATKINSON (245), Kenneth Craik Laboratory, Department of Experimental Psychology, University of Cambridge, Cambridge CB2 3EB, England

MARK A. BERKLEY (197), Department of Psychology, Florida State University, Tallahassee, Florida 32306

RANDOLPH BLAKE (95), Cresap Neuroscience Laboratory, Department of Psychology, Northwestern University, Evanston, Illinois 60201

RONALD G. BOOTHE (217), Infant Primate Laboratory, Department of Psychology, University of Washington, Seattle, Washington 98195

OLIVER BRADDICK (245), Kenneth Craik Laboratory, Department of Experimental Psychology, University of Cambridge, Cambridge CB2 3EB, England

ROBERT FOX (335), Department of Psychology, Vanderbilt University, Nashville, Tennessee 37240

BARBARA GORDON (157), Department of Psychology, University of Oregon, Eugene, Oregon 97403

RICHARD HELD (279), Department of Psychology, Massachusetts Institute of Technology, Cambridge, Massachusetts 02139

DONALD E. MITCHELL* (3), National Vision Research Institute of Australia, Carlton, Victoria 3053, Australia

* Present address: Department of Psychology, Dalhousie University, Halifax, Nova Scotia B3H 4J1, Canada.

THOMAS T. NORTON (113), Department of Physiological Optics, School of Optometry/The Medical Center, The University of Alabama in Birmingham, Birmingham, Alabama 35294

BARRY E. STEIN (157), Department of Physiology, Medical College of Virginia, Richmond, Virginia 23298

DAVIDA Y. TELLER (297), Department of Psychology, University of Washington, Seattle, Washington 98195

ALBERT YONAS (313), Institute of Child Development, University of Minnesota, Minneapolis, Minnesota 55455

General Preface

The study of perceptual development has been approached from many different levels (from neurons to behavior), in different sensory modalities, and in a wide variety of species, and contemporary research has tended to travel down increasingly esoteric and reductionistic paths. Thus, articles, books, and research strategies are organized around rarified techniques, particular sensory modalities, or singular levels of analysis. We believe there is much to be gained by looking at perceptual development as a more broadly defined "field." Stepping back from the idiosyncracies of our own research and seeking out the commonalities that have been found across species and sensory modalities, we hope that overriding organizational principles will emerge to guide future research. The chapters in these volumes, disparate in origin and discipline, reflect a new surge of interest and activity in what can indeed be considered a field of scientific inquiry: the development of perception.

This two-volume set is a unique assemblage of chapters covering vision, audition, olfaction, taste, tactile sensitivity, and sensory-motor activity during ontogenesis. The chapters provide a comprehensive collection of overviews and an assortment of case histories that summarize the progress made in recent years. Within each sensory modality or content area there are different levels of analysis, varied research goals, and distinctive blends of theoretical integration. Our bias, as reflected in the title of this work, is to emphasize approaches to perceptual development that incorporate a psychobiological perspective, a term that we define to include analyses of phenomena at the mechanistic, physiological, behavioral, and evolutionary levels. Accordingly, the discussion of sensory and perceptual development must involve consideration of the multileveled network of causal factors that generate a unique, yet species-typical, organism. Studies of nonhuman species are essential, not only for ethical and methodological reasons, but also because the comparative approach allows us to take advantage of "natural experiments"—instances in which the timing, degree, and function of different developmental events can be varied by the appropriate choice of species. We hope that this broadened perspective will open new vistas for inquiry and encourage new methodologies with which we can address the persistent questions of perceptual development.

Acknowledgments

Many of the chapters in these volumes are outgrowths of a four-day meeting, the Brown County Conference, held in Nashville, Indiana, during October 7–12, 1979. More than sixty researchers from the United States, Canada, England, and Australia were assembled to share their data and thoughts on the complex interactions between genetic and experiential factors in determining the course of perceptual development. We want to thank the many people who made both the conference and the book possible. Support for the conference was provided by grants from the National Science Foundation (BNS 79-06204) and the Sloan Foundation (B1979-12). To those agencies we express our sincere appreciation. The mechanics of the conference were organized and coordinated in large part by Nancy Layman, who also provided invaluable assistance in the preparation of manuscripts during the succeeding months. We are most grateful for her efforts. Special thanks are also due to David Pisoni, one of the primary instigators of the conference, who helped to obtain funding and to oversee many of the organizational duties. Finally, we thank the graduate students at Indiana University who devoted their time and effort as hosts and shuttle bus drivers.

Preface

This volume brings together a number of topics of critical importance to the process of understanding the visual system. It is organized into three parts, each focusing on a broad set of questions in visual development. Part A includes three chapters (Mitchell, Aslin, and Blake) that are addressed to the theoretical and interpretive issues involved in designing and drawing conclusions from research on the development of the visual system. In Part B, Norton, Stein and Gordon, Berkley, and Boothe review the neural and behavioral characteristics of the cat and monkey visual system during the early postnatal period. In Part C, Atkinson and Braddick, Held, Teller, Yonas, and Fox review recent findings on the development of visual functioning in human infants. Together, these three parts offer a comprehensive coverage of major issues in the structure and function of the developing mammalian visual system. In each chapter, the *behavioral* consequences of developing visual functions are emphasized, an emphasis that in recent years has been overwhelmed by a push toward more reductionistic approaches to the study of the visual system.

Contents of Volume 1
Audition, Somatic Perception, and the Chemical Senses

DEVELOPMENT OF PERCEPTION

VOLUME 2
THE VISUAL SYSTEM

Theoretical and Interpretive Issues

The visual system has provided researchers with a rich source of data, as well as a model system for studies of other sensory modalities. The *development* of the visual system, both at the neural and behavioral levels, has likewise been a topic of considerable interest. A developmental perspective not only provides information concerning the ontogeny of structures and functions, but it also constrains the types of processes that might be proposed as underlying the adult visual system. As a result of the abundant data base that has emerged over the past two decades, theoretical issues in visual development have been formulated and refined; these issues both guide research programs and offer explanations of complex developmental phenomena. For example, the concept of a sensitive period (Hubel & Weisel, 1970) has generated a wide variety of research directed to issues at the neurochemical, electrophysiological, behavioral, and perceptual levels (see reviews in Held, Leibowitz, & Teuber, 1978, and Schmitt & Worden, 1974).

As in any area of science, theoretical principles, as well as methodological and interpretive issues, can greatly influence the types of questions asked by researchers studying visual development. Moreover, a theoretical perspective can assist in the organization of data bases into coherent descriptive and explanatory systems. In the past few years there has been an awakening of interest in conceptual and theoretical problems pertinent to the understanding of development in general and perceptual development in particular. The three chapters in this first section confront three of the major issues that have arisen in the study of visual development during the past decade (see also Freeman, 1979). Mitchell (Chapter 1) reviews the concept of a sensitive period in the visual development of neural and behavioral systems. Aslin (Chapter 2) offers a model of the manner in which experience influences the course of perceptual development. Finally, Blake (Chapter 3) tackles the difficult issue of how we can draw meaningful conclusions concerning the mechanisms underlying perceptual and behavioral development from studies of deficient neural systems. It will become apparent that these discussions reach beyond any single perceptual system or sensory modality. The concepts, theoretical considerations, and interpretive issues pertain to virtually all contemporary research in perceptual development.

REFERENCES

Freeman, R. D. (Ed.), *Developmental neurobiology of vision.* New York: Plenum Press, 1979.
Held, R., Leibowitz, H., & Teuber, H. L. (Eds.), *Handbook of sensory physiology.* Volume VIII. New York: Springer-Verlag, 1978.
Hubel, D. H., & Wiesel, T. N. The period of susceptibility to the physiological effects of unilateral eye closure in kittens. *Journal of Physiology (London),* 1970, **206,** 419–436.
Schmitt, F. O., & Worden, F. G. (Eds.), *The neurosciences: Third study program.* Cambridge, Massachusetts: M.I.T. Press, 1974.

1

Sensitive Periods in Visual Development

Donald E. Mitchell
National Vision Research Institute of Australia

I. INTRODUCTION

The notion of a "sensitive" or "critical" period in visual development has been one of the central concepts to emerge over the last 15 years from the many studies on the effects of various manipulations of the early visual input on the development of the visual pathways. Although there are obvious clinical antecedents (Duke-Elder & Wybar, 1973), the conviction that visual experience can exert a greater influence on the

3

DEVELOPMENT OF PERCEPTION
Volume 2

development of the visual pathways at certain stages of life than at others, arose from Hubel and Wiesel's observations on the effects of periods of monocular occlusion imposed on animals of different ages (Hubel & Wiesel, 1970; Wiesel & Hubel, 1963). However, as they pointed out, the observation of a restricted period of sensitivity to abnormal experience is by no means new: The concept of sensitive, critical, or susceptible periods in development is, in fact, deeply rooted in a number of different areas of research. Although other terms have been coined, such as critical moments, optimal or impressionable periods, or vulnerable or crucial stages, the underlying idea is the same; namely, that certain characteristics or behaviors of an animal can be influenced by environmental factors to a greater extent at one stage of development than at any other later stage. The concept of sensitive periods in development originated in embryology (e.g., Stockard, 1921) but it has subsequently permitted an understanding of a wide range of phenomena in behavioral development, especially those of imprinting and socialization (e.g., Scott, 1978; Sluckin, 1972). The concept of sensitive periods has now been incorporated into accounts of development in a diverse range of other phenomena. For example, malnourishment or teratogenic agents have permanent stunting effects on brain and somatic growth and function if present during certain crucial stages of development, but not at other times (e.g., Dobbing, 1968, 1976; Widdowson & McCance, 1960). Similarly, the masculinizing influence of androgens on rodents and monkeys is only found at particular times in life (e.g., Goldman, 1978). Finally, it has been known for some time that there is a sensitive period for the development of bird song (e.g., Konishi, 1978; Thorpe, 1961b). Systematic surveys of the evidence for sensitive periods in development have been made by Thorpe (1961a), Scott (1962), and Hess (1973), and Bateson (1979) has provided a most readable discussion of the general issue of sensitive periods in behavioral development.

In this chapter, I shall examine the experimental evidence for sensitive period(s) in visual development as well as recent experiments that challenge current opinion concerning the duration and nature of the period of susceptibility of the visual cortex to various forms of early visual deprivation. Some of the issues raised by these latter experiments find parallels with well established principles of the concept of sensitive periods in other disciplines. The chapter concludes with some speculation concerning the general principles that may be employed to delineate the duration of the sensitive period in visual development in species that have not been analyzed as extensively as the cat and monkey. Any review of sensitive periods in visual development naturally touches upon the old debate concerning the role that visual experience plays in visual cortical development and perception. The reader is referred to a number of reviews for a more complete account of the issues involved in this dispute (e.g., Barlow, 1975; Blakemore, 1978; Grobstein & Chow, 1975; Morgan, 1977; Movshon & Van Sluyters, 1981; Pettigrew, 1978).

II. DELINEATION OF SENSITIVE PERIODS IN VISUAL DEVELOPMENT

Prior to describing the experimental evidence for sensitive periods in visual development, it is helpful to discuss the assumptions that underlie the general experimental approaches that have been employed in the past to provide this evidence. Three basic approaches have been used to determine the duration of the sensitive period in visual cortical development that can be defined as the period during which neural connections in the visual cortex can be altered by manipulation of visual input. The first two of these approaches follow directly from this definition, whereas the third is an indirect approach.

A. Imposition of Fixed Periods of Deprivation

The first, and most common approach, as well as the one that is closest to the term "sensitive period" itself, is derived from examination of the effects of periods of abnormal visual exposure imposed on animals of different ages. This was the experimental design employed by Hubel and Wiesel (1970) in their pioneering investigation of the period of susceptibility of binocular connections in the visual cortex to monocular visual deprivation. If the duration of the period of anomalous visual exposure is held constant across animals, this method has the additional advantage of providing information concerning the *degree* of susceptibility of the visual cortex to deprivation at different ages. With the exception of the studies by Olson and Freeman (1978, 1980), Freeman (1978), and Wilkinson (1980), the majority of investigators that have employed this approach, including Hubel and Wiesel (1970), have imposed periods of deprivation of widely different durations on animals at various ages. Whereas this may assist in the determination of the physiological effects of the period of deprivation, it makes it difficult to assess the profile of the sensitive period of the cortex to the particular deprivation condition in question. The principle of the approach is well illustrated by the recent results of Olson and Freeman (1980) shown in Fig. 1.1, in which an index of the physiological effect of a fixed

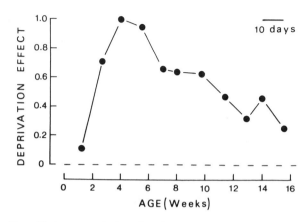

Fig. 1.1 The effects on cortical ocular dominance (ordinate) of a short period of monocular occlusion of 10–12 days duration imposed on kittens at different ages. Recordings were always made from the visual cortex ipsilateral to the formerly occluded eye. The physiological effects of the period of deprivation on each animal are given in the form of an index defined as the percentage of cortical neurons dominated by the deprived (ipsilateral) eye ($[(\%$ cells in Groups 5–7) $- N]/[100\% - N]$, where N was the average for four normal kittens of the percentage of cells in Groups 5–7 [36%]). The horizontal bar depicts the duration of the period of deprivation (10 days). (Redrawn from Olson & Freeman, 1980.)

period of 10–12 days duration of monocular occlusion imposed on various animals at different ages is plotted as a function of the age of the animals at the time it was imposed.

B. Imposition of Reverse Deprivation at Different Ages

The second approach, first employed by Hubel and Wiesel (1965), and later more extensively by Blakemore and Van Sluyters (1974), is to examine the extent of any recovery from the anatomical, physiological, or behavioral effects of an early period of visual deprivation following restoration of either normal visual input, or the imposition of a second period of what could be termed "reverse" deprivation, a period of visual exposure that is biased in the opposite direction to the visual exposure imposed during the initial period of deprivation. Underlying this general approach is the assumption that the sensitive period is not only a period in the animal's life during which the visual pathways can be altered by visual experience, but that it is also a period during which the neural connections formed during a prior period of biased visual exposure can be altered subsequently following either the restoration of normal visual input or by the imposition of a second period of biased visual exposure. This particular design has been employed for delineating the sensitive period for the effects of monocular deprivation in kittens (Blakemore & Van Sluyters, 1974) and for the effect of exposure to unidirectional motion (Daw & Wyatt, 1976). The design of the former study is illustrated diagrammatically in Fig. 1.2. The right eyes of five kittens were monocularly deprived by eyelid suture from the time of natural eye opening (8–10 days) until the ages shown, at which point they were subjected to reverse deprivation by reversal of the eyelid suture, so that at the time the initially sutured eyelids of the deprived eye were opened, those of the other eye were sutured shut. This is analogous to the common clinical practice of "patching" in amblyopia where the child is forced to employ the amblyopic eye by occluding the normal eye. Although the particular experimental design employed by Blakemore and Van Sluyters (1974) utilized a constant period (9 weeks) of reverse occlusion for each animal, the length of the initial period of deprivation was different. Because the age of reverse suture is thus confounded with the length of the initial period of deprivation, their particular design makes it difficult to define accurately the time course of the latter part of the sensitive period.

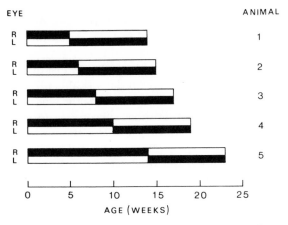

Fig. 1.2 The design of the experiment of Blakemore and Van Sluyters (1974). The horizontal bars represent the visual histories of each of five kittens whose right eyes were occluded by eyelid suture from near birth until the ages shown, at which time they were reverse sutured. Each animal received 9 weeks of vision using its right eye during the period of reverse suture, when the left eyelids were closed. Physiological recordings were made from the right visual cortex immediately following the 9-week period of reverse suture.

Although not widely utilized, experiments in which visual input is simply restored to both eyes following an initial period of deprivation can also assess the duration of the sensitive period. It is known, for example, that considerable recovery can occur from the effects of a period of monocular deprivation following restoration of visual input to the initially deprived eye without any concurrent obstruction being placed upon the visual input to the nondeprived eye (Blasdel & Pettigrew, 1978; Mitchell, Cynader, & Movshon, 1977; Olson & Freeman, 1978).

C. Relation to Periods of Rapid Neural Growth

The third approach to documenting the duration of the sensitive period in the visual pathways is indirect and borrows heavily from studies of the effects of malnutrition and teratogenic agents on brain development. A recurrent assertion in these studies is that the period of life during which the organism is maximally susceptible to lasting structural and functional deformities as a consequence of malnutrition, growth retardation, or teratogenic agents, coincides with periods of fastest neural growth (e.g., Dobbing, 1968, 1976). Consistent with these earlier studies, an accumulating body of data exists that suggests a close relationship between the period in life during which various visual structures show rapid development and the time during which these structures are susceptible to alteration from environmental influences. Neurons in the cat lateral geniculate nucleus (LGN) grow extremely rapidly during the first 4 weeks of life (Garey, Fiskin, & Powell, 1973) and are essentially fully grown by 56 days (Kalil, 1978). This period of rapid growth in the LGN coincides reasonably well with the time at which the cat's visual system is most susceptible to monocular visual deprivation (at about 4 weeks of age). The timing of synaptic development in the cat visual cortex follows a parallel time course, beginning about 3 weeks before birth and increasing to adult values at about 37 days after birth (Cragg, 1975). Thus, on the basis of teratological studies and the known close relationship between periods of rapid growth in the visual system of the cat and the period in life during which its visual system is susceptible to visual deprivation, it is possible to estimate the sensitive period for other species simply from observations of the rate of growth of neurons in various visual structures. This particular approach is especially useful with species for which it is either impossible or impractical to define the sensitive period by experimental manipulation of the early visual input. In a pioneering study utilizing this approach, Hickey (1977) provided some interesting pointers to the duration of the sensitive period in the human visual system from studies of cell growth in the parvocellular and magnocellular layers of the LGN.

At this point, it is appropriate to inject a note of caution that applies to all three approaches to the study of sensitive periods in visual development. The very field from which the rationale for the third approach to the study of sensitive periods is derived includes a large body of data that indicate quite unequivocally that brain development not only can be delayed, but may also be permanently compromised by seemingly minor restrictions on growth of a degree common in human populations (e.g., Davison & Dobbing, 1968; Dobbing, 1968, 1976; Irvine & Timiras, 1966). It has been repeatedly demonstrated, for example, that comparatively small differences in nutrition, as can exist between litters of slightly different sizes, can produce permanent structural and functional differences in brain development that remain permanently throughout life despite ad lib feeding after the animals are weaned (e.g., Dobbing, 1968; Irvine & Timiras, 1966). This finding has very important implications for studies of sensitive periods in visual development. It is obviously important in such studies to employ animals from the same litter who are also of the same weight, or animals of comparable size from different litters. However, despite explicit cautionary remarks such as those of Davison and Dobbing (1968:254) against failure to standardize environmental conditions of developing litters "so that animals of the same chronological age acquire widely different developmental ages," virtually all experimental attempts to define sensitive periods in visual development have failed to take these simple precautions. The absence of these controls could contribute to the differences observed between animals in the magnitude of the effects of brief periods of various forms of early visual deprivation. These differences are frequently attributed to the difficulties associated with recording from a valid sample of neurons in the cortex, but it is just as likely that they could be attributed to differences in nutrition. There is, in fact, some evidence that the effect of differences in litter size on sensory development can be quite dramatic. It has been reported that barrel formation in the rat somatosensory cortex can be delayed by 2 days in rats from large litters whose mothers were fed on a low-protein diet in comparison to rats from litters of normal size (Vongdokmai, 1980). As well as the delay in barrel formation, there were also indications that the number of cells in the somatosensory cortex was greatly reduced (see Chapter 9 by Woolsey in Volume I).

III.   EARLY EVIDENCE FOR SENSITIVE PERIODS IN
VISUAL CORTICAL DEVELOPMENT

Sensitive periods in visual development either can be defined in terms of the type of manipulation or restriction that is applied to the animal's early visual input, or in terms of the anatomical structure or physiological property that is influenced by the particular manipulation of the visual input. The use of the first definition frequently precedes the latter, as the nature, locus, and extent of the physiological changes induced by a given form of early visual deprivation are often not immediately obvious. Eventually, it will be both possible and convenient to define sensitive periods in cellular terms, because, potentially, a large number of manipulations of the visual input may have identical physiological or anatomical effects. However, at present, both forms of specification coexist.

A.   Modification of Cortical Ocular Dominance

Although a body of clinical data stretching back over several centuries exists that is consistent with the view that the visual system may be influenced by its visual input to a greater extent in the first few years of life than later (Duke-Elder & Wybar, 1973), the experimental evidence for a sensitive period in visual development is comparatively new. Following on the heels of their pioneering characterization of neurons in the cat visual cortex, Hubel and Wiesel (1963) conducted a series of experiments to investigate the role that visual experience plays in determining the complex visual response characteristics of these cells. In addition to examining the properties of cells in neonatal kittens, they also investigated the effects on the kitten visual cortex of a 2½-month period of monocular visual deprivation induced by eyelid suture from the time of initial eye opening (Wiesel & Hubel, 1963). The reorganization of the visual cortex that results from the latter manipulation is extremely dramatic. Although, as in adults, most cortical cells in the visual cortex of very young kittens and monkeys shortly after birth receive excitatory input from both eyes (Blakemore & Van Sluyters, 1975; Hubel & Wiesel, 1963; Hubel & Wiesel, 1977; Pettigrew, 1974), following occlusion of one eye for several months from birth, the vast majority of neurons can only be excited by visual stimuli through the nondeprived eye (e.g., Hubel, Wiesel, & Le Vay, 1977; Wiesel & Hubel, 1963, 1965). Representative results from Hubel and Wiesel's early experiments on kittens are shown in Fig. 1.3 in the form of ocular dominance histograms that show the number of cells that fell into each of

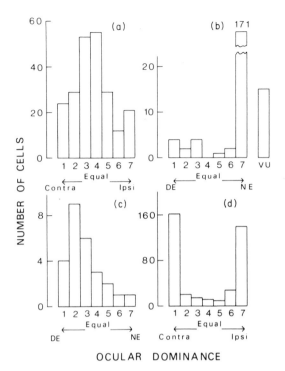

OCULAR DOMINANCE

Fig. 1.3 Classification according to ocular dominance of samples of cells recorded from the visual cortex of either normal or visually deprived animals. Ocular dominance distributions are shown for: (a) 223 cortical cells recorded from a series of normal adult animals by Hubel and Wiesel (1965); (b) 199 cortical cells recorded from five cats that were monocularly deprived from near birth until the age of recording at between 8 and 14 weeks of age. The recording electrode was located in the visual cortex contralateral to the monocularly deprived eye. (Data from Wiesel & Hubel, 1965.) (c) 26 cells recorded from the visual cortex of an adult animal that was monocularly deprived by eyelid suture for 3 months. Recordings were made from the left visual cortex contralateral to the monocularly deprived right eye. (Data from Wiesel & Hubel, 1963.) (d) 384 cells recorded from four animals reared with an artifical strabismus (exotropia) induced by section of the medial rectus muscle of the right eye. (Data from Hubel & Wiesel, 1965.)

Cells are classified into seven groups according to the relative influence of the two eyes. Cells in Groups 1 and 7 are excited exclusively by visual stimuli delivered to the eye that is respectively, contralateral and ipsilateral to the recording electrode. Cells in the other groups are binocularly driven with those classified as Group 4 being influenced equally by the two eyes. Neurons in Groups 2 and 3 are excited by the contralateral eye much stronger and slightly stronger than the other eye, respectively; cells classified in Groups 5 and 6 show a progressively stronger bias toward the ipsilateral eye. Cells classified as VU in (b) were unresponsive to visual stimuli. The arrows under the abscissae of b and c indicate increasing influence of the deprived (DE) and nondeprived (NE) eye.

seven ocular dominance classes. Cells in Groups 1 and 7 can be excited only by visual stimuli delivered to the eye, contralateral or ipsilateral, respectively, to the recording electrode. Neurons in Group 4 can be excited equally by the two eyes. Cells in Groups 5 and 6 exhibit a progressively stronger bias toward the ipsilateral eye, whereas those in Groups 2 and 3 are biased progressively more to the eye contralateral to the electrode. In normally reared adult animals (Fig. 1.3a) there is a tendency for cells to be biased toward the contralateral eye. The ocular dominance distribution shown in Fig. 1.3b represents the pooled results from five kittens that had their right eyes closed by lid suture from the time of natural eye opening until the age of recording at between 8 and 14 weeks of age. Even though the recording electrode was located in the visual cortex contralateral to the previously closed eye, only 13 of 199 cells (7%) could be excited at all through the previously closed eye (Wiesel & Hubel, 1965).

The very dramatic physiological reorganization that Wiesel and Hubel (1963:1006) observed following prolonged early monocular visual deprivation was accompanied by behavioral deficits so severe that they concluded "that there was a profound, perhaps complete, impairment of vision in the deprived eye of these animals." Subsequently, it has been shown that monocularly deprived animals eventually show a limited degree of behavioral recovery from these initially severe deficits, the rate and extent of which depend upon the length of the period of deprivation (Giffin & Mitchell, 1978).

That there must be a sensitive period for the physiological effects of monocular deprivation was immediately evident from the observation that similar periods of monocular deprivation imposed on an adult animal (see Fig. 1.3c) had no effect on the ocular dominance distribution of cortical cells (Wiesel & Hubel, 1963). Later, Hubel and Wiesel (1970) delineated the period of susceptibility to the physiological effects of monocular deprivation from examination of the effects of brief periods of monocular occlusion imposed on different animals at various ages. From observations of this sort they concluded that:

> The susceptibility begins suddenly near the start of the fourth week, at about the time a kitten begins to use its eyes, and persists until some time between the sixth and eighth week; it then begins to decline, disappearing ultimately around the end of the third month. After 4 months cats seem to be insensitive even to very long periods of monocular deprivation as tested by behavioural, physiological and morphological criteria [Hubel & Wiesel, 1970:434].

Results from representative animals from this series of experiments are shown in Fig. 1.4.

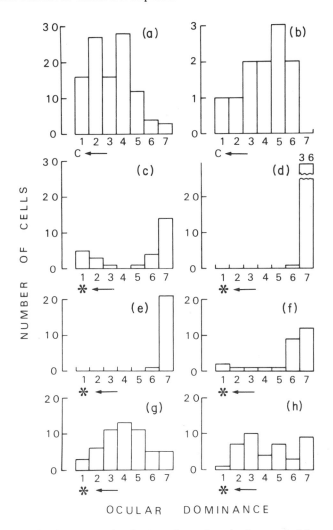

Fig. 1.4 Ocular dominance distribution of samples of cells recorded from the visual cortex of a number of normal kittens or kittens that were monocularly deprived for different times at various ages. In the latter cases, recordings were made from the visual cortex contralateral to the monocularly deprived eye. The asterisk labels the ocular dominance group in which cells are excited exclusively by the deprived eye. Classification of ocular dominance is the same as in Fig. 1.3. The ocular dominance distributions shown are for: (a) 106 cells recorded from the left striate cortex of two normal kittens, between 3 and 4 weeks old; cells in the visual cortex of seven kittens that were monocularly deprived by eyelid suture for the following periods, (b) days 9 to 19; (c) days 23 to 26; (d) days 23 to 29; (e) days 30 to 39; (f) from age 2 months to 3 months; (g) for 3 months at the age of 4 months; (h) for 4 months at 6 months of age. (Data from Hubel & Wiesel, 1963, 1970.)

Although the sample of cells was very small, a period of monocular deprivation imposed from 9 to 19 days of age (Fig. 1.4b) produced no obvious disturbance of the ocular dominance distribution of cortical cells from the pattern observed in normal animals of about the same age (Fig. 1.4a). However, a 3-day period of deprivation (Fig. 1.4c) imposed in the fourth week of life resulted in a very obvious breakdown in the proportion of binocular cells, whereas slightly longer periods of deprivation (6 days, Fig. 1.4d) caused such a dramatic shift in ocular dominance in favor of the nondeprived eye that only 1 cell out of 37 could be excited at all through the deprived eye. The cortex remains highly susceptible to monocular occlusion through the sixth week of life (Fig. 1.4e), but thereafter there is a decline in susceptibility so that a 4-week period of occlusion imposed at 2 months of age (Fig. 1.4f) results in a smaller shift in ocular dominance than that produced by only a few days of deprivation at the peak of the sensitive period in the fourth week. Current opinion concerning the duration of the sensitive period is based almost entirely on the results from the two animals of Figs. 1.4g and 1.4h. These apparently show that a period of deprivation of 3 or 4 months duration imposed at either 4 or 6 months of age, respectively, results in no obvious distortion of the ocular dominance distribution of cortical cells. However, it may be premature to conclude from the latter results that the cortex is immutable to the effects of monocular occlusion beyond 4 months of age, as the physiological recording from which the histogram of Fig. 1.4g was derived was conducted 16 months following termination of the period of monocular deprivation during which time some recovery could have occurred (Hubel & Wiesel, 1970; Fig. 6A).

The general picture of the sensitive period that emerged from these experiments was confirmed later by Blakemore and Van Sluyters (1974), who adopted the strategy described earlier (Fig. 1.2) of examining the extent of the recovery from an initial period of monocular deprivation following reverse suture. Representative results for three of their animals (reverse sutured at 5, 8, and 14 weeks) with the results from a fourth animal on which cortical recordings were made immediately on termination of a 5-week period of monocular deprivation imposed from the time of natural eye opening are shown in Fig. 1.5. In agreement with earlier results, virtually all cells recorded from the latter animal were excited exclusively through the nondeprived eye. In striking contrast to this, the results from the animal that was reverse sutured at 5 weeks were the exact opposite; nearly all cells encountered in this animal were driven exclusively by the initially *deprived* eye (Fig. 1.5b). This result demonstrates that, during the sensitive period, binocular

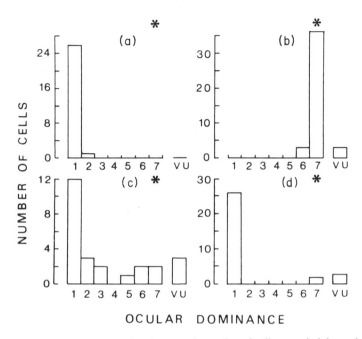

OCULAR DOMINANCE

Fig. 1.5 Ocular dominance distribution of samples of cells recorded from the right visual cortex of four kittens that were monocularly deprived in the right eye from near birth for various periods: (a) the dominance distribution from an animal that was monocularly deprived until 5 weeks of age; (b–d) results from three kittens that were monocularly deprived until either 5, 8, or 14 weeks of age, respectively, and then reverse sutured for 9 weeks (animals 1, 3, and 5 from Fig. 1.2) until the date of recording. Classification of ocular dominance groups as in Fig. 1.3. The asterisk labels the ocular dominance group in which cells are excited by only the initially deprived eye. Cells classed as VU were visually unresponsive. (Data from Blakemore & Van Sluyters, 1974.)

connections are truly plastic and can be both broken and re-established, possibly many times (Movshon, 1976). There was considerably less recovery in the cortex of the animal that was reverse sutured at 8 weeks (Fig. 1.5c) and virtually none at all in the animal on which the reverse suture was performed at 14 weeks of age. The results from these animals, together with the other animals in the series are summarized in another form in Fig. 1.6. A *reversal index*, defined as the ratio of the number of neurons dominated by the recently experienced eye (cells in Groups 5–7) to the total number of visually responsive cells, has been calculated from the results from each animal and has been plotted against the age at which they were reverse sutured. The reversal index provides a measure of the degree of recovery in the cortex so that the curve in Fig. 1.6 can be thought of as specifying the time course of the

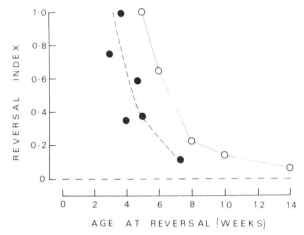

AGE AT REVERSAL (WEEKS)

Fig. 1.6 A comparison of the temporal profiles of the sensitive periods for monocular and directional deprivation in kittens derived from animals that had been reverse deprived. The reversal index is plotted on the ordinate. This index is defined in the case of monocularly deprived animals as the ratio of the number of neurons dominated by the initially deprived eye to the total number of visually responsive cells, and for the directionally deprived animals as the ratio of cells with a preference for rightward motion to the total number of unidirectional cells preferring either leftward or rightward motion.

The reversal index for reverse sutured animals as a function of the age at which the reverse suture was performed is represented by ○—○. The reversal index for directionally deprived animals as a function of the age at which the visual input of each animal was reversed from leftward to rightward moving stripes is depicted by ●—●. (Data from Blakemore & Van Sluyters, 1974; and Daw & Wyatt, 1976, respectively.)

decay in the sensitivity of neural connections in the visual cortex to modification by visual experience.

In addition to the far from subtle procedure of monocular occlusion, there are two other commonly employed manipulations that result in changes in cortical ocular dominance when applied early in life. Both of these deprivation conditions, alternating monocular occlusion (see Fig. 1.3c) and surgically induced strabismus, result in a reduction in the proportion of binocularly excitable cortical cells but leave the number of cells excited by each eye about the same. However, in kittens made esotropic by early section of the lateral rectus muscle, there is some evidence that the distribution of cortical ocular dominance may be skewed in favor of the nondeviating eye, particularly in the cortex ipsilateral to the deviating eye (Hubel & Wiesel, 1965; Kalil, Spear, & Langsetmo, 1978). Although the data are not extensive, there are suggestions that the sensitive period for the cortical effect of both these manipulations may only extend to the end of the third month of life in the kitten (Presson & Gordon, 1979; Yinon, 1976).

B. Modification of Other Visual Response Characteristics of Cortical Cells

1. Orientation Selectivity

Although the results are controversial, a number of investigators have claimed that it is possible to bias the distribution of orientation selective neurons in the visual cortex by restricting the early visual input of kittens to contours of a single orientation (for reviews, see Blakemore, 1978; Pettigrew, 1978). The possibility of a sensitive period for the cortical effects of biased exposure to stripes of a single orientation early in life has been examined by Blakemore (1974). A decided bias for the orientation preference of cortical cells to the experienced orientation was only observed in animals that had received the biased early visual exposure between 3 and 14 weeks of age, an interval that coincides well with the sensitive period for effects on cortical ocular dominance. However, because of certain procedural difficulties associated with the rearing of older animals, Blakemore (1978) warns that these findings must be interpreted with caution.

2. Direction Selectivity

The evidence for modification of the cortical distribution of the preferred direction of direction-selective neurons by selective early visual exposure is quite compelling. Following exposure of kittens to either spots or to stripes that move in only one direction, the distribution of preferred directions of subsequently recorded cortical cells have been reported to be biased toward the direction of motion experienced by the animal early in life (Cynader, Berman, & Hein, 1975; Daw & Wyatt, 1976; Tretter, Cynader, & Singer, 1975). Interestingly, there is evidence that the sensitive period for the cortical effects of "directional deprivation" may decline faster than that for the effects of monocular deprivation. Evidence for this was provided first by Daw and Wyatt (1976), who employed the technique of reverse deprivation. Six kittens were removed from a dark room, in which they were housed with their mother, at 14 days of age and placed for 2 hours each day in the center of a cylinder on the internal surface of which were painted vertical black stripes on a white background. At first the cylinder was turned counterclockwise so that each animal viewed stripes moving to the left for 7–37 days, depending upon the animal. Following this initial exposure to leftward motion, the direction of the cylinder was reversed when the animals were from 3 to 7 weeks of age so that all subsequent visual exposure was to stripes moving toward their right. Recordings were made from each animal after exposure to rightward moving stripes for 34–65 days. Animals in which the drum rotation was reversed at either 3 or 4 weeks of age exhibited a strong bias for cortical cells to prefer rightward motion, whereas those who were reversed later showed either no cortical bias or a bias for leftward motion, which was particularly marked in the animals reversed at 7 weeks of age. The results of this experiment are summarized in Fig. 1.6, which displays the reversal index (the number of unidirectional cortical cells with preferred directions to the right expressed as a percentage of the number of unidirectional cortical cells preferring either leftward or rightward motion) as a function of the age at which the drum rotation was reversed from left to right. Note that the curve for reversal of directional selectivity is displaced to the left of that for reversal of ocular dominance by about 2 weeks.

The suggestion raised by Fig. 1.6 that the sensitive period for changes in direction selectivity of cortical cells may precede that for changes of ocular dominance has been given even greater credibility by subsequent experiments (Berman & Daw, 1977; Daw, Berman, & Ariel, 1978) in which a direct comparison was made on the same animals of the effects of both deprivation conditions and their simultaneous reversal.

C. Evidence for Sensitive Periods in the Monkey Visual Cortex

There is strong behavioral and physiological evidence from monkeys that monocular eyelid closure, of more than a few days duration and imposed between birth and 2 months of age, can have the same profound effects both on the vision of the deprived eye and on cortical ocular dominance as observed after similar deprivation in kittens (Baker, Grigg, & von Noorden, 1974; Blakemore, Garey, & Vital-Durand, 1978; Crawford, Blake, Cool, & von Noorden, 1975; Hubel et al., 1977; Hubel & Wiesel, 1977; Le Vay et al., 1980; von Noorden, 1973). There are also clear indications that surgically induced strabismus induces both amblyopia and a breakdown of cortical binocularity as well as shifts in ocular dominance toward the nondeviating eye similar to those observed in kittens (Baker et al., 1974; von Noorden & Dowling, 1970). That there must be a sensitive period for the effects of monocular occlusion was made evident by the observation that a long period ($6\frac{1}{2}$ months) of occlusion imposed on an adult monkey had no effect whatever on cortical ocular dominance (Blakemore et al., 1978).

Behavioral experiments (von Noorden, 1973; von Noorden, Dowling, & Ferguson, 1970) suggest that a persistent deficit in the visual acuity of the deprived eye is only observed in monkeys that are monocularly deprived before 2 months of age. This could be interpreted in two very different ways: Either (a) the monkey visual system is insensitive to the effects of occlusion beyond 2 months of age; or (b) sufficient plasticity remains after 2 months to allow complete behavioral recovery following termination of the period of deprivation. Recent physiological experiments lend support to the second explanation (Blakemore et al., 1978; Hubel et al., 1977 Le Vay et al., 1980).

Although results from only a very limited number of animals have been reported, physiological and anatomical studies of the effects of periods of monocular occlusion or its reversal by reverse suture emphasize that the effects of these manipulations may be different in Layer IVC of the visual cortex (the recipient layer of the geniculocortical afferents) than in other cortical layers. Indeed, there is some evidence that the effects of these manipulations may even be different for the two sublaminae within Layer IVC, namely Layers IVCα and IVCβ (Hubel et al., 1977; Le Vay et al. 1980), a point that will be considered further in a later section. In general, it would appear that layers of the cortex other than Layer IVC remain susceptible to the effects of monocular deprivation for a longer period than Layer IVC itself.

The monkey visual cortex appears to be highly susceptible to monocular occlusion in the first 2 months of life, such that reverse suture instituted at 6 weeks of age for about 4 months causes an almost complete shift in cortical ocular dominance toward the originally deprived eye (Blakemore et al., 1978). As with kittens, the later reverse suturing is delayed, the less is the extent of functional recovery of the originally deprived eye. Unfortunately, the number of conditions studied by this procedure is small so that the end of the sensitive period cannot be precisely defined. However, results from one monkey that was monocularly deprived for 5 months at 11 months of age suggests that the sensitive period outside of Layer IVC may extend beyond 11 months of age.

These conclusions have been confirmed very recently in a more extensive study of Le Vay et al. (1980) performed on a different species of monkey (Macaca mulatta). In addition to determining the physiological effects of monocular deprivation on cortical ocular dominance, LeVay et al. also documented the effects of deprivation on the relative width of anatomically visualized ocular dominance bands within layer IVC. It was found that monocular deprivation imposed at any time during the first 6 weeks of postnatal life had about the same effect; in layer IVC, afferents from the nondeprived eye were greatly expanded at the expense of those from the deprived eye, and in layers other than IVC virtually all cells were completely dominated by the nondeprived eye. Deprivation imposed after 10 weeks produced little or no effects on layer IVC but still resulted in substantial shifts of cortical ocular dominance in other layers. Subtle effects on these other layers were even observed in an animal that was monocularly deprived when 1 year old.

IV. CHANGING CONCEPTS OF THE SENSITIVE PERIOD

The last few years have seen a number of important changes in our understanding of sensitive periods. New data not only challenge current thinking concerning the duration of the sensitive period, but also indicate that the sensitive period may not just be defined in terms of the animal's age, but may also depend upon environmental factors. Finally, there is a rapidly emerging body of evidence from diverse sources that suggests a multiplicity of sensitive periods in the visual system. These new twists are considered individually in what follows.

A. Duration of the Sensitive Period for Modification of Cortical Ocular Dominance

The first suggestion that the sensitive period for modification of the ocular dominance of cortical cells in the kitten may be longer than previously thought arose from studies I made in collaboration with F. Griffin and B. Timney of the extent of the recovery from extended periods of monocular occlusion imposed from birth. By means of a jumping stand (Mitchell, Giffin, & Timney, 1977), we documented the recovery of vision in the deprived eye in terms of its visual acuity for square wave gratings following restoration of visual input to the monocularly deprived eye. Although, as expected, kittens deprived for about a month eventually showed a good recovery of vision, we were surprised to find that animals that were monocularly deprived throughout the conventionally defined 3–14 week sensitive period to 4 months of age eventually recovered some vision in their formerly deprived eye, although for a period of about 1 month, they appeared completely blind when forced to employ this eye. The time course of the behavioral recovery for three animals monocularly deprived from birth to about 4 months of age is shown in Fig. 1.7. The ordinate indicates visual acuity in terms of the number of cycles (the width of one black plus one white bar of the grating) per degree of visual angle. For reference, the acuity of a normal adult cat under the conditions of these measurements would be about 7 c/deg and that of a human about 50 c/deg.

Although all three animals initially appeared blind when forced to use their deprived eye, they all eventually recovered an acuity in this eye in excess of 2.5 c/deg. The two animals that were reverse sutured

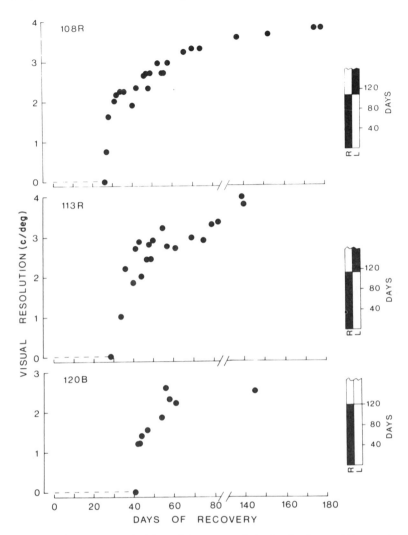

Fig. 1.7 The recovery of vision of the monocularly deprived eye of three animals, 108R, 113R, and 120B, that were monocularly deprived by eyelid suture from the time of natural eye opening until, respectively, 108, 113, or 120 days of age. Following the period of monocular occlusion, the animal was either forced to use the formerly deprived eye by reversing the eyelid suture (108R and 113R), or, as was the case for 120B, visual input was allowed to both eyes. The horizontal interrupted line indicates the period of time that the animals appeared to be functionally blind when using their deprived eye. (Reprinted with permission from Timney & Mitchell, 1979.)

following the early period of deprivation eventually attained acuities close to 4 c/deg. Although it could be argued that the improvement of the vision of the deprived eye reflected recovery of function in structures other than the visual cortex, the very high acuities that were attained by these animals argues otherwise. An acuity of 4 c/deg strongly implies that the vision is mediated by a visual area that receives input from X-type retinal ganglion cells (Enroth-Cugell & Robson, 1966), as the spatial resolution of the other classes of ganglion cells is lower (e.g., Cleland et al., 1979, 1980). Because the striate cortex is the only major cortical visual area that receives heavy projections from retinal X-cells, it is likely that the recovery of vision is mediated by the striate cortex. To check whether some recovery had occurred in the visual cortex, we recorded from the cortex of one of the animals of Fig. 1.7 (120B) that had been monocularly deprived from birth to 120 days of age, some 12 months following termination of the period of monocular deprivation. Recordings were also made from a second animal, 160B, that was monocularly deprived until 5 months (160 days) of age. In this case, 6 months were allowed to elapse following the period of deprivation before recording. The behavioral recovery observed in these two animals is shown in Fig. 1.8, with the ocular dominance distribution of 84 cells encountered on four electrode penetrations in the visual cortex of 120B, and of 30 cells encountered in the course of a single penetration in the cortex of 160B contralateral to the deprived eye. In the case of 120B, many cells could be driven by the formerly deprived eye, indicating that considerable recovery had occurred during the year that elapsed after the initial deprivation. However, from the limited number of cells that were sampled, there was little evidence of any recovery in the cortex of 160B. Nevertheless, the considerable recovery observed in the cortex of 120B suggests very strongly that it is possible to influence the ocular dominance distribution of cortical cells after 4 months of age.

This possibility was explored in a different way in the next set of experiments in which we assessed the effects on cortical ocular dominance of 3 months of monocular occlusion imposed on otherwise normally reared animals at either 4, 5, 6, 7, or 8 months of age (Cynader, Timney, & Mitchell, 1980). The distribution of ocular dominance of a sample of cells recorded in the cortex contralateral to the deprived eye of animals reared under these conditions is shown in Fig. 1.9. Many more cells were dominated by the experienced eye (Groups 5–7) of the animals that were deprived at 4, 5, and 6 months of age than by the deprived eye (Groups 1–3). The proportion of cells dominated by the deprived eye of the animals monocularly occluded at either 4, 5, or 6 months of age were in fact both similar and low, ranging from 29.2% in the animals deprived at 4 months to 31.25% in the animals deprived

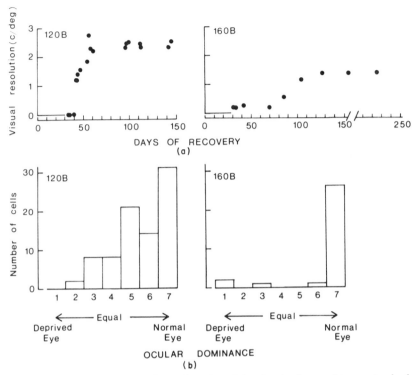

Fig. 1.8 (a) The recovery of visual acuity of the deprived eye of two animals that were monocularly deprived from the time of natural eye opening until either 120 (120B) or 160 (160B) days of age, at which time the sutured eyelids were parted to allow vision to both eyes. Throughout the period indicated by the horizontal line, neither animal exhibited any sign of vision when using its deprived eye. (b) The distribution of ocular dominance of a sample of cells recorded from the visual cortex of these animals either 6 months (160B) or 12 months (120B) following termination of the period of monocular occlusion. The recording electrode was situated in the hemisphere contralateral to the formerly deprived eye with the exception of two of the five penetrations made in 120B. The results for these two penetrations have been incorporated into the ocular dominance distributions as if the recordings had been made from the contralateral hemisphere. Ocular dominance groups are as defined in Fig. 1.3. (Reprinted with permission from Cynader *et al.*, 1980.)

at 5 months of age. This trend runs counter to the bias observed in normal animals (Figs. 1.3a, 1.4a) for cells to be dominated by the eye contralateral to the electrode, a tendency that is obvious in the animal deprived at 8 months where the proportion of cells dominated by the deprived (contralateral) eye is 55.8%, but not in the animal deprived at 7 months, in which only 41.3% of cells were dominated by the contralateral eye. The very apparent bias toward the experienced eye observed in the cortex of the animal deprived at 6 months of age

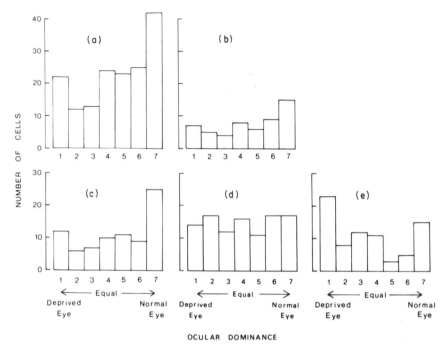

Fig. 1.9 Ocular dominance distributions from a sample of cells recorded in the visual cortex of a number of animals that were monocularly deprived for a period of 3 months at either (a) 4, (b) 5, (c) 6, (d) 7, or (e) 8 months of age. In every case the recordings were made from the hemisphere contralateral to the deprived eye. (Reprinted with permission from Cynader *et al.*, 1980.)

indicates that the cortex remains susceptible to monocular occlusion until at least this time. Moreover, the lack of any bias toward the contralateral (deprived) eye in the animal deprived at 7 months of age argues that the cortex retains some plasticity even at 7 months.

It might be thought that this finding conflicts with results obtained by Hubel and Wiesel (1970) on one animal deprived for 3 months beginning at 4 months of age (see Fig. 1.4). However, cortical recording from this animal was made 16 months after the period of deprivation, leaving open the possibility that some recovery may have occurred during this extended period. Indeed there is good behavioral evidence that considerable and rapid recovery does occur under these circumstances. Measurements of the visual acuity of the deprived eye of an animal that was monocularly deprived for 3 months, beginning at 4 months of age, revealed that although the acuity of this eye was initially poor following restoration of visual input to this eye (2.9 c/deg), thereafter, the visual acuity rapidly improved. After about 3 weeks, the vision of the deprived eye was comparable to that of the other eye, a result suggesting that considerable physiological recovery may also have occurred from the cortical effects of the period of deprivation (Timney, Mitchell, & Cynader, 1980).

The results shown in Fig. 1.9 indicate that the decline in the sensitivity of the visual cortex to the effect of monocular deprivation imposed at or beyond 4 months of age is very gradual, which makes it difficult to define the end of the sensitive period with any precision. Estimates of the duration of the sensitive period depend critically upon the sensitivity of the assay that is employed as an index of cortical plasticity. However, even the relatively crude assay of plasticity represented by observable shifts in cortical ocular dominance indicates that cortical binocular connections may be influenced by monocular occlusion for at least twice as long as previously thought, to between 6 and 8 months of age. However, behavioral measurements of the recovery of vision after long periods of monocular deprivation suggest that it may last even longer. The evidence for this can be derived from Fig. 1.10, which shows the visual acuity that was eventually attained by the deprived eye of various animals that were monocularly occluded from birth as a function of the duration of the period of occlusion (logarithmic scale). With increasing length of deprivation there is a progressive and regular reduction in the acuity that is eventually attained. The data obtained

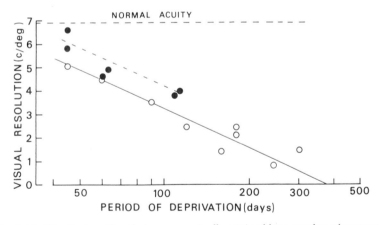

Fig. 1.10 The final acuities that were eventually attained by a number of monocularly deprived animals that had been deprived from birth to various ages. Data obtained from animals that had both eyes opened after the period of monocular occlusion are shown by ○; results obtained from animals that were reverse sutured are depicted by ●. Dashed and continuous lines of best fit have been fitted by eye through the data from reverse sutured animals and those that had both eyes open after the period of monocular eyelid suture.

to date for periods of deprivation of up to 10 months duration are well fitted by a straight line. Because of the very regular nature of the decline in the final acuities attained by the animals of Fig. 1.10, it is tempting to speculate that the recovery observed in all the animals reflected the operation of a single process, possibly occurring in the same visual area. On the basis of this assumption, the point at which the line drawn through the data of Fig. 1.10 meets the abscissa may provide an indication of the duration of the sensitive period for recovery from the effects of monocular occlusion. According to this argument, some very slight plasticity to monocular occlusion remains in the kitten visual cortex until 1 year of age.

In addition to the new information concerning the end of the sensitive period, recent findings suggest that the onset of the sensitive period may occur earlier than previously thought. Freeman (1978) imposed a similar 4 day period of monocular deprivation on a group of four animals at either 9, 13, 17, or 21 days of age. Cortical recordings were performed immediately on termination of the period of occlusion. Whereas no effects were observed on cortical ocular dominance on the animal deprived at 9 days, in each of the other animals there was a substantial reduction in the proportion of binocular cells, along with a decided bias toward the experienced eye. However, although substantial, these effects of deprivation on cortical ocular dominance in the third week of life were still much less than those observed in the fourth week (Freeman, 1978; Hubel & Wiesel, 1970).

B. Extension of the Sensitive Period in Animals Reared in Total Darkness

There is now very good evidence that the sensitive periods for phenomena as diverse as imprinting as well as birdsong development and crystallization are not solely defined in terms of the animal's age. It has been repeatedly demonstrated that animals raised in isolation remain susceptible to imprinting for a much longer period than communally reared animals (e.g., Sluckin 1972). A similar phenomenon exists for the development and crystallization of birdsong. Song crystallization takes a longer time with birds that are either tutored with an unacceptable model or raised in isolation (Marler, 1970). In addition, there is evidence in one species of song bird, the male chaffinch, that the duration of the sensitive period for the song of this species can be altered by manipulation of androgen levels (Nottebohm, 1969). Therefore, the sensitive periods for these two phenomena do not simply reflect age-dependent changes, but are partly governed by environmental factors. Recent evidence suggests that this may also be true of sensitive periods in visual development.

The first indication that the decline in the plasticity of the visual cortex may be partly governed by environmental factors arose from studies of the behavioral and physiological recovery from the effects of extended periods of total visual deprivation imposed on kittens from birth. Kittens reared with binocular lid suture or in total darkness from birth until the age of 4 months or longer initially appear completely blind on first exposure to illuminated surroundings. Nevertheless, simple visuomotor behaviors begin to appear in piecemeal fashion over the course of the next 2 weeks in the case of animals deprived for 4 months, and 6 weeks in animals deprived for 6 months (Timney et al., 1978; van Hof-van Duin, 1976). There is general consensus that cortical cells in binocularly deprived animals are quite abnormal. Typically, cells respond very poorly, if at all, to visual stimuli. The vast majority of cells that are visually responsive are extremely broadly tuned for orientation and other stimulus parameters (for review, see Blakemore, 1978). However, even animals that have been raised from birth in total darkness for a year eventually show considerable recovery of stimulus specificity in the visual cortex after several months of exposure to illuminated surroundings (Cynader et al., 1976).

This recovery of selectivity in the visual cortex is accompanied by a regular improvement in visual acuity. Fig. 1.11 shows the time course of recovery of acuity in two animals taken from an earlier study (Timney, Mitchell, & Giffin, 1978) that were dark reared from birth to either 4 or 6 months of age, with results from two additional animals that were dark reared until either 8 or 10 months of age. Following a period of apparent blindness of progressively longer duration with increasing length of visual deprivation, there was a gradual recovery of visual acuity. Animals deprived for 4 months eventually attained acuities that were close to those of normally reared animals, but those deprived for longer periods never recovered normal vision.

The behavioral and physiological recovery observed in animals binocularly deprived for long periods from birth poses a challenge to the concept of the sensitive period as a period of neural plasticity that ends at some fixed, genetically determined age. The considerable, but nevertheless incomplete, physiological and behavioral recovery observed after long periods of binocular visual deprivation suggests that dark rearing delays the decline in the sensitivity of the cortex to modification by environmental factors. This possibility was examined more directly in the next set of physiological and behavioral experiments conducted in collaboration with M. Cynader and B. Timney, in which we examined

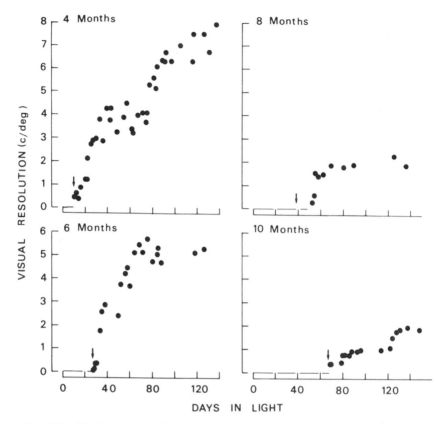

Fig. 1.11 The time course of development of visual acuity of four dark-reared animals following introduction to an illuminated environment at either 4, 6, 8, or 10 months of age. The arrows indicate the first day on which the animal showed evidence of visual behavior on the jumping stand, defined as the ability to locate a closed from an open door on the stand. Throughout the period indicated by the discontinuous line, the animals were unable to discriminate between a grating and a uniform field of the same mean luminance.

the effects of periods of monocular occlusion imposed on animals that had been dark reared from birth for 4 or more months. It was thought that if the visual cortex did retain considerable plasticity after extended periods of binocular visual deprivation, it would show a heightened susceptibility to monocular occlusion in comparison to light reared animals of the same age.

Figure 1.12 displays ocular dominance histograms for a sample of cells recorded from the visual cortex of a number of animals that had been monocularly deprived by eyelid suture for 3 months after being

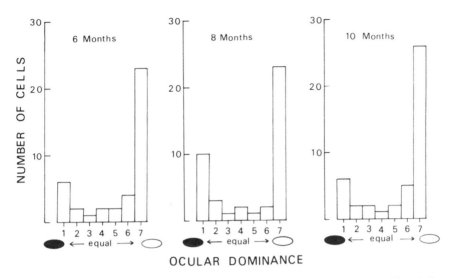

Fig. 1.12 Effects of 3 months of monocular eyelid closure beginning at either 6, 8, or 10 months of age on a number of kittens that had been reared from birth to the time of eyelid suture in total darkness. Recordings were made from the visual cortex contralateral to the formerly occluded eye. The nonoccluded eye influences many more cells than did the formerly occluded eye in every case. (Redrawn from Cynader & Mitchell, 1980.)

reared from birth in total darkness until either 6, 8, or 10 months of age (Cynader & Mitchell, 1980). The effects on ocular dominance were dramatic: Most cortical cells were driven only through the nondeprived eye. The proportion of cells dominated by the deprived (contralateral) eye of these groups of animals were only 22.5%, 33.3% and 22.7%, respectively. Comparison with Fig. 1.9 shows that the shifts in ocular dominance observed in these dark reared animals of Fig. 1.12 were very much greater than the small effects of a similar period of monocular deprivation imposed on light reared animals of the same age. The enhanced effects of monocular occlusion as well as the similarity of the effects observed after different periods of dark rearing indicate that the degree of susceptibility of the visual cortex to monocular deprivation is not solely dependent on the animal's age, but also on the state of cortical maturity as influenced by the nature of the animal's early visual experience.

The physiological findings just described have been complemented by behavioral measurements of visual acuity made on a number of animals reared in a similar manner to those of Fig. 1.12. Figure 1.13 shows the results of measurements of the visual acuity made on both

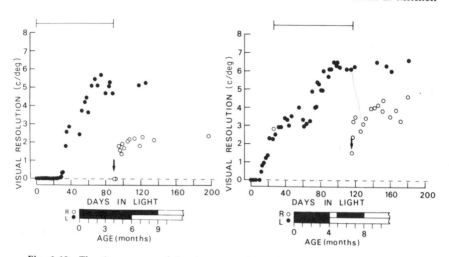

Fig. 1.13 The time course of development of visual acuity in both eyes of two dark reared animals upon introduction to an illuminated environment. The results on the left are from an animal that was monocularly deprived by eyelid suture for 3 months immediately on first exposure to light at 6 months of age. The animal whose results are shown on the right was also subjected to monocular eyelid closure for 3 months after it had spent one month in the light after having spent the first 4 months of life in darkness.

The visual histories of the two animals are depicted schematically below each graph. The acuity of the eye that was not subjected to monocular occlusion, is depicted by ●; the acuity of the formerly monocularly deprived eye is shown by ○. The arrows indicate the results obtained on testing the vision of the deprived eye immediately on termination of the period of monocular occlusion. In the case of the animal whose results are shown on the right, all measurements of acuity prior to the period of monocular occlusion were made with both eyes open with the single exception of one monocular measurement that was made of the acuity of the right eye immediately prior to it being occluded by eyelid suture (⊘). The horizontal bar at the top of each graph indicates the period of monocular occlusion. (Data from Timney et al., 1980.)

eyes of two animals that had been reared from birth in total darkness until either 4 or 6 months of age. One animal was monocularly deprived by eyelid suture for 3 months immediately after it was exposed to light, whereas the other was allowed 1 month in the light before it was monocularly deprived for a similar period. Following the period of monocular occlusion, visual input was allowed to both eyes. The time course of development of vision upon exposing the animals to illuminated surroundings was documented by regular measurements of acuity on a jumping stand (filled symbols). In the case of the animal that was monocularly occluded 1 month after being first exposed to light, all measurements of acuity were binocular with the exception of a single measurement (indicated by an open symbol) of the monocular acuity of the right eye that was made immediately prior to it being occluded by eyelid suture for 3 months. Open symbols show the results of measurements of the acuity of the formerly occluded eye following termination of the period of deprivation (Timney et al., 1980).

The effect of the period of monocular occlusion was profound in both animals, particularly the one that was monocularly deprived immediately upon being brought into the light. This particular animal initially appeared blind when forced to use its formerly occluded eye. Physiological recordings made from the cortex of this animal 24 hours later precluded behavioral testing for another 4 days at which time the animal was clearly able to see with this eye, although the acuity was poor. Thereafter the vision of this eye improved only very slightly to 2.3 c/deg.

The behavioral effects of the period of occlusion on the other animal was not as profound but, nevertheless, there was a substantial acuity deficit. On first testing the vision of the monocularly deprived eye, it was obvious that the animal was considerably worse than it had been 3 months earlier immediately prior to the period of occlusion. Thereafter the vision of the eye improved rapidly, but the acuity always remained considerably less than that of the other eye. This result suggests quite strongly that the visual cortex retains considerable plasticity even after exposure to light for 1 month. Behavioral measurements made on another animal that was also dark reared until 4 months of age indicated that a period of monocular deprivation imposed after the animal had spent 2 months in the light still produced a profound deficit in acuity (Timney et al., 1980). The fact that monocular occlusion exerts such severe behavioral effects on dark-reared animals even after being exposed to light suggests that the period of dark rearing truly retards the decline in the susceptibility of the cortex to visual deprivation, rather than simply weakening the strength of binocular cortical connections that would account equally well for the dramatic effects of a period of monocular occlusion imposed immediately after animals are exposed to light (Fig. 1.12).

Another example of the enhanced behavioral effects of monocular occlusion imposed on dark reared animals is shown in Fig. 1.14 with the effects of a period of monocular occlusion of *twice* the duration (3 months) imposed on a light reared animal when exactly the same age. Whereas the period of monocular deprivation on the latter animal produced only a temporary reduction in acuity, which all but disappeared in 3 weeks, the effect on the dark reared animal was far more dramatic. Initially, this animal appeared blind when forced to employ the formerly

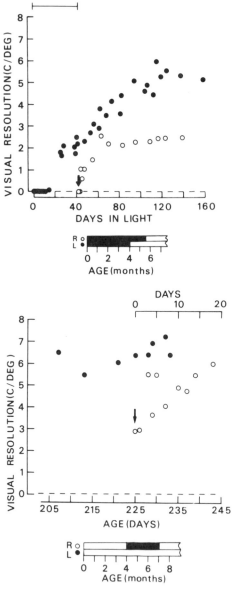

Fig. 1.14 Comparison of the behavioral effects of a period of monocular occlusion imposed on dark reared and light reared animals of the same age. The results shown on top are from an animal that was monocularly deprived for 6 weeks (as indicated by the horizontal bar on top) immediately on introduction to illuminated surroundings at 4 months of age. The results shown below are from a light reared animal that was monocularly deprived for twice the period (3 months) at the same age, namely, 4 months.

occluded eye, and even though some vision was subsequently re-covered by this eye, it never attained an acuity as good as that mediated by the deprived eye of the light reared animal immediately upon ter-mination of a period of occlusion that was twice as long.

C. Sensitive Periods in Visual Development: One or Many?

It is becoming increasingly apparent that it is not possible to postulate the existence of a single sensitive period in visual development during which all neural connections of cells in the visual pathway (and there-fore the functional properties of those cells) are all equally sensitive at the same time to environmental manipulation. As discussed earlier, even within any one cortical visual area, such as the visual cortex, there is good evidence that certain visual response characteristics of cortical neurons are sensitive to visual deprivation at a different time than are others (Daw & Wyatt, 1976; see Fig. 1.7). In addition, there are good reasons to believe, on both anatomical and physiological grounds, that the sensitive period for even one particular environmental manipula-tion, monocular occlusion, may not be the same for all cortical layers. In the monkey, monocular closure can produce changes in the ocular dominance distribution of cells outside Layer IVC when imposed as late as one year if the eye is closed for a sufficiently long time (Le Vay et al., 1980). The bias observed in the ocular dominance distribution of cortical cells is accompanied by a shrinkage of the width (assessed by physiological recording) of the deprived eye's ocular dominance columns outside of Layer IVC. However, there is good evidence that monocular deprivation imposed after about 10 weeks of age leaves the anatomical width (Hubel et al., 1977; Le Vay et al., 1980) and physio-logical size (Blakemore et al., 1978) of ocular dominance bands within Layer IVC unchanged. Thus, there is good reason to believe that the sensitive period may end earlier in Layer IVC than in the other cortical layers, a possibility that has also been raised for the cat (Le Vay, Stryker, & Shatz, 1978).

In addition to this direct anatomical evidence, there is further evi-dence of an indirect nature for a multiplicity of sensitive periods in visual development that rests merely upon the assumption that the

In both cases, filled symbols depict the acuity of the eye that was not subjected to monocular occlusion, and open symbols show the results obtained when the animal was forced to employ the formerly occluded eye. The arrows indicate the results obtained when the vision of this eye was first tested on termination of the period of occlusion. The horizontal discontinuous line indicates the absence of any sign of pattern vision. (Data from Timney et al., 1980.)

time of the period of greatest susceptibility to visual deprivation is related to periods of rapid postnatal neural growth. Even within a given visual nucleus or area, different cell types in different layers grow at different rates. For example, within the human LGN, cells in the parvocellular layers attain their adult dimensions by 6 months of age, whereas neurons in the magnocellular laminae grow at a much slower rate and do not reach their final size until 2 years of age (Hickey, 1977). On this basis, Hickey argues that the sensitive period for the latter laminae, which possibly receive their input from Y-type retinal ganglion cells, must be longer than that for the parvocellular layers, which most likely receive axons from X-type ganglion cells.

Recent studies of the development of various visual and oculomotor functions in both cats and humans also point to the existence of a number of different sensitive periods in visual development. Interocular alignment in the cat, for example, appears to exhibit a well defined sensitive period. Whereas animals reared from birth in the dark to 60 days of age exhibit normal torsional alignment, the pupils of kittens reared in the dark for 4 months or more are characteristically incyclotorted in comparison to normally reared animals (Cynader, 1979). This result suggests that the torsional alterations in interocular alignment develop between 2 and 4 months of age, at least 1 month later than the time the visual cortex exhibits its peak sensitivity to monocular deprivation.

A number of very recent investigations of human infant vision, some of which are reviewed in later chapters, point to the existence of different sensitive periods for the effects of various forms of visual deprivation. Certain peripheral obstructions to vision produce long-lasting visual deficits within the first few months of life, whereas others apparently do not result in any visual deficits until nearly 3 years of age. Infants born with a strabismus exhibit no acuity loss in the deviating eye until between 4 and 5 months of age, at which time the acuity of this eye remains apparently static or even falls, resulting in strabismic amblyopia (Mohindra, Jacobson, Thomas, & Held, 1980). Permanent profound deficits in acuity arising from monocular obstructions to vision in the first few months of life due to conditions such as unilateral cataract, ptosis, or corneal insults that require temporary patching, have been reported by von Noorden (1973); Awaya, Miyake, Imaizumi, Shoise, Kanda, and Komuro (1973); Enoch & Rabinowicz (1976); and Vaegan & Taylor (1979). However, the characteristic meridional acuity loss associated with high astigmatism that remains optically uncorrected throughout childhood, known as meridional amblyopia (Mitchell, Freeman, Millodot, & Haegerstrom, 1973), does not apparently develop in infants until they are almost 3 years old (Mohindra, Held, Gwiazda, & Brill, 1978). These findings suggest that the sensitive period for the effects of peripheral obstructions to concordant binocular vision, such as early cataract or strabismus, begin earlier than the period in life during which the human visual system is susceptible to high astigmatism. However, as yet only limited data are available concerning the duration and time course of the sensitive periods for these deprivation conditions (Banks, Aslin, & Letson, 1975; Cobb & MacDonald, 1978; Vaegan & Taylor, 1979).

V. FUNCTIONAL SIGNIFICANCE OF SENSITIVE PERIODS IN VISUAL DEVELOPMENT

Although by no means the only suggestion (Blakemore, 1974; Lund, 1978), a common and persistent assertion is that the plasticity manifested by the visual system of certain species early in life is related in some way to the specific requirements of stereoscopic vision (e.g., Blakemore, 1978; Blakemore & Van Sluyters, 1974, 1975; Pettigrew, 1974, 1978). Stereopsis requires the detection by the visual system of tiny horizontal disparities between the positions of identical images on the two retinas, which in man can be as small as 5 sec of arc (Ogle, 1962). It seems inconceivable that the neural connectivity underlying this amazing ability can be genetically programmed with sufficient precision to allow such an acute sensitivity and at the same time accommodate slight and unpredictable imbalances between the optical systems of the two eyes, in eye size and position, or imbalances in oculomotor control that could arise during periods of rapid somatic growth. Obviously, the capacity to alter binocular neural connections during this period in life could potentially permit accommodation of such perturbations of growth. But more importantly, it has been argued that the guiding hand of visual experience may be indispensible for the actual development of the neural machinery underlying the detection of the retinal disparity that is a necessary requirement for stereopsis (e.g., Blakemore & Van Sluyters, 1974, 1975; Pettigrew, 1974, 1978).

One of the most attractive lines of evidence for this hypothesis has emerged recently from evolutionary and comparative considerations. Central neural plasticity does not appear to be confined to the cat and monkey visual cortex. Research by Pettigrew and Konishi (1976b) and Pettigrew (1978) indicates that it is also a property of the visual Wulst of the owl, the cells of which bear an amazing similarity to visual cortical cells of the cat and monkey including being highly specific for

retinal disparity (Pettigrew & Konishi, 1976a). Thus, despite its very
different evolutionary history, the geniculostriate pathway of the owl
appears to have evolved the capacity for stereoscopic processing, and
at the same time manifests a high degree of plasticity in early life. This
considerably strengthens the argument that early plasticity is linked to
the special demands during development of a system involved in stereoscopic depth processing (Pettigrew, 1978:327).

Although the special demands of stereopsis provide a plausible explanation for early plasticity, they do not provide a ready explanation
for the time course of this plasticity aside from the prediction that the
time of greatest sensitivity should coincide with periods of rapid growth
of the eyes and head. However, recent considerations of another aspect
of the special demands of binocular vision during development, apart
from stereopsis, provide an insight into the duration of the sensitive
period in various species. This insight has been provided by neurophysiological investigations of the system of binocular correspondence
of certain species (Cooper & Pettigrew, 1979), a system that is characterized by a theoretical surface called the horopter.

The horopter is simply defined as the locus of points in space that
stimulate corresponding points on the two retinae (Ogle, 1962). Objects
lying on the horopter surface are seen as single, whereas those lying
considerably in front or behind may be seen as double (diplopic). Because of the special requirements for stereopsis, namely, the detection
of small horizontal retinal disparities, most attention has been focused
on the shape of the horizontal section of the horopter, particularly that
section that lies in the plane of the fixation point and the nodal points
of the two eyes, referred to as the longitudinal horizontal horopter.
Because the horopter surface in general represents the locus of all points
in space that stimulate corresponding points, it represents the locus of
points in space around which stereoscopic processing is possible. The
position of this surface in space thus defines the region in which the
animal may possess stereopsis. Recent considerations of the shape of
this surface in the vertical dimension not only provide insights into the
need for plasticity in the visual cortex, but also the time course of that
sensitivity.

For some time it has been known that the main vertical retinal meridians of the human (the zero azimuthal meridian passing through the
fovea of each eye and dividing the nasal from the temporal retinas) are
not exactly vertical, but are in fact extorted with respect to each other.
This means that the line space whose images simultaneously fall along
these two meridians (the vertical horopter) is a tilted line in the midsagittal plane passing through the fixation point that slopes away from

the observer at the top (Cogan, 1979; Helmholtz, 1925). Recent neurophysiological determinations of the zero azimuthal meridian for the
two eyes of the cat and of the burrowing owl indicate that in life they
are not vertical and parallel, but also are extorted with respect to each
other. This means that the locus of points in space whose images
simultaneously lie on these meridians is a line tilted backwards in just
the same way as the vertical horopter of the human. The geometry of
the situation is illustrated in Fig. 1.15. The inclined plane LEFLE'B
represents the projection of the zero azimuthal meridian from the left
eye into space, and the plane REFRE'B represents the equivalent plane
from the right eye. These two planes intersect in the midsagittal plane
along the line BF, which represents the vertical horopter. Note that the
projections of the two zero azimuthal meridians onto a coronal plane
(such as a tangent screen) are sheared with respect to each other by
the angle, θ, which has been exaggerated in this figure for the sake of

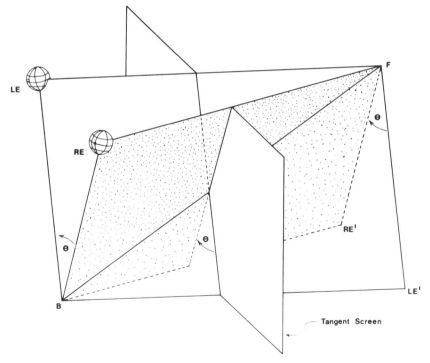

Fig. 1.15 The geometric relationships that define the slope of the vertical horopter.
The zero meridians of the left (LE) and right (RE) eyes are out-torted with respect to
each other by the angle θ during fixation of the point F. (From Cooper & Pettigrew,
1979, reprinted with permission.)

clarity. It is possible to show (Cooper & Pettigrew, 1979) that the point, B, at which the vertical horopter intersects the coronal plane that contains both eyes can be calculated solely from knowledge of the interpupillary separation and the angle of shear between the zero meridians. Helmholtz (1925) pointed out that the vertical horopter of the human passes through the observer's feet. Calculations made for the cat and burrowing owl indicate that the vertical horopters of these two species do likewise (Cooper & Pettigrew, 1979, Fig. 9). Thus, for as yet some unknown reason, there appears to be strong evolutionary pressure for the vertical horopter of at least three species (cat, burrowing owl, and human) to pass through the feet. If this is also a requirement throughout development, as the animal grows in height and the separation of the eyes changes, the angle of shear of the zero meridians must also change for the vertical horopter still to pass through the feet. Such a requirement *demands* plasticity of binocular connections in the geniculostriate pathway to prevent the visual world from breaking into diplopia as the shear between the zero meridians alters.

According to this formulation, the geniculostriate pathway must retain considerable plasticity not only throughout the period in life during which the separation of the eyes changes, but as long as an animal's height is changing. This predicts that some plasticity must be retained into adolescence. It is thus intriguing that recent physiological work indicates that the sensitive period in visual development in the cat lasts much longer than previously thought, to at least 6 months of age (Fig. 1.9). With even more sensitive assays (e.g., Fig. 1.10), it is possible to discern evidence of some plasticity up to 1 year of age, at which time an animal has virtually reached its adult size. Thus, although the plasticity of binocular connections in the kitten visual cortex is greatest during the fourth week of life, the subsequent decline in plasticity is quite gradual, extending into late adolescence. The same line of argument suggests that binocular connections in the human visual cortex might also retain some residual plasticity for a longer period than was previously thought (e.g., Banks *et al.*, 1975; Duke-Elder & Wybar, 1973; Vaegan & Taylor, 1979) possibly even until adult height is achieved in the mid teen-age years.

As Pettigrew (1978) has so cogently argued, central binocular connections of species that possess stereoscopic vision must be plastic early in life, not only to achieve initially the intricate connectivity that underlies the exquisitely fine sensitivity characteristic of stereopsis, but also to compensate for changes in the geometry of visual space consequent upon changes in interocular separation and height during growth. Unfortunately, however, the very plasticity that permits the development of stereoscopic vision potentially places the visual system at risk to permanent "damage" from accidental peripheral obstructions to concordant binocular visual input early in life. Detailed knowledge of the time course of sensitive periods in visual development is an obvious clinical first step toward the functional treatment of such developmental visual disorders.

ACKNOWLEDGMENTS

The research work reported in this chapter was generously supported by grants from the National Science and Engineering Research Council of Canada (AP7660) and from the National Health and Medical Research Council of Australia. I wish to thank all my colleagues at Dalhousie University, particularly Drs. Brian Timney and Max Cynader with whom I collaborated in much of the research. I would also like to express my appreciation of very many helpful discussions with my colleagues at the National Vision Research Institute of Australia, Dr. J. D. Pettigrew, Drs. Sheila and David Crewther and Dr. Ed Howell.

REFERENCES

Awaya, S., Miyake, Y., Imaizumi, Y., Shoise, Y., Kanda, T., & Komuro, K. Amblyopia in man suggestive of stimulus deprivation amblyopia. *Japanese Journal of Ophthalmology*, 1973, **17**, 69–82.

Baker, F. H., Grigg, P., & von Noorden, G. K. Effects of visual deprivation and strabismus on the responses of neurons in the visual cortex of the monkey, including studies on the striate and prestriate cortex in the normal animal. *Brain Research*, 1974, **66**, 185–208.

Banks, M. S., Aslin, R. N., & Letson, R. D. Sensitive period for the development of human binocular vision. *Science*, 1975, **190**, 675–677.

Barlow, H. B. Visual experience and cortical development. *Nature*, 1975, **258**, 199–204.

Bateson, P. How do sensitive periods arise and what are they for? *Animal Behaviour*, 1979, **27**, 470–486.

Berman, N., & Daw, N. W. Comparison of the critical periods for monocular and directional deprivation in cats. *Journal of Physiology*, 1977, **265**, 249–259.

Blakemore, C. Developmental factors in the formation of feature extracting neurons. In F. O. Schmitt & F. G. Worden (Eds.), *The neurosciences: Third study program.* Cambridge, Mass: MIT Press, 1974, pp. 105–113.

Blakemore, C. Maturation and modification in the developing visual system. In R. Held, M. W. Leibowitz, & H. L. Teuber (Eds.), *Handbook of sensory physiology* VIII. *Perception.* New York: Springer-Verlag, 1978, pp. 377–436.

Blakemore, C., & Van Sluyters, R. C. Reversal of the physiological effects of monocular deprivation in kittens: Further evidence for a sensitive period. *Journal of Physiology*, 1974, **237**, 195–216.

Blakemore, C., & Van Sluyters, R. C. Innate and environmental factors in the development of the kitten's visual cortex. *Journal of Physiology,* 1975, **248,** 663–716.

Blakemore, C., Garey, L. T., & Vital-Durand, F. The physiological effects of monocular deprivation and their reversal in the monkey's visual cortex. *Journal of Physiology,* 1978, **283,** 223–262.

Blasdel, G. G., & Pettigrew, J. D. Effect of prior visual experience on cortical recovery from the effects of unilateral eyelid suture in kittens. *Journal of Physiology,* 1978, **274,** 601–619.

Cleland, B. G., Harding, T. H., & Tulunay-Keesey, U. Visual resolution and receptive field size: Examination of two kinds of cat retinal ganglion cell. *Science* 1979, **205,** 1015–1017.

Cleland, B. G., Mitchell, D. E., Crewther, S. G., & Crewther, D. P. Visual resolution of retinal ganglion cells in monocularly-deprived cats. *Brain Research,* 1980, **192,** 261–266.

Cobb, S. R., & MacDonald, C. F. Resolution acuity in astigmats: Evidence for critical period in the human visual system. *British Journal of Physiological Optics,* 1978, **32,** 38–49.

Cogan, A. I. The relationship between the apparent vertical and the vertical horopter. *Vision Research,* 1979, **19,** 655–665.

Cooper, M. L., & Pettigrew, J. D. A neurophysiological determination of the vertical horopter in the cat and owl. *Journal of Comparative Neurology,* 1979, **194,** 1–26.

Cragg, B. G. The development of synapses in the visual system of the cat. *Journal of Comparative Neurology,* 1975, **160,** 147–166.

Crawford, M. L. J., Blake, R., Cool, S. J., & von Noorden, G. K. Physiological consequences of unilateral and bilateral eye closure in macaque monkeys: Some further observations. *Brain Research,* 1975, **84,** 150–154.

Cynader, M. Interocular alignment following visual deprivation in the cat. *Investigative Ophthalmology & Visual Science,* 1979, **18,** 726–741.

Cynader, M., Berman, N., & Hein, A. Cats raised in a one-directional world: Effects on receptive fields in visual cortex and superior colliculus. *Experimental Brain Research,* 1975, **22,** 267–280.

Cynader, M., Berman, N., & Hein, A. Recovery of function in cat visual cortex following prolonged deprivation. *Experimental Brain Research,* 1976, **25,** 139–156.

Cynader, M., & Mitchell, D. E. Prolonged sensitivity to monocular deprivation in dark reared cats. *Journal of Neurophysiology,* 1980, **43,** 1026–1040.

Cynader, M., Timney, B. N., & Mitchell, D. E. Period of susceptibility of kitten visual cortex to the effects of monocular deprivation extends beyond 6 months of age. *Brain Research,* 1980, **191,** 545–550.

Davison, A. N., & Dobbing, J. The developing brain. In A. N. Davison & J. Dobbing (Eds.), *Applied neurochemistry.* Oxford: Blackwell, 1968, 253–286.

Daw, N. W., & Wyatt, M. J. Kittens reared in a unidirectional environment: Evidence for a critical period. *Journal of Physiology,* 1976, **257,** 155–170.

Daw, N. W., Berman, N. E. J., & Ariel, M. Interaction of critical periods in the visual cortex of kittens. *Science,* 1978, **199,** 565–567.

Dobbing, J. Vulnerable periods in developing brain. In A. N. Davison & J. Dobbing (Eds.), *Applied neurochemistry.* Oxford: Blackwell, 1968, pp. 287–316.

Dobbing, J. Vulnerable periods in brain growth and somatic growth. In D. F. Roberts & A. M. Thomson (Eds.), *The biology of human fetal growth.* London: Taylor & Francis, 1976.

Duke-Elder, S., & Wybar, K. Ocular motility and strabismus. In S. Duke-Elder (Ed.), *System of ophthalmology* VI. London: Henry Kimpton, 1973.

Enoch, J. M., & Rabinowicz, I. M. Early surgery and visual correction of an infant born with unilateral eye lens opacity. *Documenta Ophthalmologica*, 1976, **41**, 371–382.

Enroth-Cugell, C., & Robson, J. G. The contrast sensitivity of retinal ganglion cells of the cat. *Journal of Physiology*, 1966, **187**, 517–552.

Freeman, R. D. Some neural and non-neural factors in visual development of the kitten. *Archives Italiennes de Biologie*, 1978, **116**, 338–351.

Garey, L. J., Fisken, R. A., & Powell, T. P. S. Observations on the growth of cells in the lateral geniculate nucleus of the cat. *Brain Research*, 1973, **52**, 359–362.

Giffin, F., & Mitchell, D. E. The rate of recovery of vision after early monocular deprivation in kittens. *Journal of Physiology*, 1978, **274**, 511–537.

Goldman, B. D. Developmental influences of hormones on neuroendocrine mechanisms of sexual behaviour: Comparisons with other sexually dimorphic behaviors. In J. B. Hutchison (Ed.), *Biological determinants of sexual behaviour*. Chichester: Wiley, 1978, pp. 127–152.

Grobstein, P., & Chow, K. L. Receptive field development and individual experience. *Science*, 1975, **190**, 352–358.

Helmholtz, H. von. [*Treatise on physiological optics* III.] (J. P. C. Southall, Ed. and trans. of third German ed.) New York: Optical Society of America, 1925.

Hess, E. H. *Imprinting*. New York: Van Nostrand Reinhold, 1973.

Hickey, T. L. Postnatal development of the human lateral geniculate nucleus: Relationship to a critical period for the visual system. *Science*, 1977, **198**, 836–838.

Hubel, D. H., & Wiesel, T. N. Receptive fields of cells in striate cortex of very young, visually inexperienced kittens. *Journal of Neurophysiology*, 1963, **26**, 994–1002.

Hubel, D. H., & Wiesel, T. N. Binocular interaction in striate cortex of kittens reared with artificial squint. *Journal of Neurophysiology*, 1965, **28**, 1041–1059.

Hubel, D. H., & Wiesel, T. N. The period of susceptibility to the physiological effects of unilateral eye closure in kittens. *Journal of Physiology*, 1970, **206**, 419–436.

Hubel, D. H., & Wiesel, T. N. Ferrier Lecture. Functional architecture of macaque monkey visual cortex. *Proceedings of the Royal Society of London B*, 1977, **198**, 1–59.

Hubel, D. H., Wiesel, T. N., & Le Vay, S. Plasticity of ocular dominance columns in monkey striate cortex. *Philosophical Transactions of the Royal Society of London B*, 1977, **278**, 377–409.

Irvine, G. L., & Timaras, P. S. Litter size and brain development in the rat. *Life Sciences*, 1966, **5**, 1577–1582.

Kalil, R. Development of the dorsal lateral geniculate nucleus in the cat. *Journal of Comparative Neurology*, 1978, **182**, 265–292.

Kalil, R. E., Spear, P. D., & Langsetmo, A. Response properties of striate cortex neurons in cats raised with divergent or convergent strabismus. *ARVO abstracts*, 1978, **269.**

Konishi, M. Auditory environment and vocal development in birds. In R. D. Walk & H. L. Pick (Eds.), *Perception and experience*, New York: Plenum, 1978, pp. 105–118.

Le Vay, S., Stryker, M. P., & Shatz, C. J. Ocular dominance columns and their development in layer IV of the cat's visual cortex: A quantitative study. *Journal of Comparative Neurology*, 1978, **179**, 223–244.

Le Vay, S., Wiesel, T. N., & Hubel, D. H. The development of ocular dominance columns in normal and visually deprived monkeys. *Journal of Comparative Neurology*, 1980, **191**, 1–51.

Lund, R. D. *Development and plasticity of the brain*. New York: Oxford University Press, 1978.

Marler, P. A comparative approach to vocal learning: Song development in white-crowned sparrows. *Journal of Comparative and Physiological Psychology Monograph*, 1970, **71**(3), 1–25.

Mitchell, D. E., Cynader, M., & Movshon, J. A. Recovery from the effects of monocular deprivation in kittens. *Journal of Comparative Neurology*, 1977, **6**, 181–193. (a)

Mitchell, D. E., Freeman, R. D., Millodot, M., & Haegerstrom, G. Meridional amblyopia: Evidence for modification of the human visual system by early visual experience. *Vision Research*, 1973, **13**, 535–558.

Mitchell, D. E., Giffin, F., & Timney, B. A behavioural technique for the rapid assessment of the visual capabilities of kittens. *Perception*, 1977, **6**, 181–193.

Mohindra, I., Held, R., Gwiazda, J., & Brill, S. Astigmatism in infants. *Science*, 1978, **202**, 329–331.

Mohindra, I., Jacobson, S. G., Thomas, J., & Held, R. Development of amblyopia in infants. *Transactions of the Ophthalmological Societies of the United Kingdom*, 1979, **99**, 344–346.

Morgan, M. J. *Molyneux's question*. Cambridge: Cambridge University Press, 1977.

Movshon, J. A. Reversal of the physiological effects of monocular deprivation in the kitten's visual cortex. *Journal of Physiology*, 1976, **261**, 125–174.

Movshon, J. A., & Van Sluyters, R. C. Visual neural development. *Annual Review of Psychology*, 1981, **32**, 477–522.

Nottebohm, F. The "critical period" for song learning in birds. *Ibis*, 1969, **3**, 386–387.

Ogle, K. N. The optical space sense. In H. Davson (Ed.), *The eye (Vol. 4). Visual optics and the optical space sense.* New York: Academic Press, 1962.

Olson, C. R., & Freeman, R. D. Monocular deprivation and recovery during sensitive period in kittens. *Journal of Neurophysiology*, 1978, **41**, 65–74.

Olson, C. R., & Freeman, R. D. Profile of the sensitive period for monocular deprivation in kittens. *Experimental Brain Research*, 1980, **39**, 17–21.

Pettigrew, J. D. The effect of visual experience on the development of stimulus specificity by kitten cortical neurones. *Journal of Physiology*, 1974, **237**, 49–74.

Pettigrew, J. D. The paradox of the critical period for striate cortex. In C. W. Cotman (Ed.), *Neuronal plasticity*. New York: Raven, 1978, pp. 311–330.

Pettigrew, J. D., & Konishi, M. Neurons selective for orientation and binocular disparity in the visual Wulst of the barn owl. *(Tyto alba). Science*, 1976, **193**, 675–678. (a)

Pettigrew, J. D., & Konishi, M. Effects of monocular deprivation on binocular neurones in the owl's visual Wulst. *Nature*, 1976, **264**, 753–754. (b)

Presson, J., & Gordon, B. Critical period and minimum exposure required for the effects of alternating monocular occlusion in cat visual cortex. *Vision Research*, 1979, **19**, 807–811.

Scott, J. P. Critical periods in behavioral development. *Science*, 1962, **138**, 949–958.

Scott, J. P. *Critical periods.* Stroudsburg, Pa: Dowden, Hutchinson, & Ross, 1978.

Sluckin, W. *Early learning in man and animal* (2nd ed.). London: George Allen & Unwin, 1972.

Stockard, C. R. Developmental rate and structural expression: An experimental study of twins, "double monsters" and single deformities, and the interaction among embryonic organs during their origin and development. *American Journal of Anatomy*, 1921, **28**, 115–227.

Thorpe, W. M. Sensitive periods in the learning of animals and men: A study of imprinting with special reference to the induction of cyclic behaviour. In. W. M. Thorpe & O. L. Zangwill (Eds.), *Current Problems in Animal Behaviour*, Cambridge: Cambridge University Press, 1961, **11**, 194–224. (a)

Thorpe, W. H. *Bird song.* Cambridge: Cambridge University Press, 1961. (b)

Timney, B., Mitchell, D. E., & Giffin, F. The development of vision in cats after extended periods of dark rearing. *Experimental Brain Research*, 1978, **31**, 547–560.

Timney, B. & Mitchell, D. E. Behavioral recovery from visual deprivation: comments on the critical period. In R. D. Freeman (Ed.) *Developmental Neurobiology of Vision*, New York, Plenum, 1979.

Timney, B., Mitchell, D. E., & Cynader, M. Behavioral evidence for prolonged sensitivity to effects of monocular deprivation in dark reared cats. *Journal of Neurophysiology*, 1980, **43**, 1041–1054.

Tretter, F., Cynader, M., & Singer, W. Modification of direction selectivity of neurons in the visual cortex of kittens. *Brain Research*, 1975, **84**, 143–149.

Vaegan & Taylor, D. Critical period for deprivation amblyopia in children. *Transactions of the Ophthalmological Societies of the United Kingdom*, 1979, **99**, 432–439.

van Hof-van Duin, J. Development of visuomotor behaviour in normal and dark reared cats. *Brain Research*, 1976, **104**, 233–241.

Vongdokmai, R. Effects of protein malnutrition on development of mouse cortical barrels. *Journal of Comparative Neurology*, 1980, **191**, 283–294.

von Noorden, G. K. Experimental amblyopia in monkeys. Further behavioral observations and clinical correlations. *Investigative Ophthalmology*, 1973, **12**, 721–726.

von Noorden, G. K., & Dowling, J. E. Experimental amblyopia in monkeys II. Behavioral studies in strabismic amblyopia. *AMA Archives of Ophthalmology*, 1970, **84**, 215–220.

von Noorden, G. K., Dowling, J. E., & Ferguson, D. C. Experimental amblyopia in monkeys I. Behavioral studies of stimulus deprivation amblyopia. *AMA Archives of Ophthalmology*, 1970, **84**, 206–214.

Widdowson, E. M., & McCance, R. A. Some effects of accelerating growth I. General somatic development. *Proceedings of the Royal Society of London B*, 1960, **152**, 188–206.

Wiesel, T. N., & Hubel, D. H. Single-cell responses in striate cortex of kittens deprived of vision in one eye. *Journal of Neurophysiology*, 1963, **26**, 1003–1017.

Wiesel, T. N., & Hubel, D. H. Comparison of the effects of unilateral and bilateral eye closure on cortical unit responses in kittens. *Journal of Neurophysiology*, 1965, **28**, 1029–1040.

Wilkinson, F. Reversal of the behavioural effects of monocular deprivation as a function of age in the kitten. *Behavioural Brain Research*, 1980, **1**, 101–123.

Yinon, U. Age dependence of the effect of squint on cells in kitten's visual cortex. *Experimental Brain Research*, 1976, **26**, 151–157.

2

Experiential Influences and Sensitive Periods in Perceptual Development: A Unified Model

RICHARD N. ASLIN
Indiana University

I. INTRODUCTION

During the past decade, two important and wide-ranging theoretical concepts have emerged (or re-emerged) from studies of perceptual development. First, it has become quite clear that the role that environmental input (i.e., experience) plays in determining the course of perceptual development is multifaceted. Although this concept has been generally accepted, it has typically generated oversimplified dichotomies such as the nature–nurture controversy (Hochberg, 1962). As a result, the entire question of the relative contributions of genetic and experiential factors to perceptual development has floundered for cen-

DEVELOPMENT OF PERCEPTION
Volume 2

turies (Anastasi, 1958; Pastore, 1971). What has been lacking is a coherent theoretical framework within which the interaction between genetic constraints and experiential influences can be viewed. Gottlieb (1976a,b; Chapter 1 in Volume I) has provided just such a framework, and despite its after-the-fact simplicity to many, it is apparent that such a vehicle for conceptualizing the roles of experience in development has been of great benefit to a wide variety of researchers in several diverse areas of investigation.

The second key concept to emerge in the past decade is that of a sensitive period. The concept of a sensitive period in development is not new and has been discussed by several researchers with regard to various sensory, perceptual, cognitive, and social abilities and behaviors (Scott, 1978). For example, the imprinting literature has utilized this concept for several decades (see Bateson, 1979, for a recent review). Yet it has only been 10 years since Hubel and Wiesel (1970) reintroduced the concept of a sensitive period to a specific case in visual neural development. As with the general notion of a nature–nurture distinction, however, the concept of a sensitive period has received little quantitative exploration despite a rash of empirical investigations in several areas that could have provided such a detailed description. Again, the problem is not that researchers are unaware of the concept, but rather that the specific nature and timing of a sensitive period have not been integrated into a general model of perceptual development.

Despite the absence of a clear conception of how to integrate genetic and experiential factors, it can be argued that the general questions and approaches to research within the diverse areas of perceptual development are shared by the vast majority of researchers. What is lacking is a coherent framework within which one's empirical research program can be guided and one's results conceptualized and interpreted. The purpose of this chapter, therefore, is to (a) delineate the potential roles that early experience can play in perceptual development; (b) describe the important aspects of experiential timing embodied in the concept of a sensitive period; (c) present a comprehensive model of the mechanism by which experience influences perceptual development; and (d) illustrate the usefulness of this unified model with examples from several instances of perceptual development. In the final two sections, several further issues will be examined, including how developmental research should be done and what kind of explanation of developmental change we can hope to obtain from such research. These multiple goals are put forth with an overriding concern for generating testable hypotheses and stimulating other researchers to ponder the goals and strategies of their own research programs.

II. THE ROLES OF EXPERIENCE REVISITED

Although virtually no one seriously clings to a theory of perceptual development that could be classified as either purely nativist or purely empiricist, the resultant "interactional" viewpoint is frustratingly non-specific. There can be little doubt that development is determined by a combination of genetic and environmental factors operating in a complex manner. Of particular concern are (a) *how* these factors interact; and (b) *when* during development they exert their most significant influence.

Gottlieb's (1976a,b) framework for viewing experiential influences during development attempts to add some degree of specificity to the interactional viewpoint by describing three major types of developmental outcomes. The first type, *maintenance*, describes a particular perceptual preference (or ability level) that is already fully developed prior to the time when specific experiences become available to the organism. If specific experiences are present during this early receptive or sensitive period, the perceptual preference is maintained. If the specific experiences are absent, the perceptual preference declines (perhaps permanently). The second type of developmental outcome, *facilitation*, describes a perceptual preference that is only partially developed at the time when specific experiences become available to the organism. In the absence of specific experiences, the perceptual preference continues to develop. However, if specific experiences are present, the perceptual preference will develop more rapidly (or more completely). The third type of developmental outcome, *induction*, describes a perceptual preference that is absent until the time when specific experiences become available to the organism. The perceptual preference will develop only if the specific experience is provided. The timing of this experiential input, that is, its necessity at certain developmental periods, has not been delineated; but presumably the induction process is typically not open-ended during the organism's entire lifetime.

In a review of infant speech perception (Aslin & Pisoni, 1980), we attempted to offer a scheme for illustrating these possible developmental outcomes as they related to the human infant's ability to discriminate various phonetic contrasts. In a subsequent review (Aslin & Dumais, 1980), we offered a similar scheme to describe the possible developmental outcomes for the human infant's binocular visual capabilities. The most general case of this schematic representation would be to consider the development of any perceptual ability or, for that matter, any aspect of the organism's phenotype. Figure 2.1 illustrates this generalized scheme for the possible developmental outcomes re-

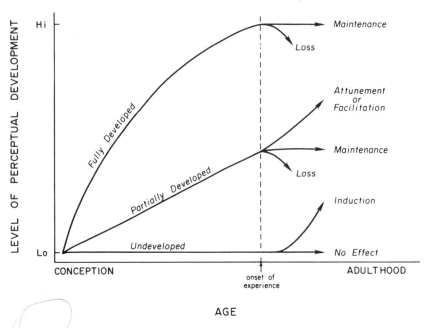

Fig. 2.1 Illustration of several possible developmental outcomes resulting from different levels of development prior to the onset of experience (dashed line) and different experiential inputs. (Adapted from Aslin and Dumais, 1980.)

sulting from different influences exerted by experience. Several key points are depicted in this figure. First, during the developmental period prior to the availability of specific experiences (e.g., prior to birth or eye opening for vision) there nevertheless is the possibility that the phenotype in question has already developed. Thus, in general, the phenotype may be fully developed, partially developed, or not developed at all when specific experiences become available to the organism. Obviously, there are an infinite number of such pre-experience developmental functions, but these three provide a sufficient categorization for illustrative purposes. Second, after the time when specific experiences become available, the level of development of the phenotype may increase, decrease, or stay the same. Thus, the three general types of developmental outcomes described by Gottlieb—maintenance, facilitation, and induction—are specific cases of the multitude of developmental outcomes illustrated in this figure.

Chapter 1 by Gottlieb in Volume I provides an updated and more elaborate illustration of the roles of experience in perceptual development. However, several issues related to that illustration remain unspecified, and the process of revising that illustration has led me to reformulate the entire scheme. Before describing that reformulation, however, a more complete form of Gottlieb's latest scheme, as well as some of the problems that it raises, will be discussed.

As described by Gottlieb (1976b), his classification of the three different roles of experience was carefully extracted from a wide array of anatomical, physiological, and behavioral studies before being applied to his own research on auditory development in ducks. The primary dependent measure in his research on ducklings is a behavioral preference for one of two auditory signals. However, in other areas of perceptual development, the primary dependent measure is somewhat different; for example, in psychophysics, a measure of discriminability such as d' or, in single unit research, a neuron's tuning curve. These examples raise a fourth type of developmental outcome that was not originally encompassed by the terms *maintenance, facilitation,* or *induction.* As in the case of facilitation, the perceptual ability may be partially developed at the time when specific experiences become available to the organism. However, the specific experience may not affect the *rate* of development. Rather, the experience may influence the absolute level or the specific characteristics of the phenotype at the developmental endpoint.

In our previous treatments of this issue (Aslin & Dumais, 1980; Aslin & Pisoni, 1980), we have, in fact, substituted this alteration in the developmental endpoint for the increase in rate characteristic of facilitation, primarily because the specific phenotypes of interest did not appear to show much variance in their rate of development. We used the term *attunement* to describe this fourth developmental outcome. However, as Gottlieb has pointed out in Chapter 1 of Volume I, attunement is, in fact, a subtype or special instance of induction. In other words, for both induction and attunement, the level of phenotypic development increases provided that certain experiences are present, either emerging (induction) or becoming more finely tuned (attunement). However, not all experiences operate as inducers or tuners of the phenotype. This constraint on the effectiveness of specific experiences has not been adequately illustrated in the past. Finally, it should be noted that a fifth type of developmental outcome is possible: a purely maturational function in which certain specific types of experiences play little or no role in the development of the phenotype being studied. All five of these types of possible developmental outcomes are illustrated in Fig. 2.2 using Gottlieb's scheme.

Figure 2.2 also illustrates a possible ordering of experiential influences, progressing from maturation (a) to induction (e), in which there

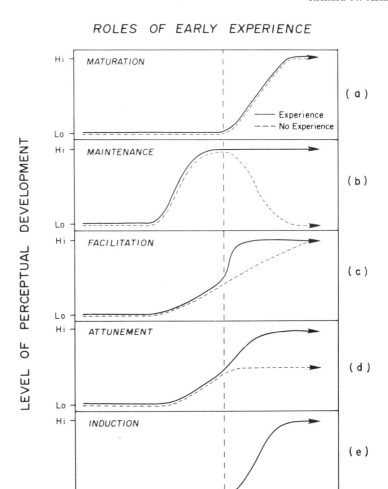

ROLES OF EARLY EXPERIENCE

Fig. 2.2 Five roles of experience in the development of a phenotype. (Adapted from Gottlieb, Chapter 1 in Volume 1.)

is an increasing dependence upon experience for the development of the phenotype. Maturation occurs with little or no experiential influence; maintenance simply stabilizes an already mature phenotype; facilitation enhances the acquisition but not the final level of the phenotype; attunement enhances the final level and/or the characteristics of a phenotype that is already partially present; and induction actually determines the presence and final level of the phenotype. Yet, if 5 types of experiential influence provide a good description, why not 6, 10, or 100? Moreover, it would seem reasonable to describe certain experiences that allow a phenotype to continue developing as "maintaining" that developmental progression. However, in the past, the use of the term *maintenance* has been applied primarily to phenotypes that are already fully developed. To abandon that restriction would introduce concepts such as "trajectory" that are not deemed appropriate by Gottlieb (personal communication, May 1980) as they are usually associated with teleological arguments about the future course of development. Nevertheless, an ambiguity raised by Gottlieb's scheme is the apparent focus on *states* of development rather than on *processes* of development.[1] A state of a phenotype can be maintained, but can a process of development be maintained? For example, in the case of attunement (Fig. 2.2d), one could argue that the species-typical process of reaching a fully developed endpoint is maintained by the presence of a specific experiential input. This issue may be largely semantic, but it raises another problematic aspect of past descriptions of experiential influence that, despite some discussion by Gottlieb (1976b), continues to lead to interpretive confusions.

Another problem in past discussions of experiential influences in perceptual development has been the invariable intermixing of several levels of explanation. For example, consider a particular species of mammal that normally begins to wean at 6 weeks of age but, if exposed to early environmental radiation, begins to wean at 4 weeks of age. In this case, the behavioral phenotype of weaning occurs whether or not the animal received "normal" or "special" early experience. Yet the animal receiving the "special" experience reaches the phenotypic level sooner. At the behavioral level, therefore, we have a clear case of facilitation. But at some underlying level there may have been a process of induction (or attunement). For example, the radiation may have affected the number of synapses that made connections in a neural structure subserving thermoregulation. If this thermoregulation system were triggered (i.e., induced), then the behavioral phenotype of weaning would follow.

The apparent maintenance of binocularity in the visual cortex of

---

[1] Admittedly, Gottlieb (1976b:28) stated that the term *maintenance* could include instances in which experience may "be required to keep an immature system intact, going and functional so that it is able to reach its full development at a later stage." However, the primary use of the term *maintenance* has been in the description of phenotypes that are already fully developed prior to the onset of experience.

mammals provides another example of the multileveled nature of experiential influences. The property of binocularity is present at the time of eye opening in kittens. Yet, binocularity can be lost if an imbalance exists in the visual input to the two eyes during the early postnatal weeks. Why, if the phenotype is mature, does the visual system remain plastic? Pettigrew (1978) has provided a possible explanation by proposing that what appears to be a fully developed phenotype may, in fact, be only partially developed. That is, the mechanism underlying the phenotype (in this case binocularity) may still be undergoing significant development (perhaps involving the formation of inhibitory connections). Thus, at the single unit level, the role of experience may be characterized by the term *maintenance*, while, at the same time, at the neurochemical level involved in the formation of synapses, the role of experience may be best described as *attunement* or *induction* (see Rakic, 1979, for a recent review).

The purpose of this discussion of levels of experiential influence is to point out that in describing the manner in which experience modifies a phenotype during development, the mechanism is only being characterized *at the level of the phenotype itself,* and not at all underlying levels. It must be the case that, for any given phenotype, there have been inductive processes operating at some preceding point(s) in development. However, for the purpose of describing perceptual development, one must be clear about keeping the level of analysis at the level of description. Failure to do so will result in an infinite reduction to lower and lower levels of explanation that push us further and further from a perceptual (or behavioral) level.

III. SENSITIVE PERIODS: WHEN IS EXPERIENCE NECESSARY?

Despite its popularity in recent discussions of sensory and perceptual development, the concept of a sensitive period has received remarkably little quantitative analysis. The basic notion of a sensitive period is that specific experiences exert a differential effect on the development of a phenotype at different times during development. In general, this should come as no surprise. Certainly, there are many (perhaps most) *serial* aspects of development that require certain specific events to allow the continuation of a developmental progression. Yet whenever we find examples of a very limited time window in which specific experiences must be present, and when the experience happens to be required in early development, we are struck by the necessary (critical) nature of the experience for the organism's later development.

Although the general concept of a sensitive period seems straightforward, it is not obvious how this concept can be clearly illustrated. The most common method of illustration has been to plot the relative importance of specific experiences to the development of a phenotype as a function of the organism's age. Clearly, the height, shape, timing, and duration of this sensitive period could vary in many ways. What is not immediately apparent is how this plot of experiential sensitivity could represent the effects of experiential deficits. Several reports, all in the literature on visual development, have attempted to describe quantitatively the effects of experiential deficits during the sensitive period (Banks, Aslin, & Letson, 1975; Blakemore & Van Sluyters, 1974; Hohmann & Creutzfeldt, 1975; Movshon, 1976; Olson & Freeman, 1980). The reversal index approach used by Blakemore and Van Sluyters (1974) and Movshon (1976) has already been discussed in Chapter 1 in this volume; the Olson and Freeman (1980) study only employed a brief period of monocular deprivation. Therefore, the sensitive period model of Banks, et al. (1975) will be reviewed here to illustrate their approach to describing the quantitative aspects of a sensitive period.

Figure 2.3 illustrates the general scheme used by Banks et al. (1975) for estimating the characteristics of a sensitive period. First, a particular "guess" at the shape and timing of the sensitive period is chosen. Then the time period during which each subject has received an experiential deficit is mapped onto this hypothesized sensitive period. In Fig. 2.3, this period of deprivation for one particular subject is represented by the shaded area. The entire area under this hypothesized sensitive period is set at 100% and the area corresponding to the period of deprivation is subtracted from this 100% value.[2] Thus, if the correct sensitive period has been chosen, each subject, regardless of the period of deprivation, will have a "predicted" phenotype (from 0 to 100%) that corresponds very closely with the actual (measured) phenotype. Obviously, if the hypothesized sensitive period is grossly incorrect, the correlation between the predicted and actual phenotypes for a group of subjects will approach zero.

---

[2] The model of Banks et al. (1975) has been simplified here. An additional parameter used in searching for the sensitive period was the subject's age at testing. The area under the function from the age at testing to the age when the ability reached maturity (e.g., 20 years after birth in the case of humans) was subtracted from 100%. This calculation was added because the sensitive period could have extended beyond the subject's age at testing. In that event, the estimate of the sensitive period would have been in error, as the normal experience required to acquire or maintain the ability would not have been accounted for. However, if the subject is tested at a mature age, presumably after the sensitive period has ended, this additional computation can be eliminated.

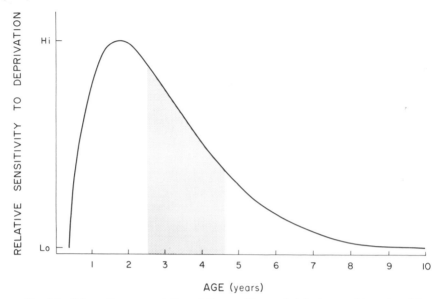

Fig. 2.3 Schematic representation of the sensitive period for human binocular vision and a period of binocular deprivation (shaded area) for a particular subject. (Adapted from Banks, Aslin, and Letson, 1975; copyright 1975 by the American Association for the Advancement of Science.)

In the Banks *et al.* (1975) study, a group of subjects, all of whom had different periods of deprivation, were tested for their current phenotype (binocular function). The hypothesized sensitive period was systematically manipulated in shape and timing to determine the particular mathematical function that generated the highest correlation between predicted and measured phenotype scores. The resultant best-fitting curve, the one actually shown in Fig. 2.3, represents the best estimate of the sensitive period for binocular vision in humans. That is, this curve depicts the relative sensitivity of the human visual system to binocular deprivation.

This general approach to quantitatively describing the sensitive period is applicable to a wide variety of phenotypes from many different species. Several important issues, however, are not encompassed within the descriptive analysis of a sensitive period as outlined. First, the characteristics of the sensitive period are independent of the status of the phenotype at any point during normal development. In other words, the phenotypic level could be fully developed, partially developed, or not developed at all prior to the onset of the sensitive period. For example, cortical binocularity is apparently fully present prior to the time of eye opening (tenth postnatal day) in kittens. The onset of the cat's sensitive period, however, does not occur until 3 or 4 weeks postnatally. Thus, binocularity in the kitten cortex follows a maintenance role for early experience. In contrast, the case of binocular vision in humans appears (perhaps coincidentally) to show a close correspondence between phenotypic onset (stereopsis appears to emerge 3–4 months postnatally; see Fox, Aslin, Shea, & Dumais, 1980; Fox, Chapter 12 in this volume) and an estimated sensitive period onset of 3–4 months postnatally (based on the function shown in Fig. 2.3). Finally, the phenotype could emerge several weeks or months *after* the sensitive period, as in the case of song acquisition in various species of songbirds (see Marler, 1970, for a general review). Thus, it is important to separate, at least conceptually, the timing of the sensitive period from the level of specificity of the phenotype during normal development.

A second issue that has rarely been addressed in past discussions of a sensitive period is the specific nature of the experience required during the sensitive period for "normal" development to occur. If the deprivation received by the organism is severe, then it is quite possible that only one of the many aspects of experiential deprivation was responsible for the failure of the phenotype to reach (or to maintain) its normal level. Clearly, careful parametric manipulations of experience, particularly those that are more subtle than dark or isolation rearing, are needed to specify the precise experiential requirements(s) for normal development.

Third, data relevant to a sensitive period are typically used to infer the experiential requirements for normal development from the results of experimentally induced experiential deficits. However, in these instances of perceptual deprivation, the system underlying the phenotype may have been forced to adopt redundant or compensatory mechanisms in an effort to counteract the loss of specific experiential input. If so, the sensitive period under conditions of *normal* experience may have a considerably different duration or a different selectivity for particular experiential inputs than the estimate of the sensitive period based on studies of severe experiential deficits.

Finally, schemes for describing a sensitive period have not offered any insight into a well-known process in development: the rebound or catch-up that occurs after a period of deprivation (Tanner, 1970). Presumably, this rebound can occur only if the period of deprivation has ended prior to the *offset* of the sensitive period. Yet, according to the sensitive period model of Banks *et al.* (1975), there are several deprivation regimens that could yield equivalent postdeprivation phenotypes (i.e., a constant loss in the area under the curve could occur in various ways). However, the process underlying these different deprivation regimens is probably quite different. Three consecutive days of monocular deprivation may operate quite differently on the visual system than three alternate days of monocular deprivation, even though the predicted loss in the phenotype based on the model may be equivalent. What, then, allows the phenotype to "recover" from deprivation during the sensitive period? What aspects of postdeprivation experiences allow for this recovery? Are those experiences that are optimal for postdeprivation recovery the same as the experiences required for "normal" development? These and other questions cannot be addressed without recourse to a more comprehensive, integrated model of development. In the next section, such a unified perspective on the process of experiential influence is presented.

IV. A UNIFIED MODEL OF EXPERIENTIAL INFLUENCE

The goal of the present model of experiential influence is to bring together, in a generalized form, the various roles of experience, as described by Gottlieb and others, and the concept of a sensitive period. To begin, consider a particular aspect of the phenotype related to the functioning of a perceptual system. At some point in development, the perceptual ability must have been absent. Yet, given a "normal" environment and the absence of a genetic deficiency, the level of specificity of the perceptual ability should eventually reach a value of 1.0 (i.e., the average of the adult population of that species). We can therefore consider a normative developmental function for any aspect of the phenotype. This normative function represents the typical progression of changes in the phenotype during development, and any deviations from this function are the result of genetic and/or experiential factors. Presumably, natural selection has determined the shape and timing of this developmental function, and different aspects of the phenotype will have their own characteristic developmental functions. Figure 2.4 shows several examples of these hypothetical normative developmental functions, all of which are scaled to asymptote at a value of 1.0. It should be emphasized here that the normative developmental function is *not* intended to represent a predetermined pathway or trajectory of phenotypic development culminating in a fixed endpoint. Rather, the function is simply a descriptive statement of the fact that a species-specific genotype and a species-typical environment will, for the average member of the species, result in a relatively uniform course of phe-

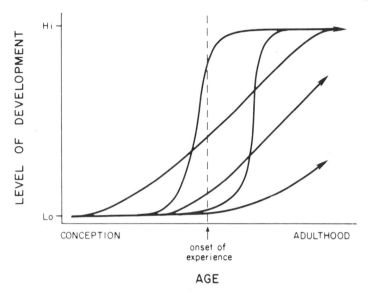

Fig. 2.4 Hypothetical normative developmental functions for various phenotypes illustrating the potential variance in age of onset and rate of development.

notypic development. The uniformity of this function across different members of a species may reflect invariant environmental conditions, a highly constrained and species-specific susceptibility to particular experiences, or both.

During the course of normal development, each particular aspect of the phenotype may be susceptible to the influences of environmental factors. The concept of a sensitive period, as previously discussed, is that the normal course of development contains one (or more) delimited time periods during which experience exerts a significant influence, even to the point of permanently altering the normative developmental function. Two important aspects of the interaction between the normative developmental function and the concept of a sensitive period deserve special mention. First, for a given aspect of the phenotype, it is possible that the sensitive period could be located at any region along the age axis of the developmental function. If the sensitive period occurred early, we would tend to view experience as inducing the phenotype. If the sensitive period occurred during the transition in the level of specificity of the phenotype, we would tend to view experience as facilitating or tuning the phenotype. And if the sensitive period occurred after the level of phenotypic specificity had reached an asymptote, we would tend to view experience as maintaining the phenotype. Although these interpretations seem plausible, they are not necessary conclusions, as we shall see in a later section.

Second, the time during development when experiences become available to the organism is both species- and modality-specific. Thus, in rats, for example, specific chemical stimuli are available prenatally (see Chapter 12 by Pedersen & Blass in Volume I), whereas patterned visual stimuli are not available until several days postnatally at the time of eye opening. In more visually precocious species (e.g., primates), the availability of visual stimulation coincides with birth. Clearly, however, the time of birth (or hatching) is only one convenient milestone that may have only an indirect relation to the age when specific experiences become available to the developing organism. For example, it is possible that, for a given species, sensitivity to experiences in a particular modality precedes the typical availability of such experiences. As a result of this species-typical absence of experiential inputs, the "effective" sensitive period is delayed. The presence of this latent sensitive period could only be discovered by experimental manipulations of the timing of experiential inputs by altering the species-typical environment. In contrast, it is possible that, for a given species, the "actual" sensitive period is delayed relative to the species-typical onset of experiential inputs in a particular modality.

In summary, there are three aspects of the interaction between a normative developmental function and a sensitive period: (a) the shape and timing of the normative developmental function for a given aspect of the phenotype; (b) the postconceptional age when specific experiences become available to the organism; and (c) the timing of the sensitive period. Each of these three aspects of development are potentially independent of one another. For example, by manipulating the organism's species-typical environment, it is possible to present experiences important for development before, during, or after the sensitive period. Moreover, these important experiences could be presented to the organism at any time during the course of the normative developmental function. And, as mentioned previously, it is possible that, for specific aspects of the phenotype, the sensitive period could occur during different portions of the normative developmental function for different species. The task of integrating these three aspects into a coherent model of development is extremely complex. Often, in theoretical discussions, it is useful to employ a metaphor to more clearly illustrate, by analogy, an underlying process that is likely to be involved in the phenomenon of interest. In the following section, such a metaphoric description will be offered. It is important to note, however, that this description should *not* be taken literally as the mechanism underlying experiential influence in perceptual development. Rather, the metaphor is only intended to capture what the underlying mechanism must be doing *in some fashion.*

A. Genetic Constraints: A Filter Analogy

The concept of a filter is well known to a wide variety of researchers, particularly those in the physical sciences. In essence, a filter is a device that has the characteristic of passing (transmitting) only certain aspects of stimulation or information, while blocking (filtering) all other aspects. In optics and acoustics, filters can be constructed to pass only certain types of light and sound, respectively, and the filter's characteristics (low pass, high pass, or bandpass) along the dimensions of wavelength and frequency can be specified by a mathematical function.

By analogy, we could consider specific perceptual experiences as lying along a dimension of environmental input. For example, the orientation of high contrast edges or the dominant frequency of species-specific vocalizations could be considered to be dimensions of perceptual experience. Furthermore, only certain aspects of experience along these dimensions will exert a significant effect on the organism. A trivial example of this selectivity is the insensitivity of most humans to electromagnetic and acoustic wavelengths that are either very low (less than 400 nm or 15 Hz) or very high (greater than 700 nm or 20 kHz). A more intriguing example of this selectivity occurs when a broad range of experiential inputs is available, particularly when each of these inputs can affect the organism when presented individually. In most cases of this multiple availability of suprathreshold stimuli, the organism is affected by only a limited range of these experiential inputs, and may develop a heightened sensitivity or behavioral preference to those specific experiences. Clearly, this selectivity must be species-specific and determined, at least in part, by the genome.

Of particular importance to a model of experiential influence is the mechanism by which the organism becomes differentially responsive to specific experiences. To attempt an explanation of such a mechanism, it is necessary to make certain assumptions. The first assumption is that there is a genetically specified range of "acceptable" environmental inputs that fulfills certain basic requirements for each aspect of the developing organism's perceptual system. This range of acceptable environmental stimulation could be viewed as a filter. As illustrated in Fig. 2.5, this filter lies along a dimension of environmental stimulation (e.g., the orientation of edges) and transmits only those experiences

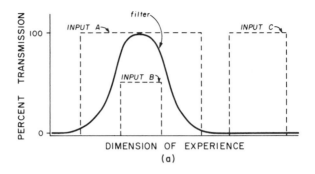

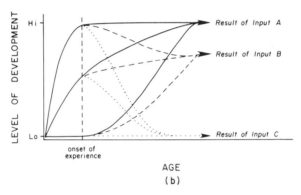

Fig. 2.5 (a) Scheme of a hypothetical experiential filter and three different experiential inputs. (b) Illustration of the effect of the transmission of different experiential inputs on the course of development.

within its range while attenuating those experiences falling outside its range. The level of attenuation is inversely proportional to the height of the filter. Thus, the filter analogy specifies a genetic constraint on the specific aspects of experience that have an effect upon the course of development.

Given this assumption of selective experiential filtering, we can also consider the result of variations in experiential input with respect to the normative developmental function. Several examples of the modified course of development resulting from variations in experiential input are illustrated in Fig. 2.5b. If the range of experiential input covers the extent of the filter (Input A), the developmental function will progress normally (solid lines). Note that, in this case, the role that experience plays in development is determined by the location of the sensitive period along the normative developmental function. If the amount (or purity) of experience, despite matching the mean of the filter, is reduced (Input B), the developmental function will be attenuated and may never reach the species-typical asymptote (dashed lines). Finally, if the experiential input does not overlap the filter (Input C), the developmental function will decline (or fail to emerge) and will not reach the species-typical asymptote (dotted lines).

The second assumption of the present model is that both the height and width of the experiential filter typically change over the course of development. The height of the filter represents the *sensitivity* of the system to experiential inputs. If sensitivity to experiential inputs shows a peak during the course of development, the duration of this peak defines the sensitive period. The assumption that the filter changes in width provides an additional conceptualization of the mechanism underlying the sensitive period. Rather than the simple assumption that, during a sensitive period the perceptual system becomes more sensitive to all experiences, it is also assumed that there may be an increase in the *selectivity* of the perceptual system to specific experiences. As shown in Fig. 2.6, the changing shape of the experiential filter, and in particular its narrowing during a limited period of development, provides an explanatory mechanism for the operation of a sensitive period. The central portion of the figure contains a representation of the experiential filter, which for ease of illustration is depicted in a discrete rather than in a continuous manner across time. The height and width of the filter at each age represents the transmission characteristics for particular

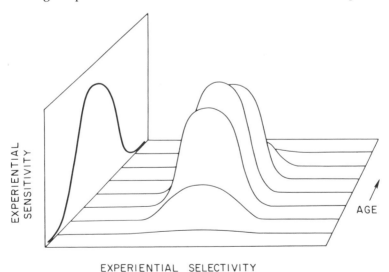

Fig. 2.6 Schematic illustration of a sensitive period showing the sensitivity and selectivity of the perceptual system to different experiences.

experiential inputs. The general importance of experience at each age is the projection of the filter onto the left panel (i.e., the traditional conception of a sensitive period). In addition, however, the filter acts in a selective manner during the sensitive period, thereby requiring specific experiential inputs to enable the perceptual system to follow the course of the normative developmental function. Only in cases of experiential deprivation, or selective experiential input that fails to match the characteristics of the filter, will the developmental function deviate significantly from the species-typical norm. Finally, it is possible that the selectivity of the filter remains very broad throughout the sensitive period. In that case, the filter is constraining the type of experiential input that will influence the development of the phenotype, but there are several alternative endpoints (all at the fully developed level) that could result from biased experiential inputs.

The final assumption of the present model is that the progressive changes in the shape (height and width) of the experiential filter during the course of development are determined by the organism's genotype. That is, the characteristics of the filter are fixed during ontogenesis, although clearly they may be altered by the process of natural selection operating across generations. The rationale for this assumption can best be explained with the aid of the following examples. Consider a species whose sensitive period is characterized by such a high degree of selectivity that only a single type of experience, visual input X, will result in the development of phenotype X'. For all members of the species, visual input X is very common in the species-typical environment, and phenotype X' typically emerges during the sensitive period, thereby describing a normative developmental function. If the presence of visual input X is made less frequent, or if it is eliminated entirely during the sensitive period, the organism's developmental function for phenotype X' will not reach the species-typical asymptote. Moreover, for this particular class of phenotypes, no related phenotype will emerge even if visual inputs similar to X (e.g., V, W, Y, or Z) are presented to the organism during the sensitive period, because the experiential filter allows only visual input X to be transmitted.

Now consider the same example except that the selectivity of the experiential filter is less constrained. Visual input X is transmitted completely (0% attenuation) during the sensitive period, and visual inputs V, W, Y, and Z are also transmitted, but less completely (50% attenuation). Given a species-typical environment in which all five types of visual inputs are presented during the sensitive period, the organism will eventually exhibit a fully developed or primary phenotype (X') as well as other less well-developed phenotypes (V', W', Y', and Z'). If the experiential input during the sensitive period is biased, the course of development for each of the five phenotypes will be altered accordingly. Thus, if only visual input V' is presented to the organism during the sensitive period, phenotypes W', X', Y', and Z' will fail to emerge, and the eventual developmental level of phenotype V' will be determined by the characteristics of the experiential filter.

These two examples emphasize the assumption of the present model that the characteristics of the experiential filter do not change during ontogeny as a result of variations in experiential input. Rather, the characteristics of the experiential filter are determined by the organism's genotype. The filter operates to constrain the types of inputs that will influence the course of phenotypic development, allowing certain phenotypes to emerge (or to be maintained) and others to be attenuated (either partially or completely). If one demonstrates that a certain phenotype which is *not* species-typical can emerge as a result of some regimen of experiential inputs, then, by definition (according to the present model), the experiential filter must have transmitted those inputs required for the development of that atypical phenotype. This does not imply that the *filter* changed, but only that the characteristics of the filter had not previously been well defined. To assume, in contrast to the present model, that the filter can undergo modifications during a given organism's lifetime not only implies that well-defined sensitive periods do not exist, but it also raises a problem of reductionism. If the filter itself were not constrained during development, a changeable filter would allow the possibility for the development of any phenotype, unless some additional process constrained the "changeability" of the filter. But this constraint on the filter (a constraint on a constraint) is in essence another filter, and this theory suffers from an assumption that is clearly reductionistic. The assumption of the present model is simply that the filter is fixed during ontogeny and the expression of the phenotype is dependent upon the interaction of the filter and the potential diversity of experiential inputs.[3]

---

[3] It is possible that a later developing phenotype is dependent upon other phenotypes that typically emerge during earlier periods of development. If the earlier phenotypes do not emerge, the later phenotype may be unable to emerge. Although this situation might imply that the experiential filter for the later phenotype has been altered during the earlier developmental period, the present model assumes that the filter for the later phenotype remains intact. It is the *input* to that filter that has been altered as a result of the failure of the earlier phenotype to emerge. For example, in human infants, visual preferences for specific faces typically emerge after several months of postnatal development. It is likely that "lower-level" phenotypes, such as attention to contours, emerge prior to the facial preference phenotype. If contour deprivation occurs during the early

There are two special cases in which evidence contrary to the assumption that the experiential filter is fixed could be obtained. First, it is possible, as mentioned previously, that a redundant or back-up system could emerge under certain conditions of experiential input, particularly if the conditions deviated greatly from the species-typical norm. If this redundant system became operative, presumably it would be characterized by its own filter, which, in turn, would account for the subsequent development of any "new" (atypical) phenotypes. Second, it is possible that the species-typical environment does *not* contain an experiential input that is transmitted by the experiential filter. Thus, the phenotype that could emerge if the experiential input were present during the sensitive period does not emerge, and the normative developmental function for that aspect of the phenotype in that species never attains either a partially or a fully developed endpoint. However, by selective manipulation of the organism's experiential inputs during the sensitive period, it would be possible to enable the "atypical" phenotype to emerge. This would not be an instance of a change in the filter. Rather, it would be an instance of releasing an external constraint on development that was determined by the characteristics of the species-typical environment.

In summary, the experiential filter analogy offers a convenient and easily conceptualized scheme for describing the process by which genetic constraints operate to selectively influence the course of perceptual development. The filter analogy, and in particular the hypothesized process by which experiential inputs are either passed or attenuated, stresses the need to study subtle variations along dimensions of experiential input. The analogy also offers a partial glimpse at the mechanism that may underlie the different roles of experience defined by Gottlieb. However, several details of the process underlying experiential influence are still missing. These details are at least partially specified by a second major property of normal perceptual development to be discussed in the next section.

B. Elasticity: Rebound from Deprivation

A term that has entered the conventional wisdom of the sensory and perceptual development areas is *plasticity*. Obviously, this term is used

---

postnatal period, there may be a deficit in the earlier phenotype (attention to contours). As a result, the subsequent development of the facial preference phenotype may also be degraded. However, the deficit in this later occurring phenotype is assumed to be the result of the inability of the lower-level phenotype to transmit inputs to the filter for the higher-level (facial preference) phenotype, rather than assuming that the filter for the higher-level phenotype has been changed during ontogeny.

metaphorically, and refers to the general observation that certain aspects of the phenotype can be modified as the result of variations in experience. The term plasticity, however, can be misleading. If something is plastic, it can be molded into a new configuration, and this new configuration remains stable unless a secondary molding process occurs. There are several examples from the sensory and perceptual development literature, however, that clearly demonstrate a return to a normal phenotypic level after a period of anomalous experiential input. Thus, the stability of the molding process, as implied by the term plasticity, is often inappropriate.

An alternative to the term plasticity is one that also implies modifiability, but with the additional property of spontaneously returning to a previous state. Such a term is *elasticity*, which, in the present case, implies that the genotype determines a normative course of development that can be modified by pressures exerted by the environment, but brief instances of anomalous experiential inputs are followed by a rebound to the normative level. One important aspect of this process of rebounding from deficits, however, is that the rebound can only occur if the experiential deficit is eliminated prior to the end of the sensitive period. If deprivation is present throughout the sensitive period, the rebound associated with the property of elasticity cannot occur.[4]

The prototypic example of the property of elasticity is the ability of developing organisms to recover from the effects of short-term nutritional deficits (Tanner, 1970). Based on large scale longitudinal studies, Tanner was able to characterize the normative aspects of physical growth. From these norms, it was possible to chart the day-to-day results of nutritional deficits. During periods of rapid growth, the absence of adequate nutrients had a severe effect, typically resulting in a decrease in the normative growth curve. If this deprivation continued throughout the period of rapid growth, the final level of growth was depressed. However, if the deprivation was eliminated prior to the end of the period of rapid growth, the growth curve would show a rebound to a near-normal level, often reaching the normative endpoint. Thus, although the phenotype (physical stature) was susceptible to the effects

---

[4] The mechanism underlying the property of elasticity could be conceptualized as a heightening of the experiential filter. That is, if during a period of deprivation, the filter transmits more at its center value and less at its outlying values, then subsequent broadband inputs would be transmitted better at this central filter value. This supranormal transmission, if it occurred after a period of deprivation but before the end of the sensitive period, could account for the rebound toward the normative developmental function. However, this alternative explanation was rejected in an effort to preserve the assumption that the characteristics of the experiential filter remain invariant during development.

of deprivation during periods of rapid development, the phenotype was resilient (elastic) and returned to a normative level, provided that the deprivation was eliminated before the end of the (sensitive) period of rapid growth.

The foregoing example of elasticity in the case of physical growth points out a disadvantage associated with many studies of perceptual development. It is often impossible to assess repeatedly the level of a phenotype during the period of rapid development. Thus, for example, in the case of recordings from single neurons in the visual cortex, it is not possible as yet to use a chronically implanted electrode to measure binocularity in kittens from birth through maturity. If recordings are made from the animal immediately after a period of deprivation, the course of any subsequent recovery cannot be assessed. It is possible to compare the final level of the phenotype in deprived animals to age matched controls who have not been deprived. However, the specific time course of any recovery process cannot be measured without repeated postdeprivation assessments.

Despite this limitation of measurement, two examples from the visual development literature provide a glimpse at the property of elasticity. Peck and Blakemore (1975) demonstrated that kittens who received as little as 6 *hours* of monocular deprivation exhibit a marked decline in cortical binocularity. If a period of binocular occlusion follows the brief monocular deprivation, the loss of binocularity remains in effect. However, Olson and Freeman (1978) showed that kittens who receive a brief period of monocular deprivation during the sensitive period recover a significant amount of binocularity if they are simply allowed normal binocular input during the remainder of the sensitive period. Thus, the initial loss of binocularity after a period of monocular deprivation appears to be transient, provided that normal binocular input is available before the end of the sensitive period.

In addition to this research on the effects of short-term monocular deprivation, other evidence for the property of elasticity comes from the work on dark rearing in cats. As described by Kalil (1978) and Mitchell (Chapter 1 in this volume) for cats and Regal, Boothe, Teller, and Sackett (1976) for monkeys, an animal that has experienced a lengthy period of dark rearing initially appears to be blind. Yet after several days of recovery in normally illuminated conditions, the animal will begin to show a gradual return to a normal level of visual functioning (acuity). If the duration of dark rearing is extremely long (i.e., for the entire sensitive period), then the property of elasticity has presumably been overcome and visual functioning will never recover to a normal level. Cynader and Mitchell (1980) have shown that the deleterious effects of monocular deprivation are exhibited in the neural responsiveness of cats who have been dark reared beyond the age when light reared cats suffer such deficits. Thus, dark rearing seems to act as an "extender" of the sensitive period, as if some minimal level of visual stimulation is required to move the normative developmental function forward. The property of elasticity, therefore, is dependent upon the level of development of the phenotype prior to deprivation, the duration of the deprivation relative to the sensitive period, and other basic requirements essential to the progression of the normative developmental function.

Figure 2.7 illustrates how the property of elasticity interacts with the normative developmental function both during and after a period of perceptual deprivation. A particular function is shown to represent the species-typical progression of the phenotype during development. Recall that the sensitive period can occur before, during, or after the transition from a low to a high phenotypic level, as depicted by the three locations I, II, and III. If there were a 100% loss of necessary experiential inputs during the sensitive period, then the developmental function would deviate from the norm, either falling to a low phenotypic level or failing to emerge from a low level. However, if the period of experiential deprivation occurred during the first half of the sensitive period, as shown in Fig. 2.7, the deviation of the normative developmental function would be dependent upon (a) where the sensitive period was located; and (b) the level of phenotypic elasticity. If elasticity were 100%, a deprivation of 50% during the sensitive period could result in no better than a final phenotypic level that was 50% lower than normal. However, the phenotype typically will exhibit a transient decrease after the period of deprivation before reaching the eventual phenotypic level at the end of the sensitive period. For example, in the Olson and Freeman (1978) study, the kittens that were monocularly deprived for 10 days during the middle portion of the 10-week sensitive period showed an initial loss of binocularity from a norm of 74% to 2%. However, kittens that received the same 10 day period of monocular deprivation followed by 30 days of normal binocular experience showed a level of binocularity of 39%. These kittens presumably exhibited a rebound from the 2 to the 39% level. Yet no amount of recovery beyond the sensitive period would have raised their binocularity back to the normal 74% level. If the level of elasticity is less than 100%, the amount of rebound after the initial lowering of the phenotypic level will be reduced accordingly. Moreover, in the case where the sensitive period precedes the onset of phenotypic development, there will be no distinct rebound, as no transient loss is measurable until the phenotype begins to emerge.

In summary, the response of a perceptual system to deprivation is

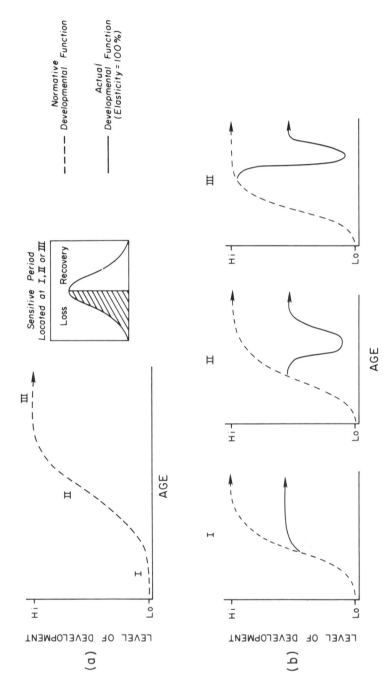

Fig. 2.7 (a) Three locations of the sensitive period along the normative developmental function and the duration of deprivation during the sensitive period. (b) Resultant developmental functions illustrating the property of elasticity.

dependent both upon the selectivity of the system to specific experiential inputs and upon the elasticity of the system to experiential influences during the sensitive period. As the system underlying the phenotype becomes more consolidated, it is more resilient to permanent influences exerted by deprivation. Although deprivation may suppress the rate or level of the phenotype, this lowered phenotypic level may not be permanent if the deprivation is eliminated prior to the end of the sensitive period. If the level of elasticity is high, the rebound to a normative level may occur quickly. If the level of elasticity is low, the rebound to a normative level may occur slowly. However, regardless of the property of elasticity, a complete recovery after a period of deprivation during the sensitive period can not occur according to the present model. In the next section, the complex interactions among the concepts of experiential filtering, selective experiential inputs, level of phenotypic development, and phenotypic elasticity will be illustrated.

C. Applications of the Unified Model

In this section, several broad characterizations will be provided to show the richness of the model and how the model's descriptions of development can encompass the roles of experience as described by Gottlieb. Figure 2.8 illustrates two general classes of experiential filtering that could occur during the sensitive period: *narrow* tuning, in which experiential inputs are selectively filtered, and *broad* tuning, in which

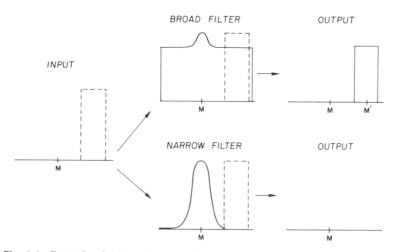

Fig. 2.8 Example of a biased experiential input during the sensitive period and its attenuation by either a broad or a narrow experiential filter.

few constraints are placed on experiential inputs. If the characteristics of the experiential input closely match the bandwidth of the filter, the course of development will closely follow the normative developmental function. However, if the characteristics of the experiential input do not closely match the filter, the "output" of the filter will be attenuated (see Fig. 2.5). Attenuation by the filter represents a decrement in the progression of the normative developmental function. That is, the level of phenotypic specificity will not reach a value of 1.0, the species-typical adult norm.

Figure 2.8 also illustrates a particular case in which the experiential input is biased. For the narrowly tuned filter, the input is completely attenuated, whereas, for the broadly tuned filter, the input is only slightly attenuated. The present model postulates that the particular characteristics of the phenotype will gravitate from a genetically specified location (the mean of the filter) to the mean value of the experiential input during the course of the sensitive period. For example, for the broadly tuned case, the biased experiential input, if present during the entire sensitive period, will move the phenotype from M to M'. If the biased experiential input is only present for part of the sensitive period, the phenotype will only move part of the distance from M to M'. And, as mentioned in the section on elasticity, the phenotype will tend to rebound from the effects of biased input if the biased input is eliminated prior to the end of the sensitive period.

In contrast to the case of a broadly tuned filter, biased experiential input will have a different effect on a narrowly tuned filter. If the input is outside the range of the filter, the phenotype will not gravitate away from the genetically specified location during the sensitive period. Rather, the level of specificity of the phenotype *at that location* will decline (or fail to emerge). The result of highly biased input, therefore, is to shut down the progression of phenotypic development. If such biased input is present during only part of the sensitive period, the level of phenotypic specificity will be only partially depressed, particularly if the property of elasticity is high and enables a partial rebound from the effects of the short-term selective input.

In summary, the characteristics of the phenotype at any time during development will be dependent upon a series of variables that interact in a relatively complex manner. Of particular importance are the following questions. First, does the phenotype have a sensitive period? Second, when during development does the sensitive period occur (before, during, or after the phenotype has reached a highly specified level)? Third, is the sensitive period characterized by a narrow or a broad experiential filter? Fourth, what is the mismatch (if any) between the characteristics of the experiential input and the filter? Fifth, what is the time course of the mismatch between the input and the filter? And sixth, how elastic is the system underlying the phenotype to modifications exerted by the specific aspects of experiential input? These questions can only be addressed by careful manipulation of the quality and quantity of experience made available to organisms at various periods during their development. In the next two sections we turn to several specific examples to illustrate the usefulness of the general model.

1. Cortical Binocularity, Disparity, and Orientation

The definition of cortical binocularity and much of the empirical evidence for its modification can be found in the preceding chapter by Mitchell, as well as in other chapters in this and other volumes (also see Freeman, 1979). From numerous empirical studies, it is clear that (*a*) there is a sensitive period for binocularity in the cat cortex; (*b*) the sensitive period is positioned after the phenotype has reached a high level of specificity (i.e., binocularity is adult-like at birth), and (*c*) the experiential filter during the sensitive period is broadly tuned. This last characteristic is illustrated in Fig. 2.9a. In this portion of the figure it is assumed that the dimension of experience most relevant to the filter is the balance of binocular inputs. Thus, the filter can be shown as a continuous cross section of the ocular dominance histogram. The rationale for depicting the filter as broad (i.e., transmitting any type of balanced or unbalanced input), is that during the sensitive period the shape of the ocular dominance histogram is extremely malleable. If a grossly unbalanced input is present during the sensitive period, the distribution will become skewed in such a way that cortical neurons only respond to stimulation delivered to the nondeprived eye. If this gross bias continues throughout the sensitive period, the eventual phenotype will be characterized by this skewed ocular dominance distribution. If the bias is present for only part of the sensitive period, the eventual shape of the ocular dominance distribution will depend on the duration of the biased input and the amount of elasticity present in the property of cortical binocularity. As discussed previously, if the level of elasticity is high, the presence of balanced binocular inputs during the remainder of the sensitive period will result in a rebound of the phenotype back toward the initial (pre-experiential) state. Based on the results of Olson and Freeman (1978), it would appear that the property of cortical binocularity in the cat is highly elastic. In fact, the rebound from the transient state of low binocularity after monocular deprivation to the state of moderate binocularity after a period of bi-

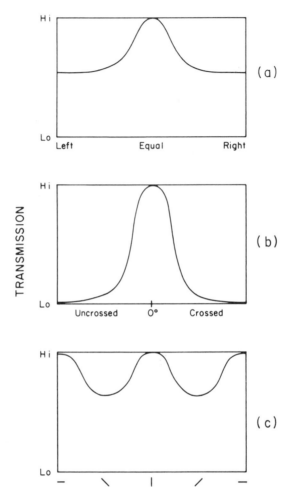

Fig. 2.9 Schematized experiential filters at the peak of the sensitive period for (a) binocularity, (b) disparity selectivity, and (c) orientation selectivity in single units from the visual cortex of the cat.

nocular "recovery," illustrates in part why the filter in Fig. 2.9a is drawn with a peak. The rebound phenomenon implies that the phenotype selects certain experiences as optimal. Clearly, this selection process must occur during nondeprived conditions as well. For example, the two eyes do not always receive balanced inputs in the natural environment. There are brief periods of monocular occlusion and slight eye misalignments that presumably have little effect on the eventual status of cortical binocularity. Extended periods of even such subtle unbalanced inputs as wearing a neutral density filter before one eye, however, can result in a permanent reduction in cortical binocularity (Blakemore, 1976). Thus, it is important to study the effect that periods of subtle experiential manipulations have on the eventual status of the phenotype.

Another example of cortical responsiveness in the cat is disparity selectivity. Disparity refers to the angular displacement of the two receptive fields (one for each eye) that are mapped from single cortical neurons. Each binocular neuron has a particular disparity value to which it responds most vigorously. Disparity values adjacent to this optimal value are responded to less vigorously, thus defining a tuning curve for each neuron (Barlow, Blakemore, & Pettigrew, 1967; Fischer & Kruger, 1980). Based on the work of Pettigrew (1974), it would appear that (a) there is a sensitive period for cortical disparity tuning; (b) the sensitive period is positioned near the beginning of the transition of the phenotype from a low to a high state; and (c) the experiential filter is narrow. The evidence for the location of the sensitive period is that disparity tuning curves for neurons in young kittens are very broad, and gross disruptions of binocular inputs required for disparity tuning (e.g., balanced and aligned) result in neurons that fail to become narrowly tuned for disparity. Thus, the period shortly after eye opening must correspond to a sensitive period not only for binocularity but also for disparity tuning.

The evidence for the narrowness of the experiential filter comes from a study by Shlaer (1971) in which slight misalignments of the eyes (approximately 2 deg) that created an altered disparity relationship resulted in a shift in the entire distribution of optimal disparity responsiveness. In other words, for normally reared cats, the mean level of disparity to which the population of binocular neurons is most sensitive is 0 deg. For kittens reared with a slight eye misalignment, however, this distribution shifts by approximately the amount corresponding to the misalignment. Yet, we know from several studies of artificially induced strabismus, in which the eyes are misaligned by more than 4 deg (Baker, Grigg, & von Noorden, 1974; Hubel & Wiesel, 1965; Smith, Bennett, Harwerth, & Crawford, 1979; Van Sluyters & Levitt, 1980; Yinon, 1976; also see Crawford & von Noorden, 1980, for similar results in monkeys), that cortical binocularity is lost (i.e., the ocular dominance distribution is as skewed as if the kitten had been monocularly deprived). If the property of binocularity is lost, the property of disparity tuning is lost, as disparity is dependent upon the presence of binocular neurons. Yet, strabismic cats receive balanced inputs insofar as the two retinal images are of normal contrast and focus. Thus, it is possible that the disparity "filter," with its narrower requirements, acts *after* the binocularity "filter" (which may be passing balanced inputs), and any gross mismatch between disparity input and the disparity filter results in a loss of binocularity as well as in a failure to finely tune the disparity mechanism.[5] Nevertheless, it remains clear from the Shlaer (1971), Pettigrew (1974), and Van Sluyters and Levitt (1980) studies, as well as numerous clinical examples (see Jampolsky, 1978), that disparity tuning is band-limited to a narrow region of acceptable inputs along the dimension of disparity.

The experiential filter shown in Fig. 2.9b, therefore, is depicted as quite narrow. Inputs during the sensitive period that fall within the range of the filter will gradually move the mean of the disparity distribution away from 0 deg to the mean of the experiential input.[6] If the input falls outside the range of the filter, however, the phenotype will remain at the level of specificity (broadly tuned; mean of 0 deg) present prior to the onset of the sensitive period. Finally, because the number of studies on disparity specificity are few, we have little information on the property of elasticity. Although a brief period of slight eye misalignment may shift the disparity tuning distribution, it is unclear whether there is a bias for subsequent normal input to result in a rebound to the zero disparity norm.

A final example from the literature on visual system neurophysiology concerns the property of orientation selectivity. The majority of single

[5] An alternative to the hypothesis that image misalignment is the cause of reduced binocularity in strabismic cats is the hypothesis that extraocular misalignment per se eliminates binocularity. Maffei and Bisti (1976) have shown that dark reared strabismic kittens fail to maintain cortical binocularity, thus contradicting the image misalignment hypothesis. They believe that the mismatch between oculomotor commands and expected sensory inputs from eye movements results in a central suppression of the input from the misaligned eye and a subsequent attenuation of its signal to binocular neurons. Further support for this extraocular proprioception hypothesis comes from Crewther, Crewther, and Pettigrew (1978) and Freeman and Bonds (1979), with the latter study showing that the deleterious effect of monocular deprivation requires active oculomotor movements. Smith, Bennett, Harwerth, and Crawford (1979) and Van Sluyters and Levitt (1980), however, have found no evidence in support of the proprioception hypothesis from their studies of optically induced strabismus. Thus, the issue of whether the loss of binocularity is partly the result of motor rather than sensory factors remains unresolved.

[6] Clinical evidence for such a slight shift in the disparity distribution comes from documented cases of anomalous retinal correspondence (Burian and von Noorden, 1974). The normal match between specific locations on the two retinas can be shifted slightly as a result of lengthy periods of early experience during which the eyes are slightly misaligned. Patients with this condition who receive corrective surgery to eliminate the misalignment often suffer from double images.

neurons in the cat visual cortex are optimally responsive to a restricted range of stimulus orientations. Although the full complement of orientation sensitive neurons is present at birth, kittens deprived of all but a single stimulus orientation during the early postnatal period lose cortical responsiveness to orientations that were not experienced (Blakemore & Cooper, 1970; Gordon, Presson, Packwood, & Scheer, 1979; Hirsch & Spinelli, 1970; Stryker, Sherk, Leventhal, & Hirsch, 1978). In addition, Pettigrew (1974) and Buisseret and Imbert (1976) have shown that the proportion of neurons that are orientation selective increases during development, presumably as a result of receiving oriented stimuli during a sensitive period.[7] A similar argument has been offered for human orientation sensitivity based on the permanent neural deficits in orientation thresholds among patients with gross astigmatism (Mitchell, Freeman, Millodot, & Haegerstrom, 1973). Finally, it appears that not all orientations are equally represented in the development of orientation selectivity. Leventhal and Hirsch (1975) have shown that vertical experience maintains vertical responsivity, horizontal experience maintains horizontal responsivity, but diagonal experience maintains diagonal *and* vertical and horizontal responsivity. These results, along with similar findings reported by Fregnac and Imbert (1978), suggest that there is a bias for vertical and horizontal inputs to be transmitted and for responsiveness to be maintained for those (primary) orientations.

These findings, although only briefly summarized and somewhat oversimplified, suggest that (*a*) there is a sensitive period for orientation selectivity; (*b*) the sensitive period is positioned near the end of the transition from nonselective to highly selective orientation neurons; and (*c*) the filter transmitting orientation experience is relatively broad. As shown in Fig. 2.9c, the filter is depicted as passing all orientations, but with a particular bias to transmit verticals and horizontals. If early experience is limited to a narrow band of orientations, the filter will attenuate little of that information, and the eventual phenotype will be characterized by biased orientation responsiveness. If all orientations are experienced, the sensitivity to orientations will conform closely to the profile of the filter. And if only diagonals are experienced, presumably the tuning curves for neurons normally most responsive to diagonals are broad enough to shift to vertical and horizontal orientations (note: Leventhal & Hirsch, 1975, only assessed the tuning of

---

[7] Sherk and Stryker (1976) have provided contradictory data on the effect of orientation experience on cortical responsiveness. They showed that dark reared kittens have orientation tuning curves that are very similar to adult cats, suggesting that experience only maintains orientation selectivity rather than also sharpening it.

neurons to plus or minus 22.5 deg).[8] Finally, the question of elasticity has been addressed by Blasdel, Mitchell, Muir, and Pettigrew (1977) who have shown that kittens receiving only a restricted range of orientations recover much of their initial deficit in cortical and behavioral responsiveness to the nonexperienced orientations. However, a specific estimate of the property of elasticity cannot be made, because to date no study has systematically manipulated the duration of selective rearing and the duration of recovery.

These three examples from the literature on visual system neurophysiology illustrate several types of experiential filtering that seem to operate during the course of perceptual development. Several important reminders are needed, however, to ensure that the model of experiential influence is not misunderstood. First, the filters shown in Fig. 2.9 are intended to represent only a single slice of time, in particular, the time when the filter is transmitting the most information (the peak of the sensitive period). At times before and after this peak, the filter is transmitting less information, and the shape of the filter (its band pass characteristics) may also be different (e.g., less peaked). Second, the filters shown in Fig. 2.9 are intended to represent the relative transmission of information to the entire visual system, not necessarily to each individual neuron. Although the filters for binocularity and orientation selectivity are broad, each neuron has only a discrete binocularity value (ocular dominance groups 1–7) and a fairly narrow band width (perhaps 20–30 deg of orientation). Similarly, the overall disparity filter is depicted as centered around 0 deg, but the mean of each neuron's disparity tuning curve is quite variable and each neuron's bandwidth is much less than the overall filter bandwidth. In summary, the model presented in this chapter is specifically directed at the perceptual (behavioral) level, and not at the neural level, although clearly many neural phenomena are intimately involved in the expression of perceptual characteristics. In the next section, we consider examples from the auditory modality that are not dependent on explanatory mechanisms drawn from the neural level, but that, nevertheless, further illustrate important aspects of genetic constraints and experiential influences on perceptual development and the usefulness of the present model.

----

[8] Additional support for the ability of neurons to accommodate to new orientations comes from the Crewther, Crewther, Peck, and Pettigrew (1980) study of eyeball rotation and the Shinkman and Bruce (1977) study of optically rotated images. Binocularity was maintained and the optimal receptive field orientations became reoriented to compensate for the novel image rotations.

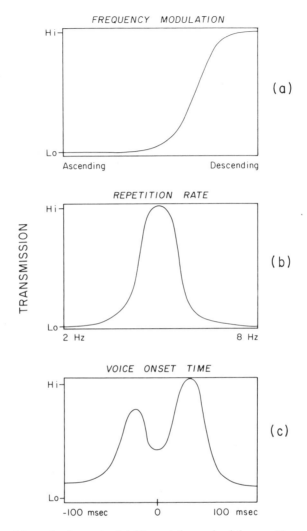

Fig. 2.10 Schematized experiential filters at the peak of the sensitive period for (a) auditory preferences in wood ducks, (b) auditory preferences in the Peking duck (mallard), and (c) auditory sensitivity in humans for speech sounds differing in VOT.

employs a preferential behavior is the necessity of assuming that the preference is mediated solely by a *perceptual* capacity. It is, of course, quite possible that the preference is not the result of any differential sensitivity to specific auditory signals, but involves some higher-level decision process. A solution to such an interpretive dilemma is to em-

2. Auditory Preferences and Sensitivities

The study of auditory preferences and sensitivities at the neura behavioral levels has a long history. Yet developmental issues ii auditory system have not received as much attention as they hav the visual system, perhaps because such dramatic experiential eff as those demonstrated for monocular deprivation have not receiv systematic study (see Chapter 2 by Clopton in Volume I for sevei exceptions). Nevertheless, the research of Gottlieb on species recog nition in ducklings and the work of Marler on the vocal production of songbirds have generated a number of developmental findings that are particularly suitable for treatment by the model outlined in this chapter.

Gottlieb's research on posthatchling wood ducks indicates that (*a*) there is a sensitive period for the development of auditory preferences; (*b*) the sensitive period is positioned near the time of hatching (including the prehatching period); and (*c*) the experiential filter for describing the effects of early auditory inputs is relatively narrow. It remains unclear whether the preference is maintained or induced because preferential behaviors have not been assessed prior to the time of hatching. However, the narrowness of the experiential filter is well documented. Figure 2.10a illustrates the estimated shape of the filter at the peak of the sensitive period. The experiential dimension of relevance to the wood duck is the direction of the frequency modulation (FM) in the wood duck vocalization (ascending or descending). There is a clear bias to transmit only the descending FM, as the ascending FM results in no preferential behavior after hatching, and the absence of either an ascending or descending FM also results in no preference. In contrast to the research on the visual system, however, these studies have not as yet provided a detailed characterization of the relative sensitivity and duration of the sensitive period. Without such information, questions about the elasticity of behavioral preferences remain unspecified.

Gottlieb's work with another species of duckling, the Peking (mallard), illustrates a different experiential filter as shown in Fig. 2.10b. The repetition rate of vocalization components appears to be the key feature determining preferential behavior in the hatchlings of this species, and the filter is shown as quite narrow. Evidence for the narrowness of the filter comes from studies showing that a restricted range of repetition rates centered at the species-typical norm is required for a preference to emerge. Again, however, questions about the exact shape and timing of the sensitive period and the elasticity of the behavioral preference are not presently known.

Perhaps the most difficult issue with regard to any research that ploy psychophysical methods in an attempt to bypass unique choice responses by the organism, such as species-specific preferences. Although psychophysical methods allow for the quantitative specification of detection or discriminative abilities independently of response biases, it is often the case that such arbitrary responses fail to engage the most acute sensory mechanisms available to the organism. Thus, both preferential and more traditional psychophysical methods suffer from interpretive difficulties.

The work of Marler and colleagues on vocal learning in songbirds provides another example of inferences that have been drawn about perceptual abilities on the basis of preferential behaviors. Marler and Peters (1980) favor the hypothesis that *perceptual* selectivity operating during the sensitive period for song learning (which occurs weeks before initial song production) is the cause of the eventual specificity of song productions. Clearly, however, there are many potential reasons for the specificity of song production, including motor, sensorimotor and attentional factors. Despite the apparently universal flexibility of the songbird syrinx, it is quite possible that, although various species are *capable* of highly variable song productions, they nevertheless find certain specific songs easier to produce. This distinction between capability and facility offers a nonsensory factor in the potential explanation of which particular song is produced among a wide array of equally salient models. Future studies of perceptual sensitivity per se will help to unravel this difficult issue. And recent evidence by Dooling and Searcy (1980) on perceptual sensitivity in prevocal songbirds strongly suggests that song production is largely influenced by perceptual rather than by motor preferences.

At the neural level, there are many issues related to auditory sensitivity that could be addressed in a developmental context. Unfortunately, many of these issues have only recently become topics of empirical investigation (Aitkin & Moore, 1975; Brugge, Javel, & Leonard, 1978; see Chapter 2 by Clopton in Volume I). However, there are many psychophysical studies of basic auditory sensitivities in human adults (see Trahiotis & Robinson, 1979, for review), and a large body of data has been accumulated on specific auditory abilities in human infants (see Eimas & Tartter, 1979; Jusczyk, 1980, for reviews). Most of these data from human infants have involved the manipulation of highly controlled acoustic parameters in synthetic speech signals. These stimuli are particularly interesting in that they bear on major questions of language learning and the role of early linguistic experience in the development of communication systems. These broader issues are dealt with in Chapters 7 and 8 by Jusczyk, and Walley, Pisoni, and Aslin in Volume 1. However, as a final example of experiential filtering, the evidence for a specific auditory ability related to speech perception will be briefly reviewed.

Much of the research on human speech perception has employed a class of speech sounds that vary along a physically specified dimension called voice onset time (VOT). VOT is an articulatory parameter that can be realized acoustically by using computer generated signals that simulate the formant (natural resonance) structure of human speech. Human adults are not equally sensitive to differences in VOT at all locations along the VOT continuum. In measurements of natural speech, Lisker and Abramson (1964) observed that different languages utilize different locations along the VOT continuum to divide particular speech sounds into categories. Two locations, however, appeared to be dominant in many of the world's languages, although only one might actually be used. Adult speakers do not spontaneously use all three of the categories resulting from these two divisions of the VOT continuum. Rather, they use only the categories required of their native language system.

One would expect, as Abramson and Lisker (1967) later confirmed, that adults' sensitivity to VOT differences would vary from language to language. Moreover, these differences in adults' sensitivity must have emerged as a result of early experience in a specific language environment. The alternative to this early experience hypothesis is a genetic explanation that would be forced to conclude that specific language groups are constrained (throughout adulthood) to specific speech categories, an obviously untenable proposal, as the phonology of natural languages must be acquired by convention. Studies of sensitivity to VOT differences in infants, therefore, offer a first glimpse at the development of experiential influences on speech categorization.

The findings in the area of infant speech perception are too numerous to cover here and are more adequately dealt with in other chapters. My particular interpretations of those findings with regard to the development of VOT are that (a) there is a sensitive period for the development of the ability to discriminate VOT differences; (b) the sensitive period is positioned near the end of the progression from poor to excellent discriminative ability; and (c) the experiential filter for VOT perception is relatively broad with two distinct peaks. Nearly all studies of VOT discrimination in infants have provided positive evidence for the ability to detect small differences in VOT. Thus, the ability is quite good shortly after birth. Although it is not precisely clear when speech signals become available to the infant (e.g., DeCasper & Fifer, 1980, have provided recent evidence suggestive of a prenatal influence), most studies of infants have been performed at least 1 month postnatally, and there appear to be few if any differences in the discriminability of VOT as a result of experiential differences in VOT input during the first 6 postnatal months. The sensitive period, therefore, is unlikely to begin until several months after birth. The relative sensitivity to specific VOT inputs, however, has not been determined, and few experiential effects are expected until the second postnatal year when infants begin in earnest the process of encoding speech sounds as meaningful units.

The experiential filter for VOT is depicted in Fig. 2.10c as broad with two peaks. The rationale for the two peaks is based on the evidence from adults whose language employs all three VOT categories. Their VOT discrimination functions have two peaks corresponding to the VOT locations at which the category boundaries occur. Moreover, adults from a language that does not employ all three VOT categories (English) show a two-peaked discrimination function for *nonspeech* signals that share a temporal parameter with VOT stimuli (Pisoni, 1977). Thus, a basic aspect of the auditory system appears to be this characteristic double-peaked function. If VOT stimuli presented during the rather lengthy sensitive period are biased, then only certain discriminative abilities will be maintained. Yet the basic ability of the auditory system to analyze temporal relations in speech and nonspeech stimuli appears to be maintained, regardless of the specific VOT content of early experience (see Pisoni, Aslin, Perey, & Hennessy, submitted). These results suggest that the sensitive period is quite lengthy, perhaps as lengthy as the one for binocularity shown in Fig. 2.3. Finally, the property of elasticity for VOT perception is unknown, and an estimate will not be forthcoming until controlled durations of selective experiential rearing are carried out. Such studies will require an animal model of auditory development analogous to the animal model of visual development employed by Boothe (see Chapter 7 in this volume).

D. Terminological Summary and Theoretical Precursors

There are several important aspects of the unified model of experiential influence outlined in this chapter that deserve brief reiteration. First, the concept of a sensitive period embodies both a delimited age range of enhanced *sensitivity* to experiential inputs and a *selectivity* for those inputs that can modify the phenotype during this age range. The sensitive period, therefore, operates like an experiential filter, transmitting some experiences and attenuating or blocking others. If the filter is broad, a variety of inputs can be transmitted (if present) and exert an influence on the quantity (level of development) or quality (type of development) of the phenotype. If the filter is narrow, the selectivity for particular experiential inputs is more restricted, and perhaps only a single type of input can be transmitted. Second, the sensitive period can occur at any location along the normative developmental function (i.e., before, during, or after the transition from a low to a high level of phenotypic specificity). The location of the sensitive period is species-specific and may vary widely for different aspects of the phenotype. Finally, if the experiential input during the sensitive period does not match the characteristics of the filter, the course of phenotypic development will deviate from the norm. The path of this deviation is dependent upon the shape of the filter, the duration of the experiential mismatch, and the amount of phenotypic elasticity. If elasticity is high and the mismatch does not extend throughout the entire sensitive period, a partial rebound from the effects of the mismatch can occur.

The roles that early experience can play in the development of perceptual abilities and preferences are obviously more complex than the triad of terms—*maintenance, facilitation,* and *induction*—offered by Gottlieb. This is not to say that those terms are without value, as they have clearly helped in delineating the multiple roles of experience, especially when contrasted with the simplistic notions of nativism and empiricism. Another advantage of using only a few terms is parsimony, as a model that relies on several dozen terms and numerous special cases will undoubtedly become too unwieldy for communicating with other researchers. Nevertheless, there are several additions and clarifications of Gottlieb's scheme that do seem to be relevant and easy to communicate.

Figure 2.11 illustrates two aspects of the present model that are particularly important for the interpretation of any research program on perceptual development. The figure shows that it is important to specify the characteristics of the experiential filter (broad versus narrow) and the nature of the experiential input with respect to the filter (match or mismatch). If the filter is broad, specific inputs within the filter will determine the eventual characteristics of the phenotype. If the specific inputs fall outside the filter, the phenotype will neither emerge nor be maintained. And if the input is broad, covering the entire filter, all of the potential phenotypes will be capable of emerging or being maintained. In this latter case, however, there may be a competition for expression of the phenotype (e.g., preferential behaviors) that results in a nonspecific phenotypic development. In contrast to the broad filter, the narrow filter predicts somewhat different outcomes. If the input matches the narrow filter, that particular phenotype will develop. If the input falls outside the filter, the phenotype will fail to emerge or be

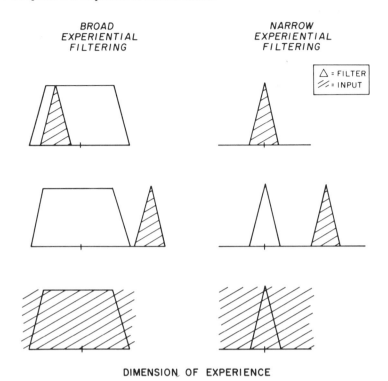

BROAD
EXPERIENTIAL
FILTERING

NARROW
EXPERIENTIAL
FILTERING

△ = FILTER
⟋⟋ = INPUT

DIMENSION OF EXPERIENCE

Fig. 2.11 Schematic illustration of two types of experiential filtering (broad and narrow) and three types of experiential inputs characterized by various degrees of mismatch with the filter.

maintained. And if the input is broad, the filter will transmit only those experiences within its range, and the phenotype will develop normally. In this latter case, however, if the diverse range of inputs are only available serially (i.e., one at a time), the phenotype may be attenuated because less experience within the filter can be transmitted per unit time.

The two basic aspects of the model illustrated in Fig. 2.11 can be combined with a final critical factor—the timing of the sensitive period— to generate labels for a description of possible developmental outcomes. Table 2.1 shows the matrix of possible developmental outcomes resulting from broad and narrow filtering, variable experiential inputs, and a sensitive period that is positioned before, during, or after the transition in the normative developmental function. First, consider the simplest situation in which the experiential input fails to overlap with the filter. If the sensitive period is located before the phenotype nor-

Table 2.1

Terminology for Describing the Roles of Experience in Cases of Broad and Narrow Experiential Filtering

| | Location of the sensitive period | | |
	Before emergence	During transition	After asymptote
Broad filtering			
Input within	Induce	Enhance or attune	Sharpen or realign
Input outside	Suppress	Decline	Decline
Broad input	Induce or suppress	Depress	Attenuate
Narrow filtering			
Input within	Activate	Sustain	Maintain
Input outside	Suppress	Decline	Decline
Broad input	Depress	Attenuate	Broaden

mally emerges, the phenotype will be suppressed. If the phenotype is already partially or fully developed before the onset of the sensitive period, the mismatch between filter and input will result in a decline in the level of phenotypic development. These outcomes—suppression and decline—will result regardless of the shape of the filter, provided that the mismatch is present for the entire sensitive period, thereby eliminating the potential for a rebound based on the property of elasticity.

Next, consider the situation in which the experiential input falls within the range of the filter. For a broad filter, there are several potential phenotypes that could emerge if the sensitive period is located before the time of normal phenotypic onset. A selective input, however, will induce the development of a specific phenotype. If the phenotype is partially developed when the sensitive period begins, a selective input will either enhance the phenotype if it matches the mean of the filter, or attune the phenotype if it falls within the filter at some point other than the mean. And if the phenotype is fully developed when the sensitive period begins, selective input will either sharpen the phenotype if it matches the mean of the filter, or realign the phenotype if it falls within the filter at some point other than the mean.

In contrast to a broad filter, consider the situation in which there is only one specific experiential input that can fall within the range of a narrow filter. If the phenotype has not emerged prior to the onset of the sensitive period, the matching input will activate the development of the phenotype. If the phenotype is partially developed prior to the onset of the sensitive period, the matching input will sustain the process of continued phenotypic development. And if the phenotype is fully developed prior to the onset of the sensitive period, the matching input will maintain the phenotype throughout the sensitive period.

Finally, consider the situation in which the input is diverse, covering more than the entire range of the filter. For the broad filter, there will be many types of specific inputs transmitted. If the phenotype has not emerged prior to the sensitive period, broad input will either induce many phenotypes (e.g., those that are not mutually exclusive) or suppress the emergence of a phenotype (e.g., a preference that is mutually exclusive if other inducers are present). If the phenotype is partially developed when the sensitive period begins, the broad input will depress the subsequent rate and endpoint of development because the concentration of matching inputs (inputs within the filter per unit time) will be reduced. And if the phenotype is fully developed when the sensitive period begins, the phenotype will be slightly attenuated as a result of the less concentrated input. Only by presenting "pure" experiential inputs of a single type that are transmitted by the filter can this attenuation be measured.

In contrast to a broad filter, a narrow filter will simply transmit a less concentrated amount of matching input. Thus, if the phenotype has not emerged or is only partially developed prior to the onset of the sensitive period, the subsequent development of the phenotype will be depressed, perhaps showing a less rapid rate and/or a lowered endpoint of development. Finally, if the phenotype is fully developed prior to the onset of the sensitive period, the less concentrated input will broaden the phenotype (i.e., prevent it from becoming sharpened by input matching the mean of the filter).

In summary, the term *induction* has been restricted to cases in which the experiential filter is broad, as, in these cases, specific inputs determine which of several possible phenotypes will emerge. If the filter is narrow, the term *activation* seems to capture the meaning of fulfilling the experiential requirement for the only possible phenotype that could emerge. The term *maintenance* has been restricted to cases in which the experiential filter is narrow. In contrast, a broad filter would allow for modification of the phenotype, processes labeled *sharpening* and *realignment*. Several other terms have been added to cover the cases in which the phenotype is partially developed prior to the onset of the sensitive period. For broad filtering, these terms are *enhancement* and *attunement*, and, for narrow filtering, the term *sustaining* appears to capture the meaning of providing an input that enables the process of development to continue. Finally, if the experiential input is very broad, the filter will transmit either multiple inputs (broad filter) or specific inputs (narrow filter), but the concentration of the transmitted output is likely to be less than if the input exactly matched the filter. Thus, additional terms—*depress, attenuate,* and *broaden*—were added to convey the fact that the course of development will be somewhat degraded.

One final term from Gottlieb's scheme deserves special mention. *Facilitation* was used by Gottlieb to characterize an experiential input that increased the normal rate of development without changing its endpoint. In the present model, facilitation would result from either of two possible interactions. First, it may be that in the typical environment of a species, a phenotype has emerged and is partially developed, but the sensitive period begins before experiences are available to the organism. Thus, if these experiential inputs were made available experimentally at an earlier age, the rate of development would appear to be accelerated. Alternatively, facilitation could result from the difference between experiential inputs that either exactly match a narrow filter versus inputs that are very broad. In other words, the species-typical environment may provide extraneous inputs that in a controlled environment could be eliminated, thereby enhancing the rate and perhaps the endpoint of development. If there is a ceiling effect for the development of the particular phenotype in question, only the rate difference will be measurable. Thus, Gottlieb's three roles of experience can be seen to be special cases of the more general model offered in this chapter. Whether these additional terms for the multiple roles of early experience prove useful remains for future determination.

Although the present model draws heavily on the earlier work of Gottlieb, there are other researchers whose ideas and writings have acted as theoretical precursors to the model's development. First, the concept of experiential filtering has been referred to extensively in the ethological literature, although typically the term *stimulus selectivity* has been used. Moreover, Marler (1961) and others have used the term *filtering,* so the idea and terminology are not novel. Nevertheless, what I believe to be new is the application of the concept of experiential filtering to simple dimensions of experience relevant to perceptual development. In the ethological literature, the concept of stimulus selectivity was applied to "elicitors" of "innate releasing mechanisms." And much of the debate concerning the animal's sensitivity to specific elicitors revolved around whether the selectivity was peripheral or central. In the present case, I am specifically concerned with what ethologists have called peripheral mechanisms, those mechanisms that involve the sensory and perceptual sensitivities of the organism, rather than those central mechanisms that involve perceptual learning, categorization, and other more cognitive processes. In this sense, then, the level of analysis that is relevant to the model in its present form involves passive experience, rather than more active encoding and information processing.

Another aspect of Marler's theorizing that has influenced the present model is his proposal that sound selectivity in songbirds is analogous to a *template* that is genetically specified (Marler, 1976). Although there are similarities between a filter and a template, the level of complexity between the two is quite different. The template for vocal learning of birdsong is very complex, involving variations in frequency, amplitude, and patterning over time. In fact, without more detailed studies, it remains unclear just exactly which of these variables is the key feature in the development of birdsong. In addition, Marler has referred to the development of song production as following a pathway or trajectory that is specified, within boundary values, by genetic factors. The present model does not make such an assumption. Rather than assuming a rigid genetically specified developmental pathway, similar to Waddington's (1957) epigenetic landscape, the present model only assumes that there are constraints placed by the genome on the timing of the sensitive period and the shape of the experiential filter. The particular time course of phenotypic development is dependent upon a multitude of factors that cannot easily be described, and any strong predictions about the development of specific phenotypes in individual members of a species must await future detailed empirical studies of these factors and their complex interaction.

Finally, there are certain similarities between the present model and that of Waddington (1957). Both share the assumption that strong genetic constraints are placed upon the process of phenotypic development. However, the concept of canalization as described by Waddington, and his use of the epigenetic landscape to illustrate his model, are quite different from the postulates of the present model. First, canalization has been used to refer to the decreasing ease with which phenotypes can be influenced by environmental pressures during the course of development. In contrast, the present model assumes neither that the period of sensitivity to experience must always come early in development, nor that significant modifications in the phenotype cannot occur once the process of development has reached an asymptote. Moreover, the use of the epigenetic landscape as an illustration of basic processes in development has certain disadvantages. For example, is the shape of the landscape predetermined? How does the "rolling ball" analogy capture the fact that many phenotypes are developing simultaneously? And, if the phenotype is diverted from the normative pathway, how does the location of the ball on the landscape illustrate the resulting difference in the qualitative *and* quantitative changes in the phenotype? Many of these problems are avoided by the present model, although clearly that opinion must await further evaluation.

Finally, there are two other sources of influence for the present model that deserve mention. Both Kuo (1967) and Lehrman (1970) have pointed out that development must be conceptualized, not in terms of simple notions of innate and learned factors, but in terms of the dynamic interplay of a complex set of factors operating against a backdrop of the organism's developmental history. Kuo (1967:128) stated that the development of behavior is characterized by a "range of potential behaviors, only a very small fraction of which can be realized during its developmental history." Three factors determine the specific phenotype that emerges from this potential range: (*a*) morphophysiological limitations that prevent the occurrence of certain actions and abilities; (*b*) ontogenetic limitations that prevent more than one of a set of mutually exclusive phenotypes from emerging; and (*c*) environmental limitations that prevent certain experiences necessary for certain phenotypes from becoming available to the organism. Much of perceptual development is undoubtedly constrained by the first two factors, allowing little variation between members of the same species. Yet the third factor can often be misinterpreted. If the range of a phenotype is very narrow, we assume that the phenotype was determined by genetic factors. Yet, as Lehrman (1970:28) has stated,

> the clearest possible genetic evidence that a characteristic of an animal is genetically determined in the sense that it has been arrived at through the operation of natural selection does not settle the question at all about the developmental processes by which the phenotypic characteristic is achieved during ontogeny.

In other words, there are many constraints placed upon environmental inputs during most periods of development, particularly prenatal development. For example, visual stimulation is not available to mammals prior to birth. However, if these constraints are species-specific, the range of phenotypes may be narrow for reasons other than strictly genetic factors related to the perceptual system per se. With these theoretical principles in mind, and with a further commitment to detailed empirical investigations of the complex process of development, answers to the questions of the role of experience in development can be meaningfully addressed.

V. CONCLUDING REMARKS

The purpose of this chapter was to raise theoretical and empirical issues related to the types of experiential influence that operate during perceptual development. The model that has been presented was designed to generate testable hypotheses and, in general, to stimulate researchers to consider broader issues as they plan and interpret their empirical studies. The concept of a sensitive period, with its dual features of sensitivity and selectivity, appears to offer a useful vehicle for describing the course of experiential influences during development. And the notion of experiential filtering during the sensitive period appears to offer a convenient analogy for conceptualizing the outcomes of various experiential inputs. Finally, the timing of the sensitive period with respect to the level of development, and the timing of any mismatch between the experiential filter and the experiential input, provides a relatively complete matrix of developmental outcomes that has general applicability to a wide variety of perceptual abilities and preferences.

Many of the ideas presented in this chapter will remain speculative until more detailed parametric studies are undertaken to "flesh out" the matrix of possible developmental outcomes (see Table 2.1). Yet pertinent studies are, in many cases, already underway as researchers begin to appreciate the fact that simple views of development cannot account for the diversity observed in the laboratory or in the wild. Of particular importance to the next decade of research on experiential influences in perceptual development will be the development of new measures that allow for the repeated assessment of neural and behavioral systems within individual subjects throughout the period of potential experiential influence. These techniques will undoubtedly involve the use of animal models of perceptual development in an effort to explain the complexities of human perceptual development. Such efforts have already begun (see Chapter 7 by Boothe in this volume) and will continue to offer new insights into the developmental processes outlined in this chapter.

Finally, it will become increasingly necessary, as more detailed empirical studies are completed, to differentiate the complex role that experience plays in development from the process by which experience exerts that role. That is, experience has been thought to maintain, facilitate, or induce different developmental outcomes. But the process may also be described as (a) supporting; (b) constraining; or (c) determining different developmental outcomes. Those experiences that are necessary for the organism to have a functioning perceptual system could be viewed as supporting experiences. Those experiences that modulate the specific aspects of a general pattern of activity in an already functioning perceptual system could be viewed as constraining experiences. Finally, those experiences that select whether a specific perceptual ability will develop among a variety of possible abilities could be viewed as determining experiences. The task of future research and theory in the area of perceptual development is to define not only what the outcomes of experiential variations are, but also the process underlying those outcomes. Judging by the interest and activity in the area, we can look forward to that task for many years to come.

ACKNOWLEDGMENTS

Preparation of this chapter was supported by a Research Career Development Award (HD–00309) from the National Institute of Child Health and Human Development. Portions of the research reported in this chapter were supported by grants from the National Science Foundation (BNS 77–04580) and the National Institute of Health (HD–11915). The helpful critical comments provided by J. Alberts, G. Bronson, G. Gottlieb, J. Juraska, P. Jusczyk, P. Marler, D. Mitchell, M. Petersen, D. Pisoni, S. Shea, and L. Smith are gratefully acknowledged.

REFERENCES

Abramson, A. S., & Lisker, L. Discriminability along the voicing continuum: Cross-language tests. *Proceedings of the Sixth International Congress of Phonetic Sciences,* Prague, 1967.

Aitkin, L. M., & Moore, D. R. Inferior colliculus II. Development of tuning characteristics and tonotopic organization in central nucleus of the neonatal cat. *Journal of Neurophysiology,* 1975, **38,** 1208–1216.

Anastasi, A. Heredity, environment, and the question "how"? *Psychological Review,* 1958, **65,** 197–208.

Aslin, R. N., & Dumais, S. T. Binocular vision in infants: A review and a theoretical framework. In H. Reese & L. Lipsitt (Eds.), *Advances in child development and behavior* (Vol. 15). New York: Academic Press, 1980.

Aslin, R. N., & Pisoni, D. B. Some developmental processes in speech perception. In G. H. Yeni-Komshian, J. Kavanagh, and C. A. Ferguson (Eds.), *Child phonology: Perception* (Vol. 2). New York: Academic Press, 1980.

Baker, F. H., Grigg, P., & von Noorden, G. K. Effects of visual deprivation on the response of neurons in the visual cortex of the monkey: including studies on the striate and prestriate cortex in the normal animal. *Brain Research,* 1974, **66,** 185–208.

Banks, M. S., Aslin, R. N., & Letson, R. D. Sensitive period for the development of human binocular vision. *Science,* 1975, **190,** 675–677.

Barlow, H. B., Blakemore, C., & Pettigrew, J. D. The neural basis of binocular depth discrimination. *Journal of Physiology,* 1967, **193,** 327–342.

Bateson, P. How do sensitive periods arise and what are they for? *Animal Behaviour*, 1979, **27**, 470–486.

Blakemore, C. The conditions required for the maintenance of binocularity in the kitten's visual cortex. *Journal of Physiology*, 1976, **261**, 423–444.

Blakemore, C., & Cooper, G. F. Development of the brain depends on the visual environment. *Nature*, 1970, **228**, 477–478.

Blakemore, C., and Van Sluyters, R. C. Reversal of the physiological effects of monocular deprivation in kittens: further evidence for a sensitive period. *Journal of Physiology*, 1974, **237**, 195–216.

Blasdel, G. G., Mitchell, D. E., Muir, D. W., & Pettigrew, J. D. A physiological and behavioral study in cats of the effect of early visual experience with contours of a single orientation. *Journal of Physiology*, 1977, **265**, 615–636.

Brugge, J. F., Javel, E., & Leonard, M. K. Signs of functional maturation of peripheral auditory system in discharge patterns of neurons in anteroventral cochlear nucleus of kitten. *Journal of Neurophysiology*, 1978, **41**, 1557–1579.

Burian, H. B., & von Noorden, G. K. *Ocular motility and strabismus*. St. Louis: C. V. Mosby, 1974.

Buisseret, P., & Imbert, M. Visual cortical cells: Their developmental properties in normal and dark reared kittens. *Journal of Physiology*, 1976, **255**, 511–525.

Crawford, M. L. J., and von Noorden, G. K. Optically induced concomitant Strabismus in monkey. *Investigative Ophthalmology and Visual Science*, 1980, **19**, 1105–1109.

Crewther, D. P., Crewther, S. G., & Pettigrew, J. D. A role for extraocular afferents in postcritical period reversal of monocular deprivation. *Journal of Physiology*, 1978, **282**, 181–195.

Crewther, S. G., Crewther, D. P., Peck, C. K., & Pettigrew, J. D. Visual cortical effects of rearing cats with monocular or binocular cyclotorsion. *Journal of Neurophysiology*, 1980, **44**, 97–118.

Cynader, M., & Mitchell, D. E. Prolonged sensitivity to monocular deprivation in dark reared cats. *Journal of Neurophysiology*, 1980, **43**, 1041–1054.

DeCasper, A. J., & Fifer, W. P. Of human bonding: Newborns prefer their mothers' voices. *Science*, 1980, **208**, 1174–1176.

Dooling, R., & Searcy, M. Early perceptual selectivity in the swamp sparrow. *Developmental Psychobiology*, 1980, **13**, 499–506.

Eimas, P. D., & Tartter, V. C. On the development of speech perception: Mechanisms and analogies. In H. W. Reese & L. P. Lipsitt (Eds.), *Advances in child development and behavior* (Vol. 13). New York: Academic Press, 1979.

Fischer, B., & Kruger, J. Disparity tuning and binocularity of single neurons in cat visual cortex. *Experimental Brain Research*, 1980, **35**, 1–8.

Freeman, R. D., & Bonds, A. B. Cortical plasticity in monocularly deprived immobilized kittens depends on eye movement. *Science*, 1979, **206**, 1093–1095.

Freeman, R. D. *Developmental neurobiology of vision*. New York: Plenum, 1979.

Fregnac, Y., & Imbert, M. Early development of visual cortical cells in normal and dark reared kittens: Relationship between orientation selectivity and ocular dominance. *Journal of Physiology*, 1978, **278**, 27–44.

Fox, R., Aslin, R. N., Shea, S. L., & Dumais, S. T. Stereopsis in human infants. *Science*, 1980, **207**, 323–324.

Gordon, B., Presson, J., Packwood, J., & Scheer, R. Alteration of cortical orientation selectivity: Importance of asymmetric input. *Science*, 1979, **204**, 1109–1111.

Gottlieb, G. Conceptions of prenatal development: Behavioral embryology. *Psychological Review*, 1976, **83**, 215–234. (a)

Gottlieb, G. The roles of experience in the development of behavior and the nervous system. In G. Gottlieb (Ed.), *Neural and behavioral specificity*. New York: Academic Press, 1976. (b)

Hirsch, H. V. B., & Spinelli, D. N. Visual experience modifies distribution of horizontally and vertically oriented receptive fields in cats. *Science*, 1970, **168**, 869–871.

Hochberg, J. Nativism and empiricism in perception. In L. Postman (Ed.), *Psychology in the making*. New York: Knopf, 1962.

Hohmann, A., & Creutzfeldt, O. D. Squint and the development of binocularity in humans. *Nature*, 1975, **254**, 613–614.

Hubel, D. H., & Wiesel, T. N. Binocular interaction in striate cortex of cats reared with artificial squint. *Journal of Neurophysiology*, 1965, **28**, 1041–1059.

Hubel, D. H., & Wiesel, T. N. The period of susceptibility to the physiological effects of unilateral eye closure in kittens. *Journal of Physiology*, 1970, **206**, 419–436.

Jampolsky, A. Unequal visual inputs and strabismus management: A comparison of human and animal strabismus. In E. M. Helveston (Ed.), *Symposium on strabismus*. St. Louis: C. V. Mosby, 1978, pp. 358–492.

Jusczyk, P. W. Infant speech perception: A critical appraisal. In P. D. Eimas & J. L. Miller (Eds.), *Perspectives on the study of speech*. Hillsdale, N. J.: Erlbaum, 1980.

Kalil, R. Dark rearing in the cat: Effects on visuomotor behavior and cell growth in the dorsal lateral geniculate nucleus. *Journal of Comparative Neurology*, 1978, **178**, 451–468.

Kuo, Z.-Y. *The dynamics of behavioral development*. New York: Random House, 1967.

Lehrman, D. S. Semantic and conceptual issues in the nature–nurture problem. In L. R. Aronson, E. Tobach, D. S. Lehrman, & J. S. Rosenblatt (Eds.), *Development and evolution of behavior*, San Francisco: Freeman, 1970.

Leventhal, A. G., & Hirsch, H. V. B. Cortical effect of early selective exposure to diagonal lines. *Science*, 1975, **190**, 902–904.

Lisker, L., & Abramson, A. S. A cross-language study of voicing in initial stops: Acoustical measurements. *Word*, 1964, **20**, 384–422.

Maffei, L., and Bisti, S. Binocular interaction in strabismic kittens deprived of vision. *Science*, 1976, **191**, 579–580.

Marler, P. The filtering of external stimuli during instinctive behavior. In W. H. Thorpe & O. L. Zangwill (Eds.), *Current problems in animal behaviour*. London: Cambridge University Press, 1961.

Marler, P. A comparative approach to vocal learning: Song development in white-crowned sparrows. *Journal of Comparative and Physiological Psychology*, 1970, **71**, 1–25.

Marler, P. Sensory templates in species-specific behavior. In J. C. Fentress (Ed.), *Simpler networks and behavior*. Sunderland, Mass.: Sinauer, 1976.

Marler, P., & Peters, S. Birdsong and speech: Evidence for special processing. In P. D. Eimas & J. L. Miller (Eds.), *Perspectives on the study of speech*. Hillsdale, N. J.: Erlbaum, 1980.

Mitchell, D. E., Freeman, R. D., Millodot, M., & Haegerstrom, G. Meridional amblyopia: evidence for modification of the human visual system by early visual experience. *Vision Research*, 1973, **13**, 535–558.

Movshon, J. A. Reversal of the physiological effects of monocular deprivation in the kitten's visual cortex. *Journal of Physiology*, 1976, **261**, 125–174.

Olson, C. R., & Freeman, R. D. Monocular deprivation and recovery during sensitive period in kittens. *Journal of Neurophysiology*, 1978, **41**, 65–74.

Olson, C. R., & Freeman, R. D. Profile of the sensitive period for monocular deprivation in kittens. *Experimental Brain Research*, 1980, **39**, 17–21.

Pastore, N. *Selective history of theories of visual perception: 1650–1950.* New York: Oxford University Press, 1971.

Peck, C. K., & Blakemore, C. Modification of single neurons in the kitten's visual cortex after brief periods of monocular visual experience. *Experimental Brain Research,* 1975, **22,** 57–68.

Pettigrew, J. D. The effect of visual experience on the development of stimulus specificity by kitten cortical neurons. *Journal of Physiology,* 1974, **237,** 49–74.

Pettigrew, J. D. The paradox of the critical period for striate cortex. In C. W. Cotman (Ed.), *Neuronal plasticity.* New York: Raven, 1978.

Pisoni, D. B. Identification and discrimination of the relative onset time of two component tones: Implications for voicing perception in stops. *Journal of the Acoustical Society of America,* 1977, **61,** 1352–1361.

Pisoni, D. B., Aslin, R. N., Perey, A. J., & Hennessy, B. L. Identification and discrimination of a new linguistic contrast: Some effects of laboratory training on speech perception. Submitted for publication.

Rakic, P. Genetic and epigenetic determinants of local neuronal circuits in the mammalian central nervous system. In F. O. Schmitt & F. G. Worden (Eds.), *The neurosciences: Fourth study program.* Cambridge, Mass.: MIT Press, 1979.

Regal, D. M., Boothe, R., Teller, D. Y:, & Sackett, G. P. Visual acuity and visual responsiveness in dark reared monkeys (*Macaca nemestrina*). *Vision Research,* 1976, **16,** 523–530.

Scott, J. P. (Ed.), *Critical periods.* Stroudsburg, Pa: Dowden, Hutchinson, & Ross, 1978.

Sherk, H., & Stryker, M. P. Quantitative study of cortical orientation selectivity in visually inexperienced kittens. *Journal of Neurophysiology,* 1976, **39,** 63–70.

Shinkman, P. G., & Bruce, C. J. Binocular differences in cortical receptive fields of kittens after rotationally disparate binocular experience. *Science,* 1977, **197,** 285–287.

Shlaer, R. Shift in binocular disparity causes compensating change in the cortical structure of kittens. *Science,* 1971, **173,** 638–641.

Smith, E. L., Bennett, M. J., Harwerth, R. S., & Crawford, M. L. J. Binocularity in kittens reared with optically induced squint. *Science,* 1979, **204,** 875–877.

Stryker, M. P., Sherk, H., Leventhal, A. G., & Hirsch, H. V. B. Physiological consequences for the cat's visual cortex of effectively restricting visual experience with oriented contours. *Journal of Neurophysiology,* 1978, **41,** 896–909.

Tanner, J. Physiological development. In P. Mussen (Ed.), *Carmichael's manual of child psychology* (3rd ed.). New York: Wiley, 1970.

Trahiotis, C., & Robinson, D. E. Auditory psychophysics. In M. R. Rosenzweig & L. W. Porter (Eds.), *Annual review of psychology* (Vol. 30). Palo Alto, Calif.: Annual Reviews, 1979.

Van Sluyters, R. C., & Levitt, F. B. Experimental strabismus in the kitten. *Journal of Neurophysiology,* 1980, **43,** 686–699.

Waddington, C. H. *The strategy of the genes.* New York: Macmillan, 1957.

Yinon, U. Age dependence of the effect of squint on cells in kittens' visual cortex. *Experimental Brain Research,* 1976, **26,** 151–157.

3

Strategies for Assessing Visual Deficits in Animals with Selective Neural Deficits

RANDOLPH BLAKE
Northwestern University

I. INTRODUCTION

Everyone knows that the brain, despite its homogeneous appearance to the naked eye, actually is divisible into specialized components, each with a unique functional assignment. Two of the real challenges in neuroscience involve understanding this division of labor within the central nervous system (CNS) and learning how activity in the various components is orchestrated to yield the integrated behavior characteristic of living organisms. One of the conventional strategies for tackling these questions of brain-behavior relationships has been to remove restricted regions of brain tissue and note the behavioral consequences of that limited lesion. In recent years, a more subtle version of this strategy has been utilized for studying the role of different categories of visual neurons in sensory tasks such as detection and discrimination. This ambitious enterprise has been inspired, in large part, by exciting discoveries concerning the effects of early visual deprivation on recep-

DEVELOPMENT OF PERCEPTION
Volume 2

tive field properties of visual neurons. In effect, visual deprivation provides a vehicle for modifying the response properties of visual neurons in interesting and suggestive ways. For several reasons, visual deprivation represents a potentially more powerful inferential strategy than lesion techniques. Unlike lesioning, which involves wholesale destruction of neural tissue, many of the deprivation paradigms only alter the underlying neural circuitry without affecting the total number of neurons. Thus it is possible to bias the response properties of visual cells or to redistribute their afferent connections (e.g., alter the ocular dominance of cortical cells) without actually destroying neural tissue. Moreover, unlike lesions that are placed at sites arbitrarily selected by an experimenter, the effects of deprivation can be localized at sites that are determined by the choice of visual stimuli to which the animal is exposed. This increases the probability that the site affected is, in fact, regularly involved in the processing of those stimuli.

This capacity to modify the visual nervous system naturally leads to questions about the sensory consequences of such modifications. In seeking answers to these sorts of questions, we typically turn to behavioral measures.

This chapter examines the extent to which various behavioral measures of sensory capacity provide information about the functional significance of different classes of visual neurons, focusing in particular on limitations on the kinds of conclusions that can be drawn from behavioral experiments on deprived animals. To begin, I shall consider the superficially compelling analogy between the properties of visual cells and the qualitative aspects of visual perception.

II. VISUAL NEURONS AND VISUAL PERCEPTION

In mature animals such as the cat and monkey, visual neurons display a remarkable degree of selectivity. Stimulus properties such as retinal position, direction of motion, and contour orientation can critically influence the activity of visual cells. These so-called neural feature detectors (e.g., Barlow, 1972) are packaged anatomically in a very orderly arrangement (Hubel, Wiesel, & Stryker, 1978), and many people believe that visual neurons become more abstract, or selective, at higher and higher stages of the visual pathways. In view of this amazing degree of neural organization, it seems natural to presume that these sophisticated neurons are involved in some crucial way in the business of visual perception. After all, the stimulus features that trigger responses in these neurons—motion, oriented contours, color, and so on—are the very same properties that underlie many of the fundamental aspects of vision. It is enticingly easy to imagine that the firing of, for example, a set of orientation-specific neurons underlies the detection of straight lines. There are various terms applied to this kind of reasoning—Teller (1980) has called it the "looking more like the response criterion," whereas Berkley (Chapter 6 in this volume) has dubbed this "reasoning by plausibility." This general idea has been most explicitly formulated by Barlow (1972) in the form of a neuronal doctrine of perception.

Now it also seems natural to assume that if particular types of visual neurons, by virtue of their stimulus selectivity, are crucially involved in seeing various perceptual features, an animal lacking a particular set of neurons should see the world differently. Here is where the work on visual deprivation enters the picture. It is well established that visual experience early in life plays an extremely important role in the development of the receptive field properties of visual neurons. Altering normal visual input during this so-called critical period can modify the properties of these neurons in intriguing ways (e.g., see review by Blakemore, 1978). In effect, the neurophysiologists have compiled a set of recipes for creating animals with specific kinds of neural deficits at sites along the visual pathways.

On the face of it, then, the visual deprivation paradigm would appear to offer the exciting opportunity to relate underlying neural mechanisms to visual performance such as detection and discrimination. I would like to demonstrate that this enterprise, although of unquestionable value, poses a number of inferential pitfalls not unlike those involved in studies of the effects of brain lesions on behavior (e.g., Gregory, 1961). To make these arguments, I shall describe three general types of behavioral strategies that have routinely been employed for studying the consequences of visual deprivation, commenting on the limitations inherent in each. Selected published data will be cited for purposes of illustration, but I have not sought to furnish anything resembling a review of this sizable literature; the interested reader may consult any of several recent reviews (e.g., Ganz, 1978). From the outset, it should be stressed that the primary concern here is to understand the role of particular classes of visual neurons in detection, recognition, and discrimination; the arguments advanced here are not necessarily applicable to more complicated behavioral processes such as visually guided motor control, visual memory, and the like. Of course, in work with animals, visual capacities must be assessed using behavioral procedures that include nonsensory components such as memory and motor performance. Indeed, it is the inclusion of those nonsensory components in the testing regime that introduces some of the interpretive complications to be discussed.

The order of presentation of these three general types of behavioral strategies is meant to reflect, in ascending rank, how conclusively results from these strategies bear on the relationship between neural events and sensory events. In this context, conclusiveness refers to the number of assumptions and qualifications that must be invoked when interpreting results from these various behavioral strategies.

III. VISUOMOTOR COORDINATION

This first class of behavioral tasks involves studying various aspects of visuomotor competence. As a rule, these tasks capitalize on reflex reactions on the part of the animal, which means that little is required in the way of formal training. This economy of time undoubtedly represents the major attraction of these techniques. Conventional behaviors that fall in this category include optokinetic nystagmus, startle reflexes, and visual placing. More omnibus behaviors such as avoiding obstacles, jumping from one height to another, and tracking moving objects would also fall under this heading.

By their nature, these sorts of tasks rely on some form of integrated motor response to gauge visual capacity. As a minor nuisance, these reflexive behaviors typically habituate rather easily, which places some real time constraints on testing. There are more serious considerations, too. For one thing, to elicit reactions on visuomotor tests, one typically employs visual stimuli that are naturally either appealing or repulsive. With such stimuli, it may be difficult to specify precisely their energic and geometric features or to vary those features along some meaningful dimension. This could preclude measuring graded effects of deprivation on behavior. (Optokinetic nystagmus may represent an exception to this rule in that the spatial frequency of the evoking stimulus may be varied to measure the acuity of the mechanism responsible for this visuomotor response). Moreover, in many instances, the motor performance itself is judged simply in terms of its presence or absence, and this too makes it difficult to evaluate any graded effects of deprivation.

Because visual competence must be inferred from motor responses, one must be cautious in assigning behavioral deficits to sensory mechanisms, as Held (1970) has forcefully warned. Inappropriate visuomotor feedback can produce deficits in coordinated, visually guided behavior even in animals receiving sufficient visual experience (Held & Hein, 1963). Hence such deficits cannot unambiguously be traced to the effects of deprivation on afferent pathways. Parenthetically, very recent physiological evidence indicates that the effectiveness of deprivation in modifying visual cortical neurons may also depend on adequate visuomotor experience (Freeman, 1978; Singer, von Gruenau, & Rauschecker, 1979). This finding underscores the potential confounding of sensory and motor contributions to the effects of deprivation.

There is also the problem of interpreting negative results from these kinds of tasks. A number of workers have commented on the remarkable ease with which deprived animals can run through a battery of tests of this sort. In our laboratory, we have had occasion to study visuomotor behavior in cats with severe impairments in visual acuity (Blake & Bellhorn, 1978; Blake & DiGianfillipo, 1980), and with rare exception these amblyopic cats were indistinguishable from normal controls on all sorts of tests of visuomotor coordination. This is not so surprising. Most tests of visuomotor performance tell us whether the animal has managed to locate and react to an event or object in its visual environment. At the same time, however, these tests indicate very little about the clarity with which an animal actually recognizes an object or the keenness of discrimination of one object from another. It may be that most tasks in this category provide at best a crude indicator that some reasonable number of visual neurons are functioning as links between sensory input and motor performance. Several studies (Blakemore & Van Sluyters, 1974; Movshon, 1976; Mitchell, Cynader, & Movshon, 1977) support this conjecture—it has been found that recovery of visuomotor performance on these kinds of tasks by reverse sutured cats nicely parallels the recapture of cortical neurons by the initially deprived eye. Visual perimetry studies (Sherman, 1973; Tumosa, Tieman, & Hirsch, 1980) provide another instance in which the number of responsive neurons is correlated with visuomotor behavior. In contrast, there is no evidence that more refined visual capacities (e.g., spatial acuity) are related to the number of responsive cells (Mitchell et al., 1977), nor is there reason to expect such a relationship. Rather, it seems more likely that performance on tasks involving visual resolution and discrimination would depend more crucially on the receptive field properties of those responsive units. Knowing just the proportion of cells responsive to stimulation provides insufficient information for making intelligent guesses about more specific perceptual consequences of a particular form of visual deprivation.

In the search for sensory consequences of neural deficits, it would be prudent to include among the arsenal of behavioral measures some tasks that focus on particular aspects of visual capacity. Toward this end there are two other behavioral strategies that may be utilized to evaluate visual function in deprived animals in a more refined fashion. One strategy, referred to as discrimination learning, involves determining the ease with which an animal is able to master a visual discrimination task; here the emphasis is on the potential to utilize visual information. The other strategy is to determine visual thresholds using any one of several psychophysical techniques that have been developed in recent years for animal testing (Stebbins, 1970).

IV. VISUAL DISCRIMINATION LEARNING

The general scheme in the case of discrimination learning is to determine the length of training required for a visually deprived aninal to achieve a level of performance comparable to that of a normally reared control animal. Often, the index of performance is the number of trials necessary to reach some asymptotic level of performance. Alternatively one might seek to determine stimulus magnitude (e.g., size of a pattern) necessary to produce some criterion level of learning. In all cases, though, it is mastery of the task that is the chief focus. There are various clever twists on this general theme but, for the moment, consider what sorts of conclusions may be drawn from various outcomes in studies of this type; these possible outcomes are shown schematically in Fig. 3.1.

First, imagine that a group of deprived animals is able to learn a discrimination task as quickly as a group of normal controls despite the fact that the visual nervous system of the deprived animals has been irreversibly altered in some seemingly important way. In this instance, one is forced to conclude that the altered neural substrate does not play a crucial role in mediating the discrimination, where crucial means only that, without that substrate, the discrimination would be impossible. Note, however, that such a result says nothing conclusive about the participation of that neural substrate in mediating discrimination performance in the normal animals. In fact, that neural substrate may be actively involved in the discrimination normally, but is replaceable by some other substrate in its absence. A trivial example should illustrate this point. Suppose we remove the left eye in a group of animals, train them to discriminate horizontal from vertical contours using their intact right eyes and discover that they learn the task as easily as their two-eyed littermates. Certainly, we would not conclude from this outcome

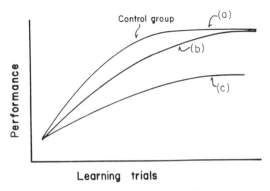

Fig. 3.1 Hypothetical outcomes on a discrimination learning task, where some index of mastery (e.g., percentage correct) is plotted as the function of training. The curve labeled (a) depicts the situation in which a group of deprived animals learns the visual discrimination as rapidly as a group of normal control animals. Curve (b) illustrates the case of retarded acquisition but ultimate achievement of the same asymptotic performance level as normals. Curve (c) depicts retarded acquisition and failure to reach the asymptotic level of normals.

that normal animals do not use the left eye on orientation discrimination tasks.

In general, a failure to find differences in learning performance between normal and deprived animals only indicates that the altered neural substrate is not absolutely crucial for the behavior under study. And the same argument holds in the case of deprived animals that display retarded learning but eventually reach a level of performance comparable to normals, the situation depicted by Curve (b) in Fig. 3.1. In this case, however, strength is added to the argument that, in normal animals, the neural substrate in question does play a role in mediating successful discrimination, and that selective alteration of that substrate forces an animal to resort to sources of visual information that are neurally less salient.

Finally, consider the situation in which a deprived animal never manages to achieve successful performance on a discrimination task that is solvable by normally reared animals, the case illustrated by Curve (c). Even in this instance the interpretation is not entirely un-equivocal—whereas this result strongly suggests a relationship between the neural deficit and the behavioral incapacity, one must be certain that the failure in discrimination performance does not stem from some more general motivational deficit or from some sensorimotor impair-ment, such as eye-movement disorders. Usually, alternative interpre-tations such as these can be ruled out by demonstrating normal performance by deprived animals on other discrimination tasks requiring comparable levels of motivation and visuomotor coordination. In general, when deficits in learning a visual discrimination are limited to one particular dimension of visual stimulation, we can conclude with more confidence that the altered neural substrate plays a crucial role in processing information about that particular dimension.

There are several variations on the discrimination learning paradigm that address issues other than the rate of learning in normal and deprived animals. One popular variation of this paradigm involves training an animal on some discrimination problem while allowing the animal to use only one eye. Once the task has been mastered, the animal is tested using just the untrained eye, a procedure known as interocular transfer. It has frequently been assumed that successful interocular transfer of learning requires the involvement of binocular visual neurons in the discrimination process. Carrying this assumption one step further, interocular transfer should be reduced or absent if the two eyes innervate separate populations of monocular visual neurons. This line of reasoning, however, seems unwarranted. It is quite conceivable for two independent sets of monocular neurons to have common access to some memory trace, just as long as this trace itself is not situated within that set of neurons. Common access to this trace would be the only requirement for transfer of learning between the eyes. To illustrate, suppose we briefly flash a visual form to the monocular visual field of your left eye and then have you select that form from a pair of stimuli flashed to the monocular field of your right eye. This "interocular transfer test" would be trivially simple, despite the fact that binocular visual neurons never entered the picture. Contrary to the opinion of some, interocular transfer of learning does not necessarily depend upon the existence of binocular neural interaction, and it is hardly surprising to learn that animals lacking binocular neurons nonetheless exhibit interocular transfer (e.g., Hirsch, 1972).

There is another version of the transfer paradigm that potentially can provide information about the features of a discriminative stimulus that are being utilized on a discrimination task. To accomplish this, an animal is trained on a particular visual discrimination problem until it reliably chooses the designated stimulus. Next, the animal is transferred to another discrimination task involving features of the original positive stimulus, now presented in a manner that pits different components of that stimulus against one another. An example of this strategy is provided by one of the experiments reported by Hirsch (1972) in his series of studies of cats reared with striped goggles. Initially, cats were trained to discriminate a square from a cross (□ versus X), with the square always being the positive, or rewarded, choice. Once trained to select the square, the cats were presented with a choice between a pair of vertical lines and a pair of horizontal lines (‖ versus =). The aim here was to determine whether, during the initial training phase, the cats selectively responded to the vertical or the horizontal components of the square, and, more to the point, whether such a preference matched the early rearing history of the cats. Unfortunately, the results from this experiment were equivocal, due to the strong position habits exhibited by the cats during the transfer testing. Another example of the discrimination transfer paradigm is provided by the work of Mitchell, Giffin, Muir, Blakemore, and Van Sluyters (1976). Using cats in which one eye had been surgically rotated about 90 deg, they initially trained the animals to discriminate horizontal from vertical stripes using the normal eye alone. Having mastered this discrimination, the cats were tested on the same problem using just the rotated eye. Remarkably, the animals continued to respond to the same distal stimulus as that chosen during initial training, implying that these cats had somehow adapted to eye rotation in a manner that preserved orientation constancy.

In summary, discrimination learning tasks can provide some idea about the kinds of visual information utilized by an animal in a learning situation. Thus, with deprived or specially reared animals, one can gain an understanding of the residual processing capacities of an altered visual nervous system. However, learning procedures pose some unique problems in experimental design (Solomon & Lessac, 1968) and, as argued here, the interpretation of results from such experiments is not always unequivocal. Gauging the effects of deprivation in terms of the ease of learning still leaves a number of inferential links between the association of neural deficits and sensory deficits.

V. PSYCHOPHYSICAL MEASURES OF VISUAL SENSITIVITY

This last category of behavioral strategies indexes an animal's visual capacities in terms of some threshold metric such as spatial resolution, flicker sensitivity, or the like. Obviously, in behavioral work with animals, it is impossible to communicate procedural instructions verbally, so one must instruct, or shape, the animal using some type of conditioning procedure. In this respect, then, there is an element of discrimination learning inherent in animal psychophysics. However, in the case of psychophysical experiments, the focus is not on the difficulty of the learning process but on the limits of visual capacity, where those limits are expressed along some stimulus dimension such as contrast, retinal disparity, and so on. The underlying strategy in animal psychophysics is essentially no different from that involved in human psychophysics: In both instances, stimulus–response relationships (Graham, 1965), or psychometric functions as they are often called, are established, and from these are derived estimates of discriminative ability. To accomplish this, an animal is trained to behave in one fashion in the presence of a stimulus (or class of stimuli) and to behave differently in its absence. Threshold is then determined by finding the stimulus value at which the animal ceases to behave differentially. The key to this strategy is that in terms of controlling the animal's behavior there is no distinction between "stimulus present but invisible" and "stimulus absent"; presumably both conditions produce equivalent neural responses (Brindley, 1970). Thus the major factor that limits the precision of threshold estimation becomes the degree to which the animal can be maintained under stimulus control at near-threshold levels of stimulation.

Of the available behavioral strategies, the psychophysical approach probably offers the most tantalizing bridge for spanning the gulf between visual capacities and neural events. Its allure stems in part from the fact that the same class of independent (i.e., stimulus) variables may be employed at both the physiological and behavioral levels of analysis. This commonality, in turn, makes it possible to look for co-variations in the dependent (i.e., response) variables measured at the two levels. Thus, for instance, one can measure the way in which apparent contrast is exaggerated at a spatial luminance gradient and compare this to the exaggeration in responsiveness of neurons when such a gradient falls within the neurons' receptive fields. In a similar vein, one may point to similarities between sensitivity functions derived psychophysically and physiologically as constituting evidence for causal linkage between the two; a prominent example here is the similarity between the scotopic spectral sensitivity curve and the action spectrum of rhodopsin. Or, linkage might be inferred based on similarities in the rates of recovery of sensitivity following visual adaptation (e.g., see Maffei, Fiorentini, & Bisti, 1973). In each of these examples it is the existence of a common stimulus dimension that furnishes the potential for inferring a relationship between neural and visual events.

This process of inference by analogy can be particularly beguiling in the case of animals with selective neural deficits. As the remainder of this section will attempt to show, one must make several strong assumptions to anticipate what kinds of psychophysical deficits are likely to accompany a neurological deficit. To exemplify the problem, suppose we are asked to evaluate the visual consequences of the neural deficit depicted in Fig. 3.2, a bias in the preferred orientation of cortical neurons. Each line in these polar plots represents the contour orientation producing the most vigorous response from a single cortical cell; both plots were fabricated by the author using a table of random numbers and two different sampling rules. For our purposes, it is irrelevant whether such a deficit can actually be produced by selective rearing; for that matter the condition could be genetically determined. Moreover, the comments that follow are not restricted to this particular kind of deficit—they apply with equal force to other selective neural losses such as a reduction in the proportion of directionally selective cells or in the spatial resolution of, for example, X-cells. The bias in orientation happens to be one of the more familiar cases of selective neural deficits (Blakemore & Cooper, 1970; Hirsch & Spinelli, 1970).

How far can we go in predicting the visual consequences for the owner of a brain that is biased in the manner illustrated in the right-hand portion of Fig. 3.2? At first glance, it is tempting to suppose that this animal would be completely blind to contours oriented around horizontal, as there are no neurons tuned to that orientation. This line of reasoning would represent a very radical form of the so-called labeled line hypothesis, which itself is an updated version of Mueller's law of specific nerve energies. Of course, common sense tells us it is unlikely that to see each and every visual object and event we must possess individual neurons optimally tuned to those occurrences. Rather, it is commonly assumed that the occurrence of an event, such as the presence of horizontal contours, is represented by the pattern of activity among an ensemble of neurons. For this scheme to work, though, some degree of overlap between the tuning curves of individual neurons

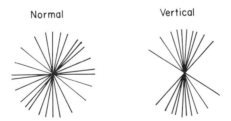

Fig. 3.2 Polar plots of preferred orientation of cortical neurons, where each line expresses the contour orientation that produces the maximum response in a single neuron. The plot on the left depicts the distribution characteristic of normally reared animals; the right-hand plot represents the distribution for animals reared in an environment of vertical contours. Both sets of data were fabricated by the author and are for illustration purposes only.

within that ensemble is required. In the case of orientation selective cortical cells, one needs information in addition to that depicted in Fig. 3.2, information about the variation of responsiveness of neurons to different orientations. This sort of information is conventionally conveyed in the form of tuning curves, plots of response magnitude (e.g., spikes/sec) as the function of orientation. Without data of this sort, one quickly encounters a dead end in trying to predict the outcome of a psychophysical experiment.

To continue this exercise, assume we have tuning curves for the neurons depicted in the right-hand portion of Fig. 3.2 and, for purposes of example, imagine the two alternative sets of curves shown in Fig. 3.3. In the top portion of the figure, neurons are rather narrowly tuned for orientation, with half-widths at half-amplitude on the order of 10 deg; the bottom portion portrays neurons with broader tuning, with half-widths of about 20 deg. The absence of neurons with peak responsiveness near horizontal is evidenced by a prominent gap in both sets of curves.

Consider first the group of narrowly tuned cells. Note that by virtue of the narrowness of their tuning a horizontal contour would evoke no increase in activity above the background level in this population of cells. Assuming this degree of narrow tuning, there would be good

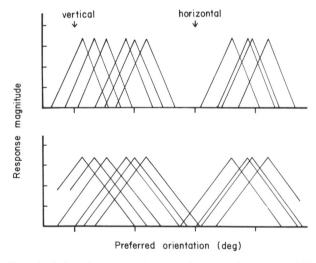

Fig. 3.3 Hypothetical tuning curves for cortical neurons in an animal like that illustrated in the right-hand portion of Fig. 3.2. Each curve shows the responsiveness of a cortical cell to contours of various orientations. The upper set of curves depicts narrow tuning, compared to the curves shown in the lower portion of the figure.

reason to expect this animal to be blind to horizontal contours,[1] for stimulation with horizontal would produce a level of neural activity that was indistinguishable from that associated with no stimulation. This represents an example of Brindley's (1970) psychophysical linking hypothesis. Hence, on a simple detection task, it is reasonable to predict considerably poorer performance for horizontal as compared to, say, vertical. This prediction assumes that visual detection depends on neural processes at or beyond the cortical level of orientation selectivity, and that those neural processes receive input exclusively via this cortical level. At the same time, however, an animal with this sort of deficit could be expected to perform quite adequately on a two-alternative discrimination task in which the choice was between horizontal and some other orientation that did evoke activity in the set of neurons. From the animal's perspective, this sort of task would boil down to a simple detection task involving the selection of the alternative that was associated with the greater level of neural activity.

Next consider the set of broadly tuned neurons in the lower portion of Fig. 3.3. In this scheme, there are neurons responsive to horizontal, but the strength of their response would be considerably weaker than for other orientations closer to their preferred value. Therefore, as in the previous example, this skewed activity profile provides a potential neural basis for discriminating horizontal from other orientations, because of the relative weakness of activity associated with horizontal. It is not obvious, however, what to expect in the case of simple detection of horizontal contours. In this situation it would be necessary to make assumptions about the minimum signal-to-background level of activity necessary to support some criterion level of detection performance. And there is no evidence bearing on this issue of threshold, a thorny problem in its own right, as signal detection theory has taught us. So it is impossible to anticipate the outcome from a detection experiment, given the model shown in the bottom portion of Fig. 3.3. But for sake of example, suppose it *is* possible to demonstrate successful detection of horizontal by an animal lacking neurons tuned to this orientation. This psychophysical outcome would support the model of broad orientation tuning and would, therefore, raise several related questions.

---

[1] This example assumes that an animal does not rotate its head to bring the horizontal contours into alignment with receptive fields elongated along nonhorizontal retinal coordinates, and it also must be assumed that the animal does not use the very ends of a horizontal contour where some vertical extent is present. Finally, it is important to remember that, at stages of visual processing prior to the emergence of orientation selectivity, horizontal contours will generate activity in excess of the background level and could therefore signal the presence of that contour.

For instance, in what way(s) would the visibility of horizontal contours differ for this animal? On most models of visual detection it would be predicted that relatively more stimulus energy (e.g., contrast) would be required for detection of horizontal, because of the absence of neurons maximally responsive to horizontal. This prediction is based on the reasonable assumption that a cell's preferred orientation also requires the least energy to evoke a response in that cell. This line of reasoning has been offered as one possible explanation of the oblique effect (Rose & Blakemore, 1974). It would also follow from this line of reasoning that any visual task on which performance varies with stimulus strength should yield poorer performance at horizontal, for more energy would be needed to evoke a criterion response.

VI. CONCLUSIONS

These considerations underscore the difficulty of making predictions about detection and discrimination performance in visually deprived animals. Intelligent predictions depend both on neurophysiological information that may not be available (e.g., tuning curves) and on assumptions that are difficult to evaluate, such as the aspects of neural activity that mediate detection and discrimination. Consequently, one is left with little in the way of firm theoretical grounds for selecting promising psychophysical measures of visual function. Rather, this selection must be guided by intuition based on reasoning by plausibility, which means that failure to demonstrate a visual deficit in a deprived animal could stem simply from a poor choice of behavioral measures. Moreover, in experiments demonstrating a visual deficit, one must be cautious in concluding that some altered neural substrate is necessary for the deficient visual capacity. For it is conceivable that performance could be restored to normal through some further manipulation of the visual nervous system. We are reminded of this by the work of Sprague (1966). In cats, he was able to produce blindness in one visual field by unilateral removal of visual cortex, yet normal visual function was restored immediately following removal of the superior colliculus contralateral to the cortical lesion. A similar postlesion recovery of visual function can be produced pharmacologically (Meyer, Horel, & Meyer, 1963). In general, it is necessary to keep in mind that experimentally induced neural losses provide information about the capacities of residual neural substrates, and do not necessarily reveal the function of the altered substrate.

Despite these limitations, the psychophysical study of deprived animals is hardly an enterprise to be abandoned, for, potentially, it still offers one of the most important strategies for gaining insight into the workings of the visual nervous system. What we must remember is that the enterprise is still largely in the atheoretical, empirical stage where there are no firm theoretical principles to channel our thinking or, for that matter, to limit our imagination.

ACKNOWLEDGMENTS

This chapter was prepared while the author held a Career Development Award from NIH (EY00106). Michael Sloane and James Zacks provided helpful discussion.

REFERENCES

Barlow, H. B. Single units and sensation: A neuron doctrine for perceptual psychology? *Perception*, 1972, **1**, 371–394.

Blake, R., & Bellhorn, R. Visual acuity in cats with central retinal lesions. *Vision Research*, 1978, **18,**, 15–18.

Blake, R., & DiGianfilippo, A. Spatial vision in cats with selective neural deficts. *Journal of Neurophysiology*, 1980, **43**, 1197–1205.

Blakemore, C. Maturation and modification in the developing visual system. In R. Held, H. W. Leibowitz, & H. - L. Teuber (Eds.), *Handbook of sensory physiology VIII. Perception.* New York: Springer-Verlag, 1978. pp. 377–436.

Blakemore, C., & Cooper, G. F. Development of the brain depends on the visual environment. *Nature*, 1970, **228**, 477–478.

Blakemore, C., & Van Sluyters, R. C. Reversal of the physiological effects of monocular deprivation in kittens: Further evidence for a sensitive period. *Journal of Physiology*, 1974, **237**, 195–216.

Brindley, G. S. *Physiology of the retina and visual pathway*, Baltimore: Williams & Wilkins, 1970.

Freeman, R. D. Visuomotor restriction of one eye in kittens reared with alternate monocular deprivation. *Experimental Brain Research*, 1978, **33**, 51–63.

Ganze, L. Sensory deprivation and visual discrimination. In R. Held, H. W. Leibowitz, & H.-L. Teuber (Eds.), *Handbook of sensory physiology VIII. Perception,* New York: Springer-Verlag, 1978. pp. 437–488.

Graham, C. H. Some basic terms and methods. In C. H. Graham, (Eds.), *Vision and visual perception.* New York: Wiley, 1965. pp. 60–67.

Gregory, R. L. The brain as an engineering problem. In W. H. Thorpe & O. L. Zangwill (Eds.), *Current problems in animal behaviour.* Cambridge: Cambridge University Press, 1961. pp. 307–330.

Held, R. Two modes of processing spatially distributed visual stimulation. In F. O. Schmitt (Ed.), *The neurosciences: second study program.* New York: Rockefeller University Press, 1970. pp. 317–324.

Held, R., & Hein, A. Movement-produced stimulation in the development of visually guided behavior. *Journal of Comparative and Physiological Psychology*, 1963, **56**, 872–876.

Hirsch, H. V. B. Visual perception in cats after environmental surgery. *Experimental Brain Research*, 1972, **15**, 405–423.

Hirsch, H. V. B., & Spinelli, D. N. Visual experience modifies distribution of horizontally and vertically oriented receptive fields in cats. *Science*, 1970, **168**, 869–871.

Hubel, D. H., Wiesel, T. N., & Stryker, M. P. Anatomical demonstration of orientation columns in macaque monkey. *Journal of Comparative Neurology*, 1978, **177**, 361–380.

Maffei, L., Fiorentini, A., & Bisti, S. Neural correlate of perceptual adaptation to gratings. *Science*, 1973, **182**, 1036–1038.

Meyer, P. M., Horel, J. A., & Meyer, D. R. Effects of dl-amphetamine upon placing responses in neodecorticate cats. *Journal of Comparative and Physiological Psychology*, 1963, **56**, 402–404.

Mitchell, D. E., Cynader, M., & Movshon, J. A. Recovery from effects of monocular deprivation in kittens. *Journal of Comparative Neurology*, 1977, **176**, 53–63.

Mitchell, D. E., Giffin, F., Blakemore, C., & Van Sluyters, R. C. Behavioural compensation of cats after early rotation of one eye. *Experimental Brain Research*, 1976, **25**, 109–113.

Movshon, J. A. Reversal of the behavioural effects of monocular deprivation in the kitten. *Journal of Physiology*, 1976, **261**, 175–187.

Rose, D., & Blakemore, C. An analysis of orientation selectivity in the cat's visual cortex. *Experimental Brain Research*, 1974, **20**, 1–17.

Singer, W. V., Gruenau, M., & Rauschecker, J. Requirements for the disruption of binocularity in the visual cortex of strabismic kittens. *Brain Research*, 1979, **171**, 536–540.

Sherman, S. M. Visual field defects in monocularly and binocularly deprived cats. *Brain Research*, 1973, **49**, 23–45.

Solomon, R. L., & Lessac, M. S. A control group design for experimental studies of developmental processes. *Psychological Bulletin*, 1968, **70**, 145–150.

Sprague, J. M. Interaction of cortex and superior colliculus in mediation of visually guided behavior in the cat. *Science*, 1966, **153**, 1544–1547.

Stebbins, W. C. *Animal psychophysics: The design and conduct of sensory experiments.* New York: Appleton-Century-Crofts, 1970.

Teller, D. Locus questions in visual science. In C. Harris, (Ed.), *Visual coding and adaptability*. Erlbaum, in press.

Tumosa, N., Tieman, S. B., & Hirsch, H. V. B. Unequal alternating monocular deprivation causes asymmetric visual fields in cats. *Science*, 1980, **208**, 421–423.

Animal Studies of Visual Development

In the past decade a wealth of empirical data has been gathered on the properties of neurons in the mammalian visual system and the behavioral correlates of neural deficits (see reviews by Blake, 1979; Daniels & Pettigrew, 1976; Grobstein & Chow, 1976). In addition, recent psychophysical studies have provided a detailed characterization of several aspects of the sensory and perceptual capacities of the developing visual system (e.g., Mitchell, 1978). The neurophysiological and behavioral approaches, as applied to the study of the visual system, provide a detailed and integrated view of brain–behavior relations. The goal of these studies is to define the structural and functional characteristics of the developing visual system, as well as the genetic and experiential mechanisms underlying neural and behavioral development.

Several species have been used in studies of visual development, with the cat and monkey providing the mechanisms most clearly analogous to the human visual system. The four chapters in this section provide a detailed summary of both the neural and behavioral aspects of visual development in cats and monkeys. Norton (Chapter 4) provides a detailed summary of neural properties and behavioral development in kittens. Stein and Gordon-Lickey (Chapter 5) describe the neural properties of the feline midbrain visual area, as well as behavioral correlates of the functioning of that visual area. Berkley (Chapter 6) reviews several psychophysical findings on the behavioral results of neural deficits in cats. Finally, Boothe (Chapter 7) offers a comprehensive review of psychophysical measures of visual capacity in both normally reared and visually deprived monkeys. These four chapters cover the major topical areas within the visual system, as well as providing a broad perspective from which future studies can be evaluated.

REFERENCES

Blake, R. The visual system of the cat. *Perception and Psychophysics*, 1979, **26**, 423–448.

Daniels, J. D., & Pettigrew, J. D. Development of neuronal responses in the visual system of cats. In G. Gottlieb (Ed.), *Neural and behavioral specificity*. New York: Academic Press, 1976.

Grobstein, P., & Chow, K. L. Receptive field organization in the mammalian visual cortex: The role of individual experience in development. In G. Gottlieb (Ed.), *Neural and behavioral specificity*. New York: Academic Press, 1976.

Mitchell, D. E. Effect of early visual experience on the development of certain perceptual abilities in animals and man. In R. D. Walk and H. L. Pick (Eds.), *Perception and experience*. New York: Plenum Press, 1978.

4

Development of the Visual System and Visually Guided Behavior

THOMAS T. NORTON
The University of Alabama in Birmingham

I. INTRODUCTION

Because the ultimate aim of visual developmental studies is to explain human visual perceptual development, one would like to study the development of neural responses to visual stimuli in human infants

113

DEVELOPMENT OF PERCEPTION
Volume 2

and simultaneously study the development of human visual perception. Obvious ethical considerations, however, restrict us to using lower animals in the invasive, often terminal experiments required for neurophysiological studies. Thus, to study the development of both visual capacities and the visual system in detail, investigators must use animal models instead of humans. Despite the importance of normal visual development, there has been surprisingly little work on it, and even less work aimed at correlating normal neural development to the development of normal perceptual abilities. Although there are many recent articles on visual development (see, e.g., Barlow, 1975; Blakemore, 1977; Hubel, 1978; Lehmkuhle, Kratz, Mangel, & Sherman, 1980), most of these have examined the consequences of environmental manipulations (visual deprivation, rearing in striped environments, etc.) on the development of the neural pathways, the functioning of neurons in the visual system and the visually guided behavior of the experimental animals. This type of experiment examines the visually guided behaviors and the visual system of adult animals only *after* they have completed their development in the experimental situation. Although these experiments have contributed significantly to our understanding of the neural basis of visual perception, it must be stressed that it is also critically important to study the *normal sequence* and *timing* of development of the visual system and of visual perception *during* the time period that they are normally developing. It is this type of experiment which will be covered in this chapter.

The majority of the work on normal visual neural and behavioral development has been done on kittens. The kitten is a useful animal for the study of the developing visual system because it shows no visually guided behavior immediately after eye opening and because it develops its full range of visual capacities within a few months after birth. Thus, both the onset and full development of visual behavior and the underlying neural responses can be examined longitudinally without waiting years for behaviors to develop. As will be discussed in Section VI of this chapter, however, care must be exercised in generalizing results obtained in kittens to human development.

An obvious lower limit on the time when visually guided responses can be demonstrated is the age at which the kitten's eyes open for the first time. As shown in Table 4.1, the time of eye opening is highly variable, occurring at 2–16 days after birth with an average of 8–9 days after birth (also see Blakemore & Cummings, 1975; Illingworth, 1980). Even before the eyes open, bright light produces constriction of the pupils (tested by opening the lid before its normal time) and produces blinking of the eyelids (Fox, 1970; Warkentin, 1938; Warkentin & Smith,

Table 4.1
Onset of Visually Guided Behaviors[a]

	Windle (1930)	Warkentin & Smith (1937)	Warkentin (1938)	Fox (1970)	Fagan (Unpublished Manuscript)	Norton (1974)	Norton & Holcombe (Unpublished Data)	van Hof-van Duin (1976)
Blink to light	7–10		1–8 (.5)	0–2				
Pupillary response	7–10		Before eyes open					
Eyes fully open	7–10	3–15 (9)	2–14 (8)	5–9	5–13 (8)		2–16 (9.8)	
Optokinetic nystagmus		12–17 (14)	8–16 (12)		8–17 (13)	(9.4)		26–38
Visual orienting	A few at 14–15, but mostly 21–28			14–16		16–21	15–23	
Visual following (large stimulus)						18–24	18–23	
Visual following (small stimulus)					17–38 (27)		18–24	24–42
Visual placing		22–28 (25)	21–30 (24)	12–16	24–32 (26)	26	23–32	28–33
Obstacle avoidance						25	20–27	26
Visual cliff				16–20	21–29 (25)	30	25–29	
Visually guided reaching					30–42 (37)	33	26–36	35–69

[a] The entries separated by dashes represent the age range over which the response was first observed. Numbers in parentheses indicate the mean day of onset of the response.

1937; Windle, 1930). Thus, at least some retinal neurons are active and functionally connected to central neurons involved in the pupillary reflex and eyelid closure.

Despite the presence of some retinal function, there is no sign of visually guided behaviors for several days after the eyelids open. The absence of visual behaviors might be due to a number of factors, including poor optics and/or poor ocular alignment, incomplete motor system development, or low motivation for the use of visual cues, as well as immaturity of the visual system. Inspection of the eyes with an ophthalmoscope shortly after eye opening reveals a vascular network, the *tunica vasculosa lentis,* covering the back of the lens. The gradual disappearance of this network during the first postnatal month, along with another vascular network (the pupillary membrane) in front of the lens, was first studied in detail by Warkentin (1938) and later by Thorn, Gollender, and Erickson (1976). In addition to the vascular regions, the optical media appear cloudy, making it extremely difficult to see more than vague outlines of retinal landmarks in young kittens (Fig. 4.1). Several investigators have questioned whether the absence of visual behavior in kittens at the time of eye opening and shortly thereafter might be due to fuzzy, low-contrast images reaching the retina. However, studies by Bonds and Freeman (1978) and Derrington (1979) using different methods have shown that the optics of the kitten visual system are not as poor from the kitten's point of view as they seem to be to an observer peering inward through an ophthalmoscope. These studies have concluded that the optics in young kittens, although poorer than those of adult cats, are not a limiting factor on the visual behavior of kittens at any stage in their development.

A second factor that might impair the use of visual cues to guide behavior is misalignment between the two eyes. Sherman (1972) and Pettigrew (1974) reported an apparent divergence of the eyes in young kittens. This divergence might be expected to produce double images (diplopia), which could generate conflicting information to the kitten and interfere with its use of visual cues. The misalignment was detected by observing the animals from directly in front (Sherman, 1972) and by measuring the locations of the receptive-field centers for each eye on a screen in front of the animal in electrophysiological recording studies (Pettigrew, 1974). As measured by these investigators, the ocular misalignment began to decrease at about 21 days, shortly before the appearance of depth perception (Table 4.1). However, a study by Olson and Freeman (1978) has contended that the ocular misalignment is only an apparent one and that images actually fall on corresponding retinal loci in young kittens as well as during later development. Thus mis-

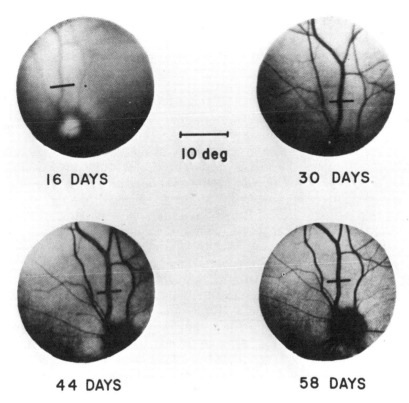

Fig. 4.1 Fundus photographs of a single kitten eye at 2-week intervals. The bars represent a 5 deg scan path used to assess the image quality of the eye. (Reprinted with permission from *Vision Research*, **18**, Bonds & Freeman, Development of optical quality in the kitten eye. Copyright 1978, Pergamon Press, Ltd.)

alignment of the eyes may not be a limiting factor in the development of visually guided behaviors in kittens.

Although the motor abilities of young kittens are obviously immature (Windle, 1930), it is not easily determined whether this immaturity limits the ability of the animals to respond to visual stimuli. In some instances, which will be mentioned later in Section II, motor responses can be produced by auditory stimuli before they will occur in response to visual stimuli. In these instances, the absence of the response to visual stimuli cannot be due to an inability of the kitten to produce the motor response. However, it is nonetheless possible that very young kittens simply may not be motivated to utilize visual cues present in their environment. Whereas this possibility might be examined by manipulation of the motivational state of the kittens, this manipulation is not simple to achieve. For instance, producing food deprivation requires separation from the mother, which can easily produce emotional responses that interfere with examination of visually guided behaviors. In addition, there are further difficulties involved in attempts to deliver reinforcement to young animals. Thus, although there is no specific evidence to support the idea, lack of motivation to use visual cues cannot be ruled out as a possible contributor to the absence of visually guided behavior in young kittens.

Despite these other factors, immaturity of the visual system seems likely to be a principal cause of the lack of visually guided behavior in young kittens. Hence, the present review concentrates on an examination of the development of the responses in the "primary" visual pathways, including retina, lateral geniculate nucleus, striate cortex, and superior colliculus (Fig. 4.4). Before examining the receptive-field properties of neurons in these structures during development, however, the normal onset of visual behaviors is first considered (Section II), as the behavioral data are what studies of the nervous system seek to explain. As will be seen, the visually guided behaviors first displayed by kittens are relatively crude. During the several weeks after their initial onset, improvements occur in the precision of the behaviors and in the ease with which they may be elicited. These improvements in visually guided behavior are briefly examined in Section III. In Section IV, the state of the visual system at the time of eye opening is assessed, with emphasis on the receptive-field properties of visual system neurons. In Section V, studies of the sequence of development of receptive-field properties of visual system neurons are reviewed, and in the final section (VI), correlations between receptive-field development and the development of visually guided behaviors are examined.

II.   ONSET OF VISUALLY GUIDED BEHAVIORS

Studies of the normal early postnatal development of visually guided behavior in kittens have been published by Windle (1930), Warkentin and Smith (1937), Walk (1965, 1968), Fox (1970), Karmel, Miller, Dettweiler, and Anderson (1970), Norton (1974), and van Hof-van Duin (1976). In addition, there are several studies existing as abstracts (Fagan, 1971), unpublished dissertations (Warkentin, 1938), manuscripts (Fagan, unpublished manuscript) or data summaries (Norton & Holcombe, unpublished data). Table 4.1 summarizes the results of all of these studies. Some older, less formal observations on the development of vision in kittens were reviewed by Warkentin & Smith (1937) and will not be presented here.

These studies show that there is a regular sequence in which visually guided behaviors develop and even generally agree as to the specific ages when these behaviors emerge. As shown in Table 4.1, the first visually guided behavior that has been reported to develop is optokinetic nystagmus (OKN). Warkentin and Smith (1937), Warkentin (1938), and Fagan (unpublished manuscript) found that at 12–14 days of age a kitten will move its head and/or eyes to follow vertically oriented black and white stripes rotated around it. The early investigations used very wide stripes (0.04 c/deg), whereas Fagan (unpublished manuscript) used slightly narrower stimuli (about 0.07–0.14 c/deg). In contrast, van Hof-van Duin (1976) did not detect OKN in her kittens until 26–38 days using similar stimulus widths (0.06 c/deg) presented at similar drift rates. Unfortunately, none of these reports includes objective eye movement records, but only subjective reports of the presence or absence of the OKN responses. Although it is important to know that these responses may occur at so young an age, it would be extremely useful to have objective eye movement records to back up the experimenter's judgments. This might help to eliminate the discrepant results on this test and would also provide quantitative measures of the improvement of the OKN responses with further development.

A day or two after optokinetic responses appear, orienting responses of the head can be elicited by presenting large visual stimuli in the peripheral visual field. These responses appear as early as about 14 days of age (about 5–6 days after eye opening) and have been found by 23 days of age in all kittens tested (Table 4.1). The onset of visual orienting in a kitten is followed within a day or two by crude, jerky following movements in response to large stimuli moved back and forth in front of the animal. Norton (1974) and Norton and Holcombe (unpublished data summarizing behavioral tests on over 100 kittens born in Norton's laboratory over a 4-year period) found the earliest following responses at 18 days, and after 24 days of age found following to be present in all animals tested. It is of interest that auditory stimuli, coupled with visual stimuli (i.e., a ball dragged along the floor), typically will elicit similar orienting and following responses a day or two before visual stimuli alone will produce them (Fig. 4.2). This indicates that the animals have the ability to make the orienting and following motor movements at a time when visual stimuli alone will not elicit them.

As is illustrated in Fig. 4.2, the development of orienting and following behaviors precedes by several days the emergence of another group of visual behaviors, including visual placing, obstacle avoidance,

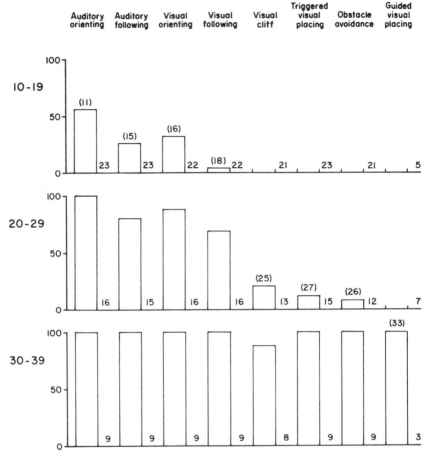

Fig. 4.2 Onset of visually guided behaviors in kittens. The presence or absence of the behaviors were tested in kittens in the three age ranges (10–19, 20–29, and 30–39 days) and listed as the percentage of kittens that responded. The number of animals tested on each behavior in each age group is given by the figure to the right of each bar. Numbers in parentheses indicate the age of the youngest animal to give a positive response on each diet. (From Norton, 1974.)

visual cliff avoidance (Walk & Gibson, 1961) and visually guided reaching (Hein & Held, 1967). In contrast with OKN, orienting, and following behaviors, which involve the localization of stimuli moving around the (more or less stationary) animal, these later developing behaviors are involved with guiding the animal as it moves through the visual environment. Visual placing, the extension of a forepaw as the kitten is lowered towards the edge of a table, has been found in six studies to first occur at about 21–25 days of age, and to occur reliably by 28–32 days. In a seventh study, Fox (1970) reported that this response develops at 12–16 days.

Obstacle avoidance, a test that has never been well quantified, but which refers to the ability of the kitten to walk through the visual environment without colliding with objects, appears during the third postnatal week (20–27 days of age, Norton, 1974; Norton & Holcombe, unpublished data; van Hof-van Duin, 1976). Depth perception, as measured with the visual cliff apparatus (Walk & Gibson, 1961) seems to develop in kittens between about 21 and 30 days, although Fox (1970) and Karmel et al. (1970) reported its development between 16 and 20 days after birth; however, Karmel et al. (1970) used extremely large (34°) checkers on the cliff apparatus. Visually guided reaching (Hein & Held, 1967), in which a kitten must guide its paw to prongs of a test apparatus as it is lowered toward them, develops at about 1 month of age (26–42 days of age).

The development of form perception has proven difficult to study in kittens because behavioral training is usually required for its estimation, and young kittens are not easy to train. Rose (1975) and Wilkinson and Dodwell (1979) have reported training kittens to discriminate light versus dark at 4–5 weeks of age. Discrimination of vertical stripes from a uniform gray target was demonstrated at 5–6 weeks of age (Mitchell, Giffin, Wilkinson, Anderson, & Smith, 1976). Wilkinson and Dodwell (1980) have succeeded in teaching more complex visual form discriminations to kittens as young as 6–7 weeks of age.

The behavioral studies reviewed here clearly show that kittens are born with immature visuomotor abilities and that there is a more or less orderly sequence in which visually guided behaviors emerge during the first month or so postnatally. The variation in the times at which different investigators first report observing various behaviors is difficult to evaluate, as there is no assurance that similar criteria were used in determining the presence or absence of particular behaviors and, in some cases, that identical tests were used. For instance, all of the visual behaviors developed relatively early in Fox's (1970) study compared with the other investigators. One wonders whether his kittens were in some way different from those studied by others, whether his tests were in some way more sensitive, or whether he used different tests or criteria. Similar questions arise about some of the tests of van Hof-van Duin (1976) who found later onset times for several behaviors. It is also possible that differences in rearing conditions might have produced acceleration or delays in the onset of visually guided behaviors. As has been shown in a series of studies by Diamond, Bennett, and

Rosenzweig (see, e.g., Diamond, Lindner, Johnson, Bennett, & Rosenzweig, 1975) rearing in "enriched" or "deprived" environments can affect the development of the brain, including the visual system. Rather subtle variations in rearing conditions such as cage size or colony lighting might have occurred in the rearing of the kittens in these studies and may have affected the onset of visually guided behaviors.

III. IMPROVEMENT OF VISUALLY GUIDED BEHAVIORS

In addition to the postnatal emergence of qualitatively different visually guided behaviors, there are quantitative improvements in the quickness, accuracy, and reliability of responses that have already emerged and/or a decrease in the size or intensity of the stimulus required to elicit the responses. For instance, as reported by Norton (1974) and confirmed by Norton and Holcombe (unpublished data), visual orienting responses, when first present, consist of small movements of the head in response to a large visual stimulus. A few days later, the movements are brisker, more easily elicited, and easier to detect. There are similar changes in visual following; when it first emerges, this response can only be elicited by a large stimulus, such as a hand moved near the kitten's head; the head jerkily follows the stimulus. About a week later, as reported by Fagan (unpublished manuscript) a smaller stimulus, consisting of a target 2 cm in diameter (Table 4.1) can elicit relatively smooth following responses (mean age, 27 days, range 17–38 days). Norton and Holcombe (unpublished data) found that a 1-mm wide string (about 0.2°) does not elicit following until still later, at 25–38 days; and van Hof-van Duin (1976) found *reliable* visual tracking of small objects to occur at 24–42 days. Warkentin (1938) noted that at about 19–31 days of age (mean = 26 days), kittens batted crudely at objects with their forepaw, an early manifestation of the play behavior that is so evident in older kittens.

Improvements in visual acuity during the first 3 postnatal months have been examined with two different techniques. The early estimates, by Warkentin and Smith (1937) and Warkentin (1938) used OKN in response to progressively finer black and white stripes as a measure of acuity. As summarized in Fig. 4.3, Warkentin (1938) found that very wide stripes (12° per stripe, or 0.04 c/deg) produced OKN responses at a mean age of 12 days (range 8–16 days). 1.5 deg stripes (0.33 c/deg) produced responses at 13.5 days (range 10–18 days) whereas 0.7 c/deg stripes elicited responses at 16 days (range 13–24) and 2.73 c/deg stripes at 20 days (range 16–18). The progressive decrease in the stimulus width needed to produce the OKN responses, along with the consistency between the results of Warkentin and Smith (1937), Warkentin (1938), and Fagan (unpublished manuscript) suggests that a reliable improvement is occurring in the sensitivity of the kittens to these stimuli.

Using a two-choice jumping stand, Mitchell et al. (1976) found that the acuity of kittens tested at 36–40 days of age was about 1.5 c/deg, a value considerably lower than that found by Warkentin (1938) for younger kittens with the OKN technique (Fig. 4.3). Mitchell et al. (1976) found a continued gradual increase in the performance of their kittens until they reached adult levels (5–6 c/deg) at about 3 months of age. These results are comparable, but not identical to the acuity estimates obtained by Freeman and Marg (1975) using evoked potentials (Fig. 4.3). The high acuity estimates and the very rapid improvement of acuity obtained by Warkentin (1938) and Warkentin and Smith (1937) at an early age suggest that the OKN test of acuity examines rather different aspects of a kitten's visual abilities than the two-choice test. The persistance of OKN responses in adult animals following removal

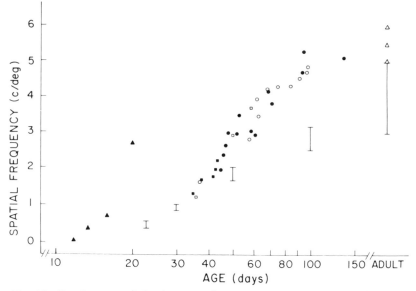

Fig. 4.3 Development of visual acuity in kittens as measured by three different tests. Estimates of acuity using optokinetic nystagmus are depicted by ▲ (Warkentin, 1938). Estimates obtained by Mitchell et al. (1976) using a two-choice jumping stand are shown by ■, □, ●, and ○. The data from three adult cats (△) are taken from Blake et al. (1974). Vertical bars summarize estimates of acuity obtained with cortical evoked potential measures by Freeman and Marg (1975). (Adapted from Warkentin, 1938, and Mitchell et al., 1976.)

of large areas of visual cortex in a variety of species (Pasik, Pasik, & Krieger, 1959; Ter Braak, 1936; Reinecke, 1961) suggests that OKN may not normally measure cortically mediated visual abilities. In contrast, acuity measures obtained on two-choice tests can be affected by neo-cortical damage (Sprague, Berkley, & Hughes, 1979). In any case, each of these tests shows a progressive improvement in the kitten's sensi-tivity to visual stimuli during the first weeks of postnatal development.

It is important to stress that the study of normal visual behavioral development in kittens is by no means complete. As Blake points out in the preceding chapter, most of the observations reported on young kittens are "visuomotor coordination tests": simple observations of the presence or absence of behavioral responses to visual stimuli at various ages. Absence of a behavior may imply that the perceptual abilities required for that behavior have not yet matured. Alternatively, as men-tioned earlier in this chapter, it may simply reflect immaturity of the motor systems required for the behavioral response. Even in instances where the motor response can be demonstrated, as in the case where orienting to an auditory stimulus can be found before orienting to a visual stimulus, it is possible that the absence of the response is due to a low level of motivation, insensitivity of the test, or to other factors unrelated to the presence or absence of the perceptual ability. Better experimental investigations involving more quantitative psychophysical tests (i.e., threshold measures) on the onset and, in particular, the improvement of the visual behaviors discussed are still needed.

The presence of a period following eye opening during which kittens appear insensitive to visual stimuli, followed by a period of several weeks when visually guided behaviors appear and improve in a fairly regular sequence, raises two questions about the visual system:

1. What is the state of the visual system in kittens at the time of eye opening such that it is unable to support visual responses?

2. What changes occur in the visual system to produce the onset and improvement of the various visually guided behaviors?

IV. THE STATE OF THE VISUAL SYSTEM AT EYE OPENING

Data on the responses and receptive-field organization of neurons in normal kittens during the first months after birth have been slowly accumulating over the past 2 decades to the point where there now have been studies of the responses of photoreceptors, retinal ganglion cells, and cells in the dorsal lateral geniculate nucleus, striate cortex, and superior colliculus (Fig. 4.4). These studies have shown that, at each level of the visual system, neurons are immature in their characteristic responses to visual stimuli, although there are some response properties that are similar to those present in adult cats.

A. Photoreceptors

Tucker, Hamasaki, Labbie, and Muroff (1979) recorded late receptor potentials from the photoreceptors of kittens 9–11 days old. They found that these potentials were very small in amplitude and that the stimulus intensity required to elicit them was about 5 log units higher than that required in adult cats (Fig. 4.5). Because these studies were performed on isolated, explanted retinas, this insensitivity was directly attributable

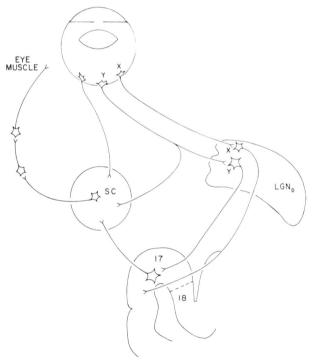

Fig. 4.4 Summary of visual system structures in which microelectrode recordings have been performed in kittens, including: retina (photoreceptors and ganglion cells), dorsal lateral geniculate nucleus (LGN$_D$), striate cortex (Area 17), and superior colliculus (SC). In addition, movement of the eyes has been elicited by stimulation of cells in the deep layers of the superior colliculus. Areas outside the striate cortex, such as cortical Area 18, have not yet been studied in kittens.

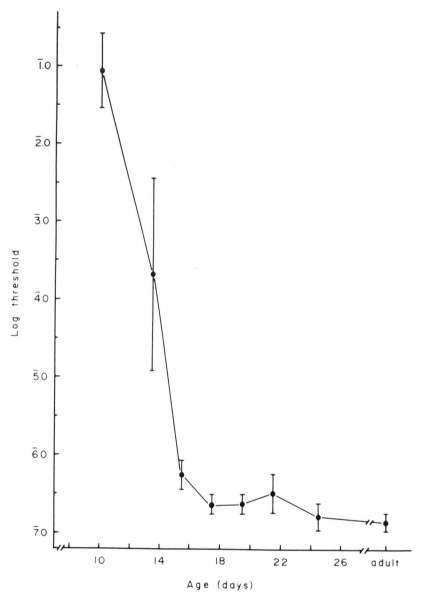

Fig. 4.5 Stimulus threshold intensity required to produce (15 θV) late receptor potentials in kitten photoreceptors. The ordinate indicates the log neutral density filter inserted in the path of the standard light source. (From Tucker *et al.*, 1979.)

to the photoreceptors, and was not due to the kitten's optics. Thus, at this very early stage in the processing of visual information, the visual system is less sensitive than in older kittens or adult cats.

B. Ganglion Cells

The results of the three studies of retinal ganglion cells (Hamasaki & Flynn, 1977; Hamasaki & Sutija, 1979; Rusoff & Dubin, 1977) are summarized in Table 4.2. Unfortunately, none of the investigators has studied cells in kittens of less than 21 days of age. At this age, the response of the photoreceptors is nearly the same as that in adult cats, and several visually guided behaviors have already developed. Rusoff and Dubin (1977) provide more information about cells in very young kittens, since they deliberately sampled cells in the region 10–30 deg outside the central portions of the retina. Since the retina develops from the area centralis toward the visual periphery (Donovan, 1966; Mooney, Dubin, & Rusoff 1979), presumably, they recorded from cells in their 3-week-old kittens that were comparable to central visual field cells in younger kittens. How much more immature these cells might have been is difficult to determine; perhaps a few days or possibly as much as a week (Donovan, 1966; Mooney et al., 1979). In the six kittens studied at 21–33 days of age by Rusoff and Dubin (1977), all the sampled cells apparently responded to visual stimuli and had a receptive field that could be plotted. The diameters of the receptive fields ranged from 2.5–6 deg, considerably larger than those measured in adult cats. Recognizing that the smaller kitten eye would have a greater number of degrees of visual angle per millimeter of retinal tissue, Rusoff and Dubin (1977) converted degrees of visual angle into millimeters on the

Table 4.2
Responses of Retinal Ganglion Cells

Adult-like	Immature
Center–surround organization	Low spontaneous activity
No fatigue	Lower peak firing rate
Normal percentage on- and off-center	Large (variable) receptive-field diameters
	Longer latency to light
	Low or absent surround response
	Weak or absent surround inhibition
	Best response to large stimuli
	Poor responses to rapid movement
	Poor grating response
	Poor responses on X- and Y-tests

retina. In the 3-week-old kittens, the large receptive-field center diameters could not quite be accounted for by the change in magnification, and may have reflected larger dendritic fields of the ganglion cells or a wider spread of excitation through laterally connecting retinal elements. Rusoff and Dubin (1977) also found that none of the cells they sampled had a demonstrable excitatory surround. The cells also had low spontaneous activities (less than 10 spikes/sec), but responded briskly (over 100 spikes/sec) to optimal visual stimuli. The optimal stimulus was typically a large target (4–10 deg in diameter) moved slowly across the receptive field. Stimulation with .5 c/deg gratings was typically ineffective, as was a radial sectored grating. None of the cells in the 3-week-old kittens could be identified as belonging to the W-, X-, or Y-cell categories found in adult cats, largely because of lack of responsiveness to the stimuli used for distinguishing these cell classes.

Hamasaki and Flynn (1977) and Hamasaki and Sutija (1979) recorded from a variety of retinal loci, including near the area centralis. Their data are in basic agreement with Rusoff and Dubin's data in the 21–24-day age range, although Hamasaki and Flynn (1977) emphasized the absence of fatigue in the retinal ganglion cells and the normal proportion of ON- and OFF-center cells sampled. Perhaps because they recorded many cells located near the area centralis, they found that the cells typically did have inhibitory surrounds, although they were much weaker than those found in adult cats (Fig. 4.6). Taken together, the data of these studies suggest that ganglion cells are capable of processing visual information at 21 days of age, are not easily exhausted by visual stimulation, and have the same basic center–surround mechanism as that in adult cats. However, they respond less briskly than adult cells, and then only to large, slowly moving stimuli, and the surround is very weak or absent in some cells. The immature ganglion cells are generally unresponsive to small spots and moderate (0.5 c/deg) gratings.

An important issue raised by Hamasaki and Flynn (1977) and by Rusoff and Dubin (1977) is whether the apparent immaturity of the ganglion cell receptive field was due, at least in part, to anesthesia or to the surgical manipulations performed on the animals. Whereas adult animals prepared and studied under similar conditions may serve as a partial control, it is not known whether the immature nervous system is more sensitive to the drugs or surgery, and is thus affected more than in adult cats. This is a valid criticism of all the recording work on anesthetized kittens, and one for which no proper control has yet been devised.

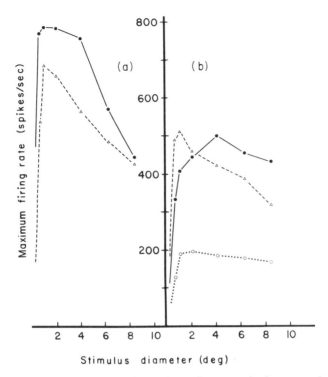

Fig. 4.6 Responses of (a) two adult ganglion cells to stimuli of successively increased diameters and (b) three 21-day-old kitten ganglion cells. For small spots, both kitten and adult cells increase their firing as the stimulus size increases. Larger spots, which stimulate both the receptive-field center and the inhibitory surrounding region, produce less firing. In comparison with the adult cells, the kitten cells have lower peak firing to the optimal stimulus size, and have weaker inhibitory surrounds. (Reprinted with permission from *Vision Research*, **17**, Hamasaki & Flynn, Physiological properties of retinal ganglion cells of 3-week-old kittens. Copyright 1977, Pergamon Press, Ltd.)

C. Lateral Geniculate Nucleus Cells

The responses of neurons in the dorsal lateral geniculate nucleus (LGN) of kittens as young as 6 days of age have been studied by Daniels, Pettigrew, & Norman (1978). As summarized in Table 4.3, these investigators found that the retinotopic projection upon the LGN is present in young kittens, as is the arrangement of the layers such that each layer receives excitatory input solely from one eye. In most other respects, however, the neurons are quite immature. Daniels *et al.* (1978) encountered fewer neurons per electrode penetration than in

Table 4.3
Responses of Dorsal Lateral Geniculate Nucleus Cells

Adult-like	Immature
Visual field topography	Few cells/penetration
Ocular dominance	Silent areas
Presence of sustained responses	Low spontaneous activity
	Fewer spikes/burst
	Many on–off cells
	Large receptive-field diameters
	Long latency to flash
	Long latency to optic chiasm shock
	Fatigable
	No transient burst
	No off inhibition
	Low surround inhibition
	Respond to slow stimulus speeds

adult animals and their electrodes passed through "silent" areas where no visually driven neurons could be detected. The spontaneous activity of the LGN cells was low, a finding that has been confirmed in awake kittens by Adrien and Roffwarg (1974) using chronically implanted microelectrodes. The number of spikes produced in a burst by the LGN cells and the peak firing rate attained in response to visual stimuli was considerably less than in adults. In addition, the cells fatigued easily upon repeated stimulation. Daniels et al. (1978) found that nearly half of the cells (42%) responded both at stimulus ON and stimulus OFF in kittens 9–13 days of age. Because the studies of retinal ganglion cells found that almost all cells were either ON- or OFF-center, the presence in the LGN of a large population of ON–OFF cells may reflect a mixing of separate ON- and OFF-center inputs in the immature LGN. Alternately, it may reflect a preponderance of ON–OFF W-cells in the immature LGN. As in the retinal studies, many cells had large receptive-field center diameters (1–30 deg) and either no surround or very weak surrounds. When the latency of response to strobe light flash was tested, the LGN cells responded with very long latencies (up to 1 sec) and about 15% did not respond at all. A high proportion of this long latency was apparently due to retinal processing time, since electrical stimulation of the optic chiasm, which directly activated the ganglion cell inputs to the LGN cells, produced responses at latencies of from 4 to 50 msec. Even this latency (mean about 20 msec) was considerably longer than the mean latency of about 3 msec found in adult cats (Hoffmann, Stone, & Sherman, 1972) and probably reflects, at least partly, the low proportion of myelinated axons in the optic nerve at this age (Moore, Kalil, & Richards, 1976).

One response property typical of some adult LGN X-cells, the ability to give a sustained response to the presence of a stationary stimulus, was present in some young LGN cells (Daniels et al., 1978). When tested with a contrast reversal stimulus, used to determine whether the cells summate light linearly within their receptive field (Enroth-Cugell & Robson, 1966), most cells in the 9–13-day age group had a location in the receptive field where they gave a minimum response, but few had either a clear-cut null point, typical of X-cells, or a doubling of responses typical of Y-cells. Of those few that could be tentatively classified, about half were X-cells and half were Y-cells. Notably absent in these X-cells, however, was the initial transient burst of spikes present to some degree in adult X-cells (Bullier & Norton, 1979). Finally, when tested with moving stimuli, most LGN cells in young kittens responded poorly, and not at all to rapid movement.

As might be expected, the properties of LGN cells at eye opening bear a strong resemblance to the properties of the retinal ganglion cells in kittens at this age. An interesting exception is the presence of mixed ON- and OFF-center cells in the LGN, which, if it truly reflects a mixing of ON- and OFF-center cells, suggests that the LGN is more immature than the retina in the segregation of responses to light ON and OFF. Whether the LGN is generally less mature than the retina is difficult to assess, because retinal cells have not been sampled systematically at as young an age as LGN cells. However, a suggestion that this is the case comes from a fortuitous instance in a 10-day-old kitten in which Daniels et al. (1978) recorded simultaneously from an LGN cell and a retinal axon that appeared to provide input to that cell. As shown in Fig. 4.7, the retinal axon responded more briskly, showing an initial transient burst to a small stationary spot of light, whereas the LGN cell responded considerably less briskly. Although a similar loss in driving (synaptic inefficiency) has been noted in the adult LGN (Fukuda & Stone, 1976), the decrement in response from the relatively brisk retinal cell to the LGN cell seems exaggerated in the kitten in comparison with the adult. This may be due to an immaturity of the neurons themselves, or to an absence of synapses, since only about 20% of the adult number of synapses are present in the LGN at the time of eye opening (Cragg, 1975). In addition, Fig. 4.7 shows that the responses of the retinal neuron were more suppressed by large spots than were the responses of the LGN cell, suggesting that the inhibitory surround was more fully developed in the retinal neuron. In this retinal–LGN pair, then, the LGN neuron seemed to be more immature than one of its retinal inputs.

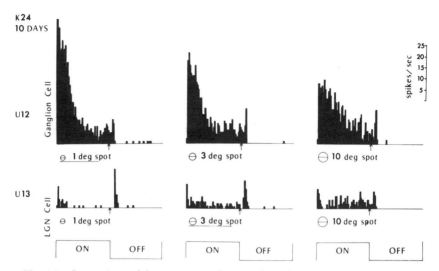

Fig. 4.7 Comparison of the responses of a retinal ganglion cell in a 10-day-old kitten (top) and a simultaneously recorded LGN cell, which apparently received input from the ganglion cell. The ganglion cell had higher spontaneous activity, responded with more spikes/sec and had a smaller receptive-field center (1 deg versus 3 deg). The initial transient burst of the retinal cell was nearly absent in the LGN cell. With larger spot sizes, the initial transient was inhibited by the inhibitory surround, whereas the LGN cell had no detectable surround inhibition. (From Daniels *et al.*, 1978.)

D. Striate Cortex Cells

There have been several studies of the receptive-field organization of neurons in the primary visual cortex (Area 17, striate cortex) of the kitten. As might be expected, given that the hallmark of the striate cortex is the presence of cells selective for the orientation of elongated visual stimuli, most studies have focused on this property. In the first of these studies, Hubel and Wiesel (1963) reported on the responses of 17 cells in two visually naive kittens 8 and 16 days of age. They reported that the cells generally had no spontaneous activity, gave "grudging" responses, and were easily fatigued. They were impressed, however, with the resemblance of the receptive-field organization in kittens to that in adult cats. The cells they studied were typically orientation-selective, binocular, and some were direction-selective as well (i.e., when tested with an optimally oriented stimulus, they responded more when the stimulus moved in one direction than in the other direction). Barlow and Pettigrew (1971) and Pettigrew (1974) agreed with Hubel and Wiesel's (1963) report that kitten striate cortex cells were immature in their spontaneous activity, unresponsiveness, and fatigability, as did Huttenlocher (1967) who recorded from unanesthetized, awake kittens. However, Barlow and Pettigrew (1971) and Pettigrew (1974) found that almost all cells in very young kittens were unselective for stimulus orientation and, when tested with moving spots of light, were not direction-selective. In addition, although most cells could be activated by visual stimuli presented to either eye, they did not have the sensitivity to retinal disparities (depth cues) found in adult cats.

Several studies by a number of investigators have subsequently examined the orientation selectivity of cells in kitten striate cortex. A major focus of these studies has been whether orientation selectivity in cortical neurons is innately determined or whether visual input is required for cells to become orientation selective. This has been assessed mainly by studying the orientation selectivity of striate cortex cells in older kittens that were prevented from seeing normal patterned visual stimuli by binocular eyelid suture or by dark rearing. Other than to mention that at least some striate cortex neurons have been found to be orientation selective in animals with no prior visual experience (Blakemore & Van Sluyters, 1975; Sherk & Stryker, 1976; Buisseret & Imbert, 1976; Frégnac & Imbert, 1978; Frégnac, 1979), this review will not dwell on this issue, as whether cells *can* have orientation selectivity innately is not as important here as the question of whether *normal* kittens typically *do* have a high proportion of orientation-selective cells.

These studies of normal young kittens (summarized in Table 4.4) have found that most striate cortex cells in normal kittens are immature

Table 4.4
Responses of Striate Cortex Cells

Adult-like	Immature
Unresponsive to diffuse illumination	Low spontaneous activity
Normal ocular dominance distribution	Many unresponsive cells
[a]Direction selective	Few cells/penetration
[a]Some orientation selective	"Grudging" responses
[a]Simple & complex cells present	Fatigable
	Generalized binocular facilitation
	Disparity tuning absent
	Nonoriented cells present
	[a]Orientation bias cells
	[a]Direction-selective cells
	[a]Few orientation-selective cells
	Broader tuning of orientation-selective cells
	Orientation-selective cells tend to be monocular

[a] There has been some disagreement on these properties. See text for discussion.

at the time of eye opening and that very few are orientation selective at that age. In a 9-day-old kitten, Blakemore and Van Sluyters (1975) found less than 20%. In another 9-day-old kitten, Frégnac and Imbert (1978) found no orientation-selective cells, whereas in kittens 12–17 days old they found 23%. A substantial proportion of cells fail to respond to any visual stimulation (Buisseret & Imbert, 1976; Blakemore & Van Sluyters, 1975). In addition, there are many cells that are immature, exhibiting some directional selectivity or tendency for orientation tuning (orientation bias), but not yet being very selective for stimulus orientation (Blakemore & Van Sluyters, 1975; Frégnac, 1979; Frégnac & Imbert, 1978). Many of these immature cells have relatively large receptive-field diameters, similar to immature retinal and LGN cells. Interestingly, the cells that are orientation-selective in young kittens typically are monocularly activated and respond preferentially to horizontal or vertical orientations (Blakemore & Van Sluyters, 1975; Frégnac & Imbert, 1978). Thus, not all optimal stimulus orientations are equally well represented in young kittens.

In addition to studies of the receptive-field properties of individual neurons in striate cortex, some attention has been paid to the development of larger functional units within this cortical region, including ocular dominance and orientation columns. LeVay, Stryker, and Shatz (1978) examined the ocular dominance of cells in layer IV, where there is strong, segregated input from each eye in the adult cat. In four kittens 10–17 days of age there was little sign of segregation of the LGN inputs as examined anatomically. Physiologically they found that most neurons were binocular and that cells with differing ocular dominances were intermingled in layer IV and in surrounding layers. In contrast, Blakemore and Van Sluyters (1975) found what appeared to be an "orderly shift" in ocular dominance in the course of long penetrations through striate cortex in a 9- and a 19-day-old kitten. However, most of the neurons were binocular, and plotted data do not show the very regular, repeated shifts of ocular dominance seen in the adult cat (Le Vay *et al.*, 1978). At best, the ocular dominance columns must be very immature at the time of eye opening, if they exist at all.

The presence or absence of orientation columns near the time of eye opening in kittens is difficult to assess, since so many of the neurons are not orientation-selective. Hubel and Wiesel (1963) reported that they were present. Blakemore and Van Sluyters (1975) reported that there was "just the slightest tendency" for nearby cells to have similar optimal stimulus orientations in a 9- and a 19-day-old normal kitten.

In conclusion, the striate cortex is quite immature at the time of eye opening. The cells are generally not very responsive to visual stimuli, do not respond to small, rapidly moving, or repeatedly presented stimuli, are insensitive to retinal disparities, although most can be activated binocularly, and generally are not orientation-selective. Two larger functional units, orientation and ocular dominance columns, are not well developed in kittens at this time.

E. Superior Colliculus Cells

The final visual structure that has been studied in young kittens is the superior colliculus (see Chapter 5 by Stein & Gordon). Although it has long been recognized as a structure involved in eye movements, recent studies have shown that the superficial layers of the superior colliculus have ascending anatomical connections in a wide variety of species (Diamond & Hall, 1969; Graybiel, 1972). These connections allow the superficial layers of the superior colliculus to relay visual sensory information rostrally to the thalamus and, potentially, to the neocortex. Stein, Labos, & Kruger (1973a,b) and Norton (1974, 1977, 1981) have examined the responses of neurons in the superior colliculus. As in other structures, the retinotopic map upon the superior colliculus appears to be present in very young kittens. As summarized in Table 4.5, the typical adult receptive-field organization of an excitatory center with a suppressive surround is also present, although the surround is extremely weak and may be absent in some cells. The proportion of cells that respond both to onset and to offset of a stationary light stimulus is about normal, and, as in adult cats, the spontaneous activity of the cells is quite low. In addition to these adult-like properties, superior colliculus neurons in young kittens are immature in many of the same ways as are cells in the visual structures just reviewed. They have fewer

Table 4.5
Responses of Superior Colliculus Cells

Adult-like	Immature
Visual field topography	Fewer spikes/burst
Excitatory center/suppressive surround	Large receptive field diameters
Low spontaneous activity	Long latency to flash
Proportion of on–off units	Long latency to optic chiasm shock
	Fatigable
	Weak surround suppression
	Respond only to stationary stimuli
	Not direction–selective
	Contralateral eye dominant
	Long stimulus durations needed

spikes per burst than adult cells, fatigue easily, and have larger than adult receptive-field diameters. Their latency to pulsed light flashes is very long (100–1100 msec, Stein *et al.*, 1973b) as is their latency to electrical stimulation of the optic chiasm (mean = 25 msec, Norton, 1977). In the very youngest kittens studied (prenatal to 13 days post-natal), Stein *et al.* (1973a) reported that most cells responded only to stationary stimuli, in contrast to adult cells which generally prefer moving stimuli. Also, long stimulus durations were needed to produce a response. Unlike adult cells, the kitten superior colliculus neurons are not direction-selective. Stein *et al.* (1973a) recorded their youngest (poorly) direction-selective cell at 10 days, and found a clearly direction-selective cell at 13 days, whereas Norton (1974) found his first at 16 days. Finally, whereas in adult cats about 80% of the cells can be activated through either eye, Stein *et al.* (1973a) found no binocular cells in animals younger than 10 days of age, and only about 30% binocular cells at 10–13 days of age.

The deep layers of the superior colliculus in adult cats appear to be involved in visuomotor coordination and in the integration of visual, auditory, and somatosensory stimuli to produce orienting movements of the head and eyes. These layers were examined in kittens by Stein *et al.* (1973a) who found that, as in adult cats, the neurons could respond to auditory and somatosensory, as well as to visual stimuli. In addition, Stein, Clamann, and Goldberg (1979) electrically stimulated the deep layers of the superior colliculus in kittens as young as 2 days of age. As in adult cats, this stimulation produced turning of the head and eyes. However, in young kittens the movements were smaller and high stimulus currents were required to produce them. Often the eye movements were not conjugate. Nonetheless, these results demonstrate that some efferent connections from the superior colliculus are present at the time of eye opening and can produce orienting movements.

F.   Summary

The immature state of the visual system at the time of eye opening in kittens may explain why kittens show no visually guided behaviors at this age: The entire primary visual system is relatively insensitive to visual stimuli, is sluggish in its responses to visual stimuli, fatigues easily, fails to respond to small, low-contrast, or rapidly moving stimuli and, when it does respond, does so immaturely. Furthermore, it ap-pears that, as one samples the responses of the visual system farther from the retina, the cells are found to be less responsive. This has important consequences for behavior, since obtaining a behavioral response to visual stimuli requires that the stimuli activate more than retinal neurons. The retinal neurons must activate LGN and superior colliculus cells, which, in turn, activate neurons further centrally in the visual system. The neural activity produced in the central visual structures must, through as yet unknown pathways, produce activation of motor system neurons that produce the response. At the time of eye opening, the visual system responds moderately to light stimulation at the retinal level, but fails to transmit more than a fraction of that activation across the synaptic connections at the LGN and superior colliculus. Thus the responses produced in the striate cortex and superior colliculus are very weak. Furthermore, as judged from the stimulation data of Stein *et al.* (1979), the motor system is also immature and requires greater activation in kittens than in adult animals to produce motor responses. Thus, it is hardly surprising that no motor responses are evoked by visual stimuli falling on the retina. In addition to being relatively unresponsive, neurons in the visual system are also rather crude and unselective in their responses to visual stimuli. Changes in stimulus dimensions do not produce alterations in the neural responses as easily as they do in adult cats. This type of immaturity may contribute to the crudeness and imprecision of the visually guided behaviors as they emerge initially in young kittens.

V. SEQUENCE OF RECEPTIVE-FIELD DEVELOPMENT IN THE VISUAL SYSTEM

Although the visual system is certainly immature at the time of eye opening, it is important to note that there are a few properties that are present as in adult animals including the retinotopic organization and (in general) the segregation of cells into either ON- or OFF-center. These properties, by themselves, are not able to produce visually guided behaviors. However, they, along with the other immature response properties form the prerequisite foundation upon which the subsequent development of the visual pathway and visual behaviors is based. All of the studies that have traced the development of the responses of the visual system have found that the region of the visual system they studied was immature at eye opening and became fully developed somewhere between 4 and 10 weeks of age. Of particular interest, given the goal of discovering causal relationships between neural and behavioral development, is whether there are differences in the time course or rate of development of receptive-field properties in different regions of the visual system and whether these differences can be regulated to differences in the onset and improvement of visually guided behaviors.

A. Photoreceptors

In the retina, Tucker *et al.* (1979) found that the photoreceptors began to develop shortly after eye opening and became adult-like in their response amplitude and threshold sensitivity at a fairly early age. As illustrated in Fig. 4.5, the threshold for evoking a late receptor potential reached adult values at 17–18 days in the area centralis and the amplitude of the potential was adult-like by 23–26 days. The development at this level of the visual system precedes that in subsequent levels of the visual system and precedes the development of almost all visually guided behaviors. Thus, photosensitivity is not a strict limiting factor on the sensitivity and responsiveness of the visual system.

B. Ganglion Cells

The physiological properties of the retinal ganglion cells are quite immature at 3 weeks of age; by 5 weeks, they are relatively mature. Figure 4.8 summarizes the development of two receptive-field prop-

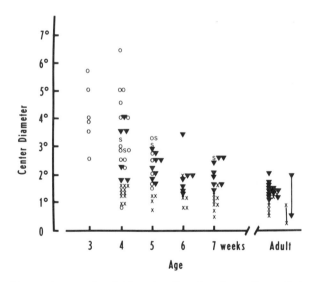

Fig. 4.8 Change in receptive-field center diameter of ganglion cells in kittens as a function of age. The progressive emergence of X and Y cells is also illustrated. Brisk X is depicted by ×, Brisk Y by ▼, sluggish by s, unknown by ○. (From Rusoff & Dubin, 1977.)

erties of ganglion cells: receptive-field center diameter and the distinctness of the cells as X- and Y-cells. At the end of 4 weeks of age (27–32 days in Rusoff & Dubin's 1977 sample) there are many cells having receptive-field diameters comparable to those in adult cats. In addition, however, there are many that retain large receptive-field diameters. Since the large-field and small-field cells are intermixed at the same retinal eccentricities, immaturities in the kittens' optics could not explain their presence. By the end of 5 weeks, Rusoff and Dubin (1977) found no large-center cells and found a gradual decrease over the next 2 weeks in center diameter toward the adult value. Rusoff (1979) has concluded that this decrease is primarily, if not entirely, due to the growth of the optical components of the eye, rather than to a change in the neural organization of the receptive-field center. Rusoff and Dubin (1977) also reported that, as cells developed an inhibitory surround, the surround was quite large. It remained large until after the fifth week and had still not decreased to adult values by the end of the seventh week. Rusoff and Dubin (1977) were not able to identify cells as either X- or Y-cells until the end of the fourth week when they found some of each along with many cells that could not be identified as either. By the end of the sixth week, all of their sample could be identified as either X- or Y-. During the fourth and fifth weeks, when some cells could be identified and some could not, the identifiable X- and Y-cells had smaller receptive-field center diameters than the unclassified cells. Hamasaki and Sutija (1979) also examined the emergence of X- and Y-retinal ganglion cells. In 3-week-old kittens, they found some cells that clearly responded as X- and some that clearly responded as Y-cells on a test of linearity. However, the vast majority did not respond like either type in adult cats. These investigators used a "null ratio" test to attempt to resolve whether the immature cells were actually X- or Y-cells. This measure suggested that they were mostly Y-cells; however without corroborative evidence from other receptive-field properties known to correlate with X- and Y-cell properties in adult animals, it seems premature to conclude that this measure successfully categorized the immature cells.

It does appear that some ganglion cells develop adult receptive-field properties earlier, and others develop these properties later in the development of the kitten. Some cells seem relatively adultlike at 3 weeks and presumably remain mature for the life of the animal. More cells have matured by 4 weeks, and this process of shifting from immature to mature receptive-field properties progresses until the entire ganglion cell population reaches adult levels of responsiveness and organization at about 8 weeks of age. This progressive development is superimposed on a gradient of development within the retina, with the central visual fields maturing before the periphery (Johns, Rusoff, & Dubin, 1979).

A problem arises in attempting to correlate the development of receptive field properties in retinal ganglion cells with the development of more central visual structures and with behavioral development because it is not known whether the ganglion cells that were studied project to the lateral geniculate nucleus and/or to the superior colliculus, or to other visual areas. It is possible, for instance, that the early developing retinal ganglion cells project to the superior colliculus, whereas the later developing ones project to the lateral geniculate nucleus, or vice versa. In addition, there has been relatively little work on the development of the largest retinal ganglion cell population, the W-cells (Rusoff & Dubin 1977).

C. Lateral Geniculate Nucleus Cells

A progressive maturation similar to that found in retinal ganglion cells is seen in the neurons of the dorsal lateral geniculate nucleus over a similar time period (3–5 weeks) as is seen for retinal ganglion cells. As in the retina, there is a large pool of immature cells in young kittens. Some of these develop earlier than other cells, forming a growing population of neurons that respond in an adult-like manner to visual stimuli. Figure 4.9 shows the progressive reduction in the latency of response of LGN neurons to optic chiasm shock along with the progressive increase in the ability of Daniels et al. (1978) to identify neurons as either X- or Y-cells. The latency of activation decreases some by the end of the second postnatal week and shows a considerable drop by the end of the third week. This decrease agrees closely with the time course of the progress of myelinization of the optic tract (Moore et al., 1976). By the end of the fifth week, the latencies approach adult levels, although they remain somewhat elevated. In kittens at about 10 days of age, Daniels et al. (1978) could identify some LGN cells as X- and as Y-cells, although the vast majority could not be classified, mostly because they did not respond to the tests used for classification. By 21–27 days, most cells could be identified as either X- or Y-, and in older animals the proportion gradually increased further. Cells that could be identified as either X- or Y- tended to have shorter latencies than unclassified cells. Furthermore, cells identified as X- seemed to reach adult latency values by the end of the third week, whereas Y-cells took longer to reach adult latencies. Also, X-cells generally had mature receptive-field properties earlier than did Y-cells, which reached maturity later than all X-cells, after 34 days of age.

Ikeda & Tremain (1978) found a similar course of development of

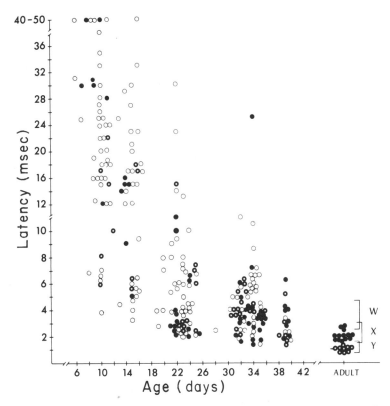

Fig. 4.9 Change in latency of response to optic chiasm shock of LGN cells as a function of age. X cells are depicted by ●, Y cells by ❂. Cells with responses too weak to allow classification as either X or Y cells by the contrast reversal null test are represented by ○. (From Daniels *et al.*, 1978.)

LGN receptive-field properties and have in addition studied the spatial resolving power of "sustained" LGN cells in kittens. At 21 days of age, the youngest age sampled, the highest spatial frequency to which the cells responded with modulated firing (contrast at 0.4) was about 0.5–1 c/deg. By 35 days of age, this increased to 1–2 c/deg and then continued to improve slowly to about 3–4 c/deg at 4 months of age.

Recordings in the adjacent medial interlaminar nucleus (MIN), which contains almost exclusively Y-cells, have been made in kittens 2–8 weeks of age by Wilson *et al.* (1981). The immature Y-cells in 2-week-old kittens have large receptive-field centers, no surround, low spatial and temporal resolution, and give long latency responses to optic chiasm stimulation. Wilson *et al.* (1981) reported that all these properties, except spatial resolution, approach adult values by 8 weeks of age. Importantly, the immature Y-cells in MIN all had linear responses to a counterphased grating. The nonlinear responses characteristic of adult Y-cells were relatively slow to develop. Since whether the cells gave linear responses was a primary test used by Daniels *et al.* (1978) to distinguish X-cells from Y-cells in the LGN, it is likely that some of the cells they characterized as X-cells in Fig. 4.9 were, in fact, immature Y cells.

Comparison of the time course of development between the retinal ganglion cells and LGN cells is impaired by the absence of retinal data from kittens younger than 21 days of age, by Rusoff and Dubin's (1977) avoidance of central retinal areas in their study, and by the absence of information about whether the retinal cells that were studied project to the LGN or to the superior colliculus or to other structures. The receptive-field center diameters in Rusoff and Dubin's (1977) kittens at the end of 3 weeks are still quite large and none of the cells could be identified as either X- or Y-, whereas Daniels *et al.* (1978), recording from many cells near the representation of the area centralis, found at a similar age that many LGN cells could be distinguished as X- or Y-, and that quite a few had optic chiasm shock latencies that were near the adult range. Logically, one would assume that retinal development would slightly precede that of the LGN. That this did not seem to be the case in these studies may be due to the possibility that some of the immature retinal ganglion cells may not have projected to the LGN, making a valid comparison of the development of these two levels of the visual system impossible without further investigation.

D.   Striate Cortex Cells

Development of single unit receptive-field properties in the striate cortex occurs during approximately the same time period (3–5 weeks) as the development of LGN neurons. As summarized in Fig. 4.10, there is an increase in the proportion of orientation-selective neurons in Area 17, which is essentially complete by about the end of the fourth post-natal week, although other investigations (Frégnac & Imbert, 1978; Pettigrew, 1974) suggest it is complete by about the end of the fifth or sixth week. The increase in orientation-selective cells is matched by a decrease in visually unresponsive, nonoriented and orientation bias (immature) cells. Presumably, during this time period, cells from these immature cell classes mature and become orientation-selective neurons. At about this same time, many of the neurons also become sensitive to retinal disparities. Given the intense interest in simple and complex cells in the striate cortex, it is surprising that none of the studies of cortical development report whether there is a differential development of these two classes of cells. The suggestion that simple cells may be

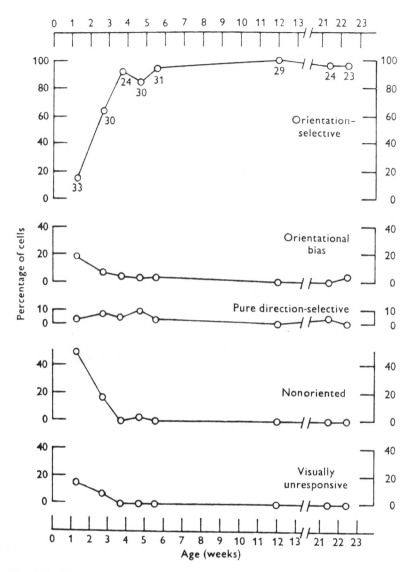

Fig. 4.10 Development of orientation-selective neurons in kitten striate cortex and the decrease in nonoriented and other immature cell types. The five curves show the percentages of each type of receptive field for 397 cells from 8 normal kittens. The numbers beneath the data points indicate the total number of cells recorded in each animal. (Adapted from Blakemore & Van Sluyters, 1975.)

preferentially tuned for horizontal and vertical stimuli (Leventhal & Hirsch, 1975), taken with the tendency for orientation-selective cells in young kittens to have either horizontal or vertical as their optimal stimulus orientation (Blakemore & Van Sluyters, 1975; Frégnac & Imbert, 1978) indicates that simple cells may develop before complex cells.

Another property of cortical cells that has been studied is sensitivity to gratings of varying spatial frequencies. Derrington (1978) has reported briefly on the contrast sensitivity and optimal spatial frequency for cells in the striate cortex of kittens 2–6 weeks of age. There was a gradual increase in the optimal spatial frequency from about 1.4–2.4 c/deg over this time period, whereas the "acuity" of the best cell (measured as the highest spatial frequency to which the cell would respond when the contrast was held at 0.5) went from 0.6 c/deg at 2 weeks to about 3 c/deg at 6 weeks of age. This acuity measure is similar to the "highest spatial frequency" measure of Ikeda and Tremain (1978) in the LGN, and the results are also in fairly close agreement. Neurons in cortex seem to be slightly better in their acuity than LGN neurons in kittens of any age, as is also the case in adult cats (Derrington, 1978).

Along with the development of individual cell receptive-field properties, ocular dominance columns have been found to gradually develop during the first several postnatal weeks (LeVay et al., 1978). At 22 days of age, there was some evidence for a partial segregation of the inputs from the two eyes. By 92 days of age, the ocular dominance pattern was indistinguishable from that of adult cats.

E. Summary of Geniculostriate Development

Whereas it is difficult, and perhaps hazardous, to condense the development of a large number of receptive-field properties into a summary statement, it does appear that some neurons in the geniculostriate pathway first begin to display adult-like properties at about 21 days of age. During the next two weeks, there is a rapid transition, with many neurons shifting from immature to mature properties. By about the fifth week, many neurons are relatively mature and the rate of maturation has slowed somewhat as the adult level is reached. The larger functional units of the cortex, ocular dominance and orientation columns, seem to develop in conjunction with the receptive-field properties of the individual neurons.

F. Superior Colliculus Cells

In the superior colliculus, the development of adult receptive-field properties overlaps extensively with the development of receptive-field properties in the geniculostriate system. However, it appears that the development of most receptive-field properties in the superior colliculus precedes slightly the development of adult-like receptive-field properties in the geniculostriate system. For instance, Norton (1974) reported that the period from 15 to 25 days of age was the time of most rapid development of several receptive-field properties, including reduction in fatigability, development of a suppressive surround, reduction in responsiveness to diffuse illumination of the receptive field, and the development of binocularly activated neurons. As shown in Fig. 4.11, Stein *et al.* (1973a) found that the initially low proportion of binocularly activated neurons rose quickly to essentially adult levels by 30 days of age. One receptive-field property, direction selectivity, starts to develop among the other properties, but seems to take longer to reach adult levels. As shown in Fig. 4.12, Norton (1974) found the proportion of direction-selective cells at 20–29 days of age to still be less than in adult cats. In kittens 30–39 days of age, the proportion was higher, and approached the adult level.

Studies in adult cats have shown that the high proportion of direction-selective, binocularly activated neurons in the superior colliculus is dependent upon the receipt of input from the striate cortex (Wickelgren

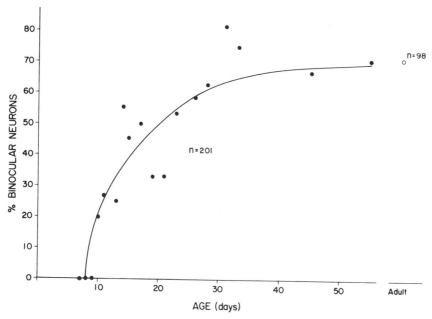

Fig. 4.11 Change in the proportion of binocular superior colliculus neurons as a function of age. The data are fitted by an exponential function with a time constant of approximately 10–12 days. (From Stein *et al.*, 1973a.)

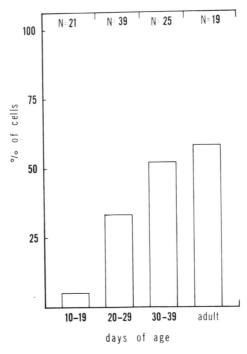

Fig. 4.12 Development of direction-selective superior colliculus neurons with age. The height of each bar represents the proportion of cells in each age group that gave direction-selective responses. The numbers at the top of the figure indicate the number of cells sampled in each age group. (From Norton, 1974.)

& Sterling, 1969). Thus the low proportion of binocular, direction-selective neurons in kittens at the time of eye opening could be due to the absence of binocular, direction-selective input from neurons in the striate cortex. This, in turn, could be due to the absence of a functional pathway from the striate cortex to the superior colliculus at this age; however, Norton (1977) showed that superior colliculus cells in kittens as young as 12 days of age respond to activation of their cortical afferents. Thus, it appears that at least a rudimentary functional pathway is present. As reviewed earlier, cortical neurons are largely binocular at the time of eye opening in kittens, but most of them are not direction-selective. It may be that the absence of binocularity in the superior colliculus at eye opening reflects inactivity of the binocular neurons, in Layer V of the striate cortex, which send their axons to the superior colliculus. As these neurons become more responsive to light, they may be able to transmit their binocular information to the superior colliculus cells. The slower development of direction selectivity in the superior colliculus may reflect the gradual development of direction selectivity in the Layer V cortical cells. If this is the case, then the property which develops most slowly in the superior colliculus, direction selectivity, is slow to develop because the cortical neurons on which the property is dependent have not yet matured. In contrast, the superior colliculus receptive-field properties which do not depend upon cortical input seem to develop relatively early, and are essentially adult-like by the end of the first postnatal month.

VI. CORRELATION OF RECEPTIVE-FIELD DEVELOPMENT WITH BEHAVIORAL DEVELOPMENT

In the introduction to this chapter, several factors were discussed (optics, motor system immaturity, motivation, etc.) that might limit the ability of young kittens to produce behavioral responses to visual stimuli. It was concluded that these factors, in most of the cases examined, did not seem to limit the ability of the animals to produce visually guided behaviors. In contrast, it is clear from the review of the state of the visual system at the time of eye opening that the visual system is sufficiently immature as to limit the ability of young kittens to respond to visual stimuli. In addition, the postnatal development of the visual system occurs during the same period (eye opening to about 2 months of age) when visually guided behaviors are emerging and improving. This is heartening; if there were not such a parallel development of the nervous system and visually guided behaviors, it would be difficult to maintain that the development of the nervous system was responsible for the development of the behaviors.

The first step in establishing a causal relationship between the development of the visual system and the development of visually guided behaviors is the establishment of correlations between the development of specific neural and behavioral responses. From the data that have been reviewed in the preceding sections, a number of potentially causal relationships are evident, and a few of these will be discussed in this section. The broadest, most obvious correlation is the increase in the activity of the visual system (both spontaneous activity and the number of spikes produced in response to a visual stimulus), which occurs concomitantly with the increased behavioral responsiveness of kittens to visual stimuli. Just as the low responsiveness of the visual system at the time of eye opening may contribute importantly to the absence of visual behaviors, so the increased responsiveness with age may allow the visual system to transmit information signaling the presence of a visual stimulus. In addition, the increased responsiveness of the primary visual system can provide a greater likelihood of activating the motor system and producing behavioral responses to the stimulus. This increase in activity is an extremely basic developmental change that has generally been neglected in the search for neural mechanisms underlying the development of visually guided behaviors.

A second, somewhat more specific correlation involves the progressive decrease in receptive-field center diameter and increasing responsiveness of neurons to small visual stimuli that develop over the same period as the increased behavioral responsiveness to small stimuli. It is certainly not surprising that young kittens, with neurons that respond poorly, if at all, to stimuli less than 5 deg in diameter, show no behavioral responses to small visual targets. As the receptive-field center diameters in the geniculostriate system decrease through the fourth and fifth weeks postnatally, the neurons respond to smaller stimuli and, behaviorally, the kittens are able to respond to stimuli of progressively smaller diameters. This parallel has been carried further by Ikeda and Tremain (1978), who have argued that there is an excellent correspondence during postnatal development between the highest spatial frequency to which neurons in the LGN will respond and the behavioral measures of acuity in the kitten (Freeman & Marg, 1975; Mitchell *et al.*, 1976). When actual numerical values are compared, however, the behavioral acuity of the kittens as they approach adulthood (about 5 c/deg) considerably exceeds the "acuity" of the LGN neurons that have been studied (about 3.6 c/deg). It is clear, however, that the improvement in neural sensitivity to grating stimuli increases at about the same rate as does the behavioral capacity.

A third correlation can be found between the development of short latency, reliable responses to repeated presentations of visual stimuli and the progressive improvement in the accuracy and reliability of visually guided behaviors. The relatively long response latencies for the immature visual system may be at least partially responsible for the crude, jerky visual following behaviors seen in young kittens. By the time the responses to even a slowly moving stimulus can produce a following response, the stimulus will have moved a considerable distance, requiring a larger movement to catch up with the stimulus than was indicated by the original stimulus position and velocity. As the response latencies in the geniculostriate pathway and superior colliculus decrease during the period from 21 to 28 days of age, this decrease may contribute to the improvements in the smoothness and accuracy of the orienting and following responses.

A fourth correlation occurs between the stimulus velocities to which visual system neurons will respond and the stimulus velocities that will elicit a behavioral response. In kittens that are beginning to show visual orienting and following responses at around 18–20 days of age, slow stimulus movement must be used to elicit a response (Norton, 1974; Norton & Holcombe, unpublished data). Neurons in all areas of the visual system show a similar restriction in the rate of stimulus velocities to which they will respond; there simply is no neural response to rapidly moving stimuli. As the visual system develops the ability to respond to more rapidly moving stimuli, a parallel improvement occurs in the ability of the kittens to respond to rapid movement.

Of particular interest in attempting to establish causal relationships between neural and behavioral development are instances where neural responses in different visual structures can be found to develop at differing times postnatally and are accompanied by differential development of specific visually guided behaviors. As has been previously noted (Norton, 1974), there is a parallel between the period of time when the neurons of the superficial layers of the superior colliculus progress from an immature to an adult-like state (generally 15–25 days) and the time when visual orienting and following behaviors emerge and begin to improve (Table 4.1, Fig. 4.2). The later emergence of visual behaviors related to the movement of the animal through the environment (25–35 days of age) can be correlated with the development of responses in the LGN and striate cortex during the same time period.

Although the presence of these neurobehavioral correlations is encouraging, a strong cautionary note must be inserted at this point: It may be that none of the specific neural changes reviewed in this section is causally related to the behavior with which it seems to be correlated. For example, the correlated development of the acuity of neurons in the striate cortex (Derrington, 1978) and behavioral acuity (Mitchell *et al.*, 1976) may not be a causal relationship, since it is now well established (Berkley & Sprague, 1979; Sprague, Berkley, & Hughes, 1979) that striate cortex removal in adult cats has only very limited effects on visual acuity. It is entirely possible that the development of responses to high spatial frequency gratings in other parts of the cortex, or even subcortical parts of the visual system is causally related to the development of this visually guided behavior. As another example, the development of receptive-field properties in the superficial layers of the superior colliculus, which occurs in parallel with the onset and improvement of visual orienting and following responses, may not be responsible for those behavioral developments. Whereas removal of the entire superior colliculus in kittens does prevent the development of visual orienting and following responses (Norton & Lindsley, 1971), it has never been shown that the neurons in the superficial layers are required for the development of the behaviors. In fact, removal of only the superficial colliculus layers in the tree shrew produces no deficits in visual orienting and following (Casagrande & Diamond, 1974). The similarity of the superior colliculus in these two species (Albano, Humphrey, & Norton, 1978) suggests that removal of only the superficial layers of the behavior colliculus in the kitten would not prevent the development of these behaviors.

As may be seen from these examples, there are many more-or-less simultaneous developmental changes in the responses of visual system neurons and in the visual abilities of kittens during the first 2 months after birth. The problem is not to find neurobehavioral correlations, but to determine which developing receptive-field property (or properties) is causally related to the onset or improvement of a specific visually guided behavior.

A partial solution to this problem could be achieved by improvements in the measures of neural and behavioral development. It would be useful if investigators in the future would (a) study behavioral development and neural development in the same animals; and (b) provide quantitative measures of the development of neural and behavioral responses rather than only the onset of a particular neural or behavioral response property. There is naturally some variability from animal to animal in the onset and improvement of visually guided behaviors and also variations across animals in the development of neural responses. Tighter correlations between neural and behavioral development can be expected if both are studied in the same individuals. Quantitative studies of neural and behavioral development would allow comparisons to be made over a more extended period of time. This could assist in determining whether the events are really as closely correlated as it might seem from comparison at one or two points during development. For instance, more complete studies of the development of contrast sensitivity and acuity of neurons and of the development of behaviorally tested contrast sensitivity and acuity would allow better estimation of whether the improvement in the neural responses really proceeds in parallel with the development of the behavior. Quantitative tests of speed and size sensitivity of visual system neurons and the tracking abilities of kittens would also be useful. Wherever possible, threshold tests of single unit responses and of the visual abilities of the animals should be employed.

Although improved quantitative measures will improve the accuracy of the neurobehavioral correlations, the establishment of causal relationships between neural development and the development of specific perceptual abilities will require more than a simple compilation of correlations. Once a tight correlation between the development of a specific neural event and a specific visually guided behavior is established, experimental manipulations must be made to alter or eliminate the development of that neural event. Then the behavior of the animal must be examined to determine whether the specific visually guided behavior has been modified or eliminated. Obviously, the large literature on the effects of visual deprivation is of considerable importance in this regard, as visual deprivation and selective rearing experiments are known to effect neural development and the development of visually guided behaviors. In addition, the long history of ablation and stimulation studies certainly points to particular brain regions being involved in certain classes of visual behaviors. By drawing on the literature of these areas as a guide, it may be possible to design experiments that can test the causality of the correlations found in careful studies of the development of the visual system and of visually guided behaviors.

It should be kept in mind that there must also be neural changes that are causally related to the development of visually guided behaviors that occur in areas beyond the visual system structures that have been studied so far. This is particularly true in the cat, which can solve visual form discrimination problems in the complete absence of Area 17, the "primary" visual cortex (Berkley & Sprague, 1979; Sprague, Berkley, & Hughes, 1979). Given the relative unimportance of this cortical area for form vision in cats, it is critically important that other cortical areas be studied more intensively in adult cats, and that the development of responses (such as acuity of the neurons, contrast sensitivity, etc.) of these areas be examined in kittens. This point is further emphasized in behavioral experiments by Held, Hein, and colleagues (Held & Hein, 1963; Hein & Diamond, 1972; Hein, Vital-Durand, Salinger, & Diamond, 1979) which have clearly shown that the development of some visually guided behaviors is dependent upon visuomotor experience obtained under conditions in which the animals can receive both visual and motor feedback entailing the perception of motion. Furthermore, the kittens must be able to move their eyes during this experience. Although the visual feedback obtained during these experiences contributes importantly to the development of the receptive-field properties of neurons in the primary visual system (Barlow, 1975; Blakemore, 1977), important changes almost certainly also occur in as yet unidentified brain regions outside the primary visual system.

Although the present review has been restricted to examining neural and behavioral development in kittens, it must be emphasized that there is a strong need for developmental neural and behavioral comparisons in other species. There have been studies of the behavioral development of vision in monkeys (Boothe, Williams, Kiorpes, & Teller, 1980; Teller, Regal, Videen, & Pulos, 1978), but there has been virtually no electrophysiological study of the sequence of postnatal development of the visual system in this species. In contrast, there has been considerable study of the neural development of the rabbit visual system (Grobstein & Chow, 1975) but very little study of the behavioral development in this species. It is extremely important to obtain this type of comparative information before attempts are made to generalize the findings from kittens to humans. Although the kitten, as the human, seems to first develop visual orienting and following behaviors before developing visual behaviors related to movement through the environment (Bronson, 1974), the specific behaviors that develop and the order in which they develop in kittens are certainly to some degree species-specific and related to the environmental niche filled by this rather specialized carniverous predator. To assume that the neural and behavioral development of this species is identical to that of the human is unwarranted without experimental verification, or at least a survey of the neural and behavioral development in several other species.

ACKNOWLEDGMENTS

I thank Drs. Vivien Casagrande, Anne Rusoff, Frances Wilkinson, Peter Dodwell, Thomas Kuyk, and Terry Hickey for their critical reading of a draft of this chapter, and Ms. Caroline Dunn for her expert assistance with the word processor. Supported by N.I.H. Grants EY02909, EY01085, and EY03039.

REFERENCES

Adrien, J., & Roffwarg, H. P. The development of unit activity in the lateral geniculate nucleus of the kitten. *Experimental Neurology*, 1974, **43**, 261–275.

Albano, J. E., Humphrey, A. L., & Norton, T. T. Laminar organization of receptive field properties in tree shrew superior colliculus. *Journal of Neurophysiology*, 1978, **41**, 1140–1164.

Barlow, H. B. Visual experience and cortical development. *Nature*, 1975, **258**, 199–204.

Barlow, H. B., & Pettigrew, J. D. Lack of specificity of neurons in the visual cortex of young kittens. *Journal of Physiology*, 1971, **218**, 98P–100P.

Berkley, M. A., & Sprague, J. M. Striate cortex and visual acuity functions in the cat. *Journal of Comparative Neurology*, 1979, **187**, 679–702.

Blake, R., Cool, S. J., & Crawford, M. L. J. Visual resolution in the cat. *Vision Research*, 1974, **14**, 1211–1217.

Blakemore, C. Genetic instructions and developmental plasticity in the kitten's visual cortex. *Philosophical Transactions of the Royal Society of London B.*, 1977, **278**, 425–434.

Blakemore, C., & Cummings, R. M. Eye opening in kittens. *Vision Research*, 1975, **15**, 1417–1418.

Blakemore, C., & Van Sluyters, R. C. Innate and environmental factors in the development of the kitten's visual cortex. *Journal of Physiology*, 1975, **248**, 663–716.

Bonds, A. B., & Freeman, R. D. Development of optical quality in the kitten eye. *Vision Research*, 1978, **18**, 391–398.

Boothe, R. G., Williams, R. A., Kiorpes, L., & Teller, D. Y. Development of contrast sensitivity in infant *Macaca nemestrina* monkeys. *Science*, 1980, **208**, 1290–1292.

Bronson, G. The postnatal growth of visual capacity. *Child Development*, 1974, **45**, 873–890.

Buisseret, P., & Imbert, M. Visual cortical cells: Their developmental properties in normal and dark reared kittens. *Journal of Physiology*, 1976, **255**, 511–525.

Bullier, J., & Norton, T. T. X- and Y-relay cells in cat lateral geniculate nucleus: Quantitative analysis of receptive field properties and classification. *Journal of Neurophysiology*, 1979, **42**, 244–273.

Casagrande, V. A., & Diamond, I. T. Ablation study of the superior colliculus in the tree shrew *(Tupaia glis)*. *Journal of Comparative Neurology*, 1974, **156**, 207–237.

Cragg, B. G. The development of synapses in the visual system of the cat. *Journal of Comparative Neurology*, 1975, **160**, 147–166.

Daniels, J. D., Pettigrew, J. D., & Norman, J. L. Development of single-neuron responses in kitten's lateral geniculate nucleus. *Journal of Neurophysiology*, 1978, **41**, 1373–1393.

Derrington, A. M. Development of selectivity in kitten striate cortex. *Journal of Physiology*, 1978, **276**, 46P–47P.

Derrington, A. M. Direct measurements of image quality in the kitten's eye. *Journal of Physiology*, 1979, **295**, 16P–17P.

Diamond, I. T., & Hall, W. C. Evolution of neocortex. *Science*, 1969, **164**, 251–261.

Diamond, M. C., Lindner, B., Johnson, R., Bennett, E. L., & Rosenzweig, M. R. Differences in occipital cortical synapses from environmentally enriched, impoverished, and standard colony rats. *Journal of Neuroscience Research*, 1975, **1**, 109–119.

Donovan, A. The postnatal development of the cat retina. *Experimental Eye Research*, 1966, **5**, 249–254.

Enroth-Cugell, C., & Robson, J. G. The contrast sensitivity of retinal ganglion cells of the cat. *Journal of Physiology*, 1966, **187**, 517–552.

Fagan, L. Development of visual responses in normal and brain-operated kittens. *Anatomical Records*, 1971, **169**, 312–313.

Fox, M. W. Reflex development and behavioral organization. In W. A. Himwich (Ed.), *Developmental neurobiology*. Springfield, Ill.: Charles C Thomas, 1970. pp. 553–580.

Freeman, D. N., & Marg, E. Visual acuity development coincides with the sensitive period in kittens. *Nature*, 1975, **254**, 614–615.

Frégnac, Y. Development of orientation selectivity in the primary visual cortex of normally and dark reared kittens. *Biological Cybernetics*, 1979, **34**, 187–193.

Frégnac, Y., & Imbert, M. Early development of visual cortical cells in normal and dark reared kittens: Relationship between orientation selectivity and ocular dominance. *Journal of Physiology*, 1978, **278**, 27–44.

Fukuda, Y., & Stone, J. Evidence of differential inhibitory influences on X- and Y-type relay cells in the cat's lateral geniculate nucleus. *Brain Research*, 1976, **113**, 188–196.

Graybiel, A. M. Some extrageniculate visual pathways in the cat. *Investigative Ophthalmology*, 1972, **11**, 322–332.

Grobstein, P., & Chow, K. L. Receptive field development and visual experience. *Science*, 1975, **190**, 352–358.

Hamasaki, D. I., & Flynn, J. T. Physiological properties of retinal ganglion cells of 3-week-old kittens. *Vision Research*, 1977, **17**, 275–284.

Hamasaki, D. I., & Sutija, V. G. Development of X- and Y-cells in kittens. *Experimental Brain Research*, 1979, **35**, 9–23.

Hein, A., & Diamond, R. M. Locomotory space as a prerequisite for acquiring visually guided reaching in kittens. *Journal of Comparative and Physiological Psychology*, 1972, **81**, 394–398.

Hein, A., & Held, R. Dissociation of the visual placing response into elicited and guided components. *Science*, 1967, **158**, 390–392.

Hein, A., Vital-Durand, F., Salinger, W., & Diamond, R. Eye movements initiate visual-motor development in the cat. *Science*, 1979, **204**, 1321–1322.

Held, R., & Hein, A. Movement-produced stimulation in the development of visually guided behavior. *Journal of Comparative and Physiological Psychology*, 1963, **56**, 872–876.

Hoffmann, K.-P., Stone, J., & Sherman, S. M. Relay of receptive field properties in dorsal lateral geniculate nucleus of the cat. *Journal of Neurophysiology*, 1972, **35**, 518–531.

Hubel, D. H. Effects of deprivation on the visual cortex of cat and monkey. *Harvey Lecture*, 1978, **72**, 1–51.

Hubel, D. H., & Wiesel, T. N. Receptive fields of cells in striate cortex of very young, visually inexperienced kittens. *Journal of Neurophysiology*, 1963, **26**, 994–1002.

Huttenlocher, P. R. Development of cortical neuronal activity in the neonatal cat. *Experimental Neurology*, 1967, **17**, 247–262.

Ikeda, H., & Tremain, K. E. The development of spatial resolving power of lateral geniculate neurones in kittens. *Experimental Brain Research*, 1978, **31**, 193–206.

Illingworth, D. J. Eye opening in kittens: further comments. *Vision Research*, 1980, **20**, 95.

Johns, P. R., Rusoff, A. C., & Dubin, M. W. Postnatal neurogenesis in the kitten retina. *Journal of Comparative Neurology*, 1979, **187**, 545–556.

Karmel, B. Z., Miller, P. N., Dettweiler, L., & Anderson, G. Texture density and normal development of visual depth avoidance. *Developmental Psychobiology*, 1970, **3**, 73–90.

Lehmkuhle, S., Kratz, K. E., Mangel, S. C., & Sherman, S. M. Spatial and temporal sensitivity of X- and Y-cells in dorsal lateral geniculate nucleus of the cat. *Journal of Neurophysiology*, 1980, **43**, 520–541.

LeVay, S., Stryker, M. P., & Shatz, C. J. Ocular dominance columns and their development in Layer IV of the cat's visual cortex: A quantitative study. *Journal of Comparative Neurology*, 1978, **179**, 223–244.

Leventhal, A. G., & Hirsch, H. V. Cortical effect of early selective exposure to diagonal lines. *Science*, 1975, **190**, 902–904.

Mitchell, D. E., Giffin, F., Wilkinson, F., Anderson, P., & Smith, M. L. Visual resolution in young kittens. *Vision Research*, 1976, **16**, 363–366.

Mooney, R. D., Dubin, M. W., & Rusoff, A. C. Interneuron circuits in the lateral geniculate nucleus of monocularly deprived cats. *Journal of Comparative Neurology*, 1979, **187**(3), 533–544.

Moore, C. L., Kalil, R., & Richards, W. Development of myelination in optic tract of the cat. *Journal of Comparative Neurology*, 1976, **165**, 125–136.

Norton, T. T. Receptive field properties of superior colliculus cells and development of visual behavior in kittens. *Journal of Neurophysiology*, 1974, **37**, 674–690.

Norton, T. T. Functional development of cortical and retinal inputs to kitten superior colliculus. *Association for Research in Vision and Ophthalmology (ARVO)*, 1977, April 25–29.

Norton, T. T. Geniculate and extrageniculate visual systems in the tree shrew. In A. R. Morrison and P. L. Strick (Eds.), *Changing Concepts of the Nervous System*. New York: Academic Press, 1981.

Norton, T. T., & Linsley, D. B. Visual behavior after bilateral superior colliculus lesions in kittens and cats. *Federation Proceedings*, 1971, **30**, 615.

Olson, C. R., & Freeman, R. D. Eye alignment in kittens. *Journal of Neurophysiology*, 1978, **41**, 848–859.

Pasik, P., Pasik, T., & Krieger, H. P. Effects of cerebral lesions upon optokinetic nystagmus in monkeys. *Journal of Neurophysiology*, 1959, **22**, 297–304.

Pettigrew, J. D. The effect of visual experience on the development of stimulus specificity by kitten cortical neurons. *Journal of Physiology*, 1974, **237**, 49–74.

Reinecke, R. D. Review of optokinetic nystagmus from 1954 to 1960. *Archives of Ophthalmology*, 1961, **65**, 609–615.

Rose, G. Discussion: CNS maturation and behavioral development. *UCLA Forum and Medical Science*, 1975, **18**, 171–178.

Rusoff, A. C. Development of ganglion cells in the retina of the cat. In R. D. Freeman (Ed.), *Developmental neurobiology of vision*. Plenum, 1979.

Rusoff, A. C., & Dubin, M. W. Development of receptive field properties of retinal ganglion cells in kittens. *Journal of Neurophysiology*, 1977, **40**, 1188–1198.

Sherk, H., & Stryker, M. P. Quantitative study of cortical orientation selectivity in visually inexperienced kittens. *Journal of Neurophysiology*, 1976, **39**, 63–70.

Sherman, S. M. Development of interocular alignment in cats. *Brain Research*, 1972, **37**, 187–203.

Sprague, J. M., Berkley, M. A., & Hughes, H. C. Visual acuity functions and pattern discrimination in the destriate cat. *Acta Neurobiologica Experimental*, 1979, **39**, 643–682.

Stein, B. E., Clamann, H. P., & Goldberg, S. J. Superior colliculus influences on eye movement in the neonatal cat. *Neuroscience Abstracts*, 1979, **5**, 809.

Stein, B. E., Labos, E., & Kruger, L. Sequence of changes in properties of neurons of superior colliculus of the kitten during maturation. *Journal of Neurophysiology*, 1973, **36**, 667–679. (a)

Stein, B. E., Labos, E., & Kruger, L. Determinants of response latency in neurons of superior colliculus in kittens. *Journal of Neurophysiology*, 1973, **36**, 680–689. (b)

Teller, D. Y., Regal, D. M., Videen, T. O., & Pulos, E. Development of visual acuity in infant monkeys *(Macaca nemestrina)* during the early postnatal weeks. *Vision Research*, 1978, **18**, 561–566.

Ter Braak, J.W.G. Untersuchungen über optokinetischen nystagmus. *Archives Neerlandaises de Physiologia*, 1936, **21**, 309–376.

Thorn, F., Gollender, M., & Erickson, P. The development of the kitten's visual optics. *Vision Research*, 1976, **16**, 1145–1150.

Tucker, G. S., Hamasaki, D. I., Labbie, A., & Muroff, J. Anatomic and physiologic development of the photoreceptor of the kitten. *Experimental Brain Research*, 1979, **37**, 459–474.

van Hof-van Duin, J. Development of visuomotor behavior in normal and dark reared cats. *Brain Research*, 1976, **104**, 233–241.

Walk, R. D. The study of visual depth and distance perception in animals. In D. S. Lehrman, R. A. Hinde, & E. Shaw (Eds.), *Advances in the study of behavior* (Vol. 1). New York: Academic Press, 1965. Pp. 99–154.

Walk, R. D. The influence of level of illumination and size of pattern on the depth perception of kitten and puppy. *Psychonomic Science*, 1968, **12**, 199–200.

Walk, R. D., & Gibson, E. J. A comparative and analytical study of visual depth perception. *Psychological Monographs: General and Applied*, 1961, **75**, 1–44.

Warkentin, J. A genetic study of vision in animals. PhD Thesis, The University of Rochester, 1938.

Warkentin, J., & Smith, K. U. The development of visual acuity in the cat. *Journal of Genetic Psychology*, 1937, **50**, 371–399.

Wickelgren, B. G., & Sterling, P. Influence of visual cortex on receptive fields in the superior colliculus of the cat. *Journal of Neurophysiology*, 1969, **32**, 16–23.

Wilkinson, F. E., & Dodwell, P. C. Visual pattern perception in very young kittens. *Investigative Ophthalmology and Visual Science*, 1979, **18**, 252.

Wilkinson, F. E., & Dodwell, P. C. Young kittens can learn complex visual pattern discriminations. *Nature*, 1980, **284**, 258–259.

Wilson, J. R., Tessin, D. E., & Sherman, S. M. Development of Y-cells in the kitten's medial interlaminar nucleus. *Investigative Ophthalmology and Visual Science (Supplement)*, 1981, **20**, 70.

Windle, W. F. Normal behavioral reactions of kittens correlated with the postnatal development of nerve fiber density in the spinal gray matter. *Journal of Comparative Neurology*, 1930, **50**, 479–503.

5

Maturation of the Superior Colliculus

BARRY E. STEIN
Medical College of Virginia

BARBARA GORDON
University of Oregon

I. INTRODUCTION

The survival of many species depends upon the precision of their visuomotor skills. These skills often develop gradually in individuals

157

and are subject to modification by environmental factors. However, alterations in the normal ontogenetic course of this development may produce permanent anomalies that limit the likelihood that a given individual will compete successfully in its "natural" setting. Because the superior colliculus plays a major role in visuomotor integration, its normal maturation and susceptibility to environmental influence is of considerable interest.

That the superior colliculus is involved in the control of eye movements and visual orientation has been known for over 100 years (Adamük, 1872). However, within the last 7–8 years our understanding of the functional organization of the colliculus has expanded dramatically. We have now become aware of the involvement of this structure in nonvisual, as well as in visual, behaviors.

Current thought places the visual role of the colliculus in facilitating shifts of gaze and perhaps attention as well. Evidence for the involvement of the colliculus in these behaviors comes from four different types of experiments.

1. Receptive field studies, described in more detail in what follows, indicate that collicular cells are well suited to signaling stimulus appearances, approximate location, and direction of movement, but are poorly suited to signaling the details of stimulus size and shape.

2. The behavior of visual collicular cells in alert, behaving primates is also consistent with their involvement in shifts of gaze and attention. Cells in the superficial layers of the monkey colliculus show an enhanced response to a visual stimulus when that stimulus is "meaningful" and is used as a target for a saccadic eye movement (Goldberg & Wurtz, 1972b; Wurtz & Mohler, 1976). Cells in the deep collicular layers fire just prior to eye movements and appear to have a role in initiating these movements (Mohler & Wurtz, 1976; Wurtz & Goldberg, 1972a).

3. Although electrical stimulation of the colliculus cannot duplicate the normal afferent input, it can evoke remarkably organized movements of the eyes, pinnae, head, and body (Clamann & Stein, 1979; Robinson, 1972; Schaefer, 1970; Stein, Goldberg, & Clamann, 1976).

4. Simple observation of monkeys with collicular lesions suggests a role for the colliculus in visuomotor behavior and attention. Staring vacantly into space, they appear inattentive and show little interest in exploring their environment (Anderson & Symmes, 1969). Nevertheless, these monkeys are quite able to move their eyes (Wurtz & Goldberg, 1972b; Mohler & Wurtz, 1976).

The conclusions drawn from lesion–behavior experiments are closely dependent on the behaviors observed, and experiments on collicular lesions are no exception. If the task requires visuomotor behavior and attention, it is likely to show that collicular lesions impair these abilities. However, it is also possible to design the task so that a pattern discrimination deficit appears as well.

Visuomotor behavior is impaired in tasks requiring complex visual search and rapid shifts of gaze, such as selecting the dimmer of two briefly presented lights (Keating, 1974; Latto, 1978). The role of the colliculus in shifts of visual attention is supported by the fact that distracting stimuli do not impair the ability of a colliculectomized rat to perform a visually guided running task; such stimuli do impair a normal rat. Thus, in the presence of distracting stimuli lesioned rats actually outperform normal rats (Goodale & Murison, 1975).

Lesion experiments also suggest that the colliculus is involved in attention to auditory and somatic as well as to visual stimuli. Cats with large collicular lesions fail to respond to visual, auditory, or somatic stimuli contralateral to the lesion (Sprague & Meikle, 1965). Electrophysiological studies (see following) have added surety and precision to our understanding of collicular integration of auditory, visual, and somatic stimuli.

Pattern discrimination deficits emerge when the animal is asked to learn new discriminations postoperatively (Anderson & Williamson, 1971; Berlucchi, Sprague, Levy, & DiBerardino, 1972). Perhaps learning new discriminations requires rapid shifts of attention to determine the distinguishing features of the stimulus. Tunkl and Berkeley (1977) tried to get evidence for this notion, but without success. Berkeley (personal communication, 1980) is not, however, satisfied that their experiment was a critical test.

Casagrande, Harting, Hall, Diamond, and Martin (1972) examined both visuomotor function and pattern discrimination in the same experiment. They found that the tree shrew colliculus is involved in both behaviors, but that the two functions are anatomically segregated. Lesions of the superficial layers caused deficits in form discrimination, whereas lesions of the deep layers caused deficits in visual tracking.

Perhaps much can be learned about colliculus function by studying how the properties of colliculus cells depend upon specific experiences. Profound changes in the properties of colliculus cells normally occur as the animal develops from infant to adult and their ultimate response characteristics reflect the animal's early sensory environment. Thus, if an animal experiences an "abnormal" environment during infancy, collicular cells develop "atypical" response characteristics.

We begin this chapter with a brief review of the anatomy and physiology of the superior colliculus. Our main goal is to describe changes in collicular physiology that may underlie changes in behavior, and vice versa. The maturation of the colliculus in normal kittens will be described first, followed by an evaluation of the consequences of abnormal rearing conditions.

II. ANATOMICAL ORGANIZATION

The superior colliculus is a laminated structure that has a similar organization in very different mammalian species. Although only two functional subdivisions (superficial and deep) are presently recognized, at least seven anatomically distinct laminae have been distinguished (see following and Fig. 5.1).

The current view of the colliculus as a bipartite structure is primarily the result of observations suggesting that superficial and deep laminar neurons have: (a) different morphological characteristics; (b) different physiological characteristics; (c) separate afferent and efferent connec-

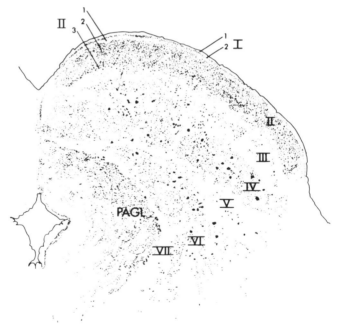

Fig. 5.1 A projection drawing of a traverse section of the cat superior colliculus. Individual laminae and sublaminae are shown. $I_{1,2}$ indicate sublaminae of stratum zonale; $II_{1,2,3}$, sublaminae of stratum griseum superficiale; III, stratum opticum; IV, stratum griseum intermediale; V, stratum album intermediale (or stratum lemnisci); VI, stratum griseum profundum; VII, stratum album profundum. (From Kaneseki & Sprague, 1970.)

tions; and (d) distinct functional roles. These differences are discussed in the following.

A. Superficial Laminae

The three laminae that compose the superficial colliculus include (a) stratum zonale; (b) stratum griseum superficiale; and (c) stratum opticum. Neurons within these laminae have the short, bushy, and non-overlapping dendrites that are typical of neurons in sensory structures (Ramon-Moliner & Nauta, 1966). Their function appears to be exclusively visual (Stein, Magalhães-Castro, & Kruger, 1976) and their major input comes from the retina and visual cortex (Gordon, 1975; Palmer, Rosenquist, & Sprague, 1972). Axons from the optic tract enter the colliculus via stratum opticum and turn upward to terminate primarily in stratum griseum superficiale. Projections are also received from the parabigeminal nucleus and pretectum (Edwards, Ginsburgh, Henkel, & Stein, 1979). Many superficial cells receive input from more than one visual source and the integration of these afferents produces the characteristic physiological profile of visual cells here. The efferents of the superficial laminae are directed to visual cortex via relays in the thalamus (Edwards, 1980; Graham, 1977; Graybiel, 1970; Harting, Hall, Diamond, & Martin, 1973; Kawamura & Kobayashi, 1975).

B. Deep Laminae

The deep colliculus consists of four main laminae: (a) stratum griseum intermediale; (b) stratum album intermediale; (c) stratum griseum profundum; and (d) stratum album profundum. In contrast to superficial cells, those of the deep laminae have long, densely overlapping dendrites and there is a pattern of interlacing axons and cell bodies (Leontovich & Zhukova, 1963). These deep layer properties also characterize the underlying reticular formation and it is usually difficult to draw the border between deep colliculus and underlying structures. These similarities as well as others between deep colliculus and underlying reticular formation have prompted Edwards (1980) to suggest classifying the deep collicular layers with the reticular core. His analysis represents a significant departure from the view of the colliculus as a bipartite structure. The lack of evidence for communication between superficial and deep laminae is taken to indicate that these divisions are not just histologically different but functionally independent. Further investigation of this possibility is certainly warranted.

The inputs to the deep laminae are derived not only from visual structures as are those to upper laminae, but from auditory, somatosensory, vestibular, and motor structures as well. In all, more than 40 subcortical structures that project to the superficial colliculus have been listed (see Edwards et al., 1979). The extensive list of ascending projections to the deep colliculus is supplemented by descending projections from widespread areas of the cerebral cortex (Garey, Jones, & Powell, 1968; Kawamura, Sprague, & Niimi, 1974).

The efferent projections of the deep laminae are also more extensive and more widely diversified than those of the superficial layers. Ascending efferents have been traced to such nonvisual thalamic areas as intralaminar nuclei, zona incerta, and reticular nucleus; descending projections have been seen terminating in reticular structures, extraocular motor nuclei, cerebellar projection nuclei, and cervical spinal segments (Edwards & Henkel, 1978; Graham, 1977; Harting et al., 1973). It appears that some segregation of efferent neurons is maintained. Cells projecting to the cervical cord and influencing head movements are found predominantly in stratum griseum intermedium, whereas those ultimately projecting to the facial nucleus and influencing ear movements are located primarily in stratum griseum profundum (Henkel & Edwards, 1978).

Because of these widespread connections, activity in the colliculus can have profound influences in the central nervous system. Attempts to evaluate these influences have involved electrical stimulation of deep layers. These studies have revealed that eye, ear, head, and limb movements can be produced and that these evoked movements are predictable on the basis of the sensory topography. For example, when the area of the colliculus representing a spot in the upper visual field is stimulated, upward deflections of the eyes, ears, and head result (Clamann & Stein, 1979; Roucoux & Crommelinck, 1976; Schaefer, 1970; Schiller, 1972; Stein et al., 1976). The saccadic eye movement brings the fovea, or area centralis, precisely to that point of the visual field represented at the stimulation site. This topographic relationship between motor and sensory representations in the colliculus seems particularly well suited for the transduction of a sensory experience into an orienting response.

III. SENSORY REPRESENTATION

A. Visual Topography

As briefly indicated in the previous section, the visual representation in the colliculus is topographic. This visuotopy has been studied in detail in the superficial laminae of numerous laboratory mammals with modern electrophysiological techniques. Despite several species-specific distortions in the visual topography (e.g., a magnification of central visual fields is pronounced in the monkey, Sparks & Pollack, 1977; and cat, Feldon, Feldon, & Kruger, 1970; more limited in the rabbit, Hughes, 1971; mouse, Dräger & Hubel, 1975; hamster, Finlay, Schneps, Wilson, & Schneider, 1978; tree shrew and squirrel, Lane, Allman, Kaas, & Miezin, 1973; and absent in the rat, Siminoff, Schwassmann, & Kruger, 1977). A consistent mammalian feature is the approximate rostral–caudal orientation of the horizontal meridian and the medial–lateral orientation of the vertical meridian. Consequently, individual visual cells of caudal colliculus have receptive fields in temporal visual space, whereas those in rostral colliculus have nasal fields. Neurons in medial colliculus have superior visual fields and those in lateral colliculus have receptive fields in inferior visual space (see Fig. 5.2a).

Visual cells are also found in the deep layers of the colliculus, but their incidence decreases dramatically with depth, and the large receptive fields (see Fig. 5.5) of deep lamina visual cells results in considerably less precision in the visuotopic representation. In part, this is due to the lack of a direct retinal projection to deep colliculus and the relatively diffuse nature of the corticotectal projection to these layers (Kawamura et al., 1974). In some mammals (e.g., cat) corticotectal afferents affect cells in both superficial and deep colliculus (Stein, 1978); in others (e.g., ground squirrel and monkey) the corticotectal influence is exerted only in deep layers (Michael, 1972b; Schiller, Stryker, Cynader, & Berman, 1974). The distribution and integration of the corticotectal afferents has a profound influence on the physiological characteristics of visual cells and differences in these characteristics are discussed in following sections.

B. Visual Receptive Fields

Visual receptive fields of collicular neurons have been studied in a variety of species, including cat, primate, rabbit, ground squirrel, mouse, and hamster (Berman & Cynader, 1972; Chalupa & Rhoades, 1977; Cynader & Berman, 1972; Dräger & Hubel, 1975; Goldberg & Wurtz, 1972a; Masland, Chow, & Stewart, 1971; Michael, 1972a,b; Rizzolatti, Camarda, Grupp, & Pisa, 1974; Schiller & Koerner, 1971; Stein & Arigbede, 1972a,b; Stein & Dixon, 1979; Sterling & Wickelgren, 1969; Tiao & Blakemore, 1976; Updyke, 1974). The properties of collicular cells are remarkably similar across species. The following summary emphasizes superficial cells in the cat colliculus because these cells are

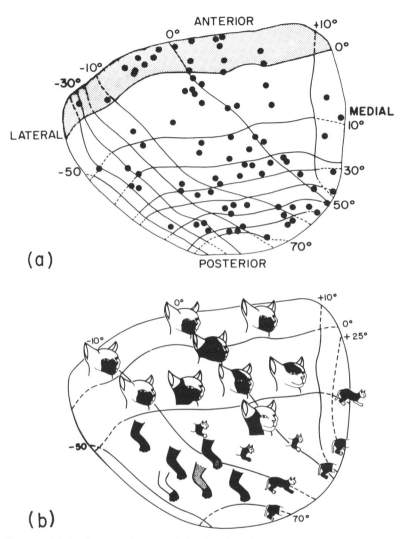

Fig. 5.2 (a) A schematic diagram of the dorsal surface of the left superior colliculus. The horizontal and vertical meridians are marked, respectively, by the vertical and horizontal degree lines, and the shaded area anterior (rostral) to the vertical meridian illustrates the representation of the ipsilateral half-field. Note the nonlinearity of the visuotopic representation with disproportionately large areas devoted to parafoveal and inferior temporal visual space. Each dot refers to a single electrode penetration; location of penetration was histologically determined. In (b), a summary of representative body sectors encountered in different areas of the superior colliculus is presented. This figure minimizes the overlap of body sectors by the choice of body sectors most heavily represented in a given area. Note the nonlinearity of the somatotopy, with disproportionately large areas devoted to trigeminal and forelimb representations. These are the same areas devoted to parafoveal and inferior temporal visual space. (From Stein *et al.*, 1976.)

the most thoroughly studied and because the cat is the animal most often used in developmental electrophysiology. Deeper cells in the cat colliculus will be described briefly at the end of this section, and occasionally interspecies comparisons will be made. Minor differences among species and among different laboratories working with the same species can perhaps be blamed on the natural variance present in the colliculus itself. Compared to the crisp and reliable responses of visual cortex cells, the responses of collicular cells can be frustratingly erratic.

In contrast to visual cortex cells whose requirements for stimulus location, size, and shape are quite stringent, collicular cells are remarkably tolerant, perhaps even lax (Berman & Cynader, 1972; Stein & Arigbede, 1972a; Sterling & Wickelgren, 1969). The activating regions of collicular receptive fields are large. Even near the area centralis they are rarely smaller than 4 deg square. Compared to visual cortex cells, collicular cells do not have very stringent requirements for stimulus shape or orientation. The receptive field of collicular cells consists of an activating region, from which responses can be elicited, and suppressive regions around all or part of the activating region. The surrounds drastically limit the size of effective stimuli. The cell responds much more poorly to stimuli invading the surround than it does to stimuli confined to the activating region. Frequently, however, the optimal stimulus is smaller than the activating region, implying the existence of a suppressive mechanism confined to the inside of the activating region. Yet, these large receptive fields responding to a wide variety of stimuli seem poorly suited to signaling the precise location or features of a visual stimulus.

An additional suppressive phenomenon has been described by Rizzolatti *et al.* (1974). They found that stimuli introduced into the visual field approximately 30 deg from the activating region can decrease the response to a second stimulus moved simultaneously through the activating region. (The ordinary suppressive surround probably never extends this far from the activating region.) Rizzolatti *et al.* suggest that the second stimulus may be a "distraction" that prevents the animals from paying attention to the stimulus moved through the activating region.

Most cells in the cat and primate superior colliculus are binocularly driven. The ocular dominance histogram from collicular cells is, if anything, more binocular than the ocular dominance histogram from cortical cells (Fig. 5.3) (Berman & Cynader, 1972; Sterling & Wickelgren, 1969). Berman, Blakemore, and Cynader (1975) state that most collicular cells are sensitive to binocular disparity but are not quite as sensitive as are cortical cells. The authors suggest that collicular disparity sensitivity might play a role in disjunctive eye movements.

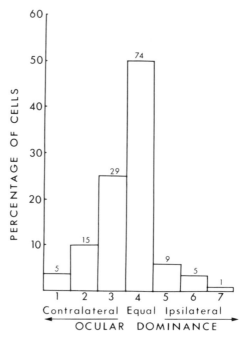

Fig. 5.3 Ocular dominance distribution of 138 units in the superior colliculus. Number over each bar gives the absolute number of cells in that category. Group 1 cells are driven only by the contralateral eye; for Group 2, the contralateral dominance is marked; for Group 3, slight. Cells in Group 4 are driven about equally by both eyes. In Group 5, the ipsilateral eye dominates slightly; in Group 6, markedly; and in Group 7, the cells respond only to the ipsilateral eye. (From Sterling and & Wickelgren, 1969.)

Rather few cells in cat colliculus respond optimally to flashed stationary stimuli even when these stimuli are confined to the activating region. Flashing diffuse light is even a poorer stimulus (Stein & Arigbede, 1972a; Sterling & Wickelgren, 1969).

Receptive fields of cat collicular cells are most easily mapped with moving stimuli. Each cell has an optimal rate of stimulus movement, but responds reasonably well to speeds half as fast or twice as fast as the optimal speed. The optimal speed can range from 1 deg/sec to over 100 deg/sec, but for most cells is less than 50 deg/sec. The cells requiring rapid movement (>50 deg/sec) tend to be those with very large indistinct receptive fields (Dreher & Hoffman, 1973; Stein & Arigbede, 1972a).

About 65% of collicular cells in the cat are directionally selective (the proportion of directionally selective cells varies widely between species), but the directional selectivity is usually somewhat different from that found in visual cortex. For cortical cells, the null direction is usually perpendicular to the preferred direction, whereas in collicular cells the null direction is usually opposite to the preferred direction. The precision of the directional selectivity varies considerably from cell to cell. Some cells respond well over a small range of directions and poorly or not at all over a wide range; others respond well over a wide range of directions and poorly or not at all over a small range (Berman & Cynader, 1972; Dreher & Hoffman, 1973; Stein & Arigbede, 1972a; Sterling & Wickelgren, 1969).

One striking difference between the cat colliculus and the colliculus of most other mammals is in the proportion of directionally selective cells. The cat has a much larger proportion than does the monkey, ground squirrel, rabbit, mouse, rat, or tree shrew. Furthermore, the specific direction of movement most often preferred by collicular cells differs among mammals. These differences probably are reflections of different ecological pressures (Ingle, 1973), but just what selective advantage they provide is unclear at present (also see Stein & Dixon, 1979).

One important difference between directional selectivity in colliculus and in visual cortex (of the cat) is a property, not of individual cells, but of the population of cells. In visual cortex, the distribution of preferred directions is uniform. In contrast, the distribution of preferred directions of collicular cells is skewed in favor of horizontal movement toward the periphery of the visual field (Berman & Cynader, 1972; Dreher & Hoffman, 1973; Stein & Arigbede, 1972a; Sterling & Wickelgren, 1969). Perhaps these cells signal that a stimulus is leaving the field and that the cat must move his head and eyes if it wants to keep the stimulus in view.

Because the development of collicular cells and their response to abnormal visual environments may reflect changes in the corticotectal tract, it is important to determine what properties of normal adult collicular cells are dependent upon the integrity of this pathway. Despite some controversy about the effects of such lesions, at least four laboratories agree that visual cortex lesions in cats increase the responsiveness of superficial collicular cells to stationary stimuli, decrease directional selectivity, and decrease binocular driving (Fig. 5.4) (Berman & Cynader, 1972, 1975, 1976; Rosenquist & Palmer, 1971; Stein & Magalhães-Castro, 1975; Wickelgren & Sterling, 1969; but cf. Hoffman & Straschill, 1971; Rizzolatti, Tradardi, & Camarda, 1970). This has also been observed in hamster (Rhoades & Chalupa, 1978; Chalupa & Rhoades, 1977).

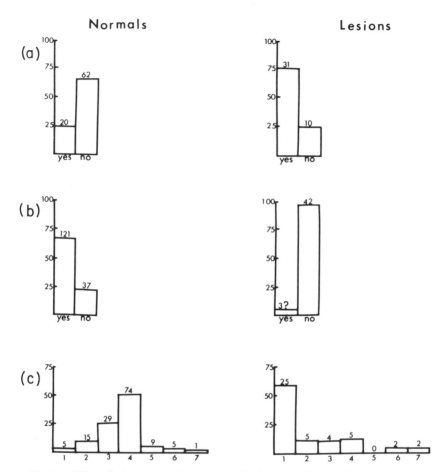

Fig. 5.4 Effect of visual cortex lesions on collicular units. Height of each bar indicates percentage of the units in the relevant category. Number over the bar gives the absolute number of units in that category. (a) Responses to stationary stimuli; (b) directional selectivity; (c) ocular dominance. Conventions as in Fig. 5.3. (From Wickelgren & Sterling, 1969a.)

The cells of the intermediate and deep gray layers exaggerate many of the properties of superficial cells (Gordon, 1973; Stein & Arigbede, 1972a,b). Many deep cells have extremely large receptive fields that may encompass an entire quadrant or even half of the visual field (Fig. 5.5). The requirement for moving stimuli is increased; these large receptive fields can rarely be mapped with flashed stationary stimuli. (As will be discussed in what follows, many of these cells respond to auditory or somatic as well as to visual stimuli.) The erratic responses

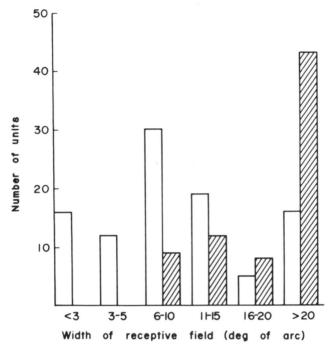

Fig. 5.5 Comparison of the receptive field widths of 98 superficial units and 72 deep units. White bars indicate superficial units, shaded bars depict deep units. (From Gordon, 1973.)

of deep layer cells are extremely frustrating. Sometimes these cells appear to habituate to repeated stimulus presentations; at other times, they seem subject to random or oscillating fluctuations in excitability (Stein & Arigbede, 1972a).

C.   Somatosensory Topography

The organization of the somatic representation in the superior colliculus of the cat has been related to the visuotopy by mapping visual and somatic receptive fields in the same electrode penetrations. The somatic representation was found to be restricted to deep colliculus and its organization was topographic: The long body axis (head to tail) was represented along the rostral–caudal extent of the colliculus and the short body axis was laid out along the medial–lateral colliculus. In a given electrode penetration, the visual and somatic receptive fields were in approximate topographical register despite their partial laminar segregation. Consequently, in penetrations in which visual fields were found near the area centralis, somatic receptive fields were generally found near the midline of the face (Fig. 5.2b). As the visual fields moved away from area centralis in subsequent electrode penetrations, somatic receptive fields moved away from the midline of the face in corresponding directions. Superior visual receptive fields were found in penetrations in which somatic receptive fields were superior on the body (e.g., the top of the head). Inferior temporal visual fields corresponded to somatic fields on the forepaw or forelimb (the forelimb may be considered the ventrolateral extreme of the body when the cat is either in a crouching or in a standing position).

A correspondence in the magnification of certain body segments and regions of the visual field was also observed. Approximately the anterior third of the colliculus is devoted to that part of the visual field within 10 deg of the area centralis and this same portion of the colliculus represents the face (Fig. 5.2b). A magnified representation of the inferior temporal visual field and forelimb representation occurs in the posterior lateral colliculus, and the trunk and tail are poorly represented. Presumably magnifying the central visual representation aids in the resolution of, and the fixation upon, the object of interest, whereas the increased tactile resolution on the face and forelimb (believed to occur as a result of this magnification) may facilitate tactile exploration (Stein et al., 1976).

Similar visuotopic–somatotopic organization have been found in the mouse and hamster (Chalupa & Rhoades, 1977; Dräger & Hubel, 1975; Finlay et al., 1978, Stein & Dixon, 1979; Tiao & Blakemore, 1976). In rodents, however, an expanded vibrissal representation is evident. As rodents use the vibrissae extensively during exploration, it should not be surprising to find that the vibrissae are very well represented in a structure intimately involved in orientation. Yet this observation does suggest that subtle differences in collicular organization are present in different species and can reflect the demands of different environments.

To examine whether these species differences represented modifications of a more ancient plan, or independent (though convergent) evolutionary trends, we studied the sensory representations in a more primitive organism, the iguana (Gaither & Stein, 1979). Presumably, the data gathered from the iguana can give us some insight into the organization of the tectum in the now extinct premammalian reptile.

The visual and somatic representations in the iguana were found to be very much like those of the mammal (see Fig. 5.6). They were in topographic register and partially segregated by layer. It seems that a general visuotopic–somatotopic plan in the midbrain antedates the appearance of mammals. The organizational differences between mam-

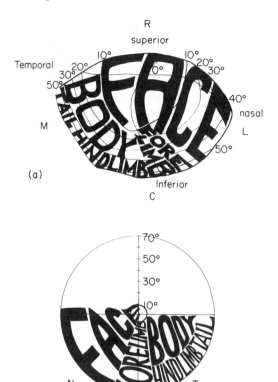

Fig. 5.6 Visual and somatic topographies in the iguana optic tectum. (a) Visual and somatic topographies illustrated on a diagram of the surface of the contralateral (right) tectum. The horizontal and vertical visual meridians are represented, and are divided by isobars representing 10 deg concentric circles of the visual field. The orientation of the visual map is indicated (*Superior, Inferior, Nasal,* and *Temporal*), and letters indicate the orientation of the tectum (*R,* rostral; *C,* caudal; *M,* medial; and *L,* lateral). The rostral pole, upon which superior visual space is represented, lies beneath the cerebral lobe and is not shown. Note the magnified representation of both the central 10 deg of the visual field and the corresponding somatic area, the face. (b) The body represented in a circular diagram of the visual field to illustrate the spatial overlapping of sensory topographies in the tectum. The location of each body sector was determined by the location of the visual receptive fields found in the same area of the tectum. (From Gaither & Stein, 1979 in *Science,* **205,** 595–597. Copyright 1979 by the American Association for the Advancement of Science.)

mals noted previously (e.g., the magnification of portions of the visual field or body) appear to reflect specific adaptations to very different ecological pressures.

D. Response Characteristics of Somatic Cells

The general characteristics of somatic collicular cells are quite similar in several different mammals. The majority of somatic cells in the superior colliculi of cats and rodents are cutaneous (Stein & Dixon, 1978, 1979; Stein et al., 1976); that is, they are activated by gentle movement of hairs or the distortion of the skin. Nocioceptive cells of the colliculus have thus far been described only in the hamster (Stein & Dixon, 1978), although there are indications that similar cells exist in the cat (Nagata & Kruger, 1979).

Even though they respond to different modalities, visual and somatic cells of the colliculus are, in some ways, quite similar to one another. For example, both visual and somatic colliculus cells exhibit decreasing responsiveness to successive identical stimuli even when such stimuli are presented at low repetition rates (Stein et al., 1976). This is a phenomenon known as "habituation." In addition, both visual and somatic cells respond in a transient manner even when a maintained stimulus is presented. Both cell types appear to be less involved in the analysis of specific stimulus features than in the detection of changes in stimulus conditions and in the location of that stimulus.

E. Auditory Representation

Comparatively little is known about the auditory representation in the superior colliculus. This is in part due to the greater technical difficulties encountered in the delivery of controlled auditory stimuli and the difficulty in identifying the "trigger" features of the auditory cells in the colliculus (Gordon, 1973; Stein & Arigbede, 1972b). Pure tones are often ineffective in reliably activating these cells and more complex stimuli are generally required. Recently, it has been reported that species-specific sounds are particularly effective in activating auditory cells in the colliculus of the monkey (Allon & Wollberg, 1978). Perhaps the use of similar "meaningful" stimuli in other animals will help to define the characteristics of auditory cells in colliculus. In addition, it may provide insight into the phylogenetic and ontogenetic modification of physiological properties of auditory cells in colliculus.

Using complex auditory signals, Gordon (1973) studied the spatial characteristics of the auditory representation in the colliculus of the cat.

She noted a correspondence between the location of the medial edges of the auditory and visual receptive fields. Although some cells had very different visual and auditory receptive fields (for many, the indistinct receptive field borders made a spatial analysis impossible), these data do suggest that a topographical register exists for the three modalities represented here. Similarities in the physiological properties of visual and auditory cells were also observed. Both visual and auditory neurons were most effectively activated by moving stimuli and both showed directional selectivity. The visual, somatic, and auditory properties of colliculus cells are consistent with the current view that the colliculus is primarily involved in detecting the presence of a stimulus and its location in space rather than in evaluating its specific features. The manner in which this detection is accomplished remains poorly understood, but there is little doubt that the process is facilitated when a variety of sensory cues can be utilized. The presence of individual colliculus cells that respond to stimuli from more than one sensory modality may facilitate stimulus detection; and maintaining topographical register between sensory representations may be the most economical way to connect the three representations to the same deep layer efferent system (Gaither & Stein, 1979).

IV. NORMAL DEVELOPMENT

Although we know a great deal about the normal response properties of superior colliculus cells, we have only begun to correlate the physiological characteristics of collicular cells with specific overt behaviors. One method currently in use is to present stimuli to alert animals and to correlate neuronal and behavioral responses (Wurtz & Goldberg, 1972a). Another method involves studying and, where possible, relating the maturation of specific behaviors and neuronal properties. In this way, the conceptual gap between neurophysiology and behavior may be narrowed. We have been using this latter approach in cats (also see Chapter 4 by T. T. Norton, in this volume).

In most animals, there is a profound increase in awareness and responsiveness to environmental stimuli during development. The newborn kitten is poorly coordinated and, although it can use tactile and olfactory cues to locate the mother's nipple, visual and auditory cues are largely ineffective. Gradually responses to auditory and then to visual cues become apparent. Because the superior colliculus is believed to be intimately involved in attentive and orienting responses to these stimuli (although it is certainly not the only structure involved), we thought that understanding the normal maturation of colliculus neurons could help us to better understand this behavioral maturation.

A. Chronology of Developing Sensory Representations

We made recordings in the colliculus of kittens from late fetal stages to 8 weeks of age (Stein, Labos, & Kruger, 1973 a,b,c). Because the eyelids are closed until 7–11 days of age, these were surgically separated to maximize the effectiveness of visual stimuli. The result of the recordings that were made in young kittens were strikingly different from those made in adult cats. In contrast to the many spontaneously active cells in the adult colliculus, the electrode traversed a near "silent" colliculus in neonatal animals. Few spontaneously active cells were encountered and few injury discharges were noted. A variety of moving and stationary visual stimuli were presented but no responses were noted to these stimuli before 7 days of age. However, on the day of birth and in late fetal stages, responses to tactile stimuli were noted in some deep lamina cells. Although responses to repeated stimuli habituated more rapidly in newborns than in adults, discharges could be readily elicited by gently moving camel's hair brushes across the hair and skin. It was not until 5 days of age that the first cell responsive to auditory stimuli appeared. At this time, a bimodal unit was also located that responded to both tactile and auditory stimuli (yet auditory cells were very poorly represented in colliculus at this stage).

Visual cells were not encountered until animals were 7 days of age. Soon after this age, multimodal visual cells were first recorded and became more common in later stages. Thus, the developmental chronology of sensory representations in the colliculus is somatic first, auditory next, and visual last. This developmental chronology is the same as that noted for the use of specific sensory cues for orientation by the kitten. Initially, orientation is based upon somatic (as well as olfactory) cues, whereas orienting to sounds begins at $3\frac{1}{2}$–$6\frac{1}{2}$ days of age (Villablanca & Olmstead, 1979). Visual orientation is delayed until after 2 weeks of age (Norton, 1974; Villablanca & Olmstead, 1979). During the first few months of postnatal life, orientation to external sensory cues shows progressive, though differential, rates of further development. It had been postulated that the different sensory representations in colliculus have access to the same efferent system. Thus, the development of orientation responses to specific sensory cues may reflect the sequential development of access to the collicular efferent system by these different sensory representations.

This hypothesis supposes that collicular efferents are already capable of effecting motor responses at, or close to, the time of birth. To test this possibility, we electrically stimulated the colliculus in kittens 2–77 days of age (Stein, Clamann, & Goldberg, 1980). Eye, ear, limb, and vibrissae movement could be elicited in even the youngest animals studied. Although stimulation was not as reliably effective as in the adult cat, and movements were usually small, it was apparent that at least portions of these efferent pathways are already developed in neonates and may play a functional role in neonatal orientation.

B. Ontogeny of Visual Cells in Colliculus

The development of visually guided behavior is delayed until long after the first visual cells become responsive in the colliculus. Estimates of the onset of visually guided orientation are from 2 to more than 4 weeks of age (Norton, 1974; Villablanca & Olmstead, 1979). In either case, this is long after the appearance of responses to visual stimuli in collicular neurons and consistent with the striking immaturity of the early visual cells. Unlike visual cells of the adult colliculus, those of 7–9-day-old animals:(a) were most responsive to stationary flashed light stimuli and either unresponsive to, or very poorly activated by, movement; (b) responded to stimulation of the contralateral eye only; (c) lacked suppressive regions at the receptive field borders; and (d) fatigued after very few presentations of a stimulus. In short, they lacked just those properties that characterize visual cells of the mature colliculus (see "Visual Receptive Fields," Section IIIB).

A maturational sequence was demonstrated for each of these response characteristics over a 6–8 week period. The first cell to respond to stimulation of the ipsilateral as well as to the contralateral eye was found in a 10-day-old kitten, and an exponential rise in the proportion of binocular cells was noted thereafter. The adult proportion of binocular neurons was reached at about 5 weeks of age. Similarly, as moving targets became more effective between 10 days and 5 weeks of age, stationary pulsed light became progressively less effective (Fig. 5.7). Whereas the movement of a target had to be well below 50 deg/sec and sometimes below 10 deg/sec to elicit responses in animals less than 2 weeks of age, the range of effective velocities increased to well over 100 deg/sec within the next few weeks. There was also a conspicuous absence of directional selectivity during the first 2 weeks of development, but this characteristic became more apparent in the next month (also see Chapter 4 by Norton, in this volume) as response latency

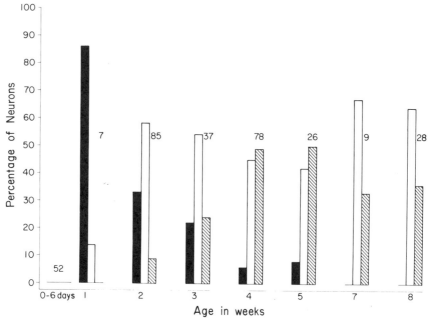

Fig. 5.7 Neurons in the superior colliculus selectively responsive to various visual stimuli as a function of age. Numbers above each set of three bars refer to the number of neurons studied during that developmental period. Black bars indicate stationary light; white, stationary light plus movement; shaded, movement only. Visually activated neurons were not encountered in kittens 6 days old and younger, and 1 (week) refers only to the 7-day-old animal. During the initial stages of visual sensitivity, many neurons were selectively responsive to stationary light, but during development, there was a progressive decrease in the proportion of these neurons, an increase in the incidence of neurons responsive to both movement and stationary light, and in those selectively responsive to movement. (From Stein *et al.*, 1973a.)

decreased from well over 1 sec in some cases to 40–60 msec. In addition, fatigability decreased progressively and suppressive regions appeared at the borders of the receptive fields during this maturational period. At about 4 weeks of age, more than 50% of the cells had adult-like characteristics, and at 7–8 weeks of age the colliculus appeared to be essentially mature.

Despite the correspondingly protracted developmental course of visual orientation and the maturation of visual cells, the profound difference between neonatal and adult visual colliculus cells was, at first, surprising. Hubel and Wiesel (1963) had shown that some visual cells in cortex are adult-like at 8 days of age (but see Blakemore & Van Sluyters, 1975; Pettigrew, 1974). Since maturation is believed to occur more rapidly in the midbrain than in the cortex (Kruger & Stein, 1973;

Tilney & Casamajor, 1924), one would expect adult-like characteristics in visual cells of the colliculus at, or before, 7 days of age. However, as noted earlier in this chapter the specialization of collicular cells depends, in part, upon a projection from cortex. When we destroyed the visual cortex in neonatal cats, the development of receptive field specialization in colliculus was arrested (Stein and Magalhães-Castro, 1975). Similar observations have been made by others (Berman & Cynader, 1976; Flandrin & Jeannerod, 1977; Mize & Murphy, 1976) and it seemed that the apparent immaturity of collicular cells in young kittens reflected the incomplete maturation of corticotectal projections.

In an attempt to determine whether or not the corticotectal pathway is present in neonates, we made injections of radioactive leucine in the visual cortex of kittens 2–23 days of age (Stein & Edwards, 1979). A dense corticotectal projection was already present in even the youngest animals studied (Fig. 5.8). In addition, a dense corticogeniculate pathway was also noted. We are now evaluating whether this pathway is functional in the neonate. In the adult cat, reversibly deactivating cortex by cooling it produces a dramatic inhibition of the responsiveness of collicular cells to all visual stimuli (Stein, 1978). By using the cooling method, we are attempting to determine whether any response changes occur in collicular cells during neonatal stages, as such changes would indicate a corticotectal influence. Thus far no evidence has been found for even nonspecific tonic influences in unspecialized collicular cells. Rather, the development of cooling induced depression in colliculus is found to parallel the development of binocularity and directional selectivity. As cells appear in the colliculus with binocularity and directional selectivity, cooling cortex inhibits their activity, but does not influence those cells that are monocular and nondirectionally selective in the same animals. Thus, despite the presence of projections from visual cortex to superior colliculus before 2 days of age, this pathway seems, for all practical purposes, to be nonfunctional at this stage and to gradually develop an influence upon individual collicular neurons. Apparently, the original suggestion is the most likely; namely that much of the maturation of physiological properties in visual cells of the colliculus from 7 days to 8 weeks of age is a reflection of corticotectal development. Perhaps this reflects the maturation of the properties of corticotectal cells themselves. Although some adult-like cortical cells in neonatal kittens have been described by Hubel and Wiesel (1963), there are many visual cortical cells that are unspecialized during the first few weeks of life (Blakemore & Van Sluyters, 1975; Pettigrew, 1974). Perhaps the corticotectal cells are within this late developing population of cells and, despite their functional synaptic contacts with collicular cells, they

Fig. 5.8 A dark field photomicrograph of an autoradiogram documenting the presence of a projection from visual cortex to the superior colliculus in a neonatal kitten. The photomicrograph shows the center of the injection site in visual cortex with the arrow indicating the needle track. Below, a dense accumulation of transported label is apparent in the anterolateral superior colliculus. This animal was injected approximately 6 hours after birth and sacrificed 24 hours later. (From Stein & Edwards, 1979.)

are unable to impress binocularity and directional selectivity upon collicular cells until they themselves "mature."

Whether the pertinent "corticotectal development" is at the corticotectal synapse, the corticotectal cell itself, or a combination of the two is unknown at present. We do know, however, that during this period the properties of most, if not all, visual cortical cells are subject to "shaping" by experiential factors, and that the ultimate response profile of corticotectal cells will profoundly influence the characteristics of superior colliculus cells receiving projections from them.

V. VISUAL DEPRIVATION IN SUPERIOR COLLICULUS

We would like to be able to argue that certain changes in visually guided behavior following deprivation can be accounted for by changes in the properties of collicular cells. This argument requires more than a demonstration of concomitant changes in collicular cells and behavior; it also requires evidence that other visual structures do not show changes that could account equally well for the behavior.

Here we attempt to compare the effects of various types of visual deprivation on the superior colliculus and the primary visual cortex. The effects of a wide range of deprivation procedures have not been studied on other visual structures. Where possible, we will make some speculative connections with behavioral deficits.

A. Monocular Lid Suture

Monocular lid suture is the archetypal form of visual deprivation. If a kitten is deprived of vision in one eye for the first 3 months of life, almost all the cells in the binocular region of the visual cortex are driven exclusively by the visually experienced eye (Hubel & Wiesel, 1970). The effect of monocular deprivation in the superior colliculus is a matter of some dispute. Wickelgren and Sterling (1969b) found that the monocularly deprived colliculus is virtually identical to the monocularly deprived cortex (Fig. 5.9). In contrast, Hoffmann and Sherman (1974) found that about 60% of the collicular units contralateral to the deprived eye are driven by this eye. Berman and Sterling (1976) obtained an intermediate result. In six out of nine monocularly deprived cats, almost all cells were driven by the experienced eye. In the other three cats, islands of cells contralateral to the deprived eye were driven by this eye. These differences might be accounted for by sampling errors; however, all cats may not respond identically to monocular deprivation.

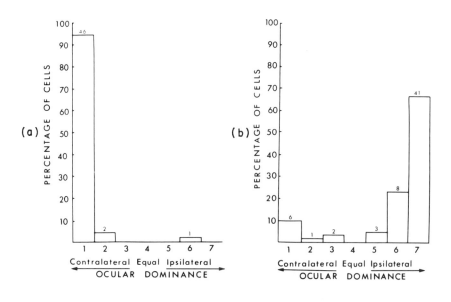

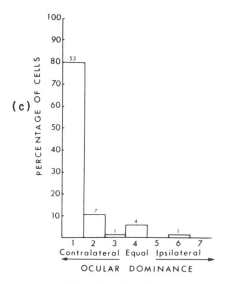

Fig. 5.9 Ocular dominance distribution of units in the superior colliculus of monocularly deprived animals. (a) Units in the colliculus contralateral to the normal eye; (b) units in the colliculus contralateral to the deprived eye; (c) units in the colliculus contralateral to the deprived eye after cortical removal. (From Wickelgren & Sterling, 1969b.)

The cells driven by the deprived eye are probably driven by direct retinal input because they lack directional selectivity. Hoffmann and Sherman (1974) verified that the deprived eye could no longer activate the corticotectal pathway by stimulating the deprived eye's optic nerve and recording in the contralateral colliculus. Latency measures show that the Y-indirect pathway from the deprived eye (the pathway relaying via visual cortex) is nonfunctional.

Behaviorally, monocularly deprived cats appear to be virtually blind in the deprived eye (except in the monocular crescent of the visual field) (Sherman, 1973, 1974; but cf. Heitlander & Hoffmann, 1978; van Hof-van Duin, 1977) and, as expected, the deprived eye drives neither cortical nor collicular cells.

B. Binocular Deprivation

Although visual cortex cells fail to respond to stimuli presented to the monocularly deprived eye, they are not inactive when both eyes are deprived. Most cells respond binocularly, although their responses are often sluggish and erratic (Wiesel & Hubel, 1965). The colliculus of binocularly deprived animals behaves as if it were relying primarily on direct retinal input. Latency measurements following electrical stimulation of the optic nerves indicate that very few cells in the binocularly deprived colliculus are driven via the corticotectal tract. The defective synapses must be between retina and cortex, because collicular cells do respond to electrical stimulation of the visual cortex (Hoffmann & Sherman, 1975).

Receptive field studies support this conclusion. The binocularly deprived colliculus resembles the decorticate colliculus in that most cells are driven only by the contralateral eye and very few are directionally selective. The binocularly deprived colliculus has another abnormality not found in the decorticate colliculus; most cells are sluggish in the face of normally adequate visual stimuli (Hoffmann & Sherman, 1975; Sterling & Wickelgren, 1970). This supports the earlier suggestion that tonic input from the corticotectal tract can inhibit collicular cells.

Cats that have been binocularly deprived for 7 months appear blind immediately upon entering a normal visual environment. Within about 10 days, some visuomotor responses such as visual placing, reaching, and following appear, and complete recovery on these specific tasks occurs in 10 weeks (van Hof-van Duin, 1976). Binocularly deprived animals have a visual field deficit. Whereas normal animals can use their entire retina to control orienting responses, binocularly deprived animals can use only their nasal retina (the portion of the retina seeing the ipsilateral visual field) (Sherman, 1973, 1974). These orienting responses seem to be dependent solely on retinotectal pathways because they are disrupted by collicular lesions but not by visual cortex lesions (Sherman, 1977). Thus, the behavior is consistent with the physiology; both indicate that only the nasal retina of binocularly deprived animals is functionally connected to the colliculus. The pathways from temporal retina appear to be much more susceptible to visual deprivation than are the pathways from nasal retina.

C. Abnormal Stimulus Movement

Cats have been deprived of abnormal stimulus movement by rearing them so that the entire visual field always moves in the same direction and by rearing them in stroboscopic illumination so that all stimuli appear stationary. Directional rearing increases the proportion of cortical cells preferring movement in the direction seen during rearing (Daw & Wyatt, 1976; Tretter, Cynader, & Singer, 1975). In the colliculus, we would not expect the same result on both sides of the brain, because most directionally selective collicular cells normally prefer movement toward the periphery of the contralateral visual field (i.e., cells in the left colliculus normally prefer rightward movement and cells in the right colliculus normally prefer leftward movement). If a cat were reared with leftward movement, the innate preference and the expected rearing induced preference would be toward the left for cells in the right colliculus. In the left colliculus, however, the innate preference for rightward movement would conflict with the expected rearing induced preference for leftward movement. Three papers describe three different results for cats reared with this conflict.

1. Cynader, Berman, and Hein (1975) found that the distribution of preferred directions is unaffected by rearing. Units in each colliculus continued to prefer movement toward the periphery of the contralateral visual field.

2. Vital-Durand and Jeannerod (1974) report that cells in both colliculi prefer movement opposite to that seen during rearing.

3. Flandrin and Jeannerod (1975) found that most cells in the colliculus that would normally prefer movement opposite to that seen during rearing were visually unresponsive.

Stroboscopic rearing causes the percentage of directionally selective cat collicular cells to decrease from 65 to 10% (a similar reduction occurs in hamster as well, Chalupa & Rhoades, 1978). Only about 25% of the cells remain binocularly driven (Flandrin, Kennedy, & Amblard, 1976). In the visual cortex, strobe rearing decreases the percentage of directionally selective cells to about 24% (Cynader, Berman, & Hein, 1973). The effect of strobe rearing on the binocularity of cortical cells has not been described. These results suggest that the effectiveness of the corticotectal pathway is greatly diminished by strobe rearing, but data on binocularity of cortical cells is required to confirm this.

The behavioral effects of abnormal stimulus movement have not yet been studied. After directional rearing, such experiments should compare detection and following of stimuli moving in the opposite direction. After strobe rearing, such experiments should compare detection of moving stimuli with detection of stationary stimuli. Relating behavioral and physiological results will, however, be difficult until the physiological effects of these manipulations are known with certainty.

D. Alternating Occlusion

Because collicular cells have larger, more diffuse receptive fields and are less precisely tuned for disparity than are cortical cells, we might expect collicular cells to be less sensitive than visual cortex cells to disruption of binocular vision by alternating occlusion during the first 3 months of life. On each day, one eye is occluded and the other eye remains open; the eye that is open is always the eye that was occluded on the previous day. The collicular ocular dominance histogram obtained from kittens reared in this way shows only a slight increase in the number of monocularly driven cells (Gordon & Presson, 1977). In contrast, alternating occlusion causes almost all cells in the visual cortex to become monocularly driven (Fig. 5.10) (Hubel & Wiesel, 1965). Perhaps collicular cells remain binocular because both Group 1 and Group 7 cortical cells converge on a single collicular cell. Surprisingly, alternating occlusion causes a marked abnormality in the distribution of ·preferred directions. The preponderance of cells preferring horizontal stimulus movement is greatly decreased.

E. Artificial Strabismus

If a cat's medial and lateral rectus muscles are cut, the cat does not receive normal visual feedback when it attempts to make horizontal eye movements. If, however, the visual world moved in the direction of the eye movement, the retinal image would remain stationary. If the medial and lateral rectus muscles are cut, the attempt to make a horizontal eye movement also results in a stationary retinal image. Perhaps

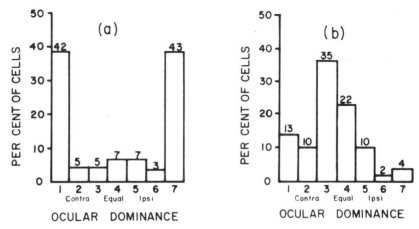

Fig. 5.10 A comparison of the effect of alternating occlusion on the ocular dominance histograms obtained from (a) visual cortex and (b) superior colliculus. (Modified from Gordon & Presson, 1977.)

the cat interprets this as movement of the visual world in the direction of the attempted eye movement.

To study the effects of perturbing the relationship between commanded eye movement and image movement, we cut the medial and lateral rectus muscles within the first 2 weeks of life. We refer to the animals receiving this surgery as strabismic because they cannot make normal eye movements, even though their operated eye is approximately centered in the orbit. The effects of strabismus on the visual cortex are similar to the effects of alternating occlusion; most cells are monocularly driven (Hubel & Wiesel, 1965). There is, however, a slight tendency for the normal eye to drive more cortical cells than the strabismic eye (Gordon & Gummow, 1975).

Although alternating occlusion and strabismus have very similar effects in the visual cortex, their effects on the colliculus are quite different. In both colliculi, alternating occlusion slightly decreases the influence of the ipsilateral eye; strabismus, however, decreases the influence of the strabismic eye regardless of whether the strabismic eye is the ipsilateral eye or the contralateral eye (Fig. 5.11). Ipsilateral to the strabismic eye its weakness is quite dramatic; the strabismic eye completely fails to drive a large number of cells. This weakness is less obvious in the colliculus contralateral to the strabismic eye, but this colliculus contains somewhat more Group 5 cells and somewhat fewer Group 3 cells than is typical of a normal animal (Gordon & Gummow, 1975).

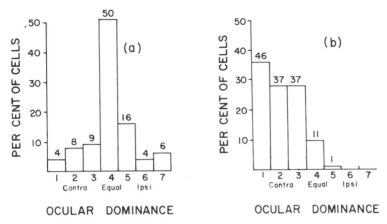

Fig. 5.11 Ocular dominance histograms obtained from the (a) left and (b) right superior colliculus of strabismic cats, right medial and lateral muscles sectioned in infancy. Conventions as in Fig. 5.9. (Modified from Gordon and Gummow, 1975.)

Strabismus causes an asymmetry between the two colliculi but not between the two visual cortices. Perhaps this fact will be useful in our search for behavioral correlates of collicular abnormalities. If the colliculus is required for orientation to visual stimuli, we might expect that, using only the strabismic eye, the animal would be unable to orient to stimuli in its contralateral visual field. (This is the portion of the visual field mapped onto the colliculus ipsilateral to the strabismic eye.)

Although we have not measured the visual fields of the strabismic cats used to obtain the ocular dominance histograms of Fig. 5.11, we have used visual perimetry to measure the visual fields of a very similar group of animals. These animals underwent section of all the extraocular muscles of one eye. The perimetry apparatus consisted of an approximate hemisphere of white cloth with white strips along the vertical and horizontal meridians. The cat was trained to fixate the center of the hemisphere: Meat was then introduced through one of the holes in the plastic strips. Only if the animal went directly toward the meat and ate it was the trial scored as positive. (For more details of the procedure see Gordon, Moran, & Presson, 1979.) Each eye was tested monocularly on both the horizontal and vertical meridians of the visual field. The strabismic eye has only a slight deficit in the contralateral visual field (Fig. 5.12a,b). Perhaps the input from the temporal retina of the right strabismic eye to the Group 2 and Group 3 cells in the right colliculus (Fig. 5.11) allows the strabismic eye to control orienting in its contralateral visual field.

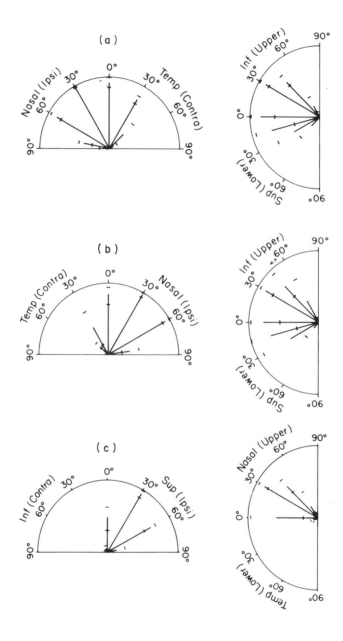

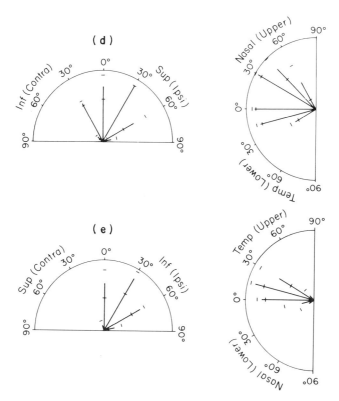

Fig. 5.12 Visual fields of cats using an eye with all extraocular muscles sectioned, a normal eye, or a rotated eye. Each semicircle represents the results of one set of perimetry measurements. Each measurement represents the average of three animals. The horizontally oriented semicircles represent measurements made along the horizontal meridian of the visual field. The vertically oriented semicircles represent measurements along the vertical meridian of the visual field. The length of each radial line is proportional to the average percentage of positive responses to stimuli placed at the angular position indicated by the direction of the line. The perpendicular tick marks indicate the range of correct responses for all cats included in the diagram. Where there is only one tick mark, at least one cat made no positive responses to stimuli presented at the angular position represented by that line. The portion of the retina used to see the stimuli is indicated just outside the perimetry map. The portion of the visual field tested is indicated in parentheses. Abbreviations: ipsi, ipsilateral; contra, contralateral; inf, inferior; sup, superior; temp, temporal. (a) Normal eye; (b) eye with all extraocular muscles cut; (c) intorted eye; (d) intorted eye with left eye sutured; (e) extorted eye. (Modified from Gordon *et al.*, 1979.)

F. Eye Rotation

We then wondered whether an exaggeration of strabismus would produce more dramatic results. We gambled that by rotating an eye 90 deg during the first two weeks of life we could produce an animal with abnormalities similar to, but more dramatic than, the abnormalities in the strabismic animals. So far, we have concentrated on the effects of eye rotation on visually guided behavior.

We examined the visual fields of four groups of eye rotated animals. Three animals had the right eye rotated from 67 to 90 deg so that the superior retina was rotated to the medial portion of the orbit (intorted). In three animals, the superior retina was rotated to the lateral portion of the orbit (extorted). In two animals, the right eye was rotated superior to medial and the left eye was sutured (intorted plus suture).

When using the rotated eye, the cats responded accurately to stimuli in the ipsilateral and upper visual fields (seen by the superior and nasal retina), but they ignored stimuli presented in the contralateral and inferior visual fields (Fig. 5.12c). The temporal and inferior retinas of the intorted eyes appeared blind. We know that these deficits require eye rotation rather than mere muscle section because animals (discussed earlier) who suffered complete section of the extraocular muscles without rotation did not have marked visual field deficits. We believe that the deficits in the intortion animals have a central rather than peripheral origin, because the intortion-plus-suture animals have a virtually normal visual field (Fig. 5.12d, Gordon et al., 1979). This fact rules out the hypothesis that the deficit in intortion animals is caused by constant errors of fixation, damage to the optic nerve during rotation, or placing the eye in the orbit so that certain portions of the retina are blocked by the face. The normal visual fields in the intortion-plus-suture animals also suggest that forcing the cat to use the rotated eye improves the ability of that eye to control visual orienting.

Very few responses were directed toward locations other than where the meat was presented. Only 5% of the responses made under control of the rotated eye and only 1% of the responses made under control of the normal eye were misdirected. In only five trials did a stimulus presented along the horizontal meridian elicit a response along the vertical meridian or vice versa.

We studied the visual fields of the three extortion animals to find out whether the deficits are specific to a portion of the retina or to a portion of the visual field. Like the intortion animals, the extortion animals had deficits in the contralateral and inferior visual fields; however, in the extortion animals, these fields are seen by the superior and nasal retinas (Fig. 5.12e).

The physiological and behavioral effects of binocular deprivation and the physiological effects of strabismus have suggested that connections from temporal retina are more susceptible to deprivation than are connections from nasal retina (Hoffmann & Sherman, 1975; Sherman, 1973, 1974, 1977; Wickelgren & Sterling, 1969b). The visual field deficits in eye rotation animals suggest that perhaps this notion should be restated as: "Connections from retina in the temporal position are more vulnerable to deprivation than are connections from retina in the nasal position."

Another possibility is that the deficit is motor rather than sensory. Perhaps the cats can see stimuli in the contralateral and lower visual fields but cannot make orienting responses toward these regions. It would not be surprising if a motor deficit were independent of the direction of retinal rotation. To test this notion, in one of our labs (B.G.'s) we are teaching cats to perform a perimetry task that does not require orienting movements. If the deficit in visual orienting, regardless of whether its origin is sensory or motor, results from a deficit in collicular function, we would predict that stimuli in the contralateral and lower visual fields would be unable to drive collicular cells normally but would drive visual cortex cells normally. (If the deficits were motor, we might expect to find the collicular deficit only in the deeper collicular layers.) Experiments to test this prediction are now under way.

VI. SUMMARY AND CONCLUSIONS

The kitten superior colliculus changes dramatically between birth and 2 months of age. Although we lack a detailed understanding of the interaction of genetics and the environment in collicular development, we have a few clues. Cells respond to somatic stimuli at birth; auditory responses appear at about Day 5, and visual responses at about Day 7 (before the eyes have opened). Therefore, at least some of the connections subserving somatic and visual responses are independent of experience, and we might guess that the same is true of auditory connections.

We know less about how the development of adult receptive field properties is controlled. This development has been studied in detail only for visual cells. During the first 2 months of life, collicular cells gradually acquire their preference for moving stimuli, their binocularity, and their directional selectivity. Two results suggest that these properties probably result from maturation of the corticotectal system. First, during intermediate states of development when both "mature" and "immature" cells are present, only mature cells are suppressed by cortical cooling. Second, lesions of visual cortex make adult cells resemble infant ones and prevent infant collicular cells from acquiring adult properties.

One way of assessing the role of the environment in normal development is to rear cats with binocular deprivation. Because binocular deprivation results in collicular cells that resemble immature ones, we might conclude that visual experience is necessary for normal development. Unfortunately, binocular deprivation experiments have used kittens that were deprived for many months. In these animals, deterioration might follow normal maturation. A more conclusive experiment would be to deprive kittens binocularly from 2–6 weeks of age, the normal maturation period. If maturation requires visual experience, the colliculi of these kittens at 6 weeks of age should consist entirely of immature cells.

In addition to preventing maturation, abnormal environments can alter the course of development of collicular cells in ways not readily predictable from the effects of the same environment on visual cortex cells. After monocular strabismus, the normal eye overwhelmingly dominates its contralateral colliculus but not its contralateral visual cortex. We cannot name the synapse at which the effectiveness of the normal eye is increased and the effectiveness of the strabismic eye is decreased. We are, however, fairly sure that it involves the corticotectal pathways because we have never succeeded in altering the retinotectal pathway by deprivation. We think that this change in ocular dominance is a qualitative change in the development of the corticotectal tract rather than a mere failure of maturation because most of the affected monocular cells have normal directional selectivity.

Thus, we know that the very existence of sensory inputs to collicular cells is genetically controlled and independent of the environment. We suspect, but do not really know, that the development of normal adult receptive fields requires normal visual input. Finally, an abnormal environment can cause development to proceed abnormally.

REFERENCES

Adamük, E. Über angeborene und erworbene. Association von F. C. Donders, Albrecht V. Graefes. *Archives of Ophthalmology*, 1872, **18**, 153–164.

Allon, N., & Wollberg, Z. Responses of cells in the superior colliculus of the squirrel monkey to auditory stimuli. *Brain Research*, 1978, **159**, 321–330.

Anderson, K. V., & Symmes, D. The superior colliculus and higher visual functions in the monkey. *Brain Research*, 1969, **13**, 37–52.

Anderson, K. V., & Williamson, M. R. Visual pattern discrimination in cats after removal of the superior colliculi. *Psychonomic Science*, 1971, **24**, 125–127.

Berlucchi, G., Sprague, J. M., Levy, J., & DiBerardino, A. C. Pretectum and superior colliculus in visually guided behavior and in flux and form discrimination in the cat. *Journal of Comparative and Physiological Psychology*, 1972, **78**, 123–172.

Berman, N., Blakemore, C., & Cynader, M. Binocular interaction in the cat's superior colliculus. *Journal of Physiology*, 1975, **246**, 595–615.

Berman, N., & Cynader, M. Comparison of receptive field organization of the superior colliculus in Siamese and normal cats. *Journal of Physiology*, 1972, **224**, 363–389.

Berman, N., & Cynader, M. Early versus late visual cortex lesions: Effects on receptive fields in cat superior colliculus. *Experimental Brain Research*, 1976, **25**, 131–137.

Berman, N., & Cynader, M. Receptive fields in cat superior colliculus after visual cortex lesions. *Journal of Physiology*, 1975, **245**, 261–270.

Berman, N., & Sterling, P. Cortical suppression of the retinocollicular pathway in the monocularly deprived cat. *Journal of Physiology*, 1976, **255**, 263–273.

Blakemore, C., & Van Sluyters, R. C. Innate and environmental factors in the development of the kitten's visual cortex. *Journal of Physiology*, 1975, **248**, 663–716.

Casagrande, V. A., Harting, J. K., Hall, W. C., Diamond, I. T., & Martin, G. F. Superior colliculus of the tree shrew: A structural and functional subdivision into superficial and deep layers. *Science*, 1972, **177**, 444–447.

Chalupa, L. M., & Rhoades, R. W. Responses of visual, somatosensory, and auditory neurones in the golden hamster's superior colliculus. *Journal of Physiology*, 1977, **270**, 596–626.

Chalupa, L. M., & Rhoades, R. W. Modification of visual responses properties in the superior colliculus of the golden hamster following stroboscopic rearing. *Journal of Physiology*, 1978, **274**, 571–592.

Clamann, H. P., & Stein, B. E. Stimulation of the cat superior colliculus evokes ear movements which parallel eye movements. *Society for Neuroscience*, 1979, **5**, 779.

Cynader, M., & Berman, N. Receptive field organization of monkey superior colliculus. *Journal of Neurophysiology*, 1972, **35**, 187–201.

Cynader, M., Berman, N., & Hein, A. Cats reared in stroboscopic illumination: Effects on receptive fields in visual cortex. *Proceedings of the National Academy of Sciences*, 1973, **70**, 1353–1354.

Cynader, M., Berman, N., & Hein, A. Cats raised in a one-directional world: effects on receptive fields in visual cortex and superior colliculus. *Experimental Brain Research*, 1975, **22**, 267–280.

Daw, N. W., & Wyatt, H. J. Kittens reared in a unidirectional environment: Evidence for a critical period. *Journal of Physiology*, 1976, **257**, 155–170.

Dräger, U. C., & Hubel, D. Responses to visual stimulation and relationship between visual, auditory, and somatosensory inputs in mouse superior colliculus. *Journal of Neurophysiology*, 1975, **38**, 690–713.

Dreher, B., & Hoffmann, K.-P. Properties of excitatory and inhibitory regions in the receptive fields of single units in the cat's superior colliculus. *Experimental Brain Research*, 1973, **16**, 333–353.

Edwards, S. B. The deep cell layers of the superior colliculus: Their reticular characteristics and structural organization. In A. Hobson & M. A. B. Brazier (Eds.), *The reticular formation revisited*. New York: Raven Press, 1980.

Edwards, S. B., Ginsburgh, C. L., Henkel, C. K., & Stein, B. E. Sources of subcortical projections to the superior colliculus in the cat. *Journal of Comparative Neurology*, 1979, **184**, 309–330.

Edwards, S. B., & Henkel, C. K. Superior colliculus connections with the extraocular motor nuclei in the cat. *Journal of Comparative Neurology,* 1978, **179**, 451–468.

Feldon, S., Feldon, P., & Kruger, L. Topography of the retinal projection upon the superior colliculus of the cat. *Vision Research,* 1970, **10**, 135–143.

Finlay, B. L., Schneps, S. E., Wilson, K. G., & Schneider, G. E. Topography of visual and somatosensory projections to the superior colliculus of the golden hamster. *Brain Research,* 1978, **142**, 223–235.

Flandrin, J. M., & Jeannerod, M. Superior colliculus: Environmental influences on the development of directional responses in the kitten. *Brain Research,* 1975, **89**, 348–352.

Flandrin, J. M., & Jeannerod, M. Lack of recovery in collicular neurons from the effects of early deprivation or neonatal cortical lesion in the kitten. *Brain Research,* 1977, **120**, 362–366.

Flandrin, J. M., Kennedy, H., & Amblard, B. Effects of stroboscopic rearing on the binocularity and directionality of cat superior colliculus neurons. *Brain Research,* 1976, **101**, 576–581.

Gaither, N. S., & Stein, B. E. Reptiles and mammals use similar sensory organization in the midbrain. *Science,* 1979, **205**, 595–597.

Garey, L. J., Jones, E. G., & Powell, T. P. S. Interrelationships of striate and extrastriate cortex with the primary relay sites of the visual pathway. *Journal of Neurology, Neurosurgery, and Psychiatry,* 1968, **31**, 135–157.

Goldberg, M. E., & Wurtz, R. H. Activity of superior colliculus in behaving monkey. I. Visual receptive fields of single neurons. *Journal of Neurophysiology,* 1972, **35**, 542–559. (a)

Goldberg, M. E., & Wurtz, R. H. Activity of superior colliculus in behaving monkey. II. The effect of attention on neuronal responses. *Journal of Neurophysiology,* 1972, **35**, 560–574. (b)

Goodale, M. A., & Murison, R.C.C. The effect of lesions of the superior colliculus on locomotor orientation and the orienting reflex in the rat. *Brain Research,* 1975, **88**, 243–261.

Gordon, B. G. Receptive fields in deep layers of cat superior colliculus. *Journal of Neurophysiology,* 1973, **36**, 157–178.

Gordon, B. G. Superior colliculus: Structure, physiology, and possible functions. In A. C. Guyton & C. C. Hunt (Eds.), *MTP International Review of Science,* **3**, 1975.

Gordon, B., & Gummow, L. Effects of extraocular muscle section on receptive fields in cat superior colliculus. *Vision Research,* 1975, **15**, 1011–1019.

Gordon, B., Moran, J., & Presson, J. Visual fields of cats reared with one eye intorted. *Brain Research,* 1979, **174**, 167–171.

Gordon, B., & Presson, J. Effects of alternating occlusion on receptive fields in cat superior colliculus. *Journal of Neurophysiology,* 1977, **40**, 1406–1414.

Graham, J. An autoradiographic study of the efferent connections of the superior colliculus in the cat. *Journal of Comparative Neurology,* 1977, **173**, 629–654.

Graybiel, A. M. Some thalamocortical projections of the pulvinar–posterior system of the thalamus in the cat. *Brain Research,* 1970, **22**, 131–136.

Harting, J. K., Hall, W. C., Diamond, I. T., & Martin, G. F. Anterograde degeneration study of the superior colliculus in *Tupaia glis:* Evidence for a subdivision between superficial and deep layers. *Journal of Comparative Neurology,* 1973, **148**, 361–386.

Henkel, C. K., & Edwards, S. B. The superior colliculus control of pinna movements in the cat: Possible anatomical connections. *Journal of Comparative Neurology,* 1978, **182**, 763–776.

Henkel, C. K., Edwards, S. B., & Kersey, K. S. Segregated origins for superior collicular projections based on their intended target structures. *Society for Neuroscience*, 1979, **5**, 372.

Hoffmann, K.-P., & Sherman, S. M. Effects of early monocular deprivation on visual input to cat superior colliculus. *Journal of Neurophysiology*, 1974, **37**, 1276–1286.

Hoffmann, K.-P., & Sherman, S. M. Effects of early binocular deprivation on visual input to cat superior colliculus. *Journal of Neurophysiology*, 1975, **38**, 1049–1059.

Hoffmann, K.-P., & Straschill, M. Influences of corticotectal and intertectal connections on visual responses in the cat's superior colliculus. *Experimental Brain Research*, 1971, **12**, 120–131.

Hubel, D. H., & Wiesel, T. N. Receptive fields of cells in striate cortex of very young, visually inexperienced kittens. *Journal of Neurophysiology*, 1963, **26**, 994–1002.

Hubel, D. H., & Wiesel, T. N. Binocular interaction in striate cortext of kittens reared with artificial squint. *Journal of Neurophysiology*, 1965, **28**, 1041–1059.

Hubel, D. H., & Wiesel, T. N. The period of susceptibility to the physiological effects of unilateral eye closure in kittens. *Journal of Physiology*, 1970, **206**, 419–436.

Hughes, A. Topographical relationships between the anatomy and physiology of the rabbit visual system. *Documenta Ophthalmologica*, 1971, **30**, 33–159.

Ingle, D. Evolutionary perspectives on the function of the optic tectum. *Brain Behavior and Evolution*, 1973, **8**, 211–237.

Kanaseki, T., & Sprague, J. M. Anatomical organization of pretectale nuclei and tectale laminae in the cat. *Journal of Comparative Neurology*, 1974, **158**, 319–338.

Kawamura, S., & Kobayashi, E. Identification of laminar origin of some tectothalamic fibers in the cat. *Brain Research*, 1975, **91**, 281–285.

Kawamura, S., Sprague, J. M., & Niimi, K. Corticofugal projections from the visual cortices to the thalamus, pretectum, and superior colliculus in the cat. *Journal of Comparative Neurology*, 1974, **158**, 339–362.

Keating, E. G. Impaired orientation after primate tectal lesions. *Brain Research*, 1974, **67**, 538–541.

Kruger, L., & Stein, B. E. Primordial sense organs and the evolution of sensory systems. In E. C. Carterette & M. P. Friedman (Eds.), *Handbook of perception* (Vol. 3). New York: Academic Press, 1973, pp. 63–87.

Lane, R. H., Allman, J. M., Kaas, J. H., & Miezin, F. M. The visuotopic organization of the superior colliculus of the owl monkey (*Aotus trivigatus*) and the bush baby (*Galago senegalensis*). *Brain Research*, 1973, **60**, 335–349.

Latto, R. The effects of bilateral frontal eye-field, posterior parietal, or superior collicular lesions on visual search in the rhesus monkey. *Brain Research*, 1978, **146**, 35–50.

Leontovich, T. A., & Zhukova, G. P. The specificity of the neuronal structure and topography of the reticular formation in the brain and spinal cord of carnivora. *Journal of Comparative Neurology*, 1963, **121**, 347–379.

Masland, R. H., Chow, K. L., & Stewart, D. L. Receptive field characteristics of superior colliculus neurons in the rabbit. *Journal of Neurophysiology*, 1971, **34**, 148–156.

Michael, C. R. Visual receptive fields of single neurons in superior colliculus of the ground squirrel. *Journal of Neurophysiology*, 1972, **35**, 815–832. (a)

Michael, C. R. Functional organization of cells in superior colliculus of the ground squirrel. *Journal of Neurophysiology*, 1972, **35**, 833–846. (b)

Mize, R. R., & Murphy, E. H. Alterations in receptive field properties of superior colliculus cells produced by visual cortex ablation in infant and adult cats. *Journal of Comparative Neurology*, 1976, **168**, 393–424.

Mohler, C. W., & Wurtz, R. H. Organization of monkey superior colliculus: Intermediate layer cells discharging before eye movements. *Journal of Neurophysiology*, 1976, **39**, 722–744.

Mohler, C. W., & Wurtz, R. H. Role of striate cortex and superior colliculus in visual guidance of saccadic eye movement in monkeys. *Journal of Neurophysiology*, 1977, **40**, 74–94.

Nagata, T., & Kruger, L. Tactile neurons of the superior colliculus of the cat: Input and physiological properties. *Brain Research*, 1979, **174**, 19–37.

Norton, T. T. Receptive field properties of superior colliculus cells and development of visual behavior in kittens. *Journal of Neurophysiology*, 1974, **37**, 674–690.

Palmer, L. A., Rosenquist, A. C., & Sprague, J. M. Corticotectal systems in the cat: Their structure and function. In T. Frigyesi, E. Rinvik, & M. D. Yahr (Eds.), *Corticothalamic projections and sensorimotor activities*. New York: Raven, 1972, pp. 491–523.

Pettigrew, J. D. The effect of visual experience on the development of stimulus specificity by kitten cortical neurones. *Journal of Physiology*, 1974, **237**, 49–74.

Ramon-Moliner, E., & Nauta, W.J.H. The isodendritic core of the brainstem. *Journal of Comparative Neurology*, 1966, **126**, 311–335.

Rhoades, R. W., & Chalupa, L. M. Functional and anatomical consequences of neonatal damage in superior colliculus of the golden hamster. *Journal of Neurophysiology*, 1978, **41**, 1466–1494.

Rizzolatti, G., Camarda, R., Grupp, L. A., & Pisa, M. Inhibitory effect of remote visual stimuli on visual responses of cat superior colliculus: Spatial and temporal factors. *Journal of Neurophysiology*, 1974, **37**, 1262–1275.

Rizzolatti, G., Tradardi, V., & Camarda, R. Unit responses to visual stimuli in the cat's superior colliculus after removal of the visual cortex. *Brain Research*, 1970, **24**, 336–339.

Robinson, D. A. Eye movements evoked by collicular stimulation in the alert monkey. *Vision Research*, 1972, **12**, 1795–1808.

Rosenquist, A. C., & Palmer, L. A. Visual receptive field properties of cells of the superior colliculus after cortical lesions in the cat. *Experimental Neurology*, 1971, **33**, 629–652.

Roucoux, A., & Crommelinck, M. Eye movements evoked by superior colliculus stimulation in the alert cat. *Brain Research*, 1976, **106**, 349–363.

Schaefer, K.-P. Unit analysis and electrical stimulation in the optic tectum of rabbits and cats. *Brain, Behavior and Evolution*, 1970, **3**, 222–240.

Schiller, P. H. The role of the monkey superior colliculus in eye movement and vision. *Investigative Ophthalmology*, 1972, **11**, 451–460.

Schiller, P. H., & Koerner, F. Discharge characteristics of single units in superior colliculus of the alert rhesus monkey. *Journal of Neurophysiology*, 1971, **34**, 920–936.

Schiller, P. H., Stryker, M., Cynader, M., & Berman, N. Response characteristics of single cells in the monkey superior colliculus following ablation or cooling of visual cortex. *Journal of Neurophysiology*, 1974, **37**, 181–194.

Sherman, S. M. Visual field defects in monocularly and binocularly deprived cats. *Brain Research*, 1973, **49**, 25–45.

Sherman, S. M. Permanence of visual perimetry deficits in monocularly and binocularly deprived cats. *Brain Research*, 1974, **73**, 491–501.

Sherman, S. M. The effect of cortical and tectal lesions on the visual fields of binocularly deprived cats. *Journal of Comparative Neurology*, 1977, **172**, 231–246.

Siminoff, R., Schwassmann, H. O., & Kruger, L. An electrophysiological study of the visual projection to the superior colliculus of the rat. *Journal of Comparative Neurology*, 1966, **127**, 435–444.

Sparks, D. L., & Pollack, J. G. The neural control of saccadic eye movements: The role of the superior colliculus. In B. A. Brooks & F. J. Bajandas (Eds.), *Eye movements.* New York: Plenum, 1977. Pp. 179–219.

Sprague, J. M., & Meikle, T. H., Jr. The role of the superior colliculus in visually guided behavior. *Experimental Neurology,* 1965, **11,** 115–146.

Stein, B. E. Nonequivalent visual, auditory, and somatic corticotectal influences in cat. *Journal of Neurophysiology,* 1978, **41,** 55–64.

Stein, B. E., & Arigbede, M. O. A parametric study of movement detection properties of neurons in the cat's superior colliculus. *Brain Research,* 1972, **45,** 437–454. (a)

Stein, B. E., & Arigbede, M. O. Unimodal and multimodal response properties of neurons in the cat's superior colliculus. *Experimental Neurology,* 1972, **36,** 179–196. (b)

Stein, B. E., Clamann, H. P., & Goldberg, S. J. Superior colliculus: Control of eye movements in neonatal kittens. *Science,* 1980, **210,** 78–80.

Stein, B. E., & Dixon, J. Superior colliculus cells respond to noxious stimuli. *Brain Research,* 1978, **158,** 65–73.

Stein, B. E., & Dixon, J. Properties of superior colliculus neurons in the golden hamster. *Journal of Comparative Neurology,* 1979, **183,** 269–284.

Stein, B. E., & Edwards, S. B. Corticotectal and other corticofugal projections in neonatal cat. *Brain Research,* 1979, **161,** 399–409.

Stein, B. E., Goldberg, S. J., & Clamann, H. P. The control of eye movements by the superior colliculus in the alert cat. *Brain Research,* 1976, **118,** 469–474.

Stein, B. E., Làbos, E., & Kruger, L. Long-lasting discharge properties of neurons in the kitten midbrain. *Vision Research,* 1973, **13,** 2615–2619. (a)

Stein, B. E., Làbos, E., & Kruger, L. Sequence of changes in properties of neurons of superior colliculus of the kitten during maturation. *Journal of Neurophysiology,* 1973, **36,** 667–679. (b)

Stein, B. E., Làbos, E., & Kruger, L. Determinants of response latency in neurons of superior colliculus in kittens. *Journal of Neurophysiology,* 1973, **36,** 680–689. (c)

Stein, B. E., & Magalhães-Castro, B. Effects of neonatal cortical lesions upon the cat superior colliculus. *Brain Research,* 1975, **83,** 480–485.

Stein, B. E., Magalhães-Castro, B., & Kruger, L. Relationship between visual and tactile representations in cat superior colliculus. *Journal of Neurophysiology,* 1976, **39,** 401–419.

Sterling, P., & Wickelgren, B. G. Visual receptive fields in the superior colliculus of the cat. *Journal of Neurophysiology,* 1969, **32,** 1–15.

Sterling, P., & Wickelgren, B. G. Function of the projection from the visual cortex to the superior colliculus. *Brain, Behavior and Evolution,* 1970, **3,** 210–218.

Tiao, Y. C., & Blakemore, C. Functional organization in the superior colliculus of the golden hamster. *Journal of Comparative Neurology,* 1976, **168,** 483–504.

Tilney, F., & Casamajor, L. Myelinogeny as applied to the study of behavior. *Archives of Neurology and Psychiatry,* 1924, **12,** 1–66.

Tretter, F., Cynader, M., & Singer, W. Modification of direction selectivity of neurons in the visual cortex of kittens. *Brain Research,* 1975, **84,** 143–149.

Tunkl, J. E., & Berkeley, M. A. The role of superior colliculus in vision: Visual form discrimination in cats with superior colliculus ablations. *Journal of Comparative Neurology,* 1977, **176,** 575–588.

Updyke, B. V. Characteristics of unit responses in superior colliculus of the *Cebus* monkey. *Journal of Neurophysiology,* 1974, **37,** 896–909.

van Hof-van Duin, J. Development of visuomotor behavior in normal and dark-reared cats. *Brain Research,* 1976, **104,** 233–241.

van Hof-van Duin, J. Visual field measurements in monocularly deprived and normal cats. *Experimental Brain Research*, 1977, **30**, 353–368.

Villablanca, J. R., & Olmstead, C. E. Neurological development of kittens. *Developmental Psychobiology*, 1979, **12**, 101–127.

Vital-Durand, F., & Jeannerod, M. Role of visual experience in the development of optokinetic response in kittens. *Experimental Brain Research*, 1974, **20**, 297–302.

Wickelgren, B. G., & Sterling, P. Influences of visual cortex on receptive fields in the superior colliculus of the cat. *Journal of Neurophysiology*, 1969, **32**, 16–23. (a)

Wickelgren, B. G., & Sterling, P. Effect on the superior colliculus of cortical removal in visually deprived cats. *Nature*, 1969, **224**, 1032–1033. (b)

Wiesel, T. N., & Hubel, D. H. Comparison of the effects of unilateral and bilateral eye closure on cortical unit responses in kittens. *Journal of Neurophysiology*, 1965, **28**, 1029–1040.

Wurtz, R. H., & Goldberg, M. E. Activity of superior colliculus in behaving monkey. III. Cells discharging before eye movements. *Journal of Neurophysiology*, 1972, **35**, 575–586. (a)

Wurtz, R. H., & Goldberg, M. E. Activity of superior colliculus in behaving monkey. IV. Effects of lesions on eye movements. *Journal of Neurophysiology*, 1972, **35**, 587–596. (b)

Wurtz, R. H., & Mohler, C. W. Enhancement of visual responses in monkey striate cortex and frontal eye fields. *Journal of Neurophysiology*, 1976, **39**, 766–772.

6

Animal Models of Visual Development: Behavioral Evaluation of Some Physiological Findings in Cat Visual Development

MARK A. BERKLEY
Florida State University

I. INTRODUCTION

In recent years, exciting discoveries concerning the development of the visual system have been made (e.g., see Freeman, 1979, for review). The study of the development of the neural–visual system has proceeded along two major, but separate lines: The more traditional lines, which might be called the longitudinal approach, has looked at the condition of the normal visual system at various ages of the organism starting from its inception (e.g., Conel, 1963; Rakic, 1977). The second line, which might be called the perturbation line, introduces manipu-

197

lations of the normal visual environment of the animal during the period of its development to gauge the effects of the change at a subsequent age (e.g., Wiesel & Hubel, 1963a,b; 1965).

II. VISUAL DEPRIVATION

Two perturbations that have been used effectively in studying the development of the visual system are: (*a*) contour deprivation; and (*b*) binocularity deprivation. The contour deprivation paradigm, while representative of a class of studies, has employed several different types of visual deprivation. In general, contour deprivation studies have employed either selective or nonselective procedures. In the latter, all contour, color, and intensity information is withheld from the organism during some period of time (e.g., via dark rearing or binocular lid suture). In the selective deprivation paradigm, procedures designed to deprive the visual system of specific inputs are used (e.g., selective contour deprivation or movement deprivation (via strobe rearing).

Binocularity deprivation procedures employ methods designed to prevent congruent, simultaneous binocular visual input using manipulations such as monocular lid suture, alternating monocular occlusion and experimentally induced strabismus. The choice of these manipulations has been governed, of course, by the discovery that the visual system undergoes dramatic changes in physiology (e.g., Wiesel & Hubel, 1963a,b) and anatomy (e.g., Guillery & Stelzner, 1970) after many of these manipulations.

The behavioral analysis of the effects of visual environment perturbation, however, has not kept pace with anatomical and physiological studies. To some extent, this lag can be attributed to the difficulty in testing deprived animals and partly to uncertainties regarding what visual capacities should be tested (e.g., Dews & Wiesel, 1970; Ganz & Fitch, 1968). In addition, the interpretation of behavioral effects of deprivation are also difficult. For example, are the alterations in visual capacity observed after deprivation due to changes in the visual system, per se, or are the visual deficits observed due to indirect mechanisms—mechanisms such as learning, memory, and visuomotor coordination. These indirect mechanisms may be affected by deprivation and produce effects on measured visual capacity, but may not necessarily reflect any direct effects on the visual system. An additional complication has been the lack of complete agreement as to the precise nature of the physiological or anatomical changes (e.g., Eysel, Grusser, & Hoffmann, 1979) observed after deprivation.

To minimize these problems, we have chosen to study a single visual capacity after manipulations that have been shown to produce unambiguous anatomical and physiological changes in the visual system. Specifically, we have been interested in the behavioral effects of the dramatic changes in anatomy and physiology that have been described after monocular deprivation (Guillery & Stelzner, 1970; Sherman, 1973; Wiesel & Hubel, 1963a,b).

III. EFFECTS OF BINOCULARITY DEPRIVATION

Numerous studies have demonstrated that a majority of neurons in visual cortex are binocular (respond to stimulation of either eye) (e.g., Bishop, 1973; Hubel & Wiesel, 1965). This high degree of binocular interaction appears to depend upon congruent visual input during the first few postnatal months (Wiesel & Hubel, 1963a,b). If congruent binocular input is prevented via monocular lid suture, deviation of the visual axes or alternating monocular occlusion, most cells in the visual cortex will be activated only by one eye (Hubel & Wiesel, 1965; Wiesel & Hubel, 1963a,b).

In the case of monocular deprivation, the physiological consequences are dramatic in that almost all neurons are driven by the nonoccluded eye, whereas less than 10% can be activated via the deprived eye (Kratz & Spear, 1976; Wiesel & Hubel, 1963). This shift in binocularity does not occur after binocular occlusion, suggesting that control of visual cortical neurons is determined by some type of experiential imbalance between the two eyes (Guillery & Stelzner, 1970; Wiesel & Hubel, 1963a,b). One explanation of these findings is that lateral geniculate nucleus (LGN) efferents compete for control of cortical neurons. This view holds that under normal circumstances (or with binocular occlusion) neither eye has a competitive advantage in the process of consolidating connections from the retina to the cortex. As a result, each eye gains control of an equal number of cells or has an equal influence on a population of cells. When one eye is occluded, however, the nondeprived eye gains an advantage in achieving control of cortical neurons.

As the study of the deprivation effects progressed, it became obvious that the physiological effects could be refined in ways that were not apparent when the first experiments were done. For example, the development of the physiological neuron classification scheme (the X- Y- W- system) has led to the evaluation of the changes in the system after deprivation with regard to these classes of neurons (Sherman, Hoffman,

& Stone, 1972). I will not spend any time describing these effects except to say that most studies suggest that deprivation affects these neuron subpopulations in different ways (Sherman, 1979), and these different subpopulations may play different roles in vision.

A. Mechanisms Involved in Deprivation

Two possible mechanisms have been proposed as determinants of the observed anatomical and physiological effects in the monocular deprivation paradigm. The first is the effect of contour deprivation per se (e.g., disuse), and the second mechanism involves some type of active process (e.g., takeover of synaptic space or inhibition of input from the occluded eye). The dual effects of these two mechanisms are not separable in the usual monocular deprivation paradigm in that when one eye is closed by lid suture, the central neural mechanisms are contour deprived as well as being subjected to the effects of binocular competition.

Several recent studies have attempted to examine these proposed mechanisms directly (Duffy, Snodgrass, Burchfield, & Conway, 1976; Kratz & Spear, 1976) so that a clearer picture of the influences that shape the visual system could emerge. A major finding from these studies is the hypothesis that there are competition effects due to an active suppression via the nondeprived eye. For example, cortical cells not previously excited via the deprived eye could be activated after the introduction in the nervous system of a chemical known to be an antagonist of a putative inhibitory transmitter (Duffy et al., 1976). This finding suggests that cortical cells normally activated via the deprived eye are inhibited by inputs from the experienced eye. In another series of experiments, it was demonstrated that the number of cells that could be activated via the deprived eye is increased if the experienced eye is removed (Kratz, Spear, & Smith, 1976). These studies also support the view that a considerable portion of the effect of monocular deprivation is due to the dynamic inhibition or suppression of the activation of cortical neurons from the deprived eye via the experienced eye. Because of the clinical relevance of these findings (e.g., perhaps amblyopia could be treated with drug therapy), it is particularly important to evaluate the effects of suppression release on the visual capacities of a visually deprived eye. Thus, the studies described in the following sections examined the visual capacities of monocularly deprived cats after suppression release.

B.   Behavioral Study of "Suppression Release"

To study suppression release, two methods were available: (a) chemical release procedures; and (b) enucleation procedures. The drug paradigm, although reversible, has a number of difficulties because systemic administration of the chemical antagonist produces interfering side effects. The enucleation paradigm, although not reversible, is less ambiguous and is not subject to side effects. Thus, the enucleation procedure was employed to produce suppression release. The effects of suppression release were evaluated using visual acuity tests.

The first experiment was done in collaboration (Jones, Berkley, Spear, & Tong, 1978). It may be simply described as an experiment in which monocularly deprived (MD) cats had their vision tested in the deprived eye before and after removal (enucleation) of the nondeprived eye. As a control procedure before the enucleation, vision was tested in the deprived eye after lid suturing the experienced eye. At the conclusion of the behavioral studies, the animals were evaluated electrophysiologically to determine whether they showed the same increase in number of cells drivable by the deprived eye after enucleation that had been recorded by previous investigators (Kratz *et al.*, 1976). Table 6.1 is a summary of the sequence and procedures employed. As seen in Table 6.1, we employed very long periods of monocular deprivation before enucleation. This was done to avoid possible contamination with recovery effects that might be seen if the plasticity period had not yet ended when we did our tests (Giffin & Mitchell, 1978; Spear & Hickey, 1979).

The visual task selected for evaluation was grating acuity and was measured in the apparatus shown in Fig. 6.1. The apparatus requires little locomotor activity, a minimal amount of orienting behavior, and

Table 6.1
Sequence and Duration of Procedures Employed in Experiment I[a]

	Condition	Duration
1.	Monocularly lid sutured	~12 months
2.	Normal binocular vision	~10 months
3.	Tested Monocular (DE and NE) and Binocular	~9 months
4.	Reverse lid suture	1–3 months
5.	Normal eye enucleated	10 days–1 month

[a] From Jones, Berkley, Spear, and Tong (1978).

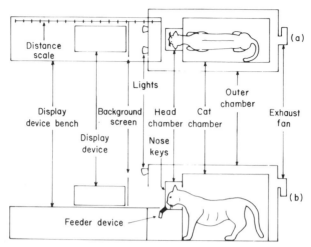

Fig. 6.1 Diagram depicting (a) top view and (b) side view of the testing apparatus employed in the current studies. For further details, see Berkley (1979). (Reprinted with permission from *Behavior Research Methods and Instrumentation*, **11**(6), Berkley, A system for behavioral evaluation of the visual capacities of cats. Copyright 1979, Pergamon Press, Ltd.)

permits fixing the viewing distance at known values. Details of the test procedures have been described elsewhere (Bloom & Berkley, 1977; Berkley, 1970, 1979). Briefly, the test stimulus consisted of a target field with two apertures. Behind one aperture was a square wave grating, and behind the other was a homogeneous field of average luminance equal to the grating. The animal's task was to select the grating from the two targets. Plots of the percentage of correct choices as a function of spatial frequency (c/deg) were made for the four animals used in this experiment. All cats were tested monocularly using opaque contact lens occluders.

Figure 6.2 shows the performance of the cats on the grating discrimination task when using their experienced eye. Their acuities ranged from about 3.5 c/deg to 7.0 c/deg, and are typical for normal animals tested in our apparatus. Testing of the cats when they were using their deprived eye was considerably more difficult. Their performance was very poor, and the few rewards they received during testing made them difficult to test. Only one animal (Squint) was able to give an estimate of acuity at this stage of testing. The acuity for this cat was about 0.5 c/deg. When stable performance was achieved with the deprived eye, the experienced eye was lid-sutured, forcing the animal to use the deprived eye all the time, not only during the test periods.

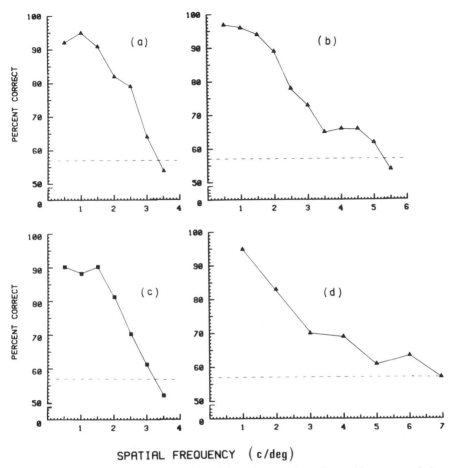

Fig. 6.2 Visual acuity estimates derived from the experienced eye of four monocularly deprived (MD) cats: (a) Squint, (b) Zuma, (c) K. J., and (d) Hannibal. The percentage of correct choices is plotted as a function of spatial frequency (abscissa). The horizontal dotted line indicates a performance level two standard deviations (SD) above chance.

Some improvements were seen in these post lid-sutured conditions and these are shown in Fig. 6.3. Note that the best acuity observed in any of the cats was just under 1 c/deg. At the completion of these tests, the experimental condition of interest was evaluated. Figure 6.3 displays the grating discrimination performance after removal of the deprived eye. Note that, although there was an improvement in overall performance, there were no significant changes in the estimated acuity of the animals after enucleation. The cause of the improvement in overall

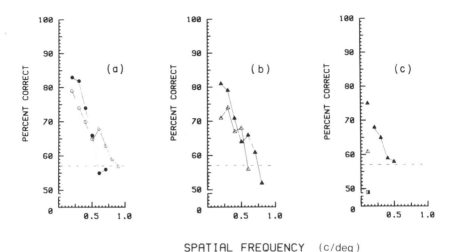

SPATIAL FREQUENCY (c/deg)

Fig. 6.3 Visual acuity estimates derived from the deprived eye of four monocularly deprived (MD) cats (a) Squint, (b) Hannibal, and (c) Zuma and K. J., after reverse lid suture (depicted by ⊙, △ and ☐) and after removal of the experienced eye depicted by ●, ▲, and ■. The percentage of correct choices is plotted against spatial frequency in cycles per degree (c/deg). The horizontal dotted line is 2 SD above chance performance. Note that in graph (c), one animal (K.J.) never performed above chance before (☐) or after (■) enucleation.

performance is not clear (e.g., it may be due to some change in the visual system or just to increased practice).

The final step in the study was to determine whether our test cats exhibited the same increased percentage of drivable cells in visual cortex as had been reported by Spear and his colleagues (Kratz *et al.*, 1976; Kratz & Spear, 1976). Thus, the cats were transported to Dr. Spear's laboratory where measures were made of the percentage of cells encountered in the cortex that were drivable via visual stimulation of the deprived eye. Figure 6.4 shows the outcome of these observations. The points around the bar on the right-hand side of the histogram of Fig. 6.4 show the percentages obtained in the present study. The first two bars represent similar measures made by Spear in other studies. Note that the percentages obtained from our four experimental animals are exactly in the range that Spear and colleagues had observed in previous studies. Because deprivation procedures such as we used ordinarily produce animals with fewer than 10% drivable cortical cells, it seems safe to assume that the animals in the present study would have had a smaller number of cells drivable by the deprived eye had they not been enucleated. Putting together the results of the behavioral and

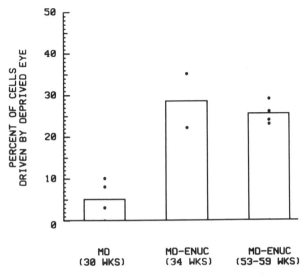

Fig. 6.4 Histograms showing the percentage of cells recorded in striate cortex that were capable of being driven via visual stimulation of the deprived eye. Each of the three groups of cats was monocularly deprived for different lengths of time during development. For the two monocularly deprived enucleated groups (MD–ENUC), the data were collected after removal of the nondeprived eye. The data for the four animals used in the present study are shown in the last right-hand column. (From Jones, *et al.*, 1978.)

electrophysiological studies, it can be concluded that, despite the fact that our test animals had a larger percentage of drivable cells in their visual cortices than do ordinary MD cats, they did not show any great improvement in acuity. Whereas this outcome would seem to argue that there is no simple relationship between activity in Area 17 neurons and acuity, it is perhaps not too surprising in light of the fact that the cells that are drivable by the deprived eye in enucleated animals are not normal (e.g., they are sluggish, have more diffuse receptive field properties, and are in other ways abnormal, Kratz *et al.*, 1976).

IV. CONTOUR DEPRIVATION

In a second set of experiments, we attempted to look at the effects of monocular deprivation, per se, without the effects of binocular competition. To do this, we adopted a paradigm developed by Guillery (1972) and Sherman, Guillery, Kaas, & Sanderson (1974). This paradigm is based on studies of the neural areas representing that portion of the visual field that is not seen by both eyes simultaneously (monocular segment). The neurons representing this portion of the field are not subject to binocular competition effects in a monocular deprivation paradigm. Thus, if vision in the monocular segment could be tested in MD cats, a good estimate of the effects of deprivation (without competition effects) could be obtained. However, because the monocular segment is in the far periphery where even normal vision is poor, it is impractical to test the visual capacity of this region. To overcome this problem, Guillery (1972) and Sherman et al. (1974) were able to create a centrally located monocular segment. They achieved this by placing a retinal lesion in the central region of one eye and lid suturing the other eye. Thus, in the region in which the lesion was made, there is no competition for those cells representing that portion of the visual field driven by the deprived eye. Using visual field testing techniques (Sherman, 1973; Sprague, 1966) Sherman et al. (1974) were able to show that such animals responded to stimuli presented in the artificial monocular segment of the monocularly deprived eye.

A summary of the effects of MD, BD, and retinal lesion + MD on the visual field is shown in Fig. 6.5, which is from Sherman & Guillery (1976). Note that the cat with a retinal lesion in the experienced eye responded to stimuli presented in the corresponding portion of the visual field of the deprived eye; that is, in the zone of the visual field that was not exposed to the effects of binocular competition. Because the artifical monocular segment can be made in the central visual field, this preparation is ideal to study the effects of deprivation, per se. Thus, an investigation of such cats was initiated in collaboration with M. Sherman.

Two cats, who each had one eye lid-sutured and the other with a retinal lesion in the central visual field were prepared, and the acuity tests described earlier were used to study these animals. They were tested using the deprived eye with a retinal lesion, the nondeprived eye only, and binocularly.

Results of the behavioral experiments were relatively clear. In the two animals that were tested in this experiment, one showed a severe acuity deficit when tested via its normal eye, whereas the other showed no deficit, having more-or-less normal visual acuity in its experienced eye. Neither animal, however, was able to give an acuity estimate via the deprived eye, even after a considerable amount of training. This was a surprising outcome, as estimates of acuity were obtained in other ordinary MD animals and the test animals did respond to stimuli pres-

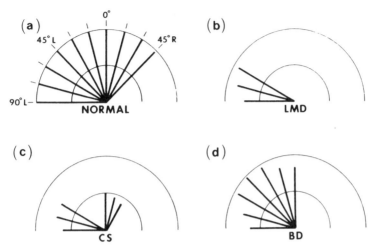

Fig. 6.5 Graphic depiction of monocular visual fields from cats exposed to different rearing conditions as measured using the food perimetry test of Sprague (1966) and Sherman (1973). Length of the bars at each angular value indicates the percentage of correct detections of food objects presented at these locations when cats are "looking" straight ahead. (a) Monocular visual field of normal eye; (b) visual field of deprived eye in monocularly deprived (MD) cat; (c) visual field of deprived eye in MD cat that had a retinal lesion placed in the central region of the retina of the nondeprived eye; (d) monocular visual field of a cat reared with both eyes lid sutured (BD). For further details, see Sherman & Guillery (1976). (From Sherman & Guillery, 1976.)

ent in the artificial monocular segment in perimetry tests. Despite the fact that an artificial monocular segment was successfully created in central vision, visual contour deprivation was sufficient to produce severe deficts in vision *without* the effects of monocular competition.

One possible explanation for the poor performance of the deprived eye is that the animals could not direct their small region of putative normal vision appropriately toward the target. To test this possibility, especially in the animal that showed poor acuity in the normal eye, the animals were tested binocularly. We reasoned as follows: The experienced eye with the retinal lesion had poor acuity because the retinal lesion was in the central visual field. The deprived eye had poor vision because it had only a small region of normal vision, which it perhaps could not direct at the appropriate portion of the stimulus panel. If the animal were permitted to put the vision of both eyes together, his acuity might improve, that is, he could fill in the scotoma of the experienced eye with the information from the artifical monocular segment of the deprived eye. Further testing revealed, however, that the animal's acuity obtained with binocular testing was the same as that obtained with monocular testing of the experienced but damaged eye (see Fig. 6.6). Thus, any information about the gratings getting into the visual system via the deprived eye's artificial monocular segment was not usable in improving acuity performance.

One of the most important conditions to be fulfilled to interpret the outcome of the foregoing experiment is to be able to describe the visual field locus and extent of the retinal lesions. This can be done via reconstructions based on fundus photography or histological preparations of whole mounts of the retina. These methods require difficult optical and histological procedures. A more direct and easily documentable method for charting the extent of the retinal lesion, however, employs the detailed maps of the projections from the retina to the LGN (Sanderson, 1971). Because a retinal lesion will produce an easily demonstrable loss of input to LGN, the zone of the visual field affected by

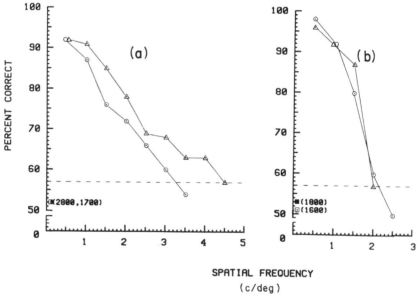

SPATIAL FREQUENCY
(c/deg)

Fig. 6.6 Visual acuity estimates derived from two monocularly deprived (MD) cats (a) Jake and (b) Joe that had retinal lesions in the nondeprived eye. The performance level achieved with the deprived eye is depicted by □ (neither animal went above chance); the performance with the experienced eye that had a retinal lesion is shown by △; performance when tested binocularly is depicted by ○. (Axes, etc., as in previous figures; from Berkley, Sherman, Warmath, & Tunkl, 1978.)

the retinal lesion can be accurately charted by plotting the input loss on maps of the LGN that depict the visual field representation. This can be done by injecting the eye containing the retinal lesion with a tritiated amino acid and observing the pattern of transported amino acid in the LGN. The retinal region where the ganglion cells have been killed in the experienced eye will transport no amino acid to the LGN. By plotting the pattern of transported amino acid onto the LGN, the region of the visual field affected by the retinal lesion can be accurately mapped.

The visual field defects as estimated from the transported amino acids were constructed and are shown in Fig. 6.7. The results of the field map are consistent with the outcome of the behavioral tests. That is, in one animal, Jake, the retinal lesion was in temporal retina, outside the *area centralis*, and produced little, if any, effect on the animal's acuity in the experienced eye. However, the other animal, Joe, had a lesion that included the *area centralis* as indicated by the fact that the region of no transported amino acid extends across the midline and, according to the projection maps of Sanderson (1971), is in the *area centralis*. This animal did show a severe acuity deficit, having an acuity of about 2 c/deg.

It is interesting to contrast the acuity of the animal with a central lesion of the retina with the acuity of animals that have suffered ablations of visual cortex that include the representation of the central visual field. Such animals were evaluated in a recent study (Berkley & Sprague, 1979) and, although they have somewhat less than normal acuity, are considerably better in their ability to resolve gratings than are the animals with central retinal lesions. The acuity data derived from three cats before and after Area 17–18 ablations and one cat with Area 17–18 spared are shown in Fig. 6.8. Reconstructions of the lesions as well as evaluation of the extent of retrograde degeneration in the LGN showed that, in all cases, the lesions included at least the cortical areas representing the central 5–7 deg, a field deficit larger than that for the cat with the central retinal lesion described earlier (Berkley & Sprague, 1979). Because the acuity deficits observed in the deprived eye of monocularly deprived enucleated cats, as well as the artificial monocular segment cats, is considerably greater than the acuity deficits observed in cats with Area 17–18 removed, the deprivation effects must extend into neural areas other than Areas 17 and 18.

From the study of cats with an artificial monocular segment, it might be concluded that deprivation alone is responsible for the visual defects observed in the deprived eye of MD animals. Studies of binocularly deprived cats, however, argue against such a view. Binocularly de-

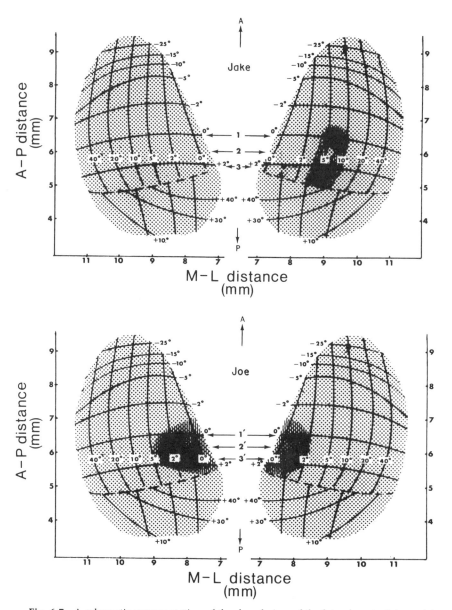

Fig. 6.7 A schematic representation of the dorsal view of the lateral geniculate nuclei with visual field projection lines drawn in as derived from Sanderson (1971). Anterior is up. Axes are in millimeters (mm) referred to Horsley–Clark stereotaxic coordinates. Darkened area shows region in geniculate Layers A or A1, which were free of transported labeled amino acid injected into the eye with the retinal lesion (nondeprived eye) for the cats Jake and Joe. (From Berkley, *et al.*, 1978.)

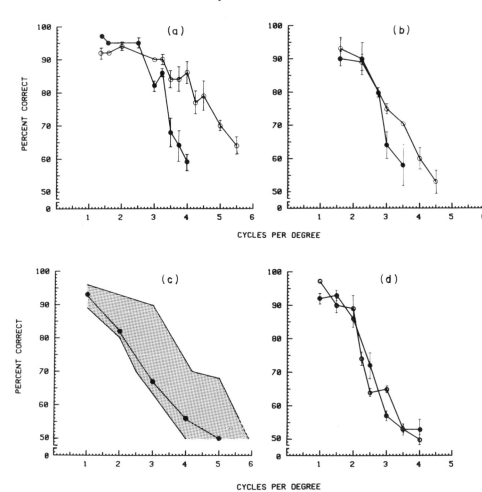

Fig. 6.8 Grating acuity estimates for four cats (a) Zelda, (b) Scarlet, (c) Francis, and (d) Arlo, before and after ablation of Areas 17–18 (Zelda, Scarlett, Francis) or more lateral cortical areas (Arlo). Preoperative performance is depicted by ○; postoperative performance by ●. Vertical bars indicate ± 1 standard deviation (SD). Cat Francis was only tested postoperatively. For comparison, shaded area depicts range of grating acuity in normal cats ($N = 5$). (From Berkley & Sprague, 1979.)

prived cats are deprived of all visual contours and presumably do not suffer the effects of binocular competition. Unlike MD cats, such animals have monocular visual fields extending to the midline (e.g., see Fig. 6.5; Sherman, 1973), and neurons drivable from each eye (Watkins, Wilson, & Sherman, 1978; Wiesel & Hubel, 1965). The visual acuity of such animals, however, has been found to be much better than that of MD cats although still considerably poorer than normal (Smith, Schwark, & Beaudry, 1979). If visual contour deprivation alone were responsible for the acuity defects, then binocularly deprived cats should have the same acuity level as the artificial monocular segment cats. As previously described, the acuity of artificial segment cats is much poorer, thus some other factors must be operating, as suggested by Watkins, et al. (1978).

The present findings have relevance to recent attempts to divide the visual system into subsystems (e.g., X-, Y-, and W-cell classification scheme). For example, the studies described in this chapter would seem to argue that the X-cell system is not required for contour discrimination as the major effect of deprivation seems to be on the Y-cell system (Sherman et al., 1972). Yet deprived animals have very poor contour vision. Ablation experiments (Berkley & Sprague, 1979) also have shown that ablation of the exclusive cortical terminus of the X-cell system only reduces acuity slightly, while still permitting the discrimination of visual forms. These findings also suggest that the Y-cell system can mediate form vision and are consistent with the deprivation studies described. Thus, MD cats with severely disrupted Y-cell systems have much poorer vision when using their deprived eye than do the animals that have extensive ablations of Areas 17 and 18, and a severely disrupted X-cell system. It must be pointed out that visual deprivation procedures produce effects not only in the structures in which effects have been electrophysiologically measured, but in other neural structures as well. At the moment, little is known of the deprivation effects in these other structures, and how they contribute to the deficits in vision that have been observed. One could predict from the present experiments, however, that the effects in other portions of the system are of more significance than we have previously guessed (Berkley, 1976).

V.   CONCLUSIONS

Several specific conclusions can be drawn based on the experiments described.

1. Release of interocular influences after monocular deprivation does not improve visual capacity as measured by grating acuity tests, a finding not consistent with electrophysiological studies.

2. Visual contour deprivation per se produces severe defects in vision but is not independent of interocular mechanisms.

More generally, these results suggest that the capacity to process visual contour information cannot be easily inferred from a consideration of the single cell data derived from Area 17 of normal or visually deprived cats, and it also calls attention to the fact that the effects of deprivation are widespread. The limited picture we have of these effects based upon electrophysiological examination of several small areas of the brain is inadequate for providing either a model of experiential influences on the visual system or for models of visual system function.

ACKNOWLEDGMENTS

The assistance of D. S. Warmath, Kenna Study and John Dishmon in the conduct of the studies is gratefully acknowledged. The work described was supported by grants from NEI (EY 00953) and NSF (BMS 75–13837).

REFERENCES

Berkley, M. A. Visual discriminations in the cat. In W. C. Stebbins (Ed.), *Animal psychophysics: The design and conduct of sensory experiments*. New York: Appleton-Century-Crofts, 1970, 231–247.

Berkley, M. A. The role of the geniculo–striate system in vision. In F. A. King (Ed.), *Handbook of behavioral neurobiology* (Vol. 1): *Sensory integration* (R. B. Masterton, Ed.). New York: Academic Press, 1976, pp. 63–120.

Berkley, M. A. A system for behavioral evaluation of the visual capacities of cats. *Behavior Research Methods and Instrumentation*, 1979, **11**, 545–548.

Berkley, M. A., Sherman, S. M., Warmath, D. S., & Tunkl, J. T. Visual capacities of adult cats which were reared with a lesion in the retina of one eye and the other occluded. *Society for Neuroscience Abstracts*, 1978, **4**, 467.

Berkley, M. A., & Sprague, J. Striate cortex and visual acuity functions in the cat. *Journal of Comparative Neurology*, 1979, **187**, 679–702.

Bishop, P. O. Neurophysiology of binocular single vision and stereopsis. In R. Jung (Ed.), *Handbook of sensory physiology VII (A)*. New York: Springer-Verlag, 1973.

Bloom, M., & Berkley, M. A. Visual acuity and the near point of accommodation in cats. *Vision Research*, 1977, **17**, 723–730.

Conel, J. *The postnatal development of the human cerebral cortex* (6 vols.). Cambridge, Mass.: Harvard University Press, 1939–1963.

Dews, P. B., & Wiesel, T. N. Consequences of monocular deprivation on visual behavior in kittens. *Journal of Physiology*, 1970, **206**, 437–455.

Duffy, F. H., Snodgrass, S. R., Burchfield, J. L., & Conway, J. L. Bicuculline reversal of deprivation amblyopia in the cat. *Nature*, 1976, **260**, 257–258.

Eysel, U. T., Grusser, O. -J., & Hoffmann, K. -P. Monocular deprivation and the signal transmission by X- and Y-neurons of the cat lateral geniculate nucleus. *Experimental Brain Research*, 1979, **34**, 521–539.

Freeman, R. D. (Ed.). *Developmental neurobiology of vision*. New York: Plenum, 1979.

Ganz, L., & Fitch, M. The effect of visual deprivation on perceptual behavior. *Experimental neurology*, 1968, **22**, 638–660.

Giffin, F., & Mitchell, D. E. The rate of recovery of vision after early monocular deprivation in kittens. *Journal of Physiology*, 1978, **274**, 511–537.

Guillery, R. W. Binocular competition in the control of geniculate cell growth. *Journal of Comparative neurology*, 1972, **144**, 117–130.

Guillery, R. W., & Stelzner, D. J. The differential effects of unilateral lid closure upon the monocular and binocular segments of the dorsal lateral geniculate nucleus in the cat. *Journal of Comparative Neurology*, 1970, **139**, 513–422.

Hubel, D., & Wiesel, T. Binocular interaction in striate cortex of kittens reared with artificial squint. *Journal of Neurophysiology*, 1965, **28**, 1041–1059.

Jones, K. R., Berkley, M. A., Spear, P., & Tong, J. Visual capacities of monocularly deprived cats for reverse lid suture and enucleation of the nondeprived eye. *Society for Neuroscience Abstracts*, 1978, **4**, 475.

Kratz, K. E., & Spear, P. D. Effects of visual deprivation and alterations in binocular competition on responses of striate cortex neurons in the cat. *Journal of Comparative Neurology*, 1976, **1970**, 141–152.

Kratz, K. E., Spear, P. D., & Smith, D. C. Post critical period reversal of effects of monocular deprivation on striate cortex cells in the cat. *Journal of Neurophysiology*, 1976, **39**, 501–511.

Rakic, P. Prenatal Development of the visual system in rhesus monkey. *Philosophical Transactions of the Royal Society of London* 1977, **278**, 245–260.

Sherman, S. M. Visual field defects in monocularly and binocularly deprived cats. *Brain Research*, 1973, **49**, 25–45.

Sherman, S. M. Development of the lateral geniculate nucleus in cats raised with monocular eyelid suture. In R. D. Freeman (Ed.), *Developmental neurobiology of vision*. New York: Plenum, 1979.

Sherman, S. M., & Guillery, R. W. Behavioral studies of binocular competition in cats. *Vision Research*, 1976, **16**, 1479–1481.

Sherman, S. M., Guillery, R. W., Kaas, J. H., & Sanderson, K. J. Behavioral, electrophysiological, and morphological studies of binocular competition in the development of the geniculocortical pathways of cats. *Journal of Comparative Neurology*, 1974, **158**, 1–18.

Sherman, S. M., Hoffman, K. -P., & Stone, J. Loss of a specific cell type from dorsal lateral geniculate nucleus in visually deprived cats *Journal of Neurophysiology*, 1972, **35,**, 532–541.

Sanderson, K. J. The projection of the visual field to the lateral geniculate and medial interlaminar nuclei in the cat. *Journal of Comparative Neurology*, 1971, **143**, 101–117.

Smith, D. C., Schwark, H. D., & Beaudry, D. M. Developmental alterations in binocular competition and visual acuity in visually deprived cats. *Society for Neuroscience Abstracts*, 1979, **5**, 635.

Spear, P. D., & Hickey, T. L. Post critical period reversal of effects of monocular deprivation on dorsal lateral geniculate cell size in the cat. *Journal of Comparative Neurology*, 1979, **185**, 317–328.

Sprague, J. M. Interaction of cortex and superior colliculus in mediation of visually guided behavior in the cat. *Science*, 1966, **153**, 1544–1547.

Watkins, D. W., Wilson, J. R., & Sherman, S. M. Receptive field properties of neurons in binocular and monocular segments of striate cortex in cats raised with binocular lid suture. *Journal of Neurophysiology*, 1978, **41**, 322–337.

Wiesel, T. N., & Hubel, D. H. Effects of visual deprivation on morphology and physiology of cells in the cat's lateral geniculate body. *Journal of Neurophysiology*, 1963, **26,**, 978–993. (2)

Wiesel, T. N., & Hubel, D. H. Single cell responses in the striate cortex of kittens deprived of vision in one eye. *Journal of Neurophysiology*, 1963, **26,** 1003–1017. (b)

Wiesel, T. N., & Hubel, D. H. Comparison of the effects of unilateral and bilateral eye closure on cortical unity responses in kittens. *Journal of Neurophysiology*, 1965, **28,** 1029–1040.

7

Development of Spatial Vision
in Infant Macaque Monkeys
under Conditions of Normal
and Abnormal Visual
Experience

RONALD G. BOOTHE
University of Washington

DEVELOPMENT OF PERCEPTION
Volume 2

I. INTRODUCTION

The term *spatial vision* refers to the ability of an organism to extract information from the environment about the spatial distribution of light in its visual field. A common measure of one aspect of spatial vision is acuity, which describes the ability of an organism to resolve fine spatial detail. A more complete description of spatial vision can be obtained by measuring contrast sensitivity for spatial sinusoidal patterns (light–dark stripes) of various spatial frequencies (stripes per visual angle) (Campbell & Robson, 1968; Schade, 1956). The relationship between contrast sensitivity and spatial frequency is described by a spatial contrast sensitivity function (CSF). Traditional measurements of grating acuity are equivalent to determining the high frequency cut-off point on the CSF. The CSF is a more powerful description of spatial vision, as it characterizes the response of the organism to all spatial frequencies, including those near its acuity level.

Numerous studies have demonstrated that human infants have poorer acuity than do adults (for review see Dobson & Teller, 1978). Measurements of CSFs in human infants have revealed a decreased contrast sensitivity over the entire adult spatial frequency range (Atkinson, Braddick, & Moar, 1977; Banks & Salapatek, 1976, 1978).

The developmental processes by which acuity and the CSF become adult-like are of importance for both theoretical and clinical reasons. Theoretically, there are important questions about whether the developmental improvements in spatial vision reflect changes in the eye's optics, structural changes in the eye, or brain, such as in the spacing between receptor elements in the retina, changes in neural processing, or some combination of these. Clinically, the development of spatial vision is important because abnormal development can result in a permanent impairment in spatial resolution (i.e., an amblyopia, von Noorden, 1980; von Noorden & Maumenee, 1968).

This chapter is restricted to behavioral studies of spatial vision in monkeys. It will be argued, on the basis of normative data, that infant monkeys provide good models for studying the development of spatial vision in human infants. It will also be argued that the development of spatial vision is influenced both by maturation and by the visual experience received during early rearing. In particular, there is evidence from a wide variety of empirical investigations that exposure to high spatial frequencies during early rearing is a necessary condition for an organism to develop the capacity to respond to these same frequencies later in life.

II. THE INFANT MONKEY AS AN ANIMAL MODEL

There are obvious advantages to having an animal model with which to study the development of spatial vision. Invasive or potentially invasive experiments such as controlled rearing studies or anatomical and physiological studies require a species similar in several appropriate ways to the developing human.

Two steps are required to demonstrate that a species can serve as an appropriate model for studying the development of spatial vision in human infants. First, it is necessary to establish that adults of the two species have similar spatial vision. Humans have a visual system that is highly developed for analyzing spatial detail, and this has been achieved through highly specialized anatomical and physiological mechanisms (e.g., the presence of the foveal depression in the retina). Such highly specialized mechanisms are not present in species with less well-developed spatial vision. Macaque monkeys have been shown to have visual systems that are structurally very similar to humans (Boycott & Dowling, 1969; Kaas, Huerta, Weber, & Harting, 1978; Polyak, 1957; Van Essen, 1979).

Parallel behavioral studies by DeValois, Morgan, and Snodderly (1974) have demonstrated that adult humans and macaque monkeys have spatial vision that is virtually identical. DeValois *et al.* presented especially convincing evidence that this is the case by conducting parametric studies. They demonstrated that, not only are the CSFs of adult humans and macaque monkeys similar under normal photopic conditions but, in addition, the CSFs in both species are modified similarly by changes in luminance.

A second step in establishing an appropriate animal model (after adults of the two species have been shown to be similar) is to show that development follows a similar developmental sequence in both species. This requires parallel developmental studies, ideally using the same procedures and apparatus. A species does not have to show the same time course of development to be an adequate model. Most species will, in fact, have shorter gestational ages and life spans than humans. However, it should be possible to superimpose their time courses by simply stretching or compressing one of the age axes. If birth does not occur at the same relative time in the two species, and development is plotted in terms of postnatal age, then simple shifts of the two time axes in relation to each other may also be required (see Allen, 1978). Parallel studies on the two species (reviewed in Section IV) provide strong evidence that infant macaque monkeys and humans do in fact follow similar developmental sequences.

III.   METHODS FOR STUDYING SPATIAL VISION IN INFANT MONKEYS

To study spatial vision in an infant monkey, one first needs to find a way of asking the infant what it can see. This requires a behavioral response. (Investigators using evoked potentials or other physiological responses may disagree with this statement but a discussion of this issue is beyond the scope of this chapter.) There are a number of behaviors in the repertoire of infant monkeys that could potentially be exploited to measure spatial vision capabilities (for review, see Boothe & Sackett, 1975). However, most of the behavioral testing methods developed for use with monkeys are limited by the fact that they either cannot be used with neonates or do not allow more than a few trials of data to be obtained per infant per day.

There are only three behavioral testing methods that have been used successfully to collect useful amounts of data regarding spatial vision from infant monkeys: optokinetic nystagmus (OKN), preferential looking (PL), and operant testing in a face mask cage apparatus. Two of these methods require no prior training of the infant and can be used from the time of birth, whereas the third can be used to test an infant only after it has first been trained on the task.

A.   Behavioral Methods that Require No Prior Training

Ordy, Samorajski, Collins, and Nagy (1965) used the OKN response to study acuity in infant monkeys during the first month after birth. This response can be elicited in infant monkeys by moving large, high-contrast stripes through the visual field. By using finer and finer stripes, it is possible to determine the narrowest stripe widths that will reliably elicit the OKN reflex, and Ordy *et al.* used this as an estimate of acuity. This procedure could probably also be used to measure a CSF, if one used sine wave gratings and varied contrast as well as spatial frequency.

A second behavioral testing method requiring no prior training that has been applied to infant monkeys is preferential looking (Fantz, 1967). This method relies on the fact that an infant given a choice between a patterned and homogeneous visual stimulus will preferentially fixate the patterned stimulus. The infant to be tested is held in front of a display containing a patterned stimulus on one side and a homogeneous field on the other. An observer watches the infant and reports to which side of the display its eyes are directed. If the side of preferential fixation is correlated with the side containing the patterned stimulus, it can be concluded that the infant detects the pattern.

A variant of the preferential looking method is Teller's forced-choice preferential looking (FPL) procedure, which has been described in detail elsewhere (Teller, 1979; Chapter 10 in this volume; Teller, Morse, Borton, & Regal, 1974; Teller, Regal, Videen, & Pulos, 1978). The FPL method differs from other versions of preferential looking in terms of the observer's response. In FPL, the observer's task is to determine the position of the patterned stimulus rather than to describe the eye movements of the infant. The observer can use any information provided by the infant (including, but not limited to, eye movements) to decide where the patterned stimulus is located. Trial-by-trial feedback is provided to the observer about whether judgments are correct or incorrect so that the observer can learn to optimize performance by making use of any available cues provided by the infant. If the observer can perform at a level significantly better than chance, it can be concluded that the infant can detect the patterned stimulus. To measure acuity or contrast sensitivity with PL, a grating (series of black–white stripes) can be used as the patterned stimulus. The spatial frequency and/or contrast of the grating can be varied to obtain either estimates of acuity or the entire CSF.

Preferential looking and OKN methods both have the advantage of being usable with neonates starting on the day of birth. Both methods also are advantageous in that they can be used with both human and monkey infants (e.g., Ordy, Latanick, Samorajski, & Massopust, 1964 for OKN; Teller et al., 1974, 1978 for FPL). This allows direct parallel comparisons between the two species using the same procedures and apparatus.

There are, however, two limitations associated with both methods. First, both methods become increasingly difficult to use with older infants. Neonates will usually sit quietly and passively in front of a visual display so that it is relatively easy to elicit OKN responses or to observe looking behavior to two predetermined stimulus positions. However, as infants get older, the increases in motor activity and exploratory behavior make it more and more difficult to obtain reliable results. Ordy et al. (1965) could not obtain reliable OKN data from their infant monkeys after one month of age. Teller et al. (1978) report increasing difficulty in obtaining FPL data from monkeys after about 2 months of age.

This limitation can be minimized by testing infants with a combination of methods. Operant methods (see Section III B) can be used with infants starting at 4 or 5 weeks. Thus, it is possible to obtain estimates of spatial vision using both of these methods within a limited age range. Studies reviewed in Section IV.D demonstrate that acuity estimates obtained by FPL and operant methods agree closely within this overlapping age range. Therefore, it is possible to measure spatial vision over the entire developmental period by starting at birth with a method requiring no training, testing infants with a combination of these methods during intermediate ages to demonstrate that both methods provide similar results, and finally continuing to follow development at older ages with operant methods.

A second limitation of both OKN and preferential looking methods is that they depend on rather primitive built-in behavioral responses. The neural pathways that subserve these responses may not be the same as those subserving behavior of a more voluntary or learned nature, and the different neural pathways may have different spatial tuning properties. For example, in the cat, X- and Y-cell pathways have somewhat different spatial properties (Sherman, 1979). If one's interest is in comparing spatial vision in infants with spatial vision in adults, it may be important to use behavioral responses that reflect the activities of neural pathways with the same (or similar) spatial properties. This limitation can also be minimized by testing infants with a combination of techniques. For example, experiments using a combination of FPL and operant techniques on the same infants have demonstrated that acuity estimates obtained with the two methods are highly similar (see Section IV.D).

In general, OKN and PL methods are probably comparable in terms of ease of use, but there is one technical advantage of preferential looking. The OKN response can only be reliably elicited if the stimulus occupies a fairly large portion of the infant's field of view. This requires fairly large stimuli (Ordy et al. used a drum 40 cm high by 55 cm in diameter placed 30 cm from the infant) that are technically difficult to construct without introducing low spatial frequency artifacts. Preferential looking responses, however, can be elicited with stimuli subtending only a few degrees of visual angle (Teller et al. used stimuli 10.5 cm in diameter at a distance of 35 cm).

B.   Operant Behavioral Methods

Use of a face mask cage for studying perception and learning in infant monkeys was first described by Sackett, Tripp, Milbrath, Gluck, and Pick (1971). A rearing cage was constructed with a face mask, molded to the shape of an infant monkey's face, mounted on one wall. There are eye holes in the face mask so that the infant can look out of the cage, and a mouth hole where a nipple can be inserted for providing milk or other liquid reinforcement. Infant monkeys can be separated from their mothers on the day of birth and permanently housed in this cage.

A shaping procedure can be used to teach the infants an operant response that can then be used in a visual discrimination task (Boothe, Teller, & Sackett, 1975; Boothe, Williams, Kiorpes, & Teller, 1980). During the first few days after birth, the infant is held up to the face mask by an experimenter, and allowed to drink every 2–4 hours around the clock. Within the first week, most infants will learn to orient themselves to the face mask and self-feed without assistance. When the infant is self-feeding, a grab bar is positioned into the cage through a hole underneath the face mask. This bar is positioned such that it will be frequently bumped by the infant's random arm movements while its face is in the mask. Milk is provided at the nipple by a pump each time the bar is moved. Infants can usually learn to self-feed by manipulating this grab bar during the second week. The grab bar is then moved in small steps through the hole in the cage wall to the outside of the cage. The final position of the grab bar is in front of a visual display positioned outside of the cage in front of the face mask. When the monkey puts its face in the cage it can look out and see a visual display with a grab bar directly in front of it. If the infant reaches out and pulls this grab bar, it receives milk reinforcement. If two bars and two visual displays are provided, the infant can be taught a discrimination task. For example, if one display is a grating and the other a homogeneous field, measurements can be made of acuity or the CSF. To date, the youngest ages at which we have been able to collect such data in our laboratory have been 4–5 weeks after birth.

The advantages of using the operant method are:

1. It can be easily automated allowing one to collect data around the clock from each infant without an experimenter being present.

2. It uses a learned motor response that can also be used in testing adults. This allows infants and adults to be tested with the same procedure.

There are two main disadvantages of the operant method. First, it cannot be used to test infants during the first few weeks after birth. This problem can be minimized, as described earlier, by testing infants with a combination of operant methods and methods requiring no prior training. Second, the operant method requires a learned motor response, and control over the infant's food supply, which cannot be used with human infants. However, operant methods suitable for use with human infants have been developed recently (Mayer & Dobson,

1980). This allows a comparison of results obtained across species with a learned operant response, although the methods are not identical (see Section IV.C).

C. Special Rearing Methods

Parallel behavioral experiments using the methods described in previous sections can be conducted on infant monkeys and infant humans to demonstrate that normal development is similar in the two species. This establishes the efficacy of the monkey as an animal model. Then the model can be used for complementary experiments (i.e., experiments that could not be conducted on human infants). One important class of such complementary experiments is one that involves special rearing conditions.

An important developmental question is whether spatial vision of adults is influenced by the properties of the visual input present during early rearing. This question can be studied within the animal model by rearing infant monkeys under conditions in which the spatial properties of the visual input can be exactly specified and carefully controlled.

A severe form of spatial pattern deprivation is dark rearing, in which the infant is allowed no visual input. This rearing method of course deprives infants of more than just spatial or patterned information. Some results obtained from dark reared infant monkeys are presented in Section VI.A.

A widely used method for depriving animals of spatial patterns without depriving them of all visual input is lid suturing (von Noorden, Dowling, & Ferguson, 1970). The lids act as diffusers, allowing little or no pattern to be transmitted to the retina. This is an effective method for depriving a developing organism of contrast information at all spatial frequencies. However, an important limitation of this method is that individual animals have differing amounts of fur on their eyelids that produces varying amounts of light loss along with the loss of spatial information.

Optical defocus can also be used to selectively deprive an organism of high spatial frequencies. This has been achieved in kittens by using a minus (concave) lens in front of one eye (Eggers & Blakemore, 1978), or by using a cycloplegic drug to relax accommodation and increase pupil size (Ikeda & Tremain, 1978). In monkeys, defocus has been achieved by removing the lens from the eye (von Noorden & Crawford, 1977) or by using a cycloplegic (Boothe, Kiorpes & Hendrickson, 1981). Results obtained from infant monkeys reared under conditions of defocus are discussed in Section VI.D.

In the last decade, several experiments have been conducted on cats using a rearing condition that selectively deprives the organism of contours in some orientations. This has been achieved by fixing the position of a striped pattern in relation to the head by forcing the animal to wear goggles (Hirsch & Spinelli, 1971); by rearing the animal in a cylinder with stripes of a particular orientation painted on the walls (Blakemore & Cooper, 1970) or by forcing the animal to view the world while looking through cylindrical lenses (Cynader & Mitchell, 1977; Freeman & Pettigrew, 1973). The crucial importance of careful stimulus and behavioral control in such studies is attested to by controversies in the literature apparently caused by differences in rearing conditions (Blasdel, Mitchell, Muir, & Pettigrew, 1977; Stryker & Sherk, 1975; Stryker, Sherk, Leventhal, & Hirsch, 1978). Results from studies with monkeys are discussed in Section VI.C.

Another kind of special rearing that, under certain conditions, can lead to a loss of sensitivity to high spatial frequencies is a surgically induced strabismus. It has been demonstrated that this leads to poor acuity in one or both eyes in cats (Jacobson & Ikeda, 1979) and monkeys (von Noorden & Dowling, 1970; von Noorden, 1973; Kiorpes & Boothe, 1980). It is not immediately obvious that this strabismic amblyopia is related to deprivation of high spatial frequencies, as both eyes presumably have normal optics. However, it has been hypothesized that the amblyopia following strabismic rearing is due to the lack of well-focused images in the fovea of the nonfixating eye during development (Ikeda, 1979; Ikeda & Tremain, 1978).

It is known that normal human infants use fixation patterns that selectively scan across contours (Salapatek & Kessen, 1966; Salapatek, 1968). Because contours contain high spatial frequency information, normal eye movements may function to ensure that the fovea is exposed to high spatial frequencies. In a strabismic animal, the nonfixating eye will be exposed to high spatial frequencies (edges) only by chance, rather than being able to seek them out continuously as the normal fixating eye does. This deprivation of high spatial frequencies in the nonfixating eye could be the cause of the abnormal development of spatial vision in that eye. Behavioral results from strabismic monkeys are discussed in Section VI.B.

All of the special rearing methods just described can be carried out effectively with infant monkeys by using the face mask cage apparatus described in Section III.B. This cage is constructed with a face mask on one wall with eye holes through which the infant looks out of the cage while its face is in the mask. Infrared emitting diodes and photodetectors can be used to detect the presence of the infants face in the mask. The cage itself can be kept in a dark room and the room lights kept off except when the face is in the mask. In this way, all visual experience is restricted to that obtained while looking through the eye holes in the mask. Dark rearing can be maintained by never turning the room lights on. Optical diffusion or defocus can be controlled in one or both eyes by placing appropriate diffusers or lenses in front of the eye holes. Viewing distance can be controlled by painting the dark room black and having all light come from a visual display at a fixed distance from the face mask. As the head cannot rotate while in the face mask, it is possible to present contours only in particular orientations or to defocus contours in particular orientations by placing cylindrical lenses in front of the eye holes. The optical effects of strabismus can be mimicked by placing prisms in front of the eye holes.

As infant monkeys can be trained to perform an operant task while in this cage, it is possible to train and test behaviorally during the rearing period rather than be forced to wait until the end of the special rearing to start behavioral testing. This allows us to conduct true development studies of abnormal development rather than to look only at the results of abnormal development after the period of deprivation. This special rearing cage also minimizes the problems of emergence trauma that are commonly encountered at the termination of the special rearing period. The animals never have to leave their home cages. At the end of the special rearing period, the special lenses are just removed from the front of the eye holes. In fact, it is easy to change, remove, or replace lenses or to alter the stimulus display repeatedly throughout the rearing period.

IV. NORMAL DEVELOPMENT OF ACUITY

A. Results Obtained with OKN

Ordy *et al.* (1965) used the OKN response to obtain an estimate of acuity in eight infant rhesus macaque monkeys. The infants were tested each day during the first 30 days after birth using four stripe widths subtending 36, 18, 9, and 4.5 minutes of visual angle. A positive response was recorded if OKN movements were seen on at least 8 out of 10 trials of drum rotation. Ordy *et al.* (1964) also used the same procedure to test 46 human infants. Examination of the Ordy *et al.* data indicates that their monkeys reached criterion to the 36 and 18 min stripes during the first week, the 9 min stripes by 2 weeks, and the 4.5 min stripes by 4 weeks. For human infants, criterion was reached to the 36 min stripes during the first month, the 18 min stripes by 2 months, the 9 min stripes by 4 months, and the 4.5 min stripes by 6 months.

B. Results Obtained with FPL

Teller *et al.* (1978) used the FPL method to measure grating acuity in 28 pigtail macaque infants ranging in age from 1 to 5 weeks. Lee and Boothe (1981) used the same FPL procedure to measure acuity in an additional 24 infant pigtails over the same age range. The best FPL estimate to date of the postnatal development of acuity in infant macaque monkeys can be obtained by combining the results of these two studies for a total of 52 infants. The results of these combined data, grouped according to age in weeks, are plotted in Fig. 7.1a with the circle symbols. Bars indicate + or − one standard error of the mean. These FPL acuity estimates show a gradual improvement from about 16 min of arc at 1 week to about 5 min at 5 weeks. There is reasonably close agreement between these results and those obtained by Ordy *et al.* (1965) with OKN.

Human infant data obtained with the FPL procedure (Allen, 1978) are shown by the circles in Fig. 7.1b. These human acuity estimates also show gradual improvement from about 32 min of arc at 2 weeks of age to about 5 min of arc at 6 months. These results are also in reasonably close agreement with those reported by Ordy *et al.* (1964) with OKN.

C. Results Obtained with Operant Methods

Ordy *et al.* (1965) trained five infant monkeys to discriminate horizontal from vertical stripes using a two-choice runway task. The infants were trained with fat stripe widths and then tested on successively narrower stripe widths to a criterion of 21 correct responses out of 25 trials for three consecutive days. The ages at which their five infants met criterion to stripes subtending 1 min of arc were 6, 7, 14, 18, and 19 weeks after birth.

Operant estimates of acuity have also been obtained for infant monkeys by using the face mask cage method (Boothe & Lee, 1980). When the infant looked out through the eye holes in the face mask it saw a visual display consisting of two cathode ray tube screens surrounded by an electroluminescent panel providing a uniform background field. The infant's task was to reach out and pull either a right or left grab

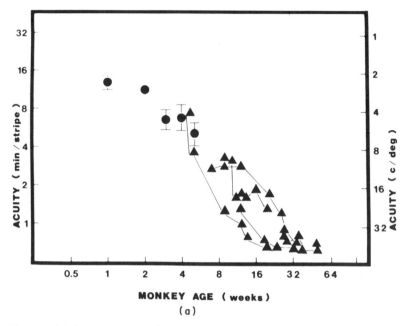

Fig. 7.1 (a) Acuity estimates obtained from infant monkeys with two separate methods are shown as a function of age in weeks. (b) Acuity estimates obtained from infant humans with two separate methods are shown as a function of age in weeks. Age in years is also indicated on top abscissa. Left-hand ordinate indicates acuity values in terms

bar corresponding to the position of a grating produced on one of the two display screens.

The procedure for estimating acuity was first to measure contrast sensitivity at a number of spatial frequencies using spatial sinusoidal patterns. The contrast sensitivity function obtained from these measurements was fit with an exponential function using a least squares criterion. This best fitting function was then extrapolated to 100% contrast at the high-frequency end, and this cut-off used as an estimate of acuity. (Results of contrast sensitivity at lower spatial frequencies are described in Section V). These operant acuity estimates for single infants as a function of age are shown by the filled triangles in Fig. 7.1a. Symbols connected by straight lines indicate repeated measures from the same infant. These operant results provide acuity estimates of about 5 min of arc at 5 weeks out to adult asymptotic levels of about 0.5 min at 30 weeks.

For comparison purposes, acuity data from human infants tested with an operant technique (Mayer, 1980; Mayer & Dobson, 1980) are

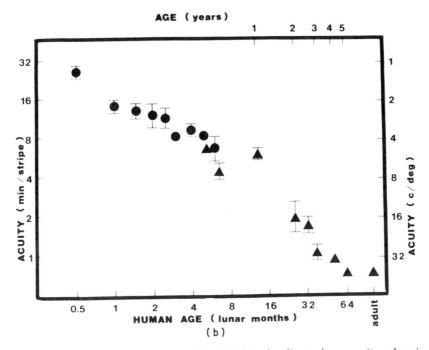

of minutes of visual angle per stripe width. Right-hand ordinate shows acuity values in terms of grating cycles per degree of visual angle. FPL estimates are indicated by ●. Estimates obtained with an operant testing method are represented by ▲.

shown by the triangle symbols in Fig. 7.1b. These human operant acuity estimates range from about 5 min of arc at 5 months after birth to about 0.5 min at 5 years.

D. The Postnatal Time Course of Acuity Development

Figures 7.1a and b summarize the time course of the development of acuity in infant monkeys and infant humans, respectively, as assessed by two methods (FPL and operant). The sequence of development is remarkably similar in the two species, with both showing a monotonic improvement in acuity from birth to adulthood. Moreover, the absolute level of acuity was very similar at birth and in adulthood in the two species. In fact, the time courses can be made the same by multiplying the monkey age axis by about a factor of four (i.e., by converting weeks to months). As a useful mnemonic device, acuity can be specified in cycles/degree (see the right-hand scale in Fig. 7.1). Then infant monkey acuity is approximately equal to age in weeks, whereas infant human acuity is approximately equal to age in months.

Note that both acuity and age are plotted on a log scale. It appears that, as a first approximation, acuity development in octaves improves approximately constantly with log age from 2 to 36 weeks in monkeys and from 2 to 36 months in humans, at which time acuity approaches adult levels. Westheimer (1979) has argued that the most appropriate scale for acuity is logarithmic rather than linear. This is because constant changes in detectability as determined psychophysically are more nearly associated with constant increments on a log scale than on a linear scale. By the same argument, the data shown in Figs. 7.1a and 7.1b may suggest that, for developmental studies of spatial vision, the most appropriate age scale is logarithmic rather than linear. On a linear age scale, a constant amount of acuity development will be associated with different amounts of time at different ages. On a log scale, however, acuity development will be associated with more nearly constant increments. Experiments concerned with measuring sensitive or critical periods should keep these implications in mind.

Finally, examination of the data in Figs. 7.1a and b and comparison of these results to those obtained by Ordy et al. (1964, 1965) reveal that within the range of ages when acuity can be estimated by more than one method, there is good agreement of results across methods. Individual differences between infants tested with the same method at a given age are always as large or larger than differences between results obtained by the different methods.

E. Comparison of Postnatal and Post-Term Results

All studies of the postnatal development of acuity have found a moderate amount of variability in acuity values among infants of the same postnatal age. One possible source of this variability is individual differences in gestational age. Casual observation of individual infant monkeys having the same postnatal age reveals large differences in physical size and maturation, as demonstrated in Fig. 7.2. To evaluate the contribution of these gestational age differences on acuity development, Lee and Boothe (1981) measured acuity in 24 pigtail macaque infants having known gestational ages. Acuity measurements were made with the FPL method during the first 6 postnatal weeks on this group. During this early period of development, a significant amount of acuity variance may be accounted for by the assumption that the relation between postnatal age and log acuity is linear. However, if the data are replotted as a function of post-term age, there is a dramatic

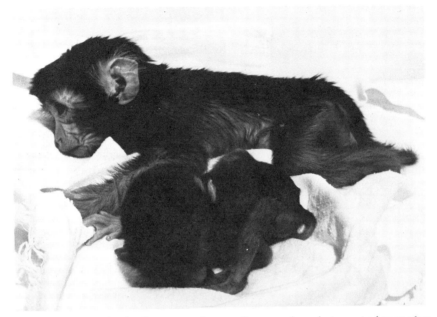

Fig. 7.2 Two male pigtail macaques born on the same day, photographed soon after birth. The infant shown on top weighed 750 gm at birth; the smaller infant's birthweight was only 240 gm.

and significant reduction in the amount of residual variability in the post-term as opposed to the postnatal plot. Whereas the postnatal regression line can account for only 12% of the acuity variance, the post-term regression line can account for 71%. It is obvious from these results that gestational age is an important determinant of acuity during development.

These results have important implications for special rearing studies that are almost always limited to small numbers of subjects. Variability in acuity values from animal to animal in such studies can be reduced by selecting subjects with similar gestational ages. It is not necessary to have timed matings to have accurate estimates of gestational ages. Highly accurate estimates can be obtained by taking X-ray photographs of the infants' bone development (Fahrenbruch, Burbacher, & Sackett, 1979; Newell-Morris, 1979).

From a theoretical point of view, the finding that acuity is closely related to gestational age is not surprising. Several structural factors such as eye size and inter-receptor spacing place limitations on acuity. These structural factors are probably determined primarily by physical maturation and little influenced by visual experience.

V. NORMAL DEVELOPMENT OF CONTRAST SENSITIVITY

A. Developmental Changes in the Shape of the CSF

Data presented in Section IV have demonstrated that acuity improves dramatically during the postnatal period. Another interesting question is how this development of acuity is related to the development of the overall contrast sensitivity function. There are a number of possible changes in the CSF that would result in improved acuity. Three of these are illustrated in Fig. 7.3a. The data points are contrast sensitivity data from a typical adult monkey. The smooth curve drawn through the data points is an exponential function that we have found adequately fits the adult CSF data from our laboratory (Williams, Boothe, Kiorpes, & Teller, 1981). The high-frequency cut-off on this function extrapolates to a predicted acuity value near 40 c/deg. Three changes

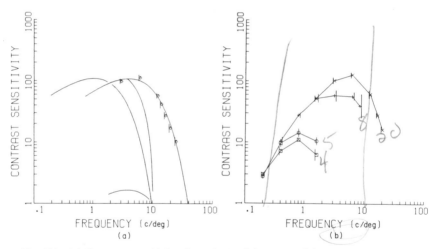

Fig. 7.3 (a) Contrast sensitivity data obtained from an adult macaque monkey are shown by ◇. Vertical bars next to each data point indicate plus and minus one standard error. The smooth curve that passes through the data points is a best fitting exponential (see text). This best fitting adult curve extrapolates to about 40 c/deg at the abscissa. Three other smooth curves are shown illustrating changes in the adult function that would result in decreased acuity values (all three curves pass through approximately 10 c/deg on the abscissa). These three curves were obtained by shifting the adult function vertically, or laterally, or by increasing the steepness of the high-frequency fall-off, respectively. (b) Contrast sensitivity data are shown for a single infant monkey tested at four separate ages. Data obtained at 4 weeks are indicated by □; at 5 weeks by ○; at 8 weeks by +; and at 20 weeks by ×. Data points obtained at the same age have been connected by straight lines. Vertical bars through or next to each data point indicate plus and minus one standard error.

in the adult CSF that would result in lower acuity values are demonstrated in Fig. 7.3a:

1. A simple vertical shift is shown that leads to a uniform change in sensitivity at all spatial frequencies along with a decrement in acuity.

2. A simple lateral shift is illustrated in which the spatial frequency of peak sensitivity changes but peak sensitivity itself remains constant.

3. A change in steepness of the high frequency fall-off is illustrated in which nonuniform changes in sensitivity occur over the high-frequency range.

These three changes illustrated in Fig. 7.3a all involve simple parametric manipulation of the normal adult function. A more complicated kind of change (not shown) would involve a shift to a different underlying function than the exponential that fits the normal adult data.

If development were to follow one of these simple kinds of changes, it would provide some clues about possible underlying physiological mechanisms. Vertical shifts are associated with changes in overall sensitivity to contrast, and could be produced by factors such as changes in the amount of center–surround antagonism. Lateral shifts are associated with changes in size and could be produced by simple growth (e.g., changes in optical magnification or growth of receptive field sizes). The high-frequency attenuation is caused by a combination of optical and neural factors (Campbell & Green, 1965) and so could be influenced by developmental changes in either.

To examine the adequacy of these simple models of CSF development, contrast sensitivity data have been obtained longitudinally from several infant monkeys at a number of different ages (Boothe, Williams, Kiorpes, & Teller, 1980; Williams & Boothe, 1979). Representative data from one infant are shown in Fig. 7.3b. These developmental data are not consistent with the simple changes, 1. or 2. alone. In addition, the CSF at each age can be reasonably well fit by changing the parameters of the adult function and therefore the fourth change, (not shown) is not necessary to describe the developmental data. As a first approximation, all of the CSFs can be modeled by a combination of changes 1. and 2.; (i.e., by a combination of vertical and lateral shifts). At present, we do not have enough data to decide whether changes of the type described under 3. (steepness of the high-frequency attenuation) are also present.

B. Evaluation of Optical Factors Influencing the CSF

These changes in the CSF during development could be totally or partially determined by changes in the eye's optics. It must be kept in

mind that the CSF plots sensitivity to the contrast in the physical stimulus as a function of spatial frequency. A decreased sensitivity for an
infant compared to an adult could reflect a decreased sensitivity of the
organism's nervous system to contrast at that frequency, or it could be
due to the fact that the eye's optics are poorer, resulting in less contrast
in the retinal image. To study changes due to neural processing, it
would be necessary to specify CSFs in terms of image contrast at the
level of the retinal image. Retinal image contrast can be determined if
the modulation transfer function of the eye's optics is known (i.e., how
well various spatial frequencies are passed through the eye's optics to
the retina).

Estimates of the optical modulation transfer function of an eye can
be obtained experimentally by measuring the light distribution in the
aerial image produced by the fundal reflection of a thin luminous line
focused upon the retina (Campbell & Gubisch, 1966; Krauskopf, 1962;
Westheimer & Campbell, 1962). The optical modulation transfer function of the eye is then derived via Fourier transformation of this measured light distribution (corrected for double passage through the
optics).

Williams and Boothe (1981) used the double pass method to measure
optical quality in infant macaque monkeys ranging in age from 2 days
to 9 months. Two main points emerge from our results. First, while
optical quality is good at birth, small age changes are present, and
adult-like optics do not emerge until several weeks after birth. Second,
optical development seems to precede neural development by such a
large factor that changes in optical quality probably have little effect
on the development of acuity or contrast sensitivity.

VI. EFFECTS OF EARLY VISUAL EXPERIENCE

A. Dark Rearing and Total Pattern Deprivation

Regal, Boothe, Teller, and Sackett (1976) reared macaque monkeys
in the dark for either 3 or 6 months. When the monkeys emerged from
the dark rearing period, they appeared, on the basis of informal observation, to be blind. These monkeys were tested with a battery of
tests designed to measure visual responsiveness, and at first these
animals appeared to be nonresponsive. For example, they would not
blink or try to avoid an impending collision. However, when their
spatial vision was assessed by measuring visual acuity with the FPL
method, these animals were found to have spatial resolution between

2.5 and 7.5 c/deg. Control monkeys tested at the same age with this method had acuity values around 15 c/deg. This reveals that the animals' spatial resolution was impaired by only one or two octaves and suggests that dark rearing is more harmful to visual responsiveness than to spatial resolution. There was no improvement in acuity during periods of up to 3 months of normal light exposure, but the visual responsiveness of several of the animals improved with time in the light.

Riesen, Ramsey, and Wilson (1964) deprived infant rhesus monkeys of pattern vision for 20 or 60 days by a combination of dark rearing and use of diffusing contact lenses. These monkeys showed effects on visual responsiveness and on acuity similar to those reported by Regal *et al.* (1976). Some recovery of acuity was found following these short deprivation periods, but acuity was not tested with stripe widths narrower than 7.5 c/deg, so it is not known whether acuity eventually reached normal adult levels.

In contrast to these rather mild effects of dark rearing and binocular pattern deprivation on spatial vision, the effects of monocular lid suture on infant monkeys are severe. This is presumably because of some mechanism involving binocular competition (Guillery & Stelzner, 1970; Hubel & Wiesel, 1965). Von Noorden, Dowling, and Ferguson (1970) and von Noorden (1973) report that monkeys with monocular lid suture during the first 1 or 2 years after birth demonstrate little or no pattern vision when tested with the deprived eye. To be effective, the lid suture must be instituted during the first 12 weeks after birth. This indicates that the visual system is more sensitive to disruptions of normal binocular patterned input during the first few months after birth than it is later in life. Even short periods of monocular lid suture during the period of maximum sensitivity are sufficient to cause severe amblyopia. von Noorden (1973) reports little or no recovery of pattern vision in the deprived eye even after extended periods of reverse suture.

Hendrickson, Boles, and McLean (1977) reported similar severe effects of monocular lid suture continued during the first 10–12 months after birth in infant monkeys. However, they found some recovery following several months of reverse suture. The reverse sutured animals eventually attained acuity values of 10–14 c/deg. Hendrickson *et al.* also found that placing a central lesion in the nondeprived retina speeded up recovery of spatial vision in the deprived eye.

B. Strabismic Amblyopia

von Noorden and Dowling (1970) utilized an experimental paradigm that involves surgically producing a strabismus in a monkey at an early age and then testing for amblyopia a year or more later. They demonstrated that an esotropia (cross eyed strabismus) produced during the first three months after birth leads to an amblyopia, whereas, if the surgery is conducted at older ages, no amblyopia occurs. This indicates that the period of susceptibility for an amblyopia produced by a deviation of the eye is similar to that for amblyopia produced by lid suture.

These experiments did not examine the time course for the development of amblyopia, but only tested older animals to demonstrate that an amblyopia had been produced. Kiorpes and Boothe (1980) examined the time course for the development of an amblyopia following a surgically induced esotropia. The developmental time course is interesting because acuity is in an immature state at the time the esotropia is induced. Therefore, the esotropia may lead to the adult amblyopia by disrupting the normal development of acuity in the deviated eye. For example, acuity could be arrested at its level at the time of the surgery. Alternatively, the deviated eye might develop normally to adult levels and then deteriorate to amblyopic levels. Kiorpes and Boothe found that the esotropia did disrupt the normal development of acuity in the deviated eye. However, it did not do so with a simple arrest of development. Both eyes showed normal acuity development for at least 4 weeks after the onset of the esotropia. Then there was a disruption of the normal pattern of acuity development, with the deviated eye following a different time course from that of the normal fixating eye.

C. Meridional Amblyopia

Boothe and Teller (1978; 1981) reared infant monkeys in a face mask cage under conditions in which their entire visual experience was limited to that obtained while looking through a +6 diopter cylindrical lens with horizontal axis. Viewing conditions were arranged so that the monkey could bring vertical contours into good focus by accommodating but could never bring horizontal contours into good focus.

These monkeys developed horizontal–vertical differences in acuity and contrast sensitivity. The direction of the effect could be predicted on the basis of the axis of defocus, and the magnitude of the effect was similar to that expected on the basis of the estimated defocus. These results support the hypothesis that exposure to high spatial frequencies (well-focused input) is necessary for normal development of contrast sensitivity to those high frequencies. The effect appears to be both orientation and spatial frequency dependent (i.e., only those spatial frequencies and orientations that were defocused were affected.

D. Defocus

Additional evidence about the necessity of high spatial frequency exposure during development for contrast sensitivity to develop normally for high frequencies comes from studies of monkeys reared with atropine given daily to one eye (Boothe, et al., 1981). The atropine causes defocus due to (a) spherical and chromatic aberration associated with large pupil sizes; and (b) lack of an ability to accommodate to overcome the hypermetropia normally found in young monkeys. To assess the amount of defocus produced by this rearing condition, CSFs were obtained from both the normal and atropinized eye during development. At the end of the rearing period, both eyes were tested with correcting lenses in place. The results were similar to those obtained with the meridional amblyopic monkeys described in the previous section except that differences are now between the two eyes instead of between orientations in the same eye. The animals show a loss of sensitivity to those spatial frequencies that were defocused during rearing.

All of the special rearing studies reviewed in this chapter have involved uniform loss of spatial frequencies (dark rearing and lid suture) or selective loss of high spatial frequencies (strabismus and defocus). Both kinds of rearing conditions produce loss of sensitivity to high frequencies (acuity loss). The defocus experiments appear to produce a nonuniform loss of contrast sensitivity that is, at least qualitatively, similar to the relative magnitude of the defocus across spatial frequencies. Measurements of contrast sensitivity at low and middle frequencies have not been reported for lid sutured primates. It would be interesting to see if the loss of spatial input at low and middle frequencies in this rearing condition causes corresponding changes in the contrast sensitivity function. It would also be interesting to see the effects of depriving a monkey of low or middle frequencies while leaving high spatial frequencies normal. Such studies have not been reported to date.

VII. SUMMARY AND CONCLUSIONS

The infant macaque monkey appears to be an excellent model for studying the development of human spatial vision. Adults of the two species have nearly identical acuity and contrast sensitivity, and they both appear to follow the same developmental sequence. In fact, their relative time courses for acuity development can be almost superimposed by making simple shifts and compressions on one of the age axes.

/ A number of useful methodologies have been developed for conducting special rearing experiments with this animal model and for assessing its visual behavioral capabilities. Behavioral studies reported to date with this animal model have demonstrated that the development of spatial vision is influenced by a combination of genetic and experiential factors. For example, acuity development in normally reared monkeys is more highly correlated with gestational than postnatal age. This indicates that within some normal range of visual environments, acuity is determined primarily by physical maturation. However, a number of special rearing studies have been reviewed that demonstrate that the visual environment present during early rearing can influence the development of spatial vision. For example, there is an accumulating amount of evidence that primates must be exposed to high spatial frequencies during early rearing to develop the capacity to respond to these same spatial frequencies as adults. These studies have important implications for theoretical reasons, and also clinically, where abnormal development of spatial vision can lead to amblyopia.

ACKNOWLEDGMENTS

Preparation of this manuscript and support of some of the unpublished studies cited in this chapter were provided by National Institutes of Health grants EY0202510 to R. B., RR00166 to the Regional Primate Research Center, NICHD02274 to the Washington Regional Child Development and Mental Retardation Center, and EY01730 to the Interdisciplinary Vision and Ophthalmic Research Center at the University of Washington.

I thank Davida Y. Teller for continuing support and collaboration in the research from our laboratories described in this chapter. Rick Williams, Lynne Kiorpes, and Clifton Lee have also collaborated fully on many of these projects as well as providing valuable comments on the manuscript. Tom Burbacher kindly provided the photograph shown in Fig. 7.2.

REFERENCES

Allen, J. L. Visual acuity development in human infants up to 6 months of age. Unpublished Doctoral Dissertation, University of Washington, Seattle, Washington, 1978.

Atkinson, J., Braddick, O., & Moar, K. Development of contrast sensitivity over the first 3 months of life in the human infant. *Vision Research*, 1977, **7**, 1037–1044.

Banks, M. S., & Salapatek, P. Contrast sensitivity function of the infant visual system. *Vision Research*, 1976, **16**, 867–869.

Banks, M. S., & Salapatek, P. Acuity and contrast sensitivity on 1-, 2-, and 3-month-old human infants. *Investigative Ophthalmology and Visual Science* 1978, **17**, 361–365.

Blakemore, C., & Cooper, G. Development of the brain depends on the visual environment. *Nature*, 1970, **228**, 477–478.

Blasdel, G. G., Mitchell, D. E., Muir, D. W., Pettigrew, J. D. A physiological and behavioural study in cats of the effect of early visual experience with contours of a single orientation. *Journal of Physiology*, 1977, **265**, 615–636.

Boothe, R., & Lee, C. The development of acuity in infant macaque monkeys having known gestational ages. *Supplement to Investigative Ophthalmology, ARVO Abstracts*, 1980, 10.

Boothe, R., & Sackett, G. P. Perception and learning in infant rhesus monkeys. In G. Bourne (Ed.), *The rhesus monkey* (Vol. 1). New York: Academic Press, 1975. Pp. 344–362.

Boothe, R., Kiorpes, L., & Hendrickson, A. Anisometropic amblyopia in *Macaca nemestrina* monkeys produced by atropinization of one eye during development. *Investigative Ophthalmology and Visual Science*, 1981, in press.

Boothe, R., & Teller, D. Y. Meridional amblyopia in monkeys reared with astigmatic lenses. *Supplement to Investigative Ophthalmology, ARVO Abstracts*, 1978, 272.

Boothe, R., & Teller, D. Y. Meridional variations in acuity and CSFs in monkeys *(Macaca nemestrina)* reared with externally applied astigmatism. Submitted to *Vision Research*, 1981.

Boothe, R., Teller, D. Y., & Sackett, G. P. Trichromacy in normally reared and light deprived infant monkeys *(Macaca nemestrina)*. *Vision Research*, 1975, **15**, 1187–1191.

Boothe, R., Williams, R., Kiorpes, L., & Teller, D. Y. Development of contrast sensitivity in infant *Macaca nemestrina* monkeys. *Science*, 1980, **208**, 1290–1292.

Boycott, B., & Dowling, J. E. Organization of the primate retina: light microscopy. *Philosophical Transactions of the Royal Society B*, 1969, **255**, 109–184.

Campbell, F. W., & Gubisch, R. W. Optical quality of the human eye. *Journal of Physiology*, 1966, **186**, 558–578.

Campbell, F. W., & Robson, J. Application of Fourier analysis to the visibility of gratings. *Journal of Physiology*, 1968, **197**, 551–556.

Campbell, F. W., & Green, D. G. Optical and retinal factors affecting visual resolution. *Journal of Physiology*, 1965, **181**, 576–598.

Cynader, M., & Mitchell, D. Monocular astigmatism effects on kitten visual cortex development. *Nature*, 1977, **270**, 177–178.

DeValois, R. L., Morgan, H. C., & Snodderly, D. M. Psychophysical studies of monkey vision III. Spatial luminance contrast sensitivity tests of macaque and human observers. *Vision Research*, 1974, **14**, 75–82.

Dobson, V., & Teller, D. Y. Visual acuity in human infants: A review and comparison of behavioral and electrophysiological studies. *Vision Research*, 1978, **18**, 1469–1483.

Eggers, H. M., & Blakemore, C. Physiological basis of anisometropic amblyopia. *Science*, 1978, **201**, 264–267.

Fahrenbruch, C. E., Burbacher, T. M., & Sackett, G. P. Assessment of skeletal growth and maturation of premature and term *Macaca nemestrina*. In G. Ruppenthal & D. Reese (Eds.), *Nursery care of nonhuman primates*. New York: Plenum, 1979. pp. 79–91.

Fantz, R. L. Visual perception and experience in early infancy: A look at the hidden side of behavior development. In H. Stevenson, E. Hess, & H. Rheingold (Eds.), *Early behavior: Comparative and developmental approaches.* New York: Wiley, 1967. pp. 181–224.

Freeman, R. D., & Pettigrew, J. D. Alteration of visual cortex from environmental asymmetries. *Nature,* 1973, **246,** 359–360.

Guillery, R. W., & Stelzner, D. J. The differential effects of unilateral lid closure upon the monocular and binocular segments of the dorsal lateral geniculate nucleus in the cat. *Journal of Comparative Neurology,* 1970, **139,** 413–422.

Hendrickson, A., Boles, J., & McLean, E. Visual acuity and behavior of monocularly deprived monkeys after retinal lesions. *Investigative Ophthalmology and Visual Science,* 1977, **16,** 469–473.

Hirsch, H. V. B., & Spinelli, D. N. Modification of the distribution of receptive field orientation in cats by selected visual exposure during development. *Experimental Brain Research,* 1971, **13,** 509–527.

Hubel, D. H., & Wiesel, T. N. Binocular interaction in striate cortex of kittens reared with artificial squint. *Journal of Neurophysiology,* 1965, **28,** 1041–1059.

Ikeda, H. Physiological basis of amblyopia. *Trends in Neuroscience,* 1979, **8,** 209–212.

Ikeda, H., & Tremain, K. E. Amblyopia resulting from penalisation: Neurophysiological studies of kittens reared with atropinisation of one or both eyes. *British Journal of Ophthalmology,* 1978, **62,** 1–8.

Jacobson, S. G., & Ikeda, H. Behavioral studies of spatial vision in cats reared with convergent squint: Is amblyopia due to arrest of development? *Experimental Brain Research,* 1979, **34,** 11–26.

Kaas, J. H., Huerta, M. F., Weber, J. T., & Harting, J. K. Patterns of retinal terminations and laminar organization of the lateral geniculate nucleus of primates. *Journal of Comparative Neurology,* 1978, **182,**

Kiorpes, L., & Boothe, R. The time course for the development of strabismic amblyopia in infant monkeys *(Macaca nemestrina). Investigative Ophthalmology and Visual Science,* 1980, **19,** 841–845.

Krauskopf, J. Light distribution in human retinal images. *Journal of the Optical Society of America,* 1962, **52,** 1046–1050.

Lee, C. P., & Boothe, R. Visual acuity development in infant monkeys *(Macaca nemestrina)* having known gestational ages. *Vision Research,* 1981, in press.

Mayer, D. L. Development of visual acuity in humans from infancy to early childhood as measured by a new operant technique. *Supplement to Investigative Ophthalmology and Visual Science, ARVO Abstracts,* 1980, 10.

Mayer, D. L., & Dobson, V. Assessment of vision in young children: A new operant approach yields estimates of acuity. *Investigative Ophthalmology and Visual Science,* 1980, **19,** 566–570.

Newell-Morris, L. Age determination in macaque fetus and neonates. In G. Ruppenthal & D. Reese (Eds.), *Nursery care of non-human primates.* New York: Plenum, 1979. Pp. 93–115.

Ordy, J. M., Latanick, A., Samorajlki, T., & Massopust, L. C. Visual acuity in newborn primate infants. *Proceedings of the Society of Experimental Biology and Medicine,* 1964, **115,** 677–680.

Ordy, J. M., Samorajski, T. S., Collins, R. L., & Nagy, A. R. Postnatal development of vision in a subhuman primate *(Macaca mulatta). Archives of Ophthalmology,* 1965, **73,** 674–686.

Polyak, S. *The vertebrate visual system.* Chicago: University of Chicago Press, 1957.

Regal, D. M., Boothe, R., Teller, D. Y., & Sackett, G. P. Visual acuity and visual responsiveness in dark reared monkeys *(Macaca nemestrina)*. *Vision Research*, 1976, **16**, 523–530.

Riesen, A. H., Ramsey, R. L., & Wilson, P. Development of visual acuity in rhesus monkeys deprived of patterned light during early infancy. *Psychonomic Science*, 1964, **1**, 33–34.

Sackett, G. P., Tripp, R., Milbrath, C., Gluck, J., & Pick, H. A method for studying visually guided perception and learning in newborn macaques. *Behavioral Research Methods and Instrumentation*, 1971, **3**, 233–236.

Salapatek, P. Visual scanning of geometric figures by the human newborn. *Journal of Comparative and Physiological Psychology*, 1968, **66**, 247–258.

Salapatek, P., & Kessen, W. Visual scanning of triangles by the human newborn. *Journal of Experimental Child Psychology*, 1966, **3**, 155–167.

Schade, O. Optical and photoelectric analog of the eye. *Journal of the Optical Society of America*, 1956, **46**, 721–739.

Sherman, S. M. The functional significance of X- and Y-cells in normal and visually deprived cats. *Trends in Neuroscience*, 1979, **8**, 192–195.

Stryker, M. P., & Sherk, H. A. Modification of cortical orientation selectivity in the cat by restricted visual experience: A re-examination. *Science*, 1975, **190**, 903–906.

Stryker, M. P., Sherk, H. A., Leventhal, A. G., & Hirsch, H. V. B. Physiological consequences for the cat's visual cortex of effectively restricting early visual experience with oriented contours. *Journal of Neurophysiology*, 1978, **41**, 896–908.

Teller, D. Y. The forced-choice preferential looking procedure: A psychophysical technique for use with human infants. *Infant Behavior and Development*, 1979, **2**, 135–153.

Teller, D. Y., Morse, R., Borton, R., & Regal, D. Visual acuity for vertical and diagonal gratings in human infants. *Vision Research*, 1974, **14**, 1433–1439.

Teller, D. Y., Regal, D., Videen, T., & Pulos, E. Development of visual acuity in infant monkeys *(Macaca nemestrina)* during the early postnatal weeks. *Vision Research*, 1978, **18**, 561–566.

Van Essen, D. C. Visual areas of the mammalian cerebral cortex. *Annual Review of Neuroscience*, 1979, **2**, 227–263.

von Noorden, G. K. *Burian-von Noorden's binocular vision and ocular motility*. St. Louis: C. V. Mosby, 1980.

von Noorden, G. K. Experimental amblyopia in monkeys. Further behavioral observations and clinical correlations. *Investigative Ophthalmology and Visual Science*, 1973, **12**, 721–726.

von Noorden, G. K., & Crawford, M. L. J. Form deprivation without light deprivation produces the visual deprivation syndrome in *Macaca mulatta*. *Brain Research*, 1977, **129**, 37–44.

von Noorden, G. K., & Dowling, J. E. Experimental amblyopia in monkeys II. Behavioral studies in strabismus amblyopia. *Archives of Ophthalmology*, 1970, **84**, 215–220.

von Noorden, G. K., Dowling, J. E., & Ferguson, D. C. Experimental amblyopia in monkeys I. Behavioral studies of stimulus deprivation amblyopia. *Archives of Ophthalmology*, 1970, **84**, 206–214.

von Noorden, G. K., & Maumenee, A. E. Clinical observations on stimulus deprivation amblyopia (amblyopia ex anopsia). *American Journal of Ophthalmology*, 1968, **65**, 220–224.

Westheimer, G. Scaling of visual acuity measurements. *Archives of Ophthalmology*, 1979, **97**, 327–330.

Westheimer, G., & Campbell, F. Light distribution in the image formed by the living human eye. *Journal of the Optical Society of America*, 1962, **52**, 1040–1045.

— Williams, R., & Boothe, R. Development of spatial contrast sensitivity in infant *Macaca nemestrina* monkeys. *Supplement to Investigative Ophthalmology and Visual Science, ARVO Abstracts*, 1979, 272.

Williams, R., & Boothe, R. Development of optical quality in the infant monkey (Macaca nemestrina) eye. *Journal of the Optical Society of America*, 1980, in press.

Williams, R., Boothe, R., Kiorpes, L., & Teller, D. Oblique effects in normally reared monkeys *(Macaca nemestrina):* Meridional variations in contrast sensitivity measured with operant techniques. Submitted to *Vision Research*, 1980.

Visual Development in Human Infants

During the past 20 years two separate areas of investigation have emerged within the field of visual development. On the one hand, there have been studies of the neural mechanisms underlying the development of vision (e.g., Hubel & Wiesel, 1977) and, on the other hand, there have been behavioral studies of visual development in human infants (see reviews by Haith, 1978; Salapatek & Banks, 1978). Recently, these two traditions have begun to overlap as neuroscientists verify through behavioral assessment the functional result of neural manipulations, and perceptual psychologists have recognized the benefits of relating their findings from human infants to animal models of visual development. The five chapters in this section cover several of the major issues in the rapidly expanding area of human visual development. Atkinson and Braddick (Chapter 8) describe the development of visual resolution, as well as its constraints, in normal infants. Held (Chapter 9) discusses his recent work on visual resolution in both normal infants and infants suffering from early visual deficits. Teller (Chapter 10) provides a summary of her program of psychophysical studies of color vision in infants. Yonas (Chapter 11) discusses the emergence of behavioral indicators of visually mediated avoidance responses to approaching objects by infants. Finally, Fox (Chapter 12) details his work on stereopsis in human infants as well as several other species. It is in these areas that we can perhaps most easily recognize the value of *integrative* analyses such as those that arise from a "psychobiological perspective."

REFERENCES

Haith, M. M. Visual competence in early infancy. In R. Held, H. Leibowitz and H. L. Teuber (Eds.), *Handbook of sensory physiology*. Volume VIII. New York: Springer-Verlag, 1978.

Hubel, D. H. and Wiesel, T. N. Functional architecture of macaque monkey visual cortex. *Proceedings of the Royal Society of London (Biology)*, 1977, **198**, 1–59.

Salapatek, P. and Banks, M. S. Infant sensory assessment: Vision. In F. D. Minifie and L. L. Lloyd (Eds.), *Communicative and cognitive abilities: early behavioral assessment.* Baltimore, Maryland: University Park Press, 1978.

8

Acuity, Contrast Sensitivity, and Accommodation in Infancy

JANETTE ATKINSON
OLIVER BRADDICK
University of Cambridge

I. INTRODUCTION

Almost every visual perceptual function depends on the visual system transmitting information about the spatial pattern in the incoming optic array. Visual acuity is a measure of the finest detail that is transmitted.

245

DEVELOPMENT OF PERCEPTION
Volume 2

The contrast sensitivity function (Campbell 1974) provides a more complete description of how the visual system transmits spatial information, as it is not restricted to the sensitivity to fine detail that is measured as acuity, but also quantifies the sensitivity to the broader distribution of light and dark in a spatial pattern.

The acuity and contrast sensitivity of infants, therefore, gives us a picture of the information that is available for the infant in gaining information about the visual world and learning the rules that govern it. These measures also provide one of the most direct sources of evidence on how the neural systems serving visual processing develop during infancy. Animal experiments show that the period in early life when acuity develops to its adult value is closely related to the period when the visual system is susceptible to environmental modification (Mitchell, Giffen, Wilkinson, Anderson, & Smith, 1976), and that acuity is a sensitive behavioral index of the changes that can occur in the visual system as a result of visual deprivation (Giffen & Mitchell, 1978). Furthermore, because it is unlikely that the visual system can be modified by stimuli that it cannot detect, the infant's sensitivity to particular components of a spatial pattern may give some indication of what aspects of the visual input could be effective in determining visual development by their presence or absence at a particular age.

The visual spatial information available to the infant does not depend only on transmission by neural pathways. The spatial pattern available for neural encoding is determined by the image-forming properties of the optics of the eye. The image may be blurred (i.e. lack certain pattern information), either because the fixed optical surfaces and dimensions of the eye are not as well matched as they are in the adult, or because the variable component of the optics, the accommodative changes in the shape of the lens that adjust the optical power of the eye for different viewing distances, is not well controlled. In this chapter, we shall first consider the evidence on how the spatial sensitivity of the infant's visual system as a whole—optics and neural pathways—develops. We shall then discuss the part played by optical factors, including the ability to control accommodation, in this development.

II. INFANT ACUITY AND CONTRAST SENSITIVITY: METHODS OF STUDY

A. Preferential Looking

The most widespread method for investigating visual sensitivity in young infants is preferential looking (PL). This method rests on the argument that infants show a preference for fixating a patterned over a blank field, and that the demonstration of this preference for a particular pattern (e.g., a grating of particular spatial frequency and contrast) is evidence that the infant can detect such a pattern. Most modern work has employed the refinement, introduced by Teller, Morse, Borton, and Regal (1974) (see also Teller, 1979), of forced choice by a blind observer (FPL). In FPL, a "psychometric function" can be constructed from the percentage of trials on which the observer, using the infant's fixation and other behavior, correctly chooses the side on which the patterned stimulus was presented. Staircase procedures similar to those of conventional psychophysics can also be used with the FPL method (see Chapter 9, by Held, in this volume).

In our laboratory (Atkinson, Braddick, & Moar, 1977a,b) stimuli are presented on a pair of oscilloscope screens in front of the infant. Before a trial, both screens are uniform bright fields, and the infant's attention is brought to the midline by flashing lights. When the observer initiates a trial, the flashing lights go out and a grating appears on one of the screens that is selected by a randomizing circuit. The mean luminance of both screens remains constant and equal. The observer can make a decision and thereby terminate the trial at any time subject to a 15-sec time-out (trial durations are commonly about 5 sec). The results of each trial are automatically printed out and, after a 5-trial block, the observer checks this record. This provides feedback and allows the observer to determine the stimulus setting (spatial frequency or contrast) for the next block according to a staircase rule (5/5 or 4/5 leads to stimulus difficulty being increased by 2/3 octave in spatial frequency or 4 dB in contrast, 3/5 to no change, and 2/5 or less to an equivalent decrease). We stop the staircase when we have two stimulus values that bracket 70% correct with at least 20 trials on each, and take the interpolated 70% point as a threshold.

If a greater number of trials is taken, a lower correct percentage will allow a statistically significant measure of detection and, if taken as a criterion, will lead to higher estimates of sensitivity. Other laboratories have used criteria as low as 58% (Gwiazda, Brill, Mohindra, & Held, 1978). However, the principal problem of working with infants is the very limited time for which their attention can be sustained and a lengthy procedure suffers in reliability and/or practicality for this reason. With our procedure, a reliable threshold estimate at the 70% criterion can be obtained in 50–90 trials over a period of 5–15 min; this is almost always practical within a single session provided a time is selected when the infant is initially in a calm and attentive state. Our automated sequencing and recording cuts down the time wasted between trials with an attentive infant and we hope to minimize this further in the future by automatic control of the stimulus parameters and hence of the staircase procedure.

The stimulus situation facing the infant before and during a trial differs between laboratories. In our set-up, both "positive" and "negative" stimuli are bright fields clearly differentiated from the darker surround, but the negative stimulus remains unchanged at trial onset. In Held's laboratory (Gwiazda et al., 1978) both the patterned and the blank field suddenly appear out of darkness at trial onset. In Teller's laboratory, the whole surround is matched in luminance to the pattern and hence from the infant's point of view there is no localized negative stimulus at all; trial onset is marked not by pattern appearance but by the infant being brought up to the viewing position. In the study by Banks and Salapatek (1978), the positive and negative stimuli together filled almost the entire visual field. Given these differences, it is the agreement rather than any differences between the various investigators' results that is striking (Dobson & Teller, 1978).

Strictly, the PL method can only provide a lower limit on estimates of visual sensitivity; it is entirely possible that some other method could demonstrate infants' detection of some stimuli for which they show no preference. The general plausibility of PL "thresholds" would be enhanced by an instance where PL results approached the likely limits of sensitivity. Such an instance is provided by the work of Regal (1981), which has shown 3-month infants' preference for a flickering over a steady field at frequencies up to 50 Hz, which is close to the adult critical flicker frequency (CFF). This result strongly suggests that the much greater differences between adult psychophysical and infant PL results on spatial sensitivity reflect real differences in capacity for visual detection.

It can also be argued that differences between performance at different ages, or for the same infants on different stimuli (e.g., contrast sensitivities at different spatial frequencies) may reflect differences in preference or in its manifestation in behavior, rather than differences in sensitivity. Between age groups, the most plausible difference would be that the youngest infants might show a greater amount of random fixation of all stimuli. This would imply a shallower psychometric function for younger infants. The one published study that has explicitly examined this question (Atkinson, Braddick, & Moar, 1977a) found no evidence for any age difference in slope of the psychometric function. The fact that age trends for low and high spatial frequency stimuli are markedly different (Atkinson et al., 1977a; Banks & Salapatek, 1978) also suggests that these changes are not the consequence of a generalized decrease in the randomness of fixation behavior. Banks and

Salapatek (in press) argue that variations in PL threshold with spatial frequency have a visual, rather than a purely preferential, basis from their finding that this function changes with luminance in the same way as adult sensitivities. This argument has some force but can hardly be general, as if it were, it would seem to imply that no qualitative difference between infant and adult vision could be validly found by the method!

In principle, a negative preference for a patterned compared to an unpatterned field could demonstrate detection just as directly as a positive preference. Held, Gwiazda, Brill, Mohindra, & Wolfe (1979) have, in fact, reported PL psychometric functions for acuity that are not monotonic, but that dip below 50% (i.e., show negative preference) for high spatial frequencies. With psychometric functions of this form, a criterion above 50% would underestimate the highest spatial frequency for which the infant shows differential behavior under the conditions of this particular test. It should be pointed out that this result may be more likely in Held's procedure than in other variants because of the relative prominence of the blank stimulus (see earlier discussion). Teller (1979) has also argued that, if the observer receives and acts on trial-by-trial feedback to maximize hit rates, systematic hit rates that are lower than chance ought not to occur, and that this is the most un-ambiguously defined version of the observer's task. An insistence on this definition of the observer's task, of course, is not compatible with the use of the PL method in cases where the positive stimulus is not defined by the experimenter, such as the paired gratings of different orientations used by Leehey, Moskowitz-Cook, Brill, & Held (1975) and Atkinson & French (1979).

Preferential looking data have been gathered from neonates (Fantz, Ordy, & Udelf, 1962; Miranda, 1970) and even from premature infants at 32 weeks gestation (Dubowitz, Dubowitz, Morante, & Verghote, in press). However, only a very small number of trials can be run in the period when such young infants are in an appropriate state, and, in practice, the youngest age at which meaningful PL thresholds can be estimated on individual infants is at about 4–5 weeks. Infants aged 8–20 weeks combine adequate periods of attentiveness with slow ha-bituation to the stimuli, making this the optimal age range for the technique. Infants older than 6 months become increasingly distractible, although there are marked individual variations, and a passive 8-month-old may prove easier to test than a restless 5-month-old. Held's labo-ratory (working in complete darkness which may optimize attention to the stimuli for older infants) has reported PL acuities up to 12 months of age (Gwiazda et al., 1978); but in our own experience the number of infants yielding usable data is low at this age and we suspect that data obtained may markedly underestimate visual acuity.

The success of PL in research studies of normal infant acuity have led to interest in its application to clinical research and assessment. Rapid versions of the procedure have been developed for this purpose (Dobson, Teller, Lee, & Wade, 1978; Gwiazda, Brill, & Held, 1978). However, our experience is that the needs of clinical assessment justify the use of our (not very lengthy) staircase procedure outlined earlier, which yields more detailed and/or more reliable measures than procedures using smaller numbers of trials. We have now used this procedure to assess acuity in about 50 cases of clinical eye disorder. In very few cases have we not been able to complete the staircase. Most of these have been infants over 6 months, although congenital nystagmus makes the PL technique difficult to use at any age.

In most clinical applications, differences between the two eyes are potentially important and often they are the principal concern. It is therefore necessary to test monocularly. We find that occluding one eye increases the fretfulness of infant subjects and makes the observer's task somewhat harder and the holder's task more critical in terms of maintaining the infant's head position. However, in the great majority of cases, satisfactory monocular threshold estimates can be obtained. Figure 8.1 shows the acuities obtained for the left and right eyes of (presumably normal) individual infants aged between 3 and 4 months (Atkinson & Braddick, 1980). The nonviewing eye was occluded with an adhesive orthoptic patch. The two estimates were obtained concurrently, that is, blocks of 25 trials were alternated between eyes, with separate staircase sequences being maintained for each eye. This method also allows the intrinsic consistency of monocular FPL thresholds to be tested. Figure 8.2 shows data in which two independent staircases, using alternate 25-trial blocks, were run concurrently on the same eye. The consistency is clearly very high; in every case the two independent estimates were within 20% of each other. Comparison with Fig. 8.1 shows that the differences found between eyes of the same individual cannot be explained as due to the variability of the method, but that real differences in acuity as large as a factor of two occur. Both figures also make clear that individual differences are a considerably larger source of variance in PL acuity measurements at this age. Some part of this variation may be due to differences in the sign, axis, or extent of the infantile astigmatism, which is marked at this age (see Section IV.D.).

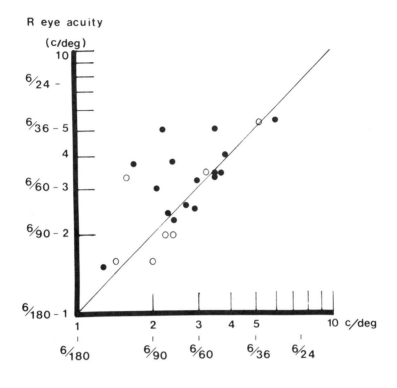

Fig. 8.1 Acuity of the left and right eyes of 23 infants aged 3–4 months, measured by preferential looking (PL) with 3 Hz drifting sinusoidal grading stimuli. Each point represents the data from one individual. The 45 deg line represents the locus for identical acuities in the two eyes. The two acuities that were determined using blocks of 25 trials, alternating between the eyes, are shown by ●. Data from the two eyes assessed in separate runs are represented by ○. (From Atkinson & Braddick, 1980.)

B. Visual Evoked Potentials

Recordings from an infant's scalp of the cortical potentials that are time-locked to pattern changes can provide evidence that the infant's visual system transmits pattern information. Either amplitude or latency measures of these potentials may be taken. Such visual evoked potentials (VEPs) have sometimes been regarded as particularly "objective" measures of visual performance. In practice, they share many of the problems of behavioral measures. Visual evoked potentials can only be recorded when an infant is in a calm state with gaze directed to the

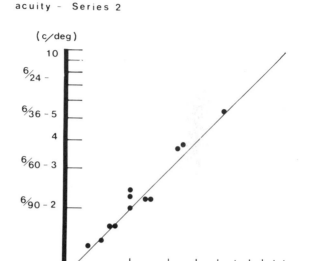

Fig. 8.2 Comparison of two independent monocular acuity measures taken for the same eye, for twelve eyes of infants aged between 3–4 months. Method as described for Fig. 8.1, with the two series interleaved in 25-trial blocks in each case. (From Atkinson & Braddick, 1980.)

stimulus for an adequate period, and some criterion has to be chosen for what response will be taken as evidence of "detection." It should also be remarked that, in normal adults, VEP results show a great deal more individual and day-to-day variability than psychophysical thresholds. However, VEPs do have the merit that an essentially identical technique may be used to compare vision in subjects across a wide age range, from neonates to adults (and, in principle, in different species, although this potential link has been remarkably little exploited).

To allow time-locked recording, the stimulus event must be transient. The simple illumination of a patterned stimulus has been used (Harter, Deaton, & Odom, 1977) but is unsatisfactory as it is difficult to unconfound pattern effects from those of luminance onset, which do not require pattern vision. The repetitive appearance of pattern in a field of equal mean luminance (e.g., Marg, Freeman, Peltzman, & Goldstein, 1976), or contrast reversal of a pattern (e.g., Atkinson, Braddick, & French, 1979; Harris, Atkinson, & Braddick, 1976; Pirchio, Spinelli,

Fiorentini, and Maffei, 1978; Sokol & Dobson, 1976) are preferable stimuli. Repetition at the rate of 1 Hz or less allows all components of the VEP wave to be observed. However, the functional significance of the different VEP components is still quite uncertain. Because the potentials from a certain number of stimulus repetitions (e.g., 100) have to be summated to achieve a given level of signal–noise separation, low stimulus frequencies lead to very prolonged trials. We have therefore preferred to work at rather high stimulus rates (8–10 Hz pattern reversal) yielding "steady state" VEPs. This stimulus rate, together with some filtering of the signal, produces an approximately sinusoidal VEP, for which an amplitude measure is, in fact, considerably more unambiguous than for the complex waveforms obtained with slow rates. It is clear that rates as high as 10 Hz yield satisfactory pattern VEPs, but the effects of varying temporal frequency at different ages are unknown, so the optimal rate for testing pattern sensitivity in infants cannot yet be stated.

Marg et al. (1976) obtained acuity estimates by taking the finest grating for which a VEP waveform was subjectively judged to be present. This is a dubious criterion, especially for small potentials of uncertain form. We have derived contrast thresholds (Harris et al., 1976) by extrapolating to zero the linear function relating VEP amplitude to the logarithm of contrast. This method has been shown (Campbell & Maffei, 1970) to predict psychophysical thresholds in the adult. (An acuity estimate may then be obtained by extrapolation of the resulting contrast sensitivity curve.) A method used by Sokol (1978) and Harter et al. (1977) is analogous but not identical: They extrapolated a plot of VEP amplitude as a function of check size to obtain an acuity value corresponding to zero VEP. This function shows a peak at intermediate values of check size, whose position changes with age. Sokol and Dobson (1979) have argued that an adult-like position and form of this peak (found by them in 6-month-olds) suggested an adult-like value of acuity. Given the evidence that the detection of different spatial frequencies develops differentially (Harris et al., 1976; Atkinson et al., 1977a; Banks & Salapatek, 1978) this suggestion must be treated with caution. A checkerboard contains a range of spatial frequency components whose role in determining the VEP at different check sizes is not known.

Working with neonates (Atkinson et al., 1979), we were unable to gather sufficient data from individual infants to use an extrapolation method. In this case we used "presence of VEP" as a criterion for detection, but defined this in terms of a signal that was statistically discriminable from that recorded in the absence of a stimulus, not in terms of subjective identification of a waveform.

Dobson and Teller (1978) have reviewed the comparison of infant acuities obtained with the PL and VEP methods. They attribute the generally higher acuities reported from VEP studies to the relatively conservative scoring criteria usually adopted in the PL method. It is, of course, true that the adoption of a suitable criterion can shift PL acuity to any point within the range of the psychometric function. It should be noted, however, that acuity estimates have been obtained from VEP data in very different ways and that the studies yielding the highest acuity estimates (Marg *et al.*, 1976; Sokol & Dobson, 1976) have involved the least secure inferences. The only studies to use PL and VEP methods on the same individual infants and with similar stimuli (Atkinson *et al.*, 1979; Harris *et al.*, 1976) have not, in fact, shown any superiority of performance as assessed by the VEP.

C. Optokinetic Nystagmus

The third method that has been used for assessment of infant acuity is the use of a moving grating stimulus to elicit optokinetic nystagmus (OKN) (Dayton, Jones, Aiu, Rawson, Steele, & Rose, 1964; Fantz *et al.*, 1962; Gorman, Cogan, & Gellis, 1957). If grating contrast rather than spatial frequency were manipulated, contrast sensitivity could be investigated by the same technique, although no such study has yet been published.

The OKN response is clearly present in the newborn and is of a peculiarly involuntary nature. OKN is thus a very promising technique for the youngest infants. The method intrinsically requires a large stimulus field, which may also be a condition for optimizing acuity estimates in the very young (see section III.A). Like the VEP, OKN should be applicable as a uniform method over a wide range of ages, although the difficulties of sustaining passive attention to a simple (possibly even a mildly aversive) stimulus apply to both methods when used with children over 6–9 months of age. It has been suggested (Dobson & Teller, 1978) that the inconvenience of eye movement recording equipment could be avoided by the use of a "blind" observer required to make a forced choice of the direction of stimulus motion, and this method has been found feasible (though not yet applied to acuity) by Atkinson (1979).

The principal obstacle to the OKN method is that of effective stimulus control. The presence of components of low spatial frequency that move with the stimulus will invalidate estimates of acuity. Such components are difficult to avoid with gratings on a physically moving surface, both because of imperfections of drawing and because of soiling or joins in the surface itself. Banks and Salapatek (in press) have shown that such problems are likely to have been present in the published neonatal OKN studies. The potential problems become more acute in testing the acuity of older infants, for whom gratings in the spatial frequency range 10–30 c/deg may be required. Electronic or optical means of generating a moving grating on a fixed surface would be greatly preferable. However, the technology to generate a grating of such high spatial frequency over a stimulus field that should subtend 70 deg or more is not yet readily available.

It should also be realized that the neural control of OKN, although not understood in detail, is known to be at least, in part, independent of the cortex (Wood, Spear, & Braun, 1973). It is therefore uncertain what is the relation between OKN acuity and the cortical information available for pattern perception. There does not, in fact, exist any published study that compares stimuli that can elicit OKN in adults with psychophysical thresholds. To add to this problem of interpretation, the work of Atkinson (1979) shows that the neural pathways involved in OKN change between 1 and 3 months of age. The asymmetry shown by this work in monocularly elicited OKN for infants under 3 months of age must also be taken into account in interpreting OKN results obtained from young infants.

III.   INFANT ACUITY AND CONTRAST SENSITIVITY: RESULTS

Fairly recent reviews of results on infant acuity (Dobson & Teller, 1978) and contrast sensitivity (Salapatek, 1979) are available: We shall concentrate here on discussing results from our own laboratory.

A.   Age Trends in Acuity and Contrast Sensitivity

Figure 8.3 combines data from a number of our studies. The neonatal results were obtained by means of VEPs produced by grating stimuli phase-reversed at 10 Hz (Atkinson et al., 1979). The other data in the figure were obtained by the PL method as described in the previous section. (Atkinson et al., 1977a,b). Each curve in the figure is a contrast sensitivity function (CSF): That is, it shows the threshold contrast (plotted inversely) for grating stimuli whose luminance profile is sinusoidal as a function of spatial position. The value of data in this form is that they are informative about the performance of the visual system for a wide range of spatial variations, coarse as well as fine, as opposed to simple acuity measures, which only reflect the performance for very

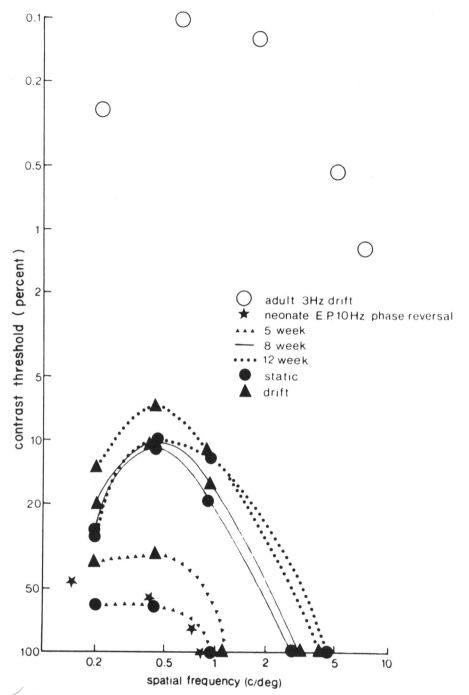

Fig. 8.3 Contrast sensitivity of 0–3 months olds. Neonate group data from visual evoked potentials from 10 Hz phase-reversing gratings (Atkinson *et al.*, 1979). Mean data from 5-, 8- and 12-week-old groups from preferential looking data using static and 3 Hz drifting gratings (Atkinson *et al.*, 1977a,b, and supplementary data). (Figure from Braddick & Atkinson, 1979.)

fine detail. The CSF may also allow the prediction of performance with quite different stimuli, as such stimuli can be analyzed as the sum of sinusoidal components (Braddick, Campbell, & Atkinson, 1978; Campbell & Robson, 1968; see Banks & Salapatek (in press) for a recent discussion of applications to infant vision). These contrast sensitivity functions include acuity measures at the point where each curve cuts the horizontal axis: These points were obtained by testing with high-contrast gratings whose spatial frequency,[1] rather than contrast, was varied.

The data of Fig. 8.3 show a clear and unsurprising age trend: Both contrast sensitivity and acuity improve progressively between birth and 3 months, but performance at 3 months falls considerably short of adult performance as measured by a forced-choice psychophysical experiment. However, from these data it appears that development does not proceed at a uniform rate during this period. The comparison of the contrast sensitivities found for newborns and 5-week-olds suggests that rather little development of spatial vision occurs in the first month of life. This conclusion must be tentative, as the neonatal data are VEP-based, whereas the 5-week data are behavioral, and the temporal conditions of display were different. The gain in performance between the 8- and 12-week groups is also rather modest. Individual data show a considerable degree of overlap between these age groups. (Figures 8.1 and 8.2 give an indication of the considerable interindividual variation at about 3 months, although in examining the actual acuity values shown in these figures, it must be remembered that performance is usually poorer in monocular viewing—Figs. 8.1 and 8.2—than in binocular, Fig. 8.3.) In contrast, individual CSFs show almost no overlap between the 5- and 8-week groups (Atkinson et al., 1977a). There appears in these data to be a marked spurt in the development of spatial visual performance in the second month of life. A number of other important developments seem to take place in the human visual system during this period, including the appearance of a low spatial frequency cut (see Section III.B), the beginning of the capacity for smooth pursuit eye movements (Aslin, in press; Dayton & Jones, 1964), of monocular OKN in a nasotemporal direction that can be ascribed to a cortical pathway (Atkinson, 1979), and the appearance of the ability to recognize features within a surrounding contour (Milewski, 1976). It is interesting to speculate whether these developmental changes might have a common origin.

[1] Spatial frequency refers to the number of grating cycles (a cycle being a paired light and dark bar) within one degree of visual angle. Acuity is therefore a measure of the highest spatial frequency for which a high-contrast grating can be detected.

The only other behavioral study of infants' CSFs is that of Banks and Salapatek (1978 & in press), which covered a very similar age range. Their data agree closely with ours for the 2- and 3-month age groups. However, at 1 month, their data show considerably better performance than ours, especially in the higher spatial frequencies. The effect of this difference is that, in their data, development between 1 and 2 months does not appear to be any more rapid than between 2 and 3 months. The discrepancy between the two sets of results can most plausibly be ascribed to the stimulus display: In our work, the stimulus fields are 15 deg across and separated by 9 deg, whereas in Banks and Salapatek's apparatus, the stimuli were generated optically rather than electronically so that the two fields could meet in the midline and extend 48 deg on either side. Salapatek (1979) has suggested that the delimiting outer contours of our display interfered with 1-month-olds' pattern detection, analogously to the interference with internal form discrimination ("externality effect") reported at this age by Milewski (1976). The finding that acuity estimates were similar for a drifting grating (Atkinson, Braddick, & Moar, 1977b) argues against this, because motion of internal features abolishes the externality effect (Bushnell, 1979). The larger field size and smaller separation may have enhanced Banks and Salapatek's 1-month sensitivities for other reasons: Fixations may be more readily elicited by stimuli that appear close to central vision (Aslin & Salapatek, 1975; Macfarlane, Harris, & Barnes, 1976; Tronick, 1972); random shifts of fixation may be more likely to fall on the stimulus if it is large, leading to the capture of visual attention; or 1-month-olds may need to integrate spatial information from a greater retinal area. Comparisons need to be undertaken in which field size and separation are varied within an otherwise standard procedure, and such studies are planned in our laboratory. Whatever the origin of the discrepancy, it is clear that some stimulus variable acts in a strikingly different way at 1 and 2 months (when large- and small-field studies agree closely). The idea of an important change in visual processing between 1 and 2 months is thus upheld, although the exact nature of that change is not yet certain.

The only other study of infant CSFs is by Pirchio et al. (1978) who tested infants aged 2–10 months by a VEP method. Their results are in good agreement with Atkinson et al.'s (1977a) and Banks & Salapatek's (1978) PL results in the age groups where they overlap. Unfortunately, Pirchio et al. did not test any infants younger than 8 weeks, so their data do not help to resolve the issue of changes between 5 and 8 weeks of age.

B. The Low Spatial Frequency Cut

The CSFs of the 8- and 12-week groups shown in Fig. 8.3, like those generally found for adults, show a decline of sensitivity to low spatial frequencies. However, this low spatial frequency cut appears to be quite absent in the data of the 5-week-olds. This striking qualitative difference appears equally prominently in the data of Banks and Salapatek (1978). The rather wide separation of the spatial frequencies used in Fig. 8.3 means that the true peak of the function, and hence the extent of the low-frequency cut, may not always have been revealed. However, more detailed investigation of the low-frequency region (Atkinson et al., 1977a) gave the results shown in Fig. 8.4, confirming that the 8- and 12-week groups show functions essentially similar in shape to the adults in this region, whereas the 5-week-olds' appear flat.

The low-frequency cut in the adult CSF is usually ascribed to the presence of lateral inhibition in the visual pathway. Artifacts associated with small numbers of cycles and with boundary effects can exaggerate the degree of low-frequency cut but cannot fully account for it (Estevez & Cavonius, 1976). The similarity of Banks and Salapatek's (1978) large-field results to ours argues strongly that such artifacts are not the

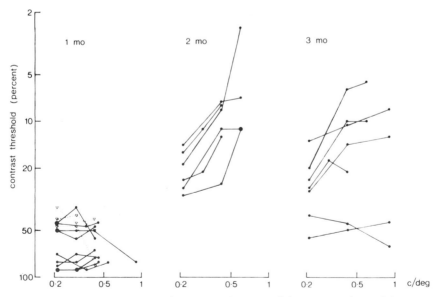

Fig. 8.4 Contrast sensitivity functions at low spatial frequencies obtained from individual infants in three age groups, using preferential looking (PL). Stimuli were static sinusoidal gratings. (Atkinson et al., 1977a.)

determining factor in the infants' low-frequency cut or its absence in 1-month-olds.

Several possibilities are open to explain the appearance of the low-frequency cut between 1 and 2 months. First, lateral inhibition may be initially absent in the infant's visual system and appear in the second month. This would be analogous to the findings of Rusoff and Dubin (1977) and Hamasaki and Flynn (1977) that retinal ganglion cells in young kittens show only weak inhibitory surrounds. The later super-imposition of an inhibitory process would serve to sharpen the spatial selectivity of the cells.

Second, the form of the CSF can be considered as the result of combining two processes, one of which imposes a low-frequency cut and the other a high-frequency cut. It is clear that, with increasing age, the high-frequency cut moves to higher frequencies. This could have the effect of "uncovering" the effects of the process that cuts low-frequency sensitivity, even if such a process had been operating un-changed throughout. If the high-frequency cut were neural in origin, this hypothesis would be very similar to the first hypothesis, of de-veloping lateral inhibition. An inhibitory process of constant spatial extent would be present but would be initially entirely "submerged" beneath an extended excitatory process, giving in net terms a receptive field that was all "excitatory center." As the excitatory process shrank in extent, the inhibitory effects would become visible in the surround. However, in principle, the low-frequency cut could be similarly sub-merged by a high-frequency cut because of optical blur with neural inhibition effective throughout. We do not, in fact, believe that the high-frequency cut in infant vision is optically imposed, for reasons to be discussed in following sections.

Third, the 1-month-olds in Figs. 8.3 and 8.4 may show no low-fre-quency cut because of the limited range of spatial frequencies used. It is possible that the whole CSF simply shifts upward and to the right as the visual system develops, and that the low cut would be observed in 1-month-olds if sensitivity to sufficiently low spatial frequencies was tested. This would correspond to both the excitatory centers and the inhibitory surrounds of receptive fields contracting during develop-ment. A test of this hypothesis would require the use of very large stimulus fields that could contain an adequate number of cycles of very low-frequency gratings. Banks and Salapatek (1978) did, in fact, mea-sure their infants' CSFs to lower spatial frequencies than those shown in Figs. 8.3 and 8.4 (0.15 c/deg as opposed to 0.2) and found no trace of a low cut; it would be useful to have the observations extended to still lower spatial frequencies.

C. Static and Dynamic Stimuli

The PL results shown in Fig. 8.3 include data obtained with two different temporal conditions: The gratings were either static, or drifting at a steady rate of 3 Hz. When a moving and a static stimulus are paired, infants preferentially fixate the moving stimulus (Volkmann & Dobson, 1976). It might be presumed, then, that dynamic stimuli are more attention-getting for the infant and that preference for them would more nearly reflect true sensitivity than preference for static stimuli. In fact, however, we find no difference in any of our age groups for *acuity* as assessed with 3 Hz and with static gratings (Atkinson *et al.*, 1977b). An analogous result has been obtained by Dobson, Teller, and Belgum (1978), who compared PL acuity for static (square wave) gratings with that for phase-reversing checkerboard patterns. There is no evidence, then, that motion or change reveals abilities to detect fine patterns that infants do not manifest with static stimuli.

At low and intermediate spatial frequencies, however, a markedly higher contrast sensitivity is found using the drifting stimulus. Temporal modulation similarly enhances low spatial frequency sensitivity for the adult observer (Robson, 1966), a result that is usually held to reflect the response of "transient channels." These are mechanisms that are sensitive to low spatial frequencies, but only if the stimulus is modulated in time (Kulikowski & Tolhurst, 1973). Presumably the difference found in infants has the same origin. There is nothing in these data to suggest that infants have any *greater* differential sensitivity to motion than do adults.

It has been proposed (Bronson, 1974) that visual changes in early infancy are the result of cortical visual function appearing later than that mediated by the superior colliculus. In the cat, the ratio of Y- or transient neurons to X- or sustained neurons is much greater in the pathway to the colliculus than in the geniculostriate pathway (Hoffman, 1973). A dominance of the collicular system might thus show up as a relatively greater advantage for detection of moving over static low-frequency gratings. However, there is no sign of such an advantage in any of the age groups we have studied, so Bronson's hypothesis must remain speculative. Current physiological evidence favors the view that, *within* the geniculostriate pathway, the X-cells develop earlier and are less modifiable than are Y-cells (Daniels, Pettigrew, & Norman, 1978; Rusoff, 1979); our data are consistent with a greater role of transient channels at 2–3 months than at 1 month.

IV. INFANT REFRACTION AND ACCOMMODATION: EFFECTS ON ACUITY

An infant's spatial visual performance is potentially constrained by the optical quality of the image on the retina. This, in turn, is determined first, by the physical parameters of the optics of the infant eye, and second, by how well those optics are behaviorally adjusted (i.e., by the accuracy of accommodation).

A. Methods of Refractive Assessment

The standard method of objectively assessing refraction[2] has been retinoscopy. In clinical practice with infants, this is usually done with accommodation paralyzed by a cycloplegic drug. The resulting estimate that infants are on average 1–2 diopters hypermetropic or far-sighted (Banks, 1980b) does not therefore give us any indication on the second point mentioned earlier, that is, where the infant's eyes are actually focused in normal viewing, as infants have a large amplitude of accommodation and could potentially use this to overcome their hypermetropia and focus at a wide range of distances. The method of "near retinoscopy" (Mohindra, 1977) does not involve cycloplegia, but is similarly intended to determine the refractive state of the eye when it is not actively accommodating. (Near retinoscopy actually measures the *resting* state of accommodation, which is not with the accommodative muscles completely relaxed.)

Retinoscopy conducted on a freely accommodating subject is known as "dynamic retinoscopy." This was the method used to study infants' accommodation by Haynes, White, and Held (1965) and more recently by Banks (1980a).

We have studied infant refraction and accommodation using the new method of "photorefraction" (Howland & Howland, 1974). In this technique, a flashed light source is centered in the camera lens, and the light reflected from the fundus of the eye is photographed through a set of cylinder lens segments. The result is a set of streak reflexes whose length in the photograph gives a direct measure of the dioptric defocus of the subject's eyes relative to the camera distance. Compared to retinoscopy, it is a simple procedure for the operator, and it has the merit

---

[2] The *refraction* of an eye refers to the distance for which the eye is focused when its accommodation is completely relaxed. It is normally expressed in diopters (the inverse of the focal distance in meters). Thus an eye which, when relaxed, is focused on objects 0.5 meters distant is described as having a refraction of 2 diopters of myopia.

for work with infants that it only requires attention to be maintained on the target for the moments when the flash photographs are taken. Another advantage is that it allows a very direct comparison of the focus of the two eyes, and of two orthogonal meridia of each eye, at the same instant. The main disadvantage is that the sign of any defocus is not usually apparent from a single photograph, although it may be inferred from a sequence of photographs.

Under conditions in which accommodative state is constant, notably in cycloplegia, retinoscopy in the hands of a skilled practitioner provides the most direct way of obtaining an estimate of refraction. However, the instantaneous nature of photorefraction makes it yield a more secure assessment of refractive state when, in the absence of cycloplegia, this may be changing from moment to moment. Also, no such changes can interfere with the comparison of two eyes or two meridia in photorefraction, whereas in retinoscopy, these comparisons require successive measurements.

B. Accuracy of Accommodation in Infants

Ophthalmoscopic observation of the infant eye shows that, unlike the kitten eye whose media are cloudy in the first few weeks, its general optical quality is very good. The modest hypermetropia that is, on average, found in infants could readily be overcome by the large amplitude of accommodation that is available in early childhood. Image quality will, therefore, be principally determined by how well infants adjust their accommodation to the stimulus.

Our photorefractive study of infant accommodation (Braddick, Atkinson, French, & Howland, 1979) used a target (the operator him-or-herself) close to the camera at two camera distances, 75 cm and 150 cm, with groups of infants aged from newborns to 12 months. Figures 8.5 and 8.6 plot the percentage of infants in each age group who met a criterion of being "in focus" at these two distances. These criteria, which were determined by physical limitations of the photorefractor, are specified in the figure legends. Each result was based on at least four photographs at a given camera distance. It was common with younger infants to find that the eyes were in focus in some but not all of these instances. These cases have been included as "inconsistent" in Figs. 8.5 and 8.6. Such infants must have the muscular capability to accommodate on a target at the distance concerned, but do not show consistent performance in doing so.

Figures 8.5 and 8.6 show that, in every case, infants aged 6 months and over met our criteria of accurate accommodation at both camera

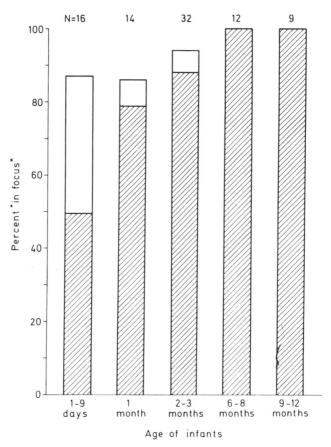

Fig. 8.5 Percentage of infants in five age groups showing "consistent" (white bar) and "inconsistent" (shaded bar) focusing at a camera distance of 75 cm. The criterion of "good focus" used corresponds to an interval of 1.2 diopters, almost entirely in front of the camera. The numbers at the top of the figure indicate the number of subjects in each group contributing to the data. (From Braddick *et al.*, 1979.)

distances. For younger infants, there was a progressive increase with age in the percentage of infants showing accurate accommodation. However, at each age, performance was better for the 75 cm distance than for 150 cm. For instance, 50% of newborns showed consistently accurate accommodation at 75 cm, whereas none did so at 150 cm. This difference is not an artifact of the criteria employed, as it appears even when less stringent criteria, designed to be comparable with that for 75 cm, are used with the 150 cm data (Columns B and C in Fig. 8.6.).

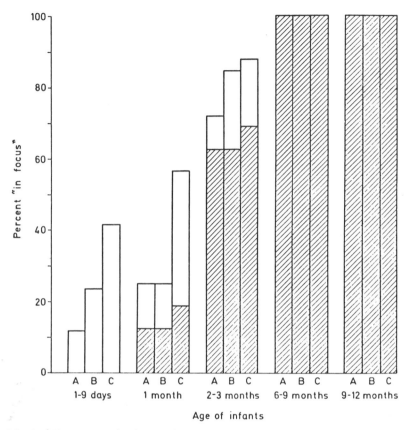

Fig. 8.6 Percentage of infants in five age groups showing "consistent" (shaded bar) and "inconsistent" (white bar) focusing at a camera distance of 150 cm. Columns A, B, and C correspond to three alternative criteria of "good focus." Criterion A corresponds to a total interval of 0.9 diopters, of which 0.6 D is in front of the camera. Criterion B corresponds to a total range of 1.2 D (as for the 75 cm criterion) but part of this range extends behind the camera. Criterion C allows a 1.2 D range in front of the camera, to correspond with the 75 cm case, but also extends behind the camera. Criterion A is thus the most stringent, whereas criteria B and C are most comparable with Fig. 8.5. (From Braddick *et al.*, 1979.)

Photographs were also taken with targets closer to the infant than the camera distance. In almost every case, infants who met the criterion of being "in focus" at the 75 cm camera distance also showed a progressive increase in defocus as the target was brought closer than 75 cm, indicating an appropriate accommodative response for these closer distances.

It appears, then, that infants are initially most likely to achieve accurate focus over a range of relatively near distances, and that this range expands to greater distances with age. Even though young infants are commonly far-sighted if their accommodation is relaxed by cycloplegia, when active accommodation is operating, they most readily set it for near distances.

Studies of infant accommodation by means of dynamic retinoscopy have led to broadly similar conclusions. Haynes *et al.* (1965) plotted accommodative response against target distance. For 3–4-month-olds this function showed a good match of accommodation to the target distance. However, for 0–1-month-olds, their function was approximately flat, implying a fixed accommodation at an average distance of around 20 cm. This is rather more static behavior than our data indicate for the youngest infants. First, we found definite evidence of accommodative response in 50% of newborns and in a larger proportion of 1-month-olds, and these met our criterion of focus at 75 cm, which would *not* have been met by infants behaving as Haynes *et al.* report. Second, infants who did not meet our criterion in many cases failed to do so because their accommodation was fluctuating over a wide range (the "inconsistent" category in Figs. 8.5 and 8.6), rather than because their focus was fixed at a particular distance.

Banks (1980a) has recently conducted an extensive retinoscopic study, using targets that he argued provided a better stimulus to accommodation than Haynes *et al.*'s. He found an accommodative response which, age for age, was better matched to target distance than that of Haynes *et al.* Some of his results are illustrated in Fig. 8.7. At 1 month, the average slope of the function relating accommodative response to target distance was 0.51 rather than flat. Accommodation was best matched to the target at this age for a target distance of about 30 cm. The average defocus given by Banks' 1-month-old function for a target distance of 75 cm would be about 0.8 diopter, which would meet the criterion of "good focus" for this distance in our experiment. Brookman (1980) has used a similar method, including infants as young as 2 weeks in his study and finding a definite accommodative response to target distance at this age. Banks explicitly demonstrated the effect of the infant's state; drowsiness could very markedly flatten these functions. This may be another reason for the differences between Haynes *et al.*'s and the later results.

The fluctuations that appear as "inconsistent" focus in our data would not be apparent in Banks' and Haynes *et al.*'s presentation of their data; in any case, the retinoscopic method is not well-suited to sampling rapidly changing accommodation.

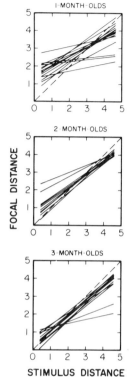

Fig. 8.7 Accommodative response functions for infants in three age groups, from Banks (1980a, reprinted with permission). Stimulus distance and response (i.e., distance of focus) are both specified in diopters (inverse of distance in meters). The lines plotted are the best straight-line fit to the data for each individual. The broken diagonal line indicates the locus of exact correspondence between stimulus distance and accommodative response.

C. Astigmatism in Infants

Infants were counted as capable of "good focus" in Figs. 8.5 and 8.6 if they met the stated criteria in at least one meridian. For many, the orthogonal meridian was not in good focus, as a large percentage of the subjects showed astigmatism of 0.75 diopters or greater (Howland, Atkinson, Braddick, & French, 1978). Mohindra, Held, Gwiazda, and Brill (1978) have found a similarly high incidence of astigmatism in infants using near retinoscopy, and despite some clinical skepticism, the finding receives support from the clinical screening data of Ingram and Barr (1979).

In most cases, the astigmatism is a transient phenomenon. Our data (Braddick & Atkinson, 1979) and those of Mohindra *et al.* (1978) agree that the amount of astigmatism shown by individual infants usually declines quite rapidly between 6 and 18 months of age, and we have found that the incidence of astigmatism at 18 months and 3 years is close to adult levels. We do not yet know whether individuals who will remain astigmatic in adulthood are distinguishable in infancy.

The scientific interest of this astigmatism lies in two questions: first, does it have any effect on visual development, and second, why does it go away? Early astigmatism is believed to be the cause of meridional amblyopia, via selective stimulus deprivation in a neural critical period (Mitchell, Freeman, Millodot, & Haegerstrom, 1973). Because such amblyopia is not common to any marked degree, we must conclude either that uncommonly large astigmatism (say, 4 diopters or more) is necessary to cause an effective degree of deprivation, or that the relevant critical period extends well into the second year of life.

The disappearance of infantile astigmatism can be regarded as one aspect of the process of "emmetropization" reviewed by Banks (1980b). Variations in the refractive effect of different components of the adult eye tend to cancel each other out, suggesting some feedback process acting during growth to optimize refraction. For the components of spherical refraction, it has been proposed that habitual accommodation (e.g., underaccommodation of a myopic eye) affects the way that axial length or refractive power change in growth, in such a way as to reduce the overall error. It is not clear how such a process could operate differently in different meridia, so if there is a feedback loop that reduces infantile astigmatism, it must involve some other, unknown route whereby retinal image quality can influence growth processes. It is not yet known how much of the early astigmatism is due to the shape of the cornea and how much to the lens, and so we do not know which of these structures requires correction during growth.

D. The Relation between Acuity and Refractive Errors in Infants

The period from birth to 6 months of age, during which accommodative accuracy is improving, is also marked by a continuous improvement in behaviorally and VEP-assessed acuity (see Section II.A). This might suggest the conclusion that, in the youngest age groups, optical defocus due to errors of accommodation is an important and perhaps the major factor limiting acuity. However, detailed consideration suggests that this is not the case.

First, most studies of infant acuity have used rather short viewing distances (e.g., 40 cm in Atkinson *et al.*, 1977a,b). Such distances are within the range of effective accommodation even for 1-month-olds, both according to our data (Braddick *et al.*, 1979) and that of Banks (1980a). Second, three studies (Atkinson *et al.*, 1977a; Fantz *et al.*, 1962;

Table 8.1
Calculated Cut-off Spatial Frequency (c/deg)[a]

	Dioptric defocus			
Pupil diameter (mm)	1 D	2 D	3 D	4 D
4	5.3	2.7	1.8	1.3
6	3.6	1.8	1.2	0.9
8	2.7	1.3	0.9	0.7

[a] These figures are calculated from the following formula derived from geometrical optics: MTF of defocused lens $= 2J_1(x)/x$ where $x = 2\pi d(NA)f$, $J_1 =$ first-order Bessel function, $d =$ defocus in mm in the eye, $NA =$ numerical aperture (pupil radius/focal length), and $f =$ spatial frequency (c/mm). The cut-off is taken as the first zero of this function, for which $x = 3.83$.

Salapatek, Bechtold, & Bushnell, 1976) have found that behaviorally assessed acuity did not change over a range of viewing distances; either accommodation was equally accurate (or inaccurate) at all distances, or variations of focus with distance were not the limiting factor for acuity.

Third, it is possible to estimate the effects of defocus on the spatial frequencies present in the retinal image. Table 8.1 gives "cut-off" spatial frequencies for various combinations of dioptric defocus and pupil size (Braddick et al., 1979), derived from geometrical optics.[3] The issue is whether the change in acuity from around 1 c/deg at 1 month to 2–5 c/deg at 2–3 months (according to our data in Fig. 8.3) can be accounted for by the constraints imposed by these values. To limit acuity to 1 c/deg would require focusing errors of 3 diopters or more, in combination with rather large pupil sizes. For a viewing distance of 40 cm, focusing errors would be expected to be within about 1 diopter of the target according to the 1-month-old data of Braddick et al. (1979) or of Banks (1980a), and even according to the poorer performance reported by Haynes et al. (1965) would be no greater than 2.5 diopters. It does not seem likely, therefore, that optical defocus is the limiting factor on 1-month-olds' acuity. Paradoxically, optical constraints may be more sig-

[3] Strictly, these spatial frequencies are not cut-offs; the transfer function of a defocused lens passes through zero at this value but has a series of lobes of diminishing height at higher spatial frequencies. These higher-frequency lobes (regions of "spurious resolution") do allow the detection of gratings by adult observers (Campbell & Green, 1965). However, because nowhere in these high-frequency lobes is the image transmitted with more than 13% of its original contrast, we argue that the low-contrast sensitivity of young infants justifies treating the first zero-crossing as an effective cut-off.

nificant in older age groups whose accommodative performance is better. This is because astigmatism of 1–3 diopters is commonplace among 2-3-month-olds. Such an infant could have an acuity of 3 c/deg or considerably better and could therefore be optically limited if the meridian brought into good focus did not coincide with the grating orientation. Preferential looking experiments by Gwiazda *et al.* (1978) and by Atkinson and French (1979) show that astigmatism can indeed have a visually significant effect in this age group.

Banks (1980a) has performed calculations essentially analogous to those embodied in Table 8.1, to arrive at estimates of the depth of focus at various ages—that is, the range of dioptric errors that would not be detectable by the infant given the estimates of acuity at each age. He shows that the accommodation functions he measured by retinoscopy are such as to maintain the target within this depth of focus. This is another way of expressing the fact that the accommodative errors found in practice remain smaller than values that would impose the observed acuity limit on a system that had potentially higher resolution.

Presumably, then, the acuity limit is determined not by optical limitations but by the ability of the infant's visual system to transmit spatial information. It is not yet known what neural structure is critical for this, if any single one is: Differentiation of the fovea, and the multiplication of cortical connections, are two plausible candidates for significant neural development over the first few months of life.

If neural information transmission is the significant limit, the argument about accommodation and acuity can be reversed. The accurate control of accommodation requires that information is available to the system about those high spatial frequencies that are most affected by defocus. If such information is not transmitted by the visual pathway, in Banks' terms, the depth of focus will be large. In-focus and out-of-focus images will not be discriminable by the infant and consequently it will not be possible to adjust accommodation accurately. The occurrence of inconsistent focusing (Figs. 8.5 and 8.6) is consistent with such an absence of control information. In this view, acuity limits accommodative accuracy rather than vice versa.

E.   The Functional Vision of Infants

The measures of visual performance reported here, especially for infants of 1 month and younger, might appear so poor in comparison to adult vision as to imply little functionally useful vision. It must be remembered, however, that young infants cannot direct effective actions toward objects more than a few feet away, and that objects of concern to them, such as the face of a parent interacting with them, are normally presented at very close range. At such distances, resolution of a spatial frequency of 1 c/degree will correspond to a useful level of object detail; for instance, it will allow the differentiation of major facial features and expressions at half a meter.

Such a range of near distances corresponds to the range over which accommodation is most nearly accurate in young infants. But the errors of accommodation at greater distances do not appear to be simply a consequence of target detail becoming harder to resolve. Banks (1980a) was careful to maintain a constant angular subtense of his target at all distances and still found accommodation less accurate in dioptric terms at greater distances. Analogously, McKenzie and Day (1972, 1976) have found that a more distant target is less likely to attract an infant's fixations, even if its angular size is unaltered. There appears to be a limited "attentional field" within which infants are prepared to apply their visual capabilities. The fact that this can be demonstrated independently of the visual angle of the stimulus implies that infants must have available, and use, other sources of distance information to determine which objects in the field shall receive fixation and hence the maximal accommodative accuracy of which they are visually capable.

V. INNATE AND EXPERIENTIAL DETERMINANTS OF SPATIAL VISION

The neural basis of acuity and contrast sensitivity is believed to lie in the orderly connection of the receptor mosaic onto retinal ganglion cells with center–surround receptive field organization, with these connecting to neurons of the visual cortex that respond to spatial contrast at a variety of spatial frequencies[4] (Robson, 1975). There is no obvious way in which the optimal arrangement of these connections would depend on environmental contingencies. The spatial precision required for the connections is high, but the principles of organization and layout required to maintain this precision are not particularly complex and do not appear to depend on extrinsic factors which it would be difficult to allow for in the maturation of the system. (This may be contrasted with, for example, the achievement of the binocular organization of the visual cortex, where independently developing pathways from the two eyes have to be targeted on common cortical neurons with at least the same degree of spatial precision, and where there is necessarily a sen-

---

[4] Both these connections, of course, involve intermediate neural relays.

sitive interplay with the muscular mechanisms that must keep the two eyes aligned in their orbits.) A priori, then, one might expect acuity and contrast sensitivity to be functions that could mature under genetic control without much need for direction by environmental variables. This view would receive some support, at least for the earliest period of infancy, from the finding that the acuity of premature infants is a function of their gestational rather than their postnatal age (Dobson, Mayer, & Lee, in press; Miranda, 1970). The support would be stronger if these data could be complemented by a similar finding on infants born after term.

There is ample evidence, however, that the development of acuity can be radically affected by anomalies of visual experience. Both physiologically and behaviorally, the occlusion of one eye during a "sensitive period" in early life results in a severe loss of acuity in animals (Giffin & Mitchell, 1978), and the analogous clinical condition of "stimulus deprivation amblyopia" is well known (von Noorden & Maumenee, 1968). These effects may be ascribed to the modifiability of binocular connections rather than to the mechanisms determining acuity per se. However, meridional amblyopia (Mitchell et al., 1973) and the loss of acuity reported in congenital bilateral myopes (Fiorentini & Maffei, 1976) imply that the absence of high spatial frequencies in the visual input can impair the development of acuity without binocular competition being involved. We do not yet know whether exposure to a specific range of high spatial frequencies is necessary to develop sensitivity to those spatial frequencies. Nor do we know how far the developmental course of these deficits is adequately described as an "arrest" of development at the point where a given level of acuity would normally be reached; in the binocular case, it is clear that development can not only be arrested, but that existing neural connections can be destroyed by visual deprivation.

A further possible role of visual experience is in the development of refraction. We have already referred to the occurrence of "emmetropization" during development. The overall refraction of the eyes depends on several parameters—corneal curvature in all axes, lens shape, and the axial length of the eye—and it is possible that these have genetically determined targets but asynchronous growth, causing early errors which are corrected when all the targets are reached. However, the fact that overall refraction shows a lower variance than would be predicted from the independent components (Sorsby, Benjamin, & Sheridan, 1961) implies either that the target values are correlated across individual variations, or that the course of growth is controlled so that variations appearing in one component are actively corrected by another. Such correction would not necessarily depend on visual experience, but it is known that visual deprivation can induce refractive errors (Raviola & Wiesel, 1978; Rose, Yinon, & Belkin, 1974; Yinon, Rose, Shapiro, Goldschmidt, & Steinschneider, 1979). Whether there is a more specific and subtle effect, that growth of the components of refraction is modulated to maximize retinal image sharpness, remains an intriguing possibility for further research.

VI. CONCLUSIONS

The work described and reviewed in this chapter has combined advances in the methodology of infant testing with modern techniques and insights derived from the study of adult vision, to give a rapidly improving understanding of the properties of the infant's visual system. The degree of agreement between the results of different research groups is encouraging. Among the findings that have received support from several independent sources are the following:

1. The first 6 months are a period of rapidly improving acuity and contrast sensitivity.

2. At age 1 month, the best performance that can be demonstrated is about 5% of adult acuity. Nonetheless, this provides the infant with functionally useful vision.

3. The 1-month-old visual system differs qualitatively from older infants and adults in the absence of a low spatial frequency drop in sensitivity.

4. There is no evidence that the infant visual system shows any greater relative sensitivity for moving over static stimuli, compared to the adult.

5. Infants show an accurate accommodative response by 4–6 months. Before that age, their errors are smallest for relatively near stimuli. The accommodative errors of young infants are not the source of their low acuity; it is more likely that neurally based acuity limitations determine the accuracy of accommodative response.

6. A significant degree of astigmatism is commonplace in the first year of life.

The achievements of this field of work so far promise that it will be possible to apply to infants wider-ranging and more subtle tests of visual function. These should improve our understanding of how visual processes develop, the nature and scope of environmental influences upon that development, and what the effective visual world of the infant is like. Applications of the techniques to questions of abnormal visual development have already begun. These will contribute to practical problems of visual assessment of infants, and to knowledge of how visual developmental processes may go wrong and possibly how they may be corrected.

ACKNOWLEDGMENTS

This work was supported by the Medical Research Council of Great Britain.

REFERENCES

Aslin, R. N. The development of smooth pursuit in human infants. In D. F. Fisher, R. A. Monty, & J. W. Senders (Eds.), *Eye movements: cognition and visual perception*. Hillsdale, N.J.: Erlbaum, in press.

Aslin, R. N., & Salapatek, P. Saccadic localization of peripheral targets by the very young human infant. *Perception & Psychophysics*, 1975, **17**, 293–302.

Atkinson, J. Development of optokinetic nystagmus in the human infant and monkey infant: An analogue to development in kittens. In R. D. Freeman (Ed.), *Developmental neurobiology of vision*, New York: Plenum, 1979.

Atkinson, J., & Braddick, O. J. Assessment of vision in infants: Applications to amblyopia. *Transactions of the Ophthalmological Societies of the United Kingdom*, 1980, **99**, 338–343.

Atkinson, J., Braddick, O., & French, J. Contrast sensitivity of the human neonate measured by the visual evoked potential. *Investigative Ophthalmology and Visual Science*, 1979, **18**, 210–213.

Atkinson, J., Braddick, O., & Moar, K. Development of contrast sensitivity over the first 3 months of life in the human infant. *Vision Research*, 1977, **17**, 1037–1044. (a)

Atkinson, J., Braddick, O., & Moar, K. Contrast sensitivity of the human infant for moving and static patterns. *Vision Research*, 1977, **17**, 1045–1047. (b)

Atkinson, J., & French, J. Astigmatism and orientation preference in human infants. *Vision Research*, 1979, **19**, 1315–1317.

Banks, M. S. The development of visual accommodation during early infancy. *Child Development*, 1980, **51**, 646–666. (a)

Banks, M. S. Infant refraction and accommodation. *International Ophthalmology Clinics*, 1980, **20**, 205–232. (b)

Banks, M. S., & Salapatek, P. Acuity and contrast sensitivity in 1-, 2- and 3-month-old human infants. *Investigative Ophthalmology and Visual Science*, 1978, **17**, 361–365.

Banks, M. S., & Salapatek, P. Infant pattern vision: a new approach based on the contrast sensitivity function. *Journal of Experimental Child Psychology*, in press.

Braddick, O., & Atkinson, J. Accommodation and acuity in the human infant. In R. D. Freeman (Ed.), *Developmental neurobiology of vision*. New York: Plenum, 1979.

Braddick, O., Atkinson, J., French, J., & Howland, H. C. A photorefractive study of infant accommodation. *Vision Research*, 1979, **19**, 1319–1330.

Braddick, O., Campbell, F. W., & Atkinson, J. Channels in vision: basic aspects. In R. Held, H. Leibowitz, & H.-L. Teuber (Eds.), *Handbook of sensory physiology VIII. Perception*. New York: Springer-Verlag, 1978.

Bronson, G. The postnatal growth of visual capacity. *Child Development*, 1974, **45**, 873–890.

Brookman, K. E. *Ocular accommodation in the human infant.* Unpublished doctoral dissertation, Indiana University, 1980.

Bushnell, I. W. R. Modification of the externality effect in young infants. *Journal of Experimental Child Psychology*, 1979, **28**, 211–229.

Campbell, F. W. The transmission of spatial information through the visual system. In F. O. Schmitt & F. G. Worden (Eds.), *The neurosciences: Third study program*, Cambridge, Mass: MIT Press, 1974.

Campbell, F. W., & Green, D. G. Optical and retinal factors affecting visual resolution. *Journal of Physiology*, 1965, **181**, 576–593.

Campbell, F. W., & Maffei, L. Electrophysiological evidence for the existence of orientation and size detectors in the human visual system. *Journal of Physiology*, 1970, **207**, 635–652.

Campbell, F. W., & Robson, J. G. Application of Fourier analysis to the visibility of gratings. *Journal of Physiology*, 1968, **197**, 551–566.

Daniels, J. D., Pettigrew, J. P., & Norman, J. L. Development of single unit responses in the kitten's lateral geniculate nucleus. *Journal of Neurophysiology*, 1978, **41**, 1373–1393.

Dayton, G. O., & Jones, M. H. Analysis of characteristics of fixation reflexes in infants by use of DC electrooculography. *Neurology*, 1964, **14**, 1152–1156.

– Dayton, G. O., Jones, M. H., Steele, B., Aiu, P., Rawson, R. A., Steele, B., & Rose, M. Developmental study of coordinated eye movements in the human infant. I: Visual acuity in the newborn human: a study based on induced optokinetic nystagmus recorded by electrooculography. *Archives of Ophthalmology*, 1964, **71**, 865–870.

Dobson, V., Mayer, D. L., & Lee, C. P. Assessment of visual acuity in preterm infants. *Investigative Ophthalmology and Visual Science*, 1980, **19**, 1498–1505.

Dobson, V., & Teller, D. Y. Visual acuity in human infants: A review and comparison of behavioral and electrophysiological studies. *Vision Research*, 1978, **18**, 1469–1485.

Dobson, V., Teller, D. Y., & Belgum, J. Visual acuity in human infants assessed with stationary stripes and phase-alternated checkerboards. *Vision Research*, 1978, **18**, 1233–1238.

– Dobson, V., Teller, D. Y., Lee, C. P., & Wade, B. A behavioral method for efficient screening of visual acuity in young infants. I. Preliminary laboratory development. *Investigative Ophthalmology and Visual Science*, 1978, **17**, 1142–1150.

Dubowitz, L.M.S., Dubowitz, V., Morante, A., & Verghote, M. Visual function in the preterm and full-term newborn infant. *Developmental Medicine & Child Neurology*, 1980, **22**, 465–475.

Estevez, O., & Cavonius, C. R. Low-frequency attenuation in the detection of gratings: sorting out the artifacts. *Vision Research*, 1976, **16**, 497–500.

Fantz, R. L., Ordy, J. M., & Udelf, M. C. Maturation of pattern vision in infants during the first 6 months. *Journal of Comparative and Physiological Psychology*, 1962, **55**, 907–917.

Fiorentini, A., & Maffei, L. Spatial contrast sensitivity of myopic subjects. *Vision Research*, 1976, **16**, 437–438.

Giffin, F., & Mitchell, D. E. Recovery of vision after monocular deprivation. *Journal of Physiology*, 1978, **274**, 511–537.

Gorman, J. J., Cogan, D. G., & Gellis, S. S. An apparatus for grading the visual acuity of infants on the basis of optokinetic nystagmus. *Pediatrics*, 1957, **19**, 1088–1092.

Gwiazda, J., Brill, S., & Held, R. Fast measurement of visual acuity in infants from 2 weeks to 1 year of age. Paper presented at annual meeting of the Association for Research in Vision and Ophthalmology, Sarasota, Florida, 1978. (Abstract)

Gwiazda, J., Brill, S., Mohindra, I., & Held, R. Infant visual acuity and its meridional variation. *Vision Research*, 1978, **18**, 1557–1564.

Hamasaki, D. I., & Flynn, J. T. Physiological properties of retinal ganglion cells of 3-week-old kittens. *Vision Research*, 1977, **17**, 275–284.

Harris, L., Atkinson, J., & Braddick, O. J. Visual contrast sensitivity of a 6-month-old infant measured by the evoked potential. *Nature*, 1976, **264**, 570–571.

Harter, M. R., Deaton, F. K., & Odom, J. V. Visual evoked potentials to checkerboard flashes in infants from 6 days to 6 months. In J. E. Desmedt (Ed.), *Developments in visual evoked potentials of the human brain*. Oxford: Oxford University Press, 1977.

Haynes, H., White, B. L., & Held, R. Visual accommodation in human infants. *Science*, 1965, **148**, 528–530.

➥ Held, R., Gwiazda, J., Brill, S., Mohindra, I., & Wolfe, J. Infant visual acuity is underestimated because near threshold gratings are not preferentially fixated. *Vision Research*, 1979, **19**, 1377–1380.

Hoffman, K. P. Conduction velocities in pathways from retina to superior colliculus in the cat: A correlation with receptive field properties. *Journal of Neurophysiology*, 1973, **36**, 409–424.

Howland, H. C., Atkinson, J., Braddick, O., & French, J. Infant astigmatism measured by photorefraction. *Science*, 1978, **202**, 331–333.

Howland, H. C., & Howland, B. Photorefraction: A technique for study of refractive state at a distance. *Journal of the Optical Society of America*, 1974, **64**, 240–249.

Ingram, R. M., & Barr, A. Changes in refraction between the ages of 1 and $3\frac{1}{2}$ years. *British Journal of Ophthalmology*, 1979, **63**, 339–342.

Kulikowski, J. J., & Tolhurst, D. J. Psychophysical evidence for sustained and transient detectors in human vision. *Journal of Physiology*, 1973, **232**, 149–162.

Leehey, S. C., Moskowitz-Cook, A., Brill, S., & Held, R. Orientational anisotropy in infant vision. *Science*, 1975, **190**, 900–902.

MacFarlane, A., Harris, P., & Barnes, I. Central and peripheral vision in early infancy, *Journal of Experimental Child Psychology*, 1976, **21**, 532–538.

McKenzie, B., & Day, R. H. Object distance as a determinant of visual fixation in early infancy. *Science*, 1972, **178**, 1108–1110.

McKenzie, B., & Day, R. H. Infants' attention to stationary and moving objects at different distances. *Australian Journal of Psychology*, 1976, **28**, 45–51.

➥ Marg, E., Freeman, D. N., Peltzman, P., & Goldstein, P. J. Visual acuity development in human infants: Evoked potential measurements. *Investigative Ophthalmology*, 1976, **15**, 150–153.

➥ Milewski, A. E. Infants' discrimination of internal and external pattern elements. *Journal of Experimental Child Psychology*, 1976, **22**, 229–246.

Mitchell, D. E., Freeman, R. D., Millodot, M., & Haegerstrom, G. Meridional amblyopia: Evidence for modification of the human visual system by early visual experience. *Vision Research*, 1973, **13**, 535–558.

Mitchell, D. E., Giffin, F., Wilkinson, F., Anderson, P., & Smith, M. L. Visual resolution in young kittens. *Vision Research*, 1976, **16**, 363–366.

Miranda, S. Visual abilities and pattern preferences of premature infants and full-term neonates. *Journal of Experimental Child Psychology*, 1970, **10**, 189–205.

Mohindra, I. A noncycloplegic refraction technique for infants and young children. *Journal of the American Optometric Association*, 1977, **48**, 518–523.

Mohindra, I., Held, R., Gwiazda, J., & Brill, S. Astigmatism in infants. *Science*, 1978, **202**, 329–331.

Pirchio, M., Spinelli, D., Fiorentini, A., & Maffei, L. Infant contrast sensitivity evaluated by evoked potentials. *Brain Research*, 1978, **141**, 179–184.

Raviola, D., & Wiesel, T. N. Effect of dark rearing on experimental myopia in monkeys. *Investigative Ophthalmology and Visual Science*, 1978, **17**, 485–488.

Regal, D. M. Development of critical flicker frequency in human infants. *Vision Research*, 1981, **21**, 549–555.

Robson, J. G. Spatial and temporal contrast sensitivity functions of the human eye. *Journal of the Optical Society of America*, 1966, **56**, 1141.

Robson, J. G. Receptive fields: Neural representation of the spatial and intensive attributes of the visual image. In E. C. Carterette & M. P. Friedman (Eds.), *Handbook of perception* (Vol. 5), *Seeing*. New York: Academic Press, 1975.

Rose, L., Yinon, U., & Belkin, M. Myopia induced in cats deprived of distance vision. *Vision Research*, 1974, **14**, 1029–1032.

Rusoff, A. C. Development of ganglion cells in the retina of the cat. In R. D. Freeman (Ed.), *Developmental neurobiology of vision*, New York: Plenum, 1979.

Rusoff, A. C., & Dubin, M. W. Development of receptive field properties of retinal ganglion cells in kittens. *Journal of Neurophysiology*, 1977, **40**, 1188–1198.

Salapatek, P. Behavioral and electrophysiological evaluation of the infant contrast sensitivity function. In E. Jampolsky & L. Proenza (Eds.), *Proceedings of the Symposium on Applications of Psychophysics to Clinical Problems*. Washington, D.C.: National Academy of Sciences, 1979.

Salapatek, P., Bechtold, A. G., & Bushnell, E. W. Infant visual acuity as a function of viewing distance. *Child Development*, 1976, **47**, 860–863.

Sokol, S. Measurement of infant visual acuity from pattern-reversal evoked potentials. *Vision Research*, 1978, **18**, 33–40.

Sokol, S., & Dobson, V. Pattern-reversal visually evoked potentials in infants. *Investigative Ophthalmology*, 1976, **15**, 58–62.

Sorsby, A., Benjamin, B., & Sheridan, M. Refraction and its components during the growth of the eye after the age of 3. *Special Report Series of the Medical Research Council*, London, 1961, No. 301.

Teller, D. Y. The forced-choice preferential looking procedure: A psychophysical technique for use with human infants. *Infant Behavior & Development*, 1979, **2**, 135–153.

Teller, D. Y., Morse, R., Borton, R., & Regal, D. Visual acuity for vertical and diagonal gratings in human infants. *Vision Research*, 1974, **14**, 1433–1439.

Tronick, E. Stimulus control and the growth of the infant's effective visual field. *Perception & Psychophysics*, 1972, **11**, 373–375.

Volkmann, F. C., & Dobson, V. Infant responses of ocular fixation to moving visual stimuli. *Journal of Experimental Child Psychology*, 1976, **22**, 86–99.

von Noorden, G. K., & Maumenee, A. E. Clinical observations on stimulus deprivation amblyopia. *American Journal of Ophthalmology*, 1968, **65**, 220–224.

Wood, C. C., Spear, P. D., & Braun, J. J. Direction-specific deficits in horizontal optokinetic nystagmus following removal of visual cortex in the cat. *Brain Research*, 1973, **60**, 231–237.

Yinon, U., Rose, L., Shapiro, A., Goldschmidt, M. M. & Steinschneider, T. Y. Refractive changes in the chicken eye following lid fusion. In R. D. Freeman (Ed.), *Developmental neurobiology of vision*, New York, Plenum, 1979.

9

Development of Acuity in Infants with Normal and Anomalous Visual Experience

RICHARD HELD
Massachusetts Institute of Technology

I. INTRODUCTION

There are two major motives for studying visual resolution in infants. The first of these is simple curiosity about what the preverbal child can see and how that capability develops. Few would doubt that, for primates, vision is the dominant sensory channel for acquiring information about the environment and, hence, for adapting to the world. Data on resolution determine minimal sizes and separations of visible entities that can be detected and, consequently, place boundary conditions on the information that can be acquired. The second motive, with both scientific and practical aspects, is to assess visual function for the purpose of detecting the onset and course of pathologies and of studying the consequences of therapeutic procedures. Studies of the consequences of ocular anomalies and of deprivation in animals provide

279

putative models of the developing visual system of the human child. Their implications must be checked by measurements made directly with noninvasive procedures in the developing child. Firm conclusions will also have clinical implications. Actually, the two motives work hand in hand, as the former impels investigators to assemble data on normal infants. Comparison with these data then makes it easier to assess the abnormal resolution that may accompany pathology. As we shall discuss, work with pathological cases is carried out, at least to some extent, in clinical settings and puts rather stringent demands on methods and procedures (Teller, in press).

Two sorts of resolution will be discussed: grating acuity, which corresponds to the common ability to distinguish fine detail and is often symbolized by the Snellen fraction; and stereoacuity, which measures the ability to distinguish differences in the distances of objects from the eyes.

Measures of resolution that are derived from either behavioral or electrophysiological responses and rely on the dioptric system of the eye to focus targets are the result of transfer of information through both optical and neural pathways. Resolution that deviates from the norm may then result from either optical or neural anomalies. The refractive properties of the optics of the eyes are readily assessed by either retinoscopy under cycloplegia or by other methods (Howland & Howland, 1974; Mohindra, 1977). Consequently, when interest centers on questions of neural processing and its development, the first requisite in interpreting any measurement of acuity is an account of the refractive state of the eyes, including accommodative abilities, at the time the acuity is measured. Only then can the contributions of the neural paths be assessed. Moreover, it is particularly important to know the refractive state of the eye at the time of measuring resolution because of the surprising lability of the optics of the infant eye over the course of the first postnatal year (Mohindra, Held, Gwiazda, & Brill, 1978; reviewed by Banks, 1980).

The state of the art of measuring the visual acuity and contrast sensitivity of infants has been reviewed a number of times in recent years (Banks & Salapatek, 1978; Dobson & Teller, 1978; Held, 1979). As discussed by Braddick and Atkinson in Chapter 8 of this volume, advances in the past few years have been impressive, and the amount of agreement among investigators augurs well for the validity of methods and usefulness of the data.

Progress in measuring stereoacuity has lagged behind that of measuring grating resolution. Only recently have reliable procedures been developed for measuring binocularity and stereopsis in infants. Although stereopsis presupposes binocularity, there is good reason to believe that binocularity—cooperative processing of the information entering the two eyes—may exist without stereopsis. We know, for example, that many observers who lack stereopsis are nevertheless quite capable of rapid and accurate convergence movements of the eyes that require binocular information. A recent example of binocular processing in the absence of stereopsis in adults is discussed in Wolfe and Held (1979). Aslin and Jackson (1979) have clearly demonstrated the use of binocular information in convergence movements of the eyes of infants as young as 2 months. Using the correlogram method (Julesz, Kropfl, & Petrig, 1980), Braddick and his colleagues have reported evidence for binocular functioning as early as the second month of life (Braddick, Atkinson, Julesz, Kropfl, Bodis-Wollner, and Raab, 1980).

Although many reports of stereoscopic discrimination in infants have been made over the last 1 or 2 decades, a consistent method for demonstrating this capability has only recently been perfected (reviewed by Aslin & Dumais, 1980). Fox, Aslin, Shea, and Dumais (1980) demonstrated that a large proportion of a sample of infants show stereopsis by the age of 4 months. They used an adaptation of the Julesz random-dot technique. The stereoscopic stimuli that were detected had retinal disparities of the order of $\frac{1}{2}$–1 deg, corresponding to large differences in depth between the objects depicted in the stereograms. Our group has just reported what is, to the best of our knowledge, the first measurements of fine stereopsis in infants. The procedure, discussed in what follows, has enabled us to trace the development of stereoacuity (Held, Birch, & Gwiazda, 1980).

A special consideration in interpreting stereoacuity is the state of the vergence mechanism of the two eyes. To achieve stereovision in general, the images on the retinae of the two eyes must fall on near-corresponding positions. Consequently, the visual axes of the two eyes must both be aligned so as to converge to the point of regard on the object of interest. Methods for assessing convergence have been developed by Slater and Findlay (1975) and Aslin & Jackson (1979). Although these methods are subject to interpretive difficulties, they appear to indicate that convergence is adequate to support stereopsis by at least as early as 2 months.

II. VISUAL RESOLUTION AND THE PREFERENCE METHOD

There are several methods of measuring resolution in the infant. They include preferential looking (PL), use of the optokinetic reflex

(OKN), visually evoked potentials (VEP), and habituation procedures. Each of these methods has its advocates and special uses and has been discussed in other chapters. It is our belief that the current state of the art makes the preferential looking procedure the most versatile and readily applied of the several methods. Consequently, we shall restrict discussion to that method.

The preference procedure was first exploited effectively to measure resolution by Fantz and his colleagues (Fantz, Ordy, & Udelf, 1962). In general, they presented the infant with two spatially separated stimuli and on the basis of its responses—first look, fixation duration, or other observable behavior—decided which of the two was preferred. Since that time, a number of variants have been introduced. Davida Teller and her colleagues introduced a forced-choice method designed to take advantage of new developments in psychophysics (Teller, Morse, Borton, & Regal, 1974). The infant is presented with a grating target of high contrast in one of two horizontally separated locations. The average luminance of the target matches that of a much larger background area of uniform luminance. The observer receives feedback for the judgment as to the location of the grating. This judgment is based upon the attentional behavior of the infant, without sharp specification as to the specific response (fixation duration, eye widening, etc.) exhibited by the infant. The observer is free to wait until the infant shows a clear preference before making the judgment. This procedure measures the correctness of the observer's decision, and provided the observer is astute, above chance performance indicates that the infant detected the grating. Either positive or negative preference for the grating by the infant is claimed to lead to above chance performance by the observer.

An alternative procedure that we have utilized consists in forcing the observer to decide upon the infant's preference between stimuli based upon several criteria of observable behavior (Gwiazda, Brill, Mohindra, & Held, 1978; Leehey, Moskowitz-Cook, Brill, & Held, 1975). In this procedure, the observer's goal is not prespecified beyond deciding which of two separate stimuli, on opposite sides of a fixation light, the infant prefers. Consequently, as Braddick and Atkinson point out in Chapter 8 of this volume, stimuli can be used for which there is no objective criterion for assessing correctness of the observer's decision. From the point of view of psychophysical method, this procedure may be less elegant (Teller, 1979), but it promotes the study of discrimination among stimuli as opposed to the detection of stimuli, and it is our impression that such discrimination can reveal a greater range of sensitivities. The following sections review some of the work that has led to that conclusion and to rapid methods of measurement that are well adapted to clinical purposes.

III. ACUITY MEASUREMENTS

To obtain measurements approximating traditional visual acuity, we presented infants with a choice of two stimuli. One of these was a circular portion of a grating; the other consisted simply of a circular field of equal size and average luminance. Each circular area subtended 11 deg of visual angle separated by 25 deg. Both areas were presented in a dark surround. In the lower range of spatial frequencies, the infants clearly show a preference for the grating. As the grating frequency increases, the preference for the grating decreases rapidly and, as we have recently discovered (Held, Gwiazda, Brill, Mohindra, & Wolfe, 1979), it usually reverses so as to favor the blank field over the grating. The result from a typical 24-week-old infant is shown in Fig. 9.1. As can be seen from this result, the slope of the psychometric function is

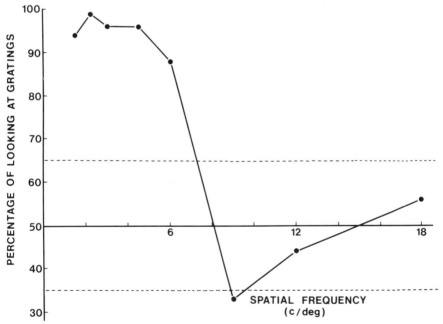

Fig. 9.1 Looking preference as a function of spatial frequency of gratings (subject E.L., 24 weeks). Percentage preferences are based on 48 trials per frequency and the dashed lines represent 95% confidence intervals. (From Held *et al.*, 1979.)

quite steep. The range in spatial frequency from 90 to 50% preference is about 1 octave. The dip below 50% and subsequent rise back toward 50% occurs in most of the infants tested with our procedure.

Using a different set of paired stimuli and the Teller technique of informing the observer on the correctness or incorrectness of response (Teller, 1979), Martin Banks, reporting results from five young infant subjects, fails to find the reversal of preference (personal communication, 1980). In his procedure, adjacent half-fields, subtending large visual angles, consist of a grating to one side with a blank field to the other. Juxtaposition of these results with ours suggests that having two stimuli clearly separated in space and distinctively differentiated as bright circular regions contributes to the reversal of preference that we find as the grating frequency nears threshold levels. Further research should clarify the conditions that produce this reversal of preference.

Perhaps the most interesting outcome of the existence of this psychometric function with its preference reversal is the stability of termination it lends to the use of a staircase-like procedure. In this procedure, successive blocks of three grating stimuli of the same frequency, each paired with a blank field, are presented in a sequence of increasing frequency. When the infant prefers the presented grating the sequence is advanced toward higher frequencies. When the blank is preferred, the sequence is reversed. Typical results using this procedure are shown for one infant tested at three ages (Fig. 9.2) and another with astig-

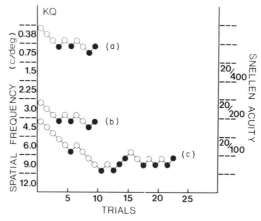

Fig. 9.2 Three typical sessions using the fast method obtained from a nonastigmatic infant tested at (a) 2 weeks (+2.75 ou), (b) 24 weeks (+1.25 ou), and (c) 36 weeks (+0.75 ou). The number of trials is shown at the bottom and the spatial frequency steps are shown in order down the left side. Note that the first three spatial frequency steps are an octave apart and the remaining steps are approximately $\frac{1}{2}$ octave apart. Correct responses are shown by $\bigcirc$, incorrect by $\bullet$.

matism (Fig. 9.4). The results demonstrate, for each infant, the consistent preference for the grating at the lower frequency and the relatively stable terminating frequency at the upper range. This procedure has the great advantage of speed and hence economy of time and effort, but it does so at some cost in accuracy. A detailed account of the procedure and its validity is contained in a recent publication (Gwiazda, Wolfe, Brill, Mohindra, & Held, 1980b). Normative acuity data obtained by using this procedure are presented in Gwiazda, Brill, Mohindra, & Held (1980a) and are reproduced in Fig. 9.3

IV. THE OBLIQUE EFFECT

The small but persistent difference in acuity between edges aligned along oblique and main (horizontal and vertical) axes is routinely observed in most adult observers and called the oblique effect. Some years ago, the claim was made that habitual exposure to the allegedly higher incidence of near vertical and near horizontal edges in the urban world was responsible for the oblique effect. This claim was bolstered by reports that the Cree Indians of northern Canada, who live in a rural environment in dwellings with dominantly oblique edges, showed less of an oblique effect (Annis & Frost, 1973). Consistent with the claim were the reports that kittens reared in environments dominated by

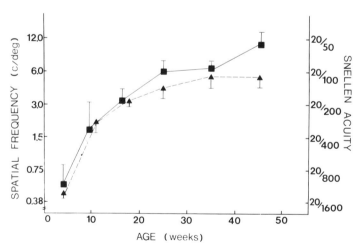

Fig. 9.3 Median spatial frequency at which infants preferred either a main axis (shown by ■) or an oblique (depicted by ▲) grating to a homogeneous (gray) field as determined by the fast method. Mean ages ranged from 4 to 45 weeks. Error bars show the semi-interquartile range.

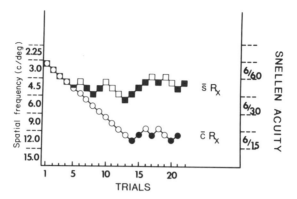

Fig. 9.4 Preference responses on successive trials to threshold criterion of a 36-week-old infant with two diopters of astigmatism (R_x: + 4.00 − 2.00 × 180). The upper plot is without correction; the lower with correction. Correct responses are shown by ○ and ☐, incorrect by ● and ■.

stripes of a particular orientation showed unusually high proportions of cortical cells responsive to that orientation (Blakemore & Cooper, 1970; Hirsch & Spinelli, 1971), although these results were qualified by Stryker, Sherk, Leventhal, & Hirsch (1978).

We were struck by the possibility that a comparison in the infant of the acuities for oblique, as opposed to main axis gratings, might reveal something of the origin of the difference. Particularly, if the acuity difference between orientations showed up sufficiently early in life, there would be a strong presumption that it did not result from exposure to a biased distribution of edge orientations.

Using the measuring procedures discussed previously, we found that the acuity for oblique gratings becomes lower than that for main axis gratings beginning at about 6 months of age (Gwiazda, et al., 1980a). The difference was also obtained using the same apparatus but with the psychophysical method of constant stimuli (Gwiazda et al., 1978).

On the hunch that direct comparision of two gratings might be a more sensitive procedure than that used in measuring acuity as just discussed, we presented these to infants in an otherwise darkened room. One grating was obliquely oriented, the other oriented along a main axis. They were matched in spatial frequency, luminance, and contrast. Spatial frequency was varied over a range including the expected acuity threshold. The results indicated that infants systematically prefer main axis to oblique gratings when, and only when, their spatial frequencies are at or near their acuity thresholds (Gwiazda et al., 1978; Leehey et al., 1975). At those frequencies, the main axis gratings are apparently more visible and consequently are preferred. At both higher and lower frequencies, preferences drop off to 50%, suggesting that the visibility differences are either minimized or absent. Moreover, using the direct comparison procedure, the oblique effect was detectable in infants of only a few weeks of age.

Apart from arguing against the thesis that exposure to the urban world produces the oblique effect (see also Switkes, Mayer, & Sloan, 1978; Timney & Muir, 1976) this result stands out in contrast to the older age (a few months versus a few weeks) at which the acuity measurements show the oblique effect (see Fig. 9.3). It suggests that the direct pairing of gratings is more sensitive to small differences in visibility than the acuity measuring procedure. In the former procedure, the infant is presented with two stimuli matched along several dimensions, that is, equivalent space-averaged luminance of the circular regions contrasting with their dark background, square wave gratings of equal frequency and equal contrast, and unmatched along the single dimension of bar orientation. In the latter procedure, the two circular regions are matched only in luminance and contrast with the background and unmatched in terms of the presence and absence of the grating. The comparison suggests that the additional number of matched dimensions shared by paired stimuli enhances sensitivity to the one difference that is presented. Other observations to be discussed are consistent with this conclusion.

V. THE INFLUENCE OF ASTIGMATISM ON ACUITY

As discussed in the previous section, the paired grating approach to testing the oblique effect has proven quite sensitive. We have also applied this procedure to examine the blurring effects of astigmatism (the presence of cylindrical power in the dioptrics of the eye). Cylindrical power has the effect of allowing a sharply focused image of an edge in only one orientation with respect to the axis of the cylinder. Edges that deviate in angle from the axis orientation are blurred (defocused) by amounts that increase with the magnitude of the deviation up to a maximum at 90 deg. The effect of astigmatic blur is to reduce the contrast of a grating and to reduce it increasingly as the grating frequency increases. Consequently, by presenting to astigmatic infants gratings whose frequency is above the acuity threshold and that differ only in bar orientation, we can test sensitivity to differences in contrast. Paired gratings, one of which is aligned with the focusable axis of astigmatism, while the other is rotated 45 deg, yield very clear evidence of the contrast reduction produced by blur. Over a considerable range of spatial frequencies, the aligned gratings are preferred to the 45 deg gratings (Held, 1978). The lowered contrast produced by blur clearly makes the latter less preferred. Moreover, it has been possible to show that even a half-diopter of blur is sufficient to alter significantly the preference in this paired comparison discrimination procedure. We have also tested the preferences between paired gratings with bar orientations at 90 deg to each other. When the range of accommodation is either insufficient to focus one of these gratings, or the amount of accommodation required to focus is large, a clear preference for one of them can be established (Atkinson & French, 1979; Held, 1978).

Previously discussed measures of preference determined acuity were all obtained on infants who had no serious refractive constraints on acuity. They had only mild spherical refractive error within the range of correction by accommodation and no significant astigmatism (less than one diopter). Having discovered that, in young infants, there is an unexpectedly high incidence of astigmatism (Mohindra *et al.*, 1978) ranging up to 50%, it was of considerable interest to test its effect on acuity. Using the acuity measuring procedure (pairing grating with blank field) it was easy to demonstrate the lowered resolution along the axis of orientation that causes blur that is not readily corrected by accommodative effort. Such a case is illustrated in Fig. 9.4. Optical correction readily returns the acuity to the norm (compare with Fig. 9.3). A similar result has been reported by Teller, Allen, Regal, & Mayer (1978).

As has already been stated, astigmatism causes blurring of the retinal image with predictable loss of acuity caused by this blur. What was not obvious until it was recently examined carefully is the long-term consequences of such habitual blur. Freeman, Mitchell, & Millodot (1972) and Mitchell, Freeman, Millodot, & Haegerstrom (1973) clearly demonstrated that many adult astigmats suffer from optically uncorrectable loss of acuity selective to the axes that are habitually blurred. They called the condition meridional amblyopia. Because it cannot be optically corrected, this loss of acuity must be attributed to abnormalities in the visual nervous system either caused by the habitual blur or accompanying it for other reasons. A partial decision over these alternatives may be obtained by studying the course of development of meridional amblyopia in infants and children. If the relation is causal, the astigmatism must antedate the amblyopia; if not, both may occur simultaneously or amblyopia may even antedate the astigmatism. The large number of infants showing astigmatism provides the essential sample, although the absolute number of highly astigmatic infants who retain their astigmatism past the first year tends to be very small. This factor may be of considerable importance, as Mitchell and his colleagues showed that the incidence of meridional amblyopia was proportionate to the strength of the astigmatism. In any event, we decided to test the acuity and preferences of astigmats throughout the first year and beyond, when possible.

Measurements of acuity were taken with and without optical correction in an attempt to detect the presence of meridional amblyopia in infant astigmats. One such case is shown in Fig. 9.4. Of the many infant astigmats tested in this fashion, not one showed convincing evidence of an uncorrectable loss of acuity during the first year of life. Using direct comparison of two gratings in different orientations, we can observe the preference for the less blurred grating as previously discussed. Optical correction, however, invariably eliminated such preferences at least during the first year of life. On the basis of this failure to detect meridional amblyopia, we have tentatively concluded that it does not develop until some time after the first year of life (Held, 1979).

VI. MEASURING STEREOACUITY

Recently, we found another convincing example of the value of our paired comparison procedure. Stereoscopic perception of depth requires central comparison between the images of objects produced on the retinas of the two eyes. Studies of the effects of binocular imbalance have demonstrated severe losses of binocularity at the single cell level of visual cortex in experimental animals (Hubel & Wiesel, 1970; Hubel, Wiesel, & LeVay, 1977). Consequently, one might expect that stereovision would provide an excellent diagnostic test of the deleterious effects of early binocular imbalance on human vision. In fact, experimental data have demonstrated such effects in adult observers who have suffered early imbalances (Mitchell & Ware, 1974; Movshon, Chambers, & Blakemore, 1972).

Several approaches to the detection of stereoscopic stimuli in infants have been taken. They are reviewed in Aslin and Dumais (1980) and by Fox, Chapter 12, in this volume. Rough agreement has been reached that stereopsis emerges within the first few months of life. We wanted to develop a technique that would allow us not only to measure the onset of gross stereoscopy, but also to measure the resolution limit of the system as it develops. Such measures of stereoacuity would not only allow us to track the development of the system but also would ultimately serve for precise clinical assessment of the consequences of binocular imbalance. We used the stimulus pairing shown in Fig. 9.5. Once again, the stimuli were equated in all dimensions except for one: the presence or absence of a relative displacement in depth of two of the three bars in one of the circular fields. The displacement in the third dimension was produced by having infants view polarized stereograms through crossed polaroid filters placed over their eyes. Infants show strong preference for the stimulus having the depth difference. By presenting them with stimuli varying in depth, preference thresholds for stereoacuity were obtained (Held *et al.*, 1980). The onset of stereoscopy using this method appears to occur between 8 and 20 weeks with a mean of 16 weeks, in rough agreement with earlier studies. Surprisingly, within another 4 weeks, on the average, the infants appear to reach a stereoacuity of 1 min or less. One min represented the limit of resolution of the apparatus then in use and not that of the infants. Actually, the acuity of adults measured more recently in the same apparatus with even smaller disparities did not exceed $\frac{1}{2}$ min of arc. Under more ideal conditions of measurement, the stereoacuity of adults is known to go down to a few seconds of arc (Foley, 1978).

The sudden onset and rapid development of stereoacuity contrasts strongly with the gradual increase of grating acuity over the course of at least the first year. Several other visual capabilities and susceptibilities

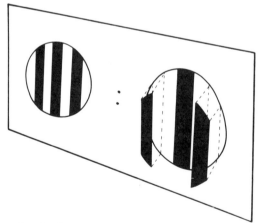

Fig. 9.5 A sample stimulus pair as it would appear to a normal adult observer. In this case, the stimulus to the left of the fixation spots contain zero disparity and the stimulus to the right contains a large crossed disparity: the bars appear in front of the screen. In the experiment, uncrossed disparities, for which the bars appear behind the screen, were also used. The dashed lines are for construction.

appear at about the time of high stereoacuity including improvement in convergence (Aslin & Jackson, 1980), accurate accommodation (Banks, 1980; Braddick, Atkinson, French, & Howland, 1979; Haynes, White, & Held, 1965), visually guided reaching (White, Castle, & Held, 1964; McDonnell, 1979), and the beginnings of what appears to be amblyopia in the deviating eye of infants suffering a form of strabismus called constant esotropia (Jacobson, Mohindra, & Held, in press; Mohindra, Jacobson, Thomas, & Held, 1979; Thomas, Mohindra, & Held, 1979). Both the capabilities of binocular vision and its susceptibility to the deleterious effects of imbalanced inputs appear to develop during this period ranging from 2 to 5 months of age.

VII. CLINICAL APPLICATIONS

With the availability of the new techniques for measuring resolution, one would like to apply them to infant patients with ocular problems more severe than the usual refractive errors found in astigmatism. A number of problems arise in clinical work that are either absent or present to only a minor degree in the laboratory: the availability of patients with appropriate pathology, the medical milieu with its emphasis on service, and the fact that research is inevitably secondary to treatment. Speed is a major issue. Whereas the time required to experiment with infants in the laboratory is a factor to contend with, it becomes critical in the clinic. The practitioner is under pressure to treat as many patients as can be accommodated. Because of this time pressure, we have used the fast procedure (see Fig. 9.2) as often as possible, although we are aware of its shortcomings as detailed in Gwiazda *et al.* (1980b). When possible, the results have been checked with the use of the more time-consuming method of constant stimuli. As there is a trade-off between speed and accuracy, some sacrifice in the latter may be justified in the interests of speed.

Through the cooperation of officers of the Massachusetts Eye and Ear Infirmary, we have been able to set up a small testing unit on the premises. By this time, a large number of infants with various clinical problems have had their grating acuities measured, usually in each eye separately. Many of these measurements have been taken before, during, and after therapeutic procedures such as patching and surgery. Perhaps the clearest results have been those from strabismic infants suffering from constant esotropia, in which one eye turns inward by a constant angle so that a point fixated by the nondeviating eye is imaged on the nasal retina of the deviating eye. In such infants, the first sign of differing acuities (monocular amblyopia) occurs no earlier than the third month, although the esotropia is seen before that time. Patching the nondeviating eye, with higher acuity, very clearly brings up the acuity of the deviating eye but reduces that of the patched eye (Mohindra *et al.*, 1979; Thomas *et al.*, 1979). This trade-off in acuities has been found in almost every patched infant that has been measured. Following release of occlusion, there is a reversal of the trade-off process, such that the formerly patched eye increases in acuity, while the deviating eye may return to its former state of lower acuity. The plasticity demonstrated by these results appears to be the rule throughout the first year and probably into at least the succeeding year.

Another type of ocular pathology that is to be found in the clinic is congenital or early cataract. These cases involve a degree of occlusion that varies with the density of the cataract and hence constitute a natural analogue to the experimental occlusion studied in animals. Surgery is frequently performed very early in these infants to eliminate the occlusion of vision. Careful optical correction is then required. We have applied our methods for studying acuity to a number of these infants, and some of the results have been reported (Mohindra, Jacobson, & Held, 1980). To sum them up, we have found that very early occlusion, during the first few weeks of life, has little or no effect on visual acuity. Enoch and Rabinowicz (1976) come to a similar conclusion based on their case. Occlusion for many weeks does, however, appear to arrest the development of acuity. Disocclusion then allows the system to develop to normal levels of resolution. Finally, the effects of monocular cataract, not surprisingly, resemble those of deliberate therapeutic occlusion (patching) as used in strabismus (see previous section). Again, as in the changes in grating acuity that accompany esotropia, they appear to be reversible during the first year.

These cataract cases pose an interesting methodological problem. We have suggested that the reversal of preference from grating to blank field observed in our testing procedure, the dip discussed earlier, may result from accommodative stress (Held *et al.*, 1979). If true, the aphakic eye lacking the lens should not show the dip when tested with the method of constant stimuli. Moreover, the stability of termination of our fast procedure should suffer if the dip is absent, and the results should become less accurate. Currently, a number of aphakic infants are being tested with both procedures in the interests of answering these questions.

Many other types of ocular pathology may be found in the clinic and tested by means of the new procedures. Although promising as a clinical tool, much more study needs to be made before this promise can be fully realized.

VIII. CONCLUSION

I have tried to sketch the major research directions of one laboratory concerned with the developing vision of infants, including those with and without ocular pathologies. Whereas the techniques preferred by the workers in this laboratory differ from those of others, and vice versa, there is a convergence of findings. They suggest that progress is being made along several lines including measurement of grating acuity, stereopsis, stereoacuity, and the effects of pathologies ranging from astigmatism to esotropia and cataract. One gets the impression that further progress will rapidly be made.

On the topic of the symposium from which this chapter originated, "Genetic and Experiential Factors in Perceptual Development," I am tempted to conclude that much of the sensory capacity that we observe develops according to a preset, presumably genetically determined program. Evidence that grating acuity measures correlate better with gestational age than with birth date (Dobson, Mayer, & Lee, 1980) is one form of evidence that bears out this conclusion. The aberrations of development that are induced by inappropriate experience appear in general to be deleterious, although they may be countered by therapeutic intervention at least in the early stages that we have examined. The variation in this plasticity with age and its termination remain to be determined.

ACKNOWLEDGMENTS

Research of the author and his colleagues has been supported by grants from the National Eye Institute (NIH–EY01191, NIH–EY02621, and NIH–EY02649) and from the Spencer Foundation (LTR–DTD–71373). The author would like to thank Jane Gwiazda and Jeremy M. Wolfe for their editorial assistance.

REFERENCES

Annis, R. C., & Frost, B. Human visual ecology and orientation anisotropies in acuity. *Science*, 1973, **182**, 729–731.
Aslin, R. N., & Dumais, S. T. Binocular vision in infants: A review and theoretical

framework. In H. Reese & L. Lipsitt (Eds.), *Advances in child development and behavior* (Vol. 15). New York: Academic Press, 1980.

Aslin, R. N., & Jackson, R. W. Accommodative convergence in young infants: Development of a synergistic sensory–motor system. *Canadian Journal of Psychology*, 1979, **33**, 222–231.

Atkinson, J., & French, J. Astigmatism and orientation preference in human infants. *Vision Research*, 1979, **19**, 1315–1317.

Banks, M. Infant ocular refraction and accommodation. In S. Sokol (Ed.), *Electrophysiology and psychophysics: Their use in ophthalmic diagnosis*. Boston: Little, Brown, 1980.

Banks, M. The development of visual accommodation during early infancy. *Child Development*, 1980, **51**, 646–666.

Banks, M., & Salapatek, P. Acuity and contrast sensitivity in 1-, 2-, and 3-month-old human infants. *Investigative Ophthalmology*, 1978, **17**, 361–365.

Blakemore, C., & Cooper, G. F. Development of the brain depends on the visual environment. *Nature*, 1970, **228**, 477–478.

Braddick, O., Atkinson, J., French, J., & Howland, H. C. A photorefractive study of infant accommodation. *Vision Research*, 1979, **19**, 1319–1330.

Braddick, O., Atkinson, J., Julesz, B., Kropfl, W., Bodis-Wollner, I., & Raab, E. Cortical binocularity in infants. *Nature*, 1980, **228**, 363–365.

Dobson, V., Mayer, D. L., & Lee, C. P. Visual acuity screening of preterm infants. *Investigative Ophthalmology*, in press.

Dobson, V., & Teller, D. Y. Visual acuity in human infants: A review and comparison of behavioral and electrophysiological studies. *Vision Research*, 1978, **18**, 1469–1483.

Enoch, J. M., & Rabinowicz, I. M. Early surgery and visual correction of an infant born with unilateral eye lens opacity. *Documenta Ophthalmologica*, 1976, **41**, 371–382.

Fantz, R. L., Ordy, J. M., & Udelf, M. S. Maturation of pattern vision in infants during the first 6 months. *Journal of Comparative and Physiological Psychology*, 1962, **55**, 907–917.

Foley, J. M. Primary distance perception. In R. Held, H. W. Leibowitz, & H.-L. Teuber (Eds.), *Handbook of sensory physiology VIII. Perception*. New York: Springer-Verlag, 1978.

Fox, R., Aslin, R. N., Shea, S. L., & Dumais, S. T. Stereopsis in human infants. *Science*, 1980, **207**, 323–324.

Freeman, R. D., Mitchell, D. E., & Millodot, M. A neural effect of partial visual deprivation in humans. *Science*, 1972, **175**, 1384–1386.

Gwiazda, J., Brill, S., Mohindra, I., & Held, R. Infant visual acuity and its meridional variation. *Vision Research*, 1978, **18**, 1557–1564.

Gwiazda, J., Brill, S., Mohindra, I., & Held, R. Preferential looking acuity in infants from 2 to 58 weeks of age. *American Journal of Optometry and Physiological Optics*, 1980, **57**, 428–432. (a)

Gwiazda, J., Wolfe, J., Brill, S., Mohindra, I., & Held, R. Quick assessment of preferential looking acuity in infants. *American Journal of Optometry and Physiological Optics*, 1980, **57**, 420–427. (b)

Haynes, H., White, B. L., & Held, R. Visual accommodation in human infants. *Science*, 1965, **148**, 528–530.

Held, R. Development of visual acuity in normal and astigmatic infants. In S. J. Cool & E. L. Smith, III (Eds.), *Frontiers in visual science*. New York: Springer-Verlag, 1978.

Held, R. Development of visual resolution. *Canadian Journal of Psychology*, 1979, **33**, 213–221.

Held, R., Birch, E., & Gwiazda, J. Stereoacuity of human infants. *Proceedings of the National Academy of Sciences*, 1980, **77**, 5572–5574.

Held, R., Gwiazda, J., Brill, S., Mohindra, I., & Wolfe, J. Infant visual acuity is underestimated because near threshold gratings are not preferentially fixated. *Vision Research*, 1979, **19**, 1377–1379.

Hirsch, H. V. B., & Spinelli, D. N. Modification of the distribution of receptive field orientation in cats by selective visual exposure during development. *Experimental Brain Research*, 1971, **12**, 509–527.

Howland, H. C., & Howland, B. Photorefraction: A technique for study of refractive state at a distance. *Journal of the Optical Society of America*, 1974, **64**, 240–249.

Hubel, D. H., & Wiesel, T. N. The period of susceptibility to the physiological effects of unilateral eye closure in kittens. *Journal of Physiology*, 1970, **206**, 419–436.

Hubel, D. H., Wiesel, T. N., & LeVay, S. Plasticity of ocular dominance columns in monkey striate cortex. *Philosophical Transactions of the Royal Society, B.* 1977, **278**, 377–409.

Jacobson, S. G., Mohindra, I., & Held, R. Age of onset of amblyopia in infants with esotropia. *Documenta Ophthalmologica*, in press.

Julesz, B., Kropfl, W., & Petrig, B. Large evoked potentials to dynamic random-dot correlograms and stereograms permit quick determination of stereopsis. *Proceedings of the National Academy of Sciences*, 1980, **77**, 2348–2351.

Leehey, S. C., Moskowitz-Cook, A., Brill, S., & Held, R. Orientational anisotropy in infant vision. *Science*, 1975, **190**, 900–902.

McDonnell, P. M. Patterns of eye–hand coordination in the first year of life. *Canadian Journal of Psychology*, 1979, **33**, 253–267.

Mitchell, D. E., Freeman, R. D., Millodot, M., & Haegerstrom, G. Meridional amblyopia: Evidence for modification of the human visual system by early visual experience. *Vision Research*, 1973, **13**, 535–558.

Mitchell, D. E., & Ware, C. Interocular transfer of a visual aftereffect in normal and stereoblind humans. *Journal of Physiology*, 1974, **236**, 707–721.

Mohindra, I. A noncycloplegic refraction technique for infants and children. *Journal of the American Optometric Association*, 1977, **48**, 518–523.

Mohindra, I., Held, R., Gwiazda, J., & Brill, S. Astigmatism in infants. *Science*, 1978, **202**, 329–331.

Mohindra, I., Jacobson, S. G., & Held, R. Development of visual acuity in infants with congenital cataracts. Abstract of presentation at meeting of Association for Research in Vision and Ophthalmology (ARVO), Orlando, Florida, May 5–9, 1980.

Mohindra, I., Jacobson, S. G., Thomas, J., & Held, R. Development of amblyopia in infants. *Transactions of the Ophthalmological Society, U.K.*, 1979, **99**, 344–346.

Movshon, J. A., Chambers, B. E. I., & Blakemore, C. Interocular transfer in normal humans, and those who lack stereopsis. *Perception*, 1972, **1**, 483–490.

Slater, A. M., & Findlay, J. M. Binocular fixation in the newborn baby. *Journal of Experimental Child Psychology*, 1975, **20**, 248–273.

Stryker, M. P., Sherk, H., Leventhal, A. G., & Hirsch, H. Physiological consequences for the cat's visual cortex of effectively restricting early visual experience with oriented contours. *Journal of Neurophysiology*, 1978, **41**, 896–909.

Switkes, E., Mayer, M. J., & Sloan, J. A. Spatial frequency analysis of the visual environment: Anisotropy and the carpentered environment hypothesis. *Vision Research*, 1978, **18**, 1393–1399.

Teller, D. Y. Infant psychophysics: The laboratory and the clinic. Invited address at

Symposium on Application of Psychophysics to Clinical Problems. Conference on Behavioral and Social Sciences, National Research Council, National Academy of Sciences, San Francisco, October 30, 1978, in press.

Teller, D. Y. The forced-choice preferential looking procedure: A psychophysical technique for use with human infants. *Infant Behavior and Development*, 1979, **2**, 135–158.

Teller, D. Y., Allen, J. L., Regal, D. M., & Mayer, D. L. Astigmatism and acuity in two primate infants. *Investigative Ophthalmology*, 1978, **17**, 344–349.

Teller, D. Y., Morse, R., Borton, R., & Regal, D. Visual acuity for vertical and diagonal gratings in human infants. *Vision Research*, 1974, **14**, 1433–1439.

Thomas, J., Mohindra, I., & Held, R. Strabismic amblyopia in infants. *American Journal of Optometry and Physiological Optics*, 1979, **56**, 197–201.

Timney, B. N., & Muir, D. W. Orientational anisotropy: Incidence and magnitude in Caucasian and Chinese subjects. *Science*, 1976, **193**, 699–700.

White, B., Castle, R., & Held, R. Observations on the development of visually directed reaching. *Child Development*, 1964, **35**, 349–364.

Wolfe, J., & Held, R. Eye torsion and visual tilt are mediated by different binocular processes. *Vision Research*, 1979, **19**, 917–920.

10

Color Vision in Infants

DAVIDA Y. TELLER
University of Washington

When most of us think of the topic of color vision, we think of the perception of hues such as those visible in the rainbow—red, orange, yellow, green, blue, and violet—and their less saturated counterparts such as pinks, light blues, and so on. These variations in perceived hue and saturation come about largely in correlation with variations in the wavelength composition of the light reaching our eyes. In the fields of visual perception and psychophysics, the term color vision has thus come to include most or all studies in which the wavelength composition of stimuli is a major independent variable.

Within the psychophysics of color vision there are two major kinds of studies: (*a*) studies of *spectral sensitivity*—the *detectability* of light as a function of its wavelength and; (*b*) studies of the *discriminability* of two lights that differ in wavelength composition. A second major division occurs between night-time, or *scotopic*, and daytime, or *photopic* vision.

In the present chapter, I shall first describe the behavioral technique developed in my laboratory for the study of visual capacities in human infants, and then describe the results of our experiments concerning

297

DEVELOPMENT OF PERCEPTION
Volume 2

scotopic spectral sensitivity, photopic spectral sensitivity, and wave-length discrimination. Our results will be compared briefly to results from other laboratories, in which other behavioral techniques and visually evoked potentials (VEPs) have been employed in related studies of infant color vision.[1]

I. THE FORCED-CHOICE PREFERENTIAL
LOOKING TECHNIQUE

The technique developed in my laboratory for the psychophysical testing of infant vision is called forced-choice preferential looking, or FPL (Teller, Morse, Borton, & Regal, 1974; Teller, 1979; cf. Fantz, 1965, 1967). In FPL testing, an infant is held by an adult in a more or less vertical position in front of a stimulus display. The display consists of a single stimulus, presented on each trial in one of two possible positions—left or right—in an otherwise homogeneous visual field. For example, in a test of an infant's absolute threshold for the detection of light, the field would be completely dark except for a single stimulus—a patch of light—that could occur in either a left or a right position.

Throughout the early postnatal months, human infants have very strong fixation and tracking responses. Thus, if the stimulus patch in the FPL experiment is of a high enough intensity, the infant will almost invariably stare at it. If the infant is rotated slowly in front of the screen, he or she will produce compensatory eye and head movements, to continue to fixate the stimulus.

The infant's looking pattern is monitored on line by an adult observer, either through a peephole in the center of the screen, or via a TV monitor. In the latter case, the observer can both hold the infant in front of the display and monitor the infant's eye and head movements on the TV monitor.

The observer is blind to the position of the stimulus. On each trial, the observer's task is to use the infant's eye and head movements and fixation patterns to judge whether the stimulus is being presented on the left or right side of the screen. Above chance performance on the part of the observer implies that information concerning the position of the stimulus passes from the screen, in through the infant's visual system, and out through the infant's behavior; i.e., that the infant can

[1] For a more comprehensive review of infant color vision, see Teller and Bornstein (1982).

see the stimulus. The formal similarity of the observer's task to a classically defined forced-choice experiment, and the logic of interpretation of the data, are discussed fully in Teller (1979).

In a detection experiment, we present the infant with 20 or more trials at each of a series of intensities. The observer's performance varies from chance, or 50% correct, for relatively dim stimuli, to virtually 100% correct for relatively intense ones. We interpolate within this psychometric function to find the intensity needed for 75% correct on the part of the observer, and use this value as an estimate of the infant's threshold.

II. SCOTOPIC SPECTRAL SENSITIVITY

Powers, Schneck, and Teller (1981) have recently studied the spectral sensitivity of 3-month-old infants under conditions of total darkness. Less extensive data were also collected on 1-month-olds. The infant's eyes were allowed to adjust to dim red light, and then to darkness, for at least 15 min before the start of each test session. The infant was tested with two or more wavelengths of light at several intensities each. The infant's fixation pattern was monitored via an infrared TV system.

Data from two 3-month-old infants tested with 502 and 608 nm light are shown in Fig. 10.1, as examples of the kinds of data obtained in FPL testing. These data are orderly within each infant and quite consistent across the two infants. The location of the function varies consistently with the wavelength of the light.

Figure 10.2 shows data for a series of wavelengths, averaged across subjects, for 1-month-olds, 3-month-olds, and adults tested in the same apparatus. Infant and adult curves have very similar shapes. The solid lines show the standard scotopic sensitivity function for adult vision— the CIE scotopic luminosity function—adjusted vertically for optimum fits to the data. Both infant and adult data are well fit by the standard function. We thus conclude that infants' relative scotopic spectral sensitivity is highly similar to that of adults, and is doubtless mediated by the same photopigment, the rhodopsin contained in the rod receptors of the retina.

Scotopic spectral sensitivity has recently been studied by means of visual evoked potential (VEP) recordings (Werner, 1979). Werner favors the interpretation that infants' relative sensitivity is slightly higher than that of adults at extremely short wavelengths. Our data on 1-month-olds show a trend in this direction, in that the infants' data fall somewhat above the CIE curve for wavelengths below 430 nm. Data from

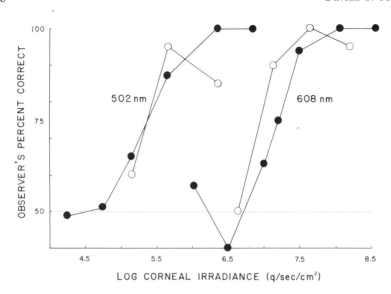

Fig. 10.1 Psychometric functions from two dark-adapted 3-month-old infants (Tyler, ●; Kyle B, ○) measured with two different wavelengths of light. In each case, the observer's percent correct is plotted as a function of the physical intensity of the light as it enters the eye (log corneal irradiance in quanta per second per square centimeter). The infants agree well with each other, and both are almost a factor of 100 more sensitive to 502 than to 608 nm. (Adapted from Powers, Schneck, & Teller, 1981.)

our 3 month-olds, however, agree with the CIE curve well throughout the spectrum. Thus, spectral sensitivity may be elevated in the short wavelength region in very early infancy, but the difference appears to be short-lived. Further data will be needed to resolve this question with certainty. In any case, Werner's study and ours are in agreement in showing that, to an excellent first approximation, infant and adult scotopic curves are highly similar.

The other notable feature of the data is that the 3-month-old infants come within about a factor of ten of the adults in absolute sensitivity, and the 1-month-olds are not far behind. The adults in our experiment are detecting the absorption of about one quantum per second per 1300 rod receptors. Using conservative assumptions concerning preretinal absorption, magnification, and so on, we calculate that, at 502 nm, the 3-month-old infants are detecting about one quantal absorption per 200 rods/sec, and the 1-month-olds about one per 56 rods/sec. Thus, dark-adapted human infants, like adults, can demonstrate exquisite sensitivity to very small amounts of light. This is a remarkable performance indeed for a visual system that was until recently thought to be barely functional.

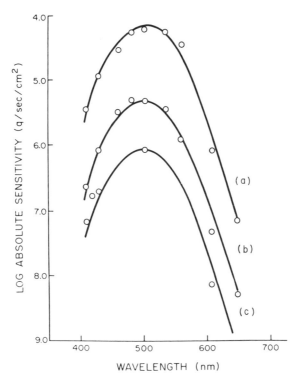

Fig. 10.2   Average scotopic spectral sensitivity curves from (a) adults, (b) 3-month-old infants, and (c) 1-month-old infants. The adults are about a factor of ten more sensitive than the 3-month-olds and about a factor of 50 more sensitive than the 1-month-olds. The solid lines are the standard adult (CIE scotopic) curve shifted vertically for best fit to each data set. All three data sets are well fit by this standard curve. (Adapted from Powers, Schneck, & Teller, 1981.)

III. PHOTOPIC SPECTRAL SENSITIVITY

Light-adapted, or *photopic*, spectral sensitivity has also been studied in young infants with the FPL technique (Peeples & Teller, 1978). In this experiment, two 2–3-month-old infants were adapted to a white screen at a luminance of 2.0 log cd/m^2—a moderately bright room illumination—to insure that light-adapted vision would be tested. A stimulus field of one of six wavelengths was presented at the center of the screen, and moved slowly outward—either leftward or rightward—from the center (cf. Chase, 1937). An adult observer watched the infant's tracking and fixation behavior and, on this basis, judged the direction of movement of the stimulus, for each of a series of intensities at each wavelength. Three adult subjects were also tested in the same apparatus.

The resulting averaged spectral sensitivity curves, for adults and infants, are shown in Fig. 10.3. The adult curve has been shifted downward by a factor of ten to coincide most closely with the infant curve. Both curves are fairly broad, as would be expected from earlier studies of adult photopic spectral sensitivity against white backgrounds (e.g., Sperling & Harwerth, 1971). The relative sensitivities of the infants and adults agree well, with the maximum difference between infants and adults being less than 0.2 log unit. Thus, under these conditions at least, infant and adult photopic relative spectral sensitivities, like scotopic ones, are highly similar.

Two other modern studies of infant photopic spectral sensitivity have been published (Dobson, 1976; Moskowitz-Cook, 1979). In both studies, VEPs rather than behavioral methods were employed, and infant and adult spectral sensitivities, tested under the same conditions, were found to be similar to a good first approximation. In both studies, young infants—the 2-month-olds studied by Dobson and the infants below 3 months of age in the Moskowitz-Cook study—were system-

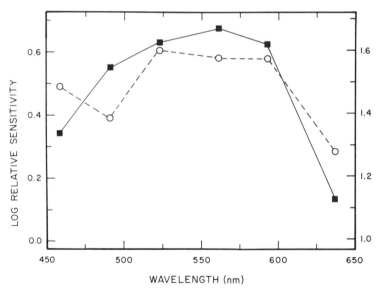

Fig. 10.3 Averaged photopic spectral sensitivity curves from two infants (represented by ■) and three adults (shown by ○), for six wavelengths of light. The adult curve (right abscissa) has been shifted vertically by a factor of ten for best fit to the infant curve (left abscissa). Both curves are broad, as expected under the white-adapted conditions used. There is good agreement between infants and adults. (Adapted from Peeples & Teller, 1978.)

atically more sensitive in the short wavelength region of the spectrum than were the adults tested. The cause for these systematic deviations, seen in the two VEP studies but not in our behavioral study, remain to be sorted out. In any case, there is good agreement across studies that, with the possible exception of short wavelength light, adult spectral sensitivities provide a reasonable first approximation to infant values across a range of neutrally adapted conditions.[2]

IV. THE EQUATING OF BRIGHTNESSES AMONG STIMULI OF DIFFERENT WAVELENGTHS

We turn now to the fundamental question of color vision—the question of discrimination among lights of different wavelength composition. Here one encounters a serious conceptual problem. It is easy to show that an infant can respond differentially to lights or objects of different wavelength composition. For example, an infant might readily learn to reach for a red milk bottle instead of a green one. The problem is that, even in a black and white photograph, an adult could almost certainly distinguish the red bottle from the green one, on the basis of a difference in brightness. The abiding problem in demonstrations of infant color vision is to prove that the infant's discrimination is made on the basis of differences in wavelength composition, rather than on the basis of brightness differences. The problem is, how can we equate two stimuli of different wavelength composition in brightness, *for the infant*, when the infant cannot make brightness matches?

The most common approach to this problem has been to equate the two stimuli for brightness by *adult* standards—for example, by having an adult make heterochromatic brightness matches *in situ*— and to assume that these brightness matches will hold to a good enough approximation for infants. In view of the good agreement between adult and infant photopic spectral sensitivity (discussed earlier), it is probably true that adult brightness matches provide a reasonable first approximation for infant matches (except possibly for short wavelength stimuli). But demonstrations of infant color vision that rest on the assumption that adult brightness matches hold for infants will always be equivocal. The two major problems are: First, that spectral sensitivities, based on detection thresholds, themselves provide only rough approximations

---

[2] The topic of photopic spectral sensitivity is a complex one in adult psychophysics, and in infant psychophysics as well. In fact, under conditions of chromatic adaptation, the similarity between infant and adult photopic spectral sensitivity is known to break down for 2-month-old infants (Pulos, Teller, & Buck, 1980). For additional discussion, see Teller and Bornstein (1982).

to brightness matches, even for adults; and second, that until recently we have had little idea how sensitive infants may be to small mismatches of brightness.

Our approach to this dilemma (Peeples & Teller, 1975) has been to vary the luminances of test stimuli systematically around the adult brightness match, in steps so small as to be certain that at least one stimulus in the luminance series confronts the infant with a brightness match. If the observer can do better than chance for *every* stimulus in such a series, it follows that the infant must have some form of color vision. The preliminary questions are, over how big a range should the luminance be varied, to insure that the infant's brightness match is included within the range; and how small must the luminance steps be, to insure that the infant's brightness match is not missed by falling between two luminance steps? Two preliminary experiments were done to estimate the answers to these two questions.

Measures of spectral sensitivity were used to choose the luminance range. In our spectral sensitivity study (Peeples & Teller, 1978), the maximum deviation between infant and adult relative spectral sensitivities was 0.16 log unit (Fig. 10.3). On this basis, we placed our bets, somewhat arbitrarily, that the infant's brightness match would fall within $\pm$ 0.4 log unit of the adult match; and tested infants at a finely spaced series of intensities across this entire range.

To choose the luminance spacing (Peeples & Teller, 1975) infants' luminance discrimination functions were determined under the exact conditions that would be used for color testing. The infants were confronted with a white screen, containing a 14 $\times$ 1 deg white bar. The white bar was presented at each of a series of intensities, ranging from 0.4 log unit above the luminance of the screen to 0.4 log unit below it, for a total of 36 trials for each intensity.

The luminance discrimination function resulting from such an experiment for a single infant is shown in Fig. 10.4. The observer's performance dropped to chance, as it must, at the point at which the bar approaches a physical match to the screen. The width of the dip at the bottom is less than 0.1 log unit; and a 0.1 log unit luminance difference, either above or below the luminance of the screen, is clearly detectable by the infant. Other infants gave similar results (Teller, Peeples, & Sekel, 1978).

The luminance discrimination function of Fig. 10.4 defines the size of the luminance steps needed in a test of infant color vision. That is, if we replace the white bar with a colored one, and search the appropriate luminance range systematically, in steps less than 0.1 log unit wide, we must somewhere confront the infant with a stimulus that does not differ discriminably from the white background in brightness.

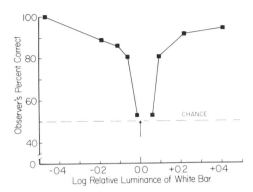

Fig. 10.4   Luminance discrimination function for a single 2-month-old infant (Katrina). The observer's percent correct is plotted as a function of the luminance of the stimulus (a 1 × 14 deg white bar) with respect to the luminance of the surrounding white screen. Zero on the abscissa represents the luminance at which the bar exactly matched the screen. The infant demonstrated excellent sensitivity to small brightness mismatches, as shown by the narrowness of the range over which the observer exhibits chance performance. (Redrawn from Peeples & Teller, 1975.)

If the infant does not have color vision, the observer's percent correct must fall to chance at that particular intensity of the colored bar.

V. DEMONSTRATIONS OF WAVELENGTH DISCRIMINATION

Using the paradigm just described, Peeples and Teller (1975) presented two 2-month-old infants with a red bar[3] contained in a white screen. The bar was presented at each of a series of luminances, spaced no more than 0.085 log unit apart, centered around the adult red–white brightness match, and spanning the range from 0.4 log unit below to 0.4 log unit above it. The observer's percent correct remained above chance for every luminance step, including, by inference, the infant's brightness match (cf. Fig. 10.5). It follows that these two 2-month-old infants can make at least one discrimination on the basis of wavelength, and thus must have some form of color vision.

More recently, Teller et al. (1978) tested 2-month-old infants' capacity to discriminate a variety of different colors from white. Fig. 10.5 shows some results from that study. Most discriminations were readily made

[3] Strictly speaking, the use of color names should be avoided in describing chromatic stimuli, because many different mixtures of wavelengths can appear to be the same color to adults and because we do not know the color appearances of stimuli for infants. The wavelength characteristics of the stimuli used are specified more fully in Teller et al. (1978).

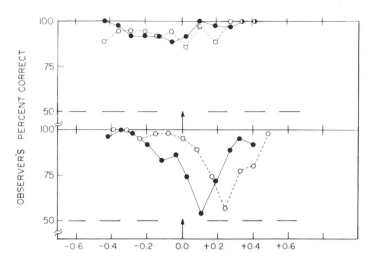

LOG RELATIVE LUMINANCE OF CHROMATIC BAR

Fig. 10.5 Chromatic discrimination functions for four 2-month-old infants. The observer's percent correct is plotted as a function of the luminance of a chromatic bar. Top: Charles (○) and Stephanie (●) tested with a blue-green bar (λ_{max} = 495 nm). Bottom: Kelly (○) and Amanda (●) tested with a yellow-green bar (λ_{max} ≈ 550 nm). Zero on the abscissa represents the luminance at which the chromatic bar matched the white screen in brightness for adult observers. The infants tested with the blue-green bar discriminated it from the screen at all luminances, and, hence, must have some form of color vision. For the yellow-green bar, the infants' performance dipped to chance, suggesting a failure of discrimination of the bar from the screen under these conditions. (Adapted from Teller, Peeples, & Sekel, 1978.)

by the infants, but on some colors—notably yellow-greens—the observer's performance fell to chance over a narrow range of luminances, yielding curves closely resembling the brightness discrimination function. The yellow-green versus white discrimination is readily made by adults. We thus conclude that, at least when tested with this stimulus configuration, the color vision of 2-month-old infants clearly differs in some respects from that of adults. Further discussion and interpretation of these findings may be found in Teller (1979) and Teller and Bornstein (1982).

Demonstrations of wavelength discriminations in young infants have also been carried out in other laboratories. For example, Schaller (1975), using an operant technique, presented 2 ½-month-old infants with red/black and green/black checkerboards. He showed that the infants could learn to stare in the direction of the reinforced (e.g., red) checkerboard, despite a wide variation in relative luminances. Bornstein (1976) showed that 3-month-old infants, habituated to a stimulus of one wavelength composition, could dishabituate to a change in wavelength composition. Thus, a number of investigators and behavioral techniques have converged upon the conclusion that young human infants have at least some form of color vision.

More recently, we (Hamer, Alexander, and Teller, in preparation) have been involved in some extensive experiments designed, as some of Bornstein's (1976) were, to see whether infants can make discriminations among stimuli chosen from the long wavelength half of the spectrum. In our experiments, the stimulus display consists of a screen illuminated with 589 nm (yellow) light from a low-pressure sodium lamp. A broadband red or a 550 nm green square, 3 deg of visual angle on a side, is contained in the screen in either a left or a right position, and takes on any one of a series of intensities, as in our earlier color testing.

We began the experiment by testing 2-month-old infants. Unfortunately for us, the results of the experiment varied from one infant to the next. Some infants gave data sets that dipped convincingly to chance over a range of luminances close to the adult brightness match; others

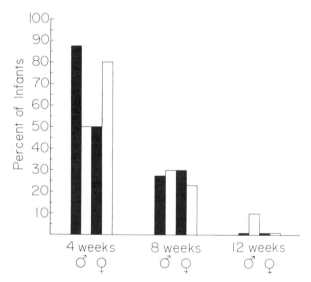

Fig. 10.6 Percentages of infants who failed to discriminate red (black bars) and green (white bars) 3 deg squares from the yellow background screen. Some infants at all ages were able to make these discriminations, but the percentage clearly increases with age. There were no systematic differences between the difficulties of the two discriminations nor any systematic sex differences. (Redrawn from Hamer, Alexander, and Teller, in preparation.)

gave data sets that stayed clearly above chance for all luminances of the red and green squares. It was thus necessary to expand the experimental population by adding 1-month-olds and 3-month-olds to the design, and to test substantial numbers of infants at each of the three ages.

The results of the experiment demonstrate clear age trends (Fig. 10.6). Most of the 1-month-olds failed to discriminate red, green, or both stimuli from the yellow background. More than half of the 2-month-olds succeeded, and from the 3-month-olds, we received only one data set in which an infant failed to make a discrimination. Thus, it looks as though the mechanisms that subserve these wavelength discriminations are in a major phase of maturation over the 1–3-month age range and that, as age increases, increasing proportions of infants reach the level of maturation necessary to perform this particular task. By 3 months postnatally, just about all infants can discriminate 3 deg red and green squares from the yellow background.

VI. GENETIC AND EXPERIENTIAL FACTORS IN COLOR VISION

To our knowledge, only a single study has been published in which color vision has been tested following any form of environmental manipulation or deprivation in primates. In that study (Boothe, Teller, & Sackett, 1975), several young infant pigtail macaque monkeys were trained to discriminate chromatic from white stimuli. The infants could discriminate many different wavelengths of light from white light by the earliest testable age—about 6 weeks. In addition, a single animal that had been dark reared from 2 weeks to 3 months after birth was trained and tested between 4 and 5 months of age. This animal too discriminated all wavelengths of light from white light.

Adult color vision in macaque monkeys closely resembles that of adult human beings (e.g., DeValois, Morgan, Polson, Mead, & Hull, 1974), and color vision testing is feasible in infant macaques. Thus, an animal model is available for studies of the development of color vision under normal and deprived conditions but, to our knowledge, this lead has never been followed up.

An approach to the topic of genetic factors arises from the fact that small percentages of the human adult population exhibit marked and often stereotypic abnormalities of color vision. Some of these are genetic (i.e., tend to run in families and are present at least from childhood), whereas others are "acquired" (i.e., have an onset beyond childhood, often associated with trauma or disease).

To the extent that one can assess the color vision of infants, one can ask some interesting questions about genetic color vision deficits. For example, one could ask whether genetic color deficiencies are always present from birth, or whether infants who will have color deficiencies in childhood and adulthood might be born with normal color vision that degenerates postnatally into color deficiency. If genetically pre-determined color deficiencies are indeed present early in infancy, it would be useful to be able to screen infants who are genetically at risk for color vision deficiencies, for clinical diagnostic purposes.

These considerations bring us back to the reasons for being especially interested in testing infants' capacities to discriminate among wavelengths from the long wavelength region of the visible spectrum, at and beyond 550 nm. Color-normal adults, of course, see these wavelengths as different colors—550 nm as yellow-green, 575 as yellow, 600 as orange, 650 as an orangey-red, and so on—and have no trouble telling the difference between any two wavelengths separated by more than a few nanometers. However, persons with either of the two most common and dramatic genetic color deficiencies—the two forms of "red-green color blindness," or protanopia and deuteranopia—are distinguished by a complete failure to discriminate among lights of this whole range of spectral wavelengths. These particular discriminations are hence used in adult color testing to diagnose the presence of these two kinds of color deficiency. This is the reason wavelengths from this range were used by Bornstein (1976) and currently in our laboratory.

Our experiments have proceeded very slowly. So far we have learned, as already discussed, that many presumably color-normal 1- and 2-month-old infants cannot make these discriminations under the conditions we have used, so our test cannot be used to discriminate color-normal from red-green color deficient infant populations below 3 months of age. We have also learned just how hard color-deficient infants are to find with certainty. Red-green color blindness occurs in only about 2% of the male population, and extremely rarely in females. It is a sex-linked recessive; that is, if a male infant's maternal grandfather has a particular form of red-green dichromacy, the odds are still only one in two that the infant will have the same condition. Both the infant and the maternal grandfather must be available and willing to be tested. Such infants should have a bimodal distribution of performances—half will be color deficient and the other half will not—but any noise in the data will blur the distinction. And finally, we will not be able to check up on which infants are which for at least 4 years, until the infants will be old enough to be retested by adult color vision tests. So, although we have seen a few interesting and suggestive cases, we are not yet able to present even preliminary data concerning techniques for clinical diagnosis of red-green color deficiencies in infancy, nor concerning the question of whether genetic red-green deficiencies are congenital.

VII. SUMMARY

In summary, we have begun to learn some preliminary answers to the fundamental questions of infant color vision. The scotopic and photopic spectral sensitivities of young infants appear to be similar to those of adults under conditions of neutral adaptation. By 2 months after birth, infants can make at least some discriminations on the basis of wavelength, and thus, by definition, have at least some form of color vision. At the same time, they also demonstrate some remarkable failures of wavelength discrimination, suggesting that important immaturities of the wavelength information-processing mechanisms remain. Finally, although we understand clearly the logical basis of methods that could be used to test for genetic color deficiencies in infants, the data as yet elude us.

ACKNOWLEDGMENTS

This research has been supported over the years in part by NIH Postdoctoral fellowship EY–04085 to David R. Peeples, NICHD Grant HD–02274, Research in Mental Retardation and Child Development, BNS–76–01503 and BNS–78–23053 from the National Science Foundation, and EY–00421 and EY–02920 from the National Eye Institute.

I thank Russell Hamer for comments on the manuscript, and Marjorie Zachow for secretarial assistance.

REFERENCES

Boothe, R. G., Teller, D. Y., & Sackett, G. Trichromacy in normally reared and light deprived infant monkeys (Macaca nemestrina). Vision Research 1975, **15,** 1187–1191.
Bornstein, M. H. Infants are trichromats. Journal of Experimental Child Psychology 1976, **21,** 425–445.
Chase, W. Color vision in infants. Journal of Experimental Psychology, 1937, **20,** 203–222.
DeValois, R., Morgan, H. C., Polson, M. C., Mead, W. R., & Hull, E. M. Psychophysical studies of monkey vision I. Macaque luminosity and color vision tests. Vision Research, 1974, **14,** 53–67.
Dobson, V. Spectral sensitivity of the 2-month-old infant as measured by the visual evoked cortical potential. Vision Research, 1976, **16,** 367–374.
Fantz, R. Visual perception from birth as shown by pattern selectivity. In Whipple (Ed.), New issues in infant development. Annals of The New York Academy of Sciences, 1965, **118,** 793–814.

Fantz, R. Visual perception and experience in early infancy: A look at the hidden side of behavior development. In Stevenson (Ed.), *Early behavior: Comparative and developmental approaches.* New York: Wiley, 1967.

Hamer, R., Alexander, K., & Teller, D. Rayleigh discriminations in young human infants. In preparation.

Moskowitz-Cook, A. The development of photopic spectral sensitivity in human infants. *Vision Research,* 1979, **19,** 1133–1142.

Peeples, D., & Teller, D. Y. Color vision and brightness discrimination in 2-month-old human infants. *Science,* 1975, **189,** 1102–1103.

Peeples, D., & Teller, D. Y. White-adapted photopic spectral sensitivity in human infants. *Vision Research,* 1978, **18,** 49–53.

Powers, M. K., Schneck, M., & Teller, D. Y. Spectral sensitivity of human infants at absolute threshold. *Vision Research,* 1981, **21,** in press.

Pulos, E., Teller, D. Y., & Buck, S. L. Infant color vision: A search for short wavelength sensitive mechanisms by means of chromatic adaptation. *Vision Research,* 1980, **20,** 485–493.

Schaller, M. J. Chromatic vision in human infants: Conditioned operant fixation to "hues" of varying intensity. *Bulletin of the Psychonomic Society,* 1975, **6,** 39–42.

Sperling, H., & Harwerth, R. Red–green cone interactions in the increment-threshold spectral sensitivity of primates. *Science,* 1971, **172,** 180–184.

Teller, D. Y., Bornstein, M. H. Color perception. In L. Cohen & P. Salapatek (Eds.), *Handbook of Infant Perception.* New York: Academic Press, 1982.

Teller, D. Y., Morse, R., Borton, R., & Regal, D. Visual acuity for vertical and diagonal gratings in human infants. *Vision Research,* 1974, **14,** 1433–1439.

Teller, D. Y., Peeples, D., & Sekel, M. Discrimination of chromatic from white light by 2-month-old human infants. *Vision Research,* 1978, **18,** 41–48.

Teller, D. Y. The forced-choice preferential looking procedure: A psychophysical technique for use with human infants. *Infant Behavior and Development,* 1979, **2,** 135–153.

Werner, J. S. Developmental change in scotopic sensitivity and the absorption spectrum of the human ocular media. Doctoral dissertation, Brown University, 1979.

11

Infants' Responses to Optical Information for Collision

ALBERT YONAS
University of Minnesota

I. INTRODUCTION

There has been a growing interest in the perception of visual phenomena that take place over time. These phenomena have traditionally been grouped under the label "motion perception," but the more generic term, "event perception," has now become popular (see Johansson, von Hofsten, & Jansson, 1980, for a review of this expanding literature). This chapter deals with the development of sensitivity to optical information for one type of optical event—the impending collision of an object with a viewer. This research is based to a large degree on the theoretical and empirical work of James Gibson (1950). Gibson argued that the optical stimulus for the perception of spatial layout consisted of spatiotemporal flow fields rather than a succession of primary, static, retinal images. Gibson challenged the assumption that

DEVELOPMENT OF PERCEPTION
Volume 2

Copyright © 1981 by Academic Press, Inc.

perception of the three-dimensional environment is necessarily a result of inferences based on two-dimensional retinal cues for depth.

In a sense, Gibson reversed the traditional view, which held that the perception of change over time was a more complex problem than the perception of a static scene, and that perception of a two-dimensional form was more basic than the perception of a three-dimensional layout. According to the traditional view, one might expect that sensitivity to optical information for a kinetic spatial event, such as collision, would develop later than sensitivity to a frozen, static, spatial layout. From the Gibsonian viewpoint, perception of kinetic spatial events is direct and might be expected to be present very early in development. In addition, the work by Gibson and his students (Schiff, 1965; Schiff, Caviness, & Gibson, 1962) on nonhuman species suggests 'that associative learning does not play a role in the development of sensitivity to optical information for collision.

This chapter explores the question of when, in the developmental history of the infant, a specific type of optical transformation evokes the perception that collision is about to occur. If we find that spatial sensitivity is present before experience in a visual environment could play a role in the development of that sensitivity, we must look to the experience of the species and not to its evolutionary history to understand the basis of that sensitivity.

Unfortunately, it is difficult to make confident inferences about the young infant's perception of a meaningful event from the small number of rather ambiguous responses the infant can perform. We have to be cautious when making inferences about what internal processes underlie the responses that we observe and to be attentive to alternate explanations for these responses. But (to give away the end of the story before I begin) there is reason to believe that, by 3 months of age and perhaps by 3 weeks, human infants are visually sensitive to the three-dimensional spatial event of collision. In contrast, there is evidence that sensitivity to binocular information for depth (Fox, Aslin, Shea, & Dumais, 1980) and to static monocular information for depth appears later in development (Yonas, Cleaves, & Pettersen, 1978).

II. HISTORICAL REVIEW

Although research on most topics in infant perception began in earnest only in the late 1950s, research began almost 100 years ago on the development of the "blinzelreflex," or blink reflex, as a defensive response to an approaching object. Peiper (1963) has summarized the early findings of several German researchers. He concluded that the newborn does not have the blink reflex, defined as the closing of the eyelids when an object is suddenly moved toward the face. Because the response was labeled a reflex, it may have been assumed that the response would have to occur with a very high probability before one could conclude that the reflex was indeed present. Thus, if the likelihood of blinking were only slightly higher to the approach of an object than to a control event (such as withdrawal), this would not have been detected by the early researchers because too few trials were given.

In general, the researchers in the late nineteenth century used informal methods, rarely including control events in the experimental design. Frequently, the object that was brought up to the child's eyes was the experimenter's hand. A description of the method for assessing responsiveness, given by Kuhlmann (1922:88), suggests the difficulty of knowing exactly what was done in the early studies: "Make a sudden pass toward the child's eyes with the flat side of a book, a hat, or other large object. Repeat several times. Scoring: passed if child winked to the threat." Given the vagueness of the method, the agreement among the research reports is surprising. Soltmann (cited in Peiper, 1963), Preyer (1909), and Raehlmann (1891) all reported that blinking to optical approach first occurred at about 8 weeks of age.

Pfister (1899) was the first to advance over the single subject, longitudinal method of the previous investigators. He studied 160 children in cross-sectional groups that spanned the period from 1 month to $2\frac{1}{2}$ years. In his method, a "shiny object of some size," which caught the child's attention, was suddenly brought toward the subject's face. Of 17 1-month-olds, none of them consistently blinked on several trials. By 2 months of age, 5 of the 13 infants blinked consistently; by 3 months, 8 of 13 infants were judged to have the reflex; and by 4 months, all 14 infants tested blinked consistently to approach. Unfortunately, "consistent" is not defined: How often did an infant have to blink at the approach of an object for the reflex to be judged as present?

Jones (1926) cites the results of two other early investigators who studied blinking responses of infants to an approaching object. She reports that Watson (1930) and Shinn (1900) found the blink reflex to appear at 9 weeks and 8 weeks, respectively, findings that corroborate the earlier reports. Jones also refers to a study by Kuhlmann (1922) of 20 3-month-old infants in which only 50% were considered to have the reflex when highly consistent blinking was the criterion, but nearly 100% were judged to have it when a lower standard for passing the test was used.

Gesell (1925) studied the "winking" response in 100 4- and 6-month-old infants. "Several" trials were presented in which the examiner's open hand was brought to within a few inches of the infant's eyes while the child was seated in the mother's lap. At 4 months of age, 84% of the group blinked to at least two presentations of the hand; at 6 months, 100% of the infants reached the criterion. No subject younger than 4 months of age was tested. Gesell (1925:102) observed that some of the younger infants who did not blink at the beginning of the procedure did respond to the presentation of the hand at the end of the examination. He states that "the visual mechanism of the four-months baby seems to be in a relatively unstable state of organization and to be highly conditioned by unknown factors."

There is some evidence to suggest that the size of the object that is brought to the eyes will affect the likelihood of blinking. Gesell performed a variation of his "winking" experiment with 4-month-old infants, in which he used a pencil rather than the open hand as the approaching object. Whereas 84% of the infants blinked at the approach of the hand, only a small percentage of them blinked when presented with the approaching pencil.

Similarly, Kasahara and Inanatsu (1931) observed blinking in 2293 2–12-month-old infants, a study in which the experimenter brought his index finger toward the infant. They reported that the reflex was present in only 2% of the 3-month-olds. That percentage rose to 20% at 4 months of age, and to 84% at 8 months. Unfortunately, we are not told how many trials were used or how many blinks were required to judge that the reflex was present.

It seems likely that the use of a small object that did not occlude the child's visual field at the time of collision was responsible for the low level of responsiveness. A small object would also be less likely than a larger approaching object to attract the attention and fixation of the infant. Raehlmann (1891) noted that, at 2 months, blinking occurs only if the child is looking at the approaching object and that it is delayed until the fifth month if the object approaches from the periphery. Due to the poor acuity of very young infants, a small object with low contrast at a distance from the infant may not even be detectable until it has approached quite close to the infant's face.

These early studies focused on the development of the blink response. It is true that several investigators pointed out that it was important not to evoke the trigeminal–facial blink reflex through touch or air currents, but little thought was given to the nature of the optical stimulation that elicits the blink response.

All the studies that have been reviewed used displays that create symmetrical expansion of the retinal image as an object approaches the infant's eyes. In an intriguing study by Jones (1926), the infant sat in his or her mother's lap facing a lighted window, while the experimenter stood behind the child and suddenly passed her hand down 6 inches in front of the baby's eyes. Although the precise number of trials varied, a maximum of 10 trials was used. Blink responses to two presentations of the hand were required for an infant to be judged as having the reflex. Thus, a blink response on about 20% of the trials was the criterion. Jones tested a total of 317 infants from 10 to 140 days of age. The first infant to pass her criterion was 46 days of age. By 11 weeks, 50% of the infants reached her criterion, and by 13 weeks, 75% of the infants were responding. This report raises the question of whether the perception of the spatial location of a rapidly moving dark contour is sufficient to produce blinking. Perhaps a rapid translation of a contour across the retina is a sufficient stimulus. It also seems possible that what Jones judged to be blinking was actually a downward tracking movement of the eyes.

There are a number of problems with the early literature on the blink reflex. The subject samples were small, often only a single subject, and the descriptions of the method were vague. Many of the studies fail to explain the criterion used to judge that the reflex is present. Nor are we told the proportion of trials during which blinking occurred, because of the assumption that a reflex is either present or absent.

But, despite the large variation in methods, a rather consistent picture emerges from the early studies: Infants from birth to 8 weeks of age generally stare at an approaching object and do not blink. At about 7 weeks, consistent blinking is observed in a small percentage of infants. This percentage increases over the next 2 months until a highly reliable response is present in almost all infants at 4 months of age.

Several of the early investigators asserted with confidence that the gradual appearance of blinking to optical information for collision was due to some form of conditioning. The pairing of tactual collision with its optical counterpart was assumed to be a requirement for the response to be learned. Jones (1926), for example, saw the defensive blink as an outgrowth of the newborn's initial blink reflex when the face is touched near the eyes. The later blink at the approach of an object is thus seen as an anticipatory reaction resulting from associations built up from experience with objects touching the face. Peiper (1963:59) professed a similar opinion. He states that, "The blinking reflex is a conditioned reflex in the Pavlovian sense: The unconditioned closing of the lids on touch will finally, after frequent repetition, be conditionally connected with the approach of an object." This may seem to be a logical explanation of how blinking at the mere sight of an approaching object develops, but it remains an assumption.

In discussing the results of her blinking study, Jones (1926) raises the question of whether blinking to a visual stimulus develops by maturation, by conditioning, or by an interaction of the two. One argument she puts forth for defensive blinking as a conditioned response is that it has been observed in some infants before 2 months of age, and in others, after 4 months of age. It would seem reasonable that the early-blinking infant may have been exposed to more experiences with touch stimuli that were preceded by the sight of the object. Or perhaps, the infants who blink are better able to make use of such information in the environment because of a greater learning capacity. Jones (1926:562) points out, however, that it is unlikely an infant would be hit in the face by an approaching object. At the time of her study, she pointed to the need for additional research on the role of maturation in blinking that would study "(a) cases which show normal development when the possibility of conditioning has been reduced to a minimum, and (b) cases which fail to accelerate in development, in spite of specific training."

III. THE MODERN PERIOD: KINETIC INFORMATION FOR IMPENDING COLLISION

The specification of optical expansion information for impending collision was made by James Gibson (1958) in an essay on the visual control of locomotion. Gibson (1958:188) pointed out that, as an animal locomotes through an environment, a continuous family of spatiotemporal transformations, or flow patterns, occurs on the retina. In the case of collision, he wrote:

> Approach to a solid surface is specified by a centrifugal flow of the texture of the optic array. Approach to an object is specified by a magnification of the closed contour in the array corresponding to the edges of the object. A *uniform* rate of approach is accompanied by an *accelerated* rate of magnification. At the theoretical point where the eye touches the object, the latter will intercept a visual angle of 180°. The magnification reaches an explosive rate in the last moments before contact. This accelerated expansion . . . specifies imminent collision.

Gibson was addressing the problem of specifying the information for collision (explosive magnification) and the information for safe contact with a surface (of the sort a pilot landing a plane would want). For a "soft" landing, Gibson pointed out that the explosive component of the magnification had to be canceled by deceleration. Gibson (1979) has stressed the importance of the loss or gain of texture in distinguishing the approach of an opening from the approach of an obstacle, but his initial analysis led to the first experimental studies in which optical expansion information for collision was systematically manipulated.

Purdy (1960), in a mathematical treatment of Gibson's hypothesis of psychological correspondence in space perception, determined that the time remaining before one collides with a surface (if velocity is not changed) is specified by the stimulus flow pattern. That is, the rate of magnification of the distance between any pair of points on a surface is proportional to the imminence of the collision. Carel (1961) tested the sensitivity of adults to this potential information by having them view a representation of a surface moving toward them. He found that subjects had some success in judging "time-to-collision" from the rate of change of the display.

IV.   MODERN EXPERIMENTAL WORK

To assess whether an optical expansion pattern with no other depth information would be perceived as providing information for collision, Schiff, Caviness, and Gibson (1962) presented infant and adult monkeys with a silhouette of an object on a rear-projection screen. A real object was moved toward and away from a point-source lamp, creating a shadow that expanded (specifying imminent collision) and contracted (specifying withdrawal). The eight infant monkeys tested were from 5 to 8 months of age. An additional 15 adult monkeys were presented with the collision and withdrawal displays. Clear avoidance responses were produced by 19 of the 23 monkeys tested. Those monkeys withdrew abruptly or ducked when presented with the explosively expanding dark silhouette. When 13 collision trials were presented in succession, no evidence of habituation was found. The display remained effective in evoking withdrawal even though no actual contact was made. The collision display clearly created an effective and powerful illusion.

Using an apparatus similar to that of the previous experiment, Schiff (1965) carried out a systematic study of the stimulus information that would evoke avoidance behavior in several species (fiddler crabs, frogs, chicks, kittens, and humans). Again, a shadow-casting device, with which an object was moved toward or away from a point-source lamp, presented expanding and contracting shadows (i.e., collision and withdrawal displays). Schiff found that most animals locomoted away from the collision display but did not avoid the withdrawal display.

The use of the inverse transformation, a contracting shadow or minification display, was an important control. Except for direction, the optical change was identical in the two conditions. In addition, Schiff found that, when the rate of approach of the occluder to the lamp was varied, it was only in the last fraction of a second of the event (when the visual angle of the display grew large) that defensive behavior occurred. He then varied the distance the occluder reached from the point-source lamp, so that the velocity and visual angle of the display at the end of an approach trial was varied. He concluded that magnification beyond 30deg of visual angle was the threshold for responses to apparent collision. Given the method used, the velocity of the expansion pattern would necessarily vary with the visual angle of the shadow; that is, the larger expansions were also the ones with higher velocity of motion. It is possible that rapid expansion that did not go beyond 30deg would also evoke avoidance behavior, but this hypothesis was not tested.

To explore the role of associative learning in the development of avoidance responses to optical information for collision, Schiff (1965) also tested chicks that had been reared in the dark after hatching. The duration of dark rearing varied from 10 min to 3 days before testing began. Regardless of the amount of dark rearing, avoidance responses were observed on approximately 50% of the magnification trials and very rarely on the minification trials. These findings suggest that, for chicks, the pick-up of optical information for collision is innate.

In another study, three kittens were reared in the dark for 26 days for 23 hours a day. For the remaining 1 hour per day, they were suspended in pouches in an illuminated room with only their heads protruding. During this period the possibility of collision was eliminated. Unlike the chicks and other animals, the responses of the kittens to magnification were far from impressive. None of the kittens locomoted away from the apparently approaching object. Only two of the kittens drew their heads back, and these responses tended to habituate quickly. Due to the small number of subjects, it is difficult to evaluate this study, but there is some suggestion that sensitivity may be present in young kittens who have never experienced optical collision.

White (1971) carried out an extensive study of the effects of enriching the stimulation available to human infants over the first 6 months of life. He found that placing infants in a prone position in front of interesting, visible displays for 45 min per day and having them wear striped mitts accelerated the development of hand regard, although it had no effect on the development of defensive blinking. It seems reasonable that making the hands more salient, visually, would bring about earlier sustained attention to the hands, but it is possible that some other type of enrichment would have been better at accelerating the development of defensive blinking.

In White's study, a red and white bull's-eye disk was dropped toward the infant from several distances. A clear Plexiglas window over the infant eliminated any changes in air pressure; the design of the apparatus minimized auditory signals. Due to the absence of a control condition, in which the disk was rapidly raised, White's study tells us little about what aspects of the stimulus event evoked the response observed, but it does provide useful norms for the development of blinking to an approaching target. The results generally agree with those of earlier studies that employed less elegant methodology. Three- to 4-week-old infants blinked on approximately 30% of the trials on which the target was dropped 30 cm (12 in.) to a distance about 5 cm (2 in.) from the face. By 8 weeks of age, response probability had increased to approximately 60%, and by 11 weeks, to 80%. Because of the absence of a control condition, it is unclear whether the low level of responding of the youngest infants was significantly higher than chance. However, there is a striking increase with age in the consistency of responding to the rapidly approaching target.

Greenberg, Uzgiris, and Hunt (1968), in a study very similar to White's, reported that 10 infants, each provided with a stabile pattern above their cribs from 5 weeks of age, blinked consistently in response to the drop of a bull's-eye target about 3 weeks earlier than did infants in a control group (whose crib did not have the pattern suspended above them). Responsiveness on more than 80% of the trials occurred at 7 rather than at 10.4 weeks when the target was dropped the maximum distance. The authors suggested that the presence of the stabile pattern accelerated blinking by speeding the development of accommodation.

V. NEW RESPONSES TO OPTICAL INFORMATION: THE PROBLEM OF INTERPRETATION

The initial study of infants' sensitivity to optical information for collision in our laboratory (Hruska & Yonas, 1971) was based on the notion that an increase in a young infant's heart rate would be a reliable indicator of a defensive response, and that a decrease in heart rate would indicate an orienting response. Such biphasic heart rate responses have been found by Campos, Hiatt, Ramsay, Henderson, and Svejda (1978) in studies testing older infants on a visual cliff. We hypothesized that these heart rate responses may be present in infants too young to exhibit other indicator responses. Infants from 2 to 10 months of age were shown a rear-projected film of an object approaching and withdrawing, as well as trials in which the object was presented at its initial and final positions in succession without motion. To our surprise, it was only the 8–10-month-old infants who gave clear evidence to differential heart rate responses to the conditions, showing consistent cardiac acceleration to the collision display and deceleration to the other conditions. For 2–4-month-old infants, all conditions evoked cardiac deceleration. Infants from 5 to 7 months responded with both heart rate acceleration and deceleration to the collision display. There are two general conclusions that might be drawn from the study. One is that, unlike the chicks studied by Schiff (1965), human infants are not sensitive to optical information for collision until rather late in development. The other is that heart rate acceleration to the type of displays we presented may be a rather late-developing response to the dangerous implications of an optical event, but simpler responses (such as blinking) may be earlier indicators that sensitivity is present. The great bulk of previous studies and our own later work support the second interpretation.

The search for new responses in newborns that could indicate sensitivity to optical information for collision was also taken up by Bower, Broughton, and Moore (1971). Surprisingly, they reported (1971:193, 194) that infants as young as 6 days of age responded to a real and optical display of an approaching object with an integrated avoidance response. "In its full form, the response consisted of three components: (1) eyes open wide; (2) the head goes back; (3) both hands come up between the object and face." Furthermore, when the real object approached within 8 cm of the infant's face, this event "produced such violent upset that after one or two cycles it was necessary to abandon the experiment."

There are several reasons to question the view that the responses they observed are defensive in character. Keeping one's eyes open wide as an object approaches within a few centimeters of the eyes, far from being adaptive, might lead to injury. Early investigators had concluded from the infrequent blinking at an approaching object that sensitivity to optical information was *absent* in young infants. The clearest outcome of these studies was a striking increase in blinking to approach over the first 4 months. If a failure to blink is adaptive, why does the probability of blinking increase with age?

Violent upset would seem to be a good indicator that a newborn is detecting a noxious event, but the small number of subjects (five) and the failure by Bower et al. to report any quantitative data makes one question whether violent upset is reliably evoked by approach. It seems unlikely that the reliable occurrence of a salient response such as upset would have gone unnoticed in all of the previous studies. In the studies since the Bower et al. report, other experimenters have not found that crying is evoked by the approach of an object (Ball & Tronick, 1971; Ball & Vurpillot, 1976; Pettersen, Yonas, & Fisch, 1980; Yonas, Bechtold, Frankel, Gordon, McRoberts, Norcia, & Sternfels, 1977; Yonas, Pettersen, & Lockman, 1979).

In contrast to violent upset, several investigators have found that upward head movements are reliably evoked when young infants are shown collision displays (Ball & Tronick, 1971; Ball & Vurpillot, 1976; Yonas et al., 1977). But this behavior is also open to an alternate interpretation. Ball, in an undergraduate honors thesis (1970) that was the basis of the Ball and Tronick (1971) study, suggested that upward rotation of the infant's head may be attributed to a tendency of the infant to follow the upward motion of the upper contours of a display with the eyes and head. In Ball's study, 28 infants from 2 to 11 weeks of age were shown real and optical collision displays. As a control condition, Ball used an asymmetrical optical expansion pattern that indicated that the approaching object would not collide but would pass to the side of the infant. In this condition, the infants clearly tracked the stimulus motion to the side. In the collision condition, contours moved symmetrically *in all directions;* thus, Ball argued that the head movements were defensive, not contour tracking, because only the contours moving upward were tracked. However, there may be other reasons why infants prefer to track upward-moving contours. In addition, the infants tested raised their arms on 24% of the collision trials and on 15% of the miss trials. Ball concluded from this rather small difference that arm raising was a part of an "integrated avoidance response" and that the Bower et al. (1971) report had been replicated.

An alternate interpretation of these results seems plausible. The infants in Ball and Tronick's (1971) study were held around the waist with their heads unsupported. In the first months of life, most infants have great difficulty controlling the movements of the head—a head that is both large and heavy in relation to the rest of the body. When a 1-month-old infant is upright, with his head unsupported, rapid upward head movements occur frequently. Most of the time, the head is oriented downward with the chin resting on the chest or is turned upward toward the ceiling. Staring straight ahead with the head held steady is a difficult accomplishment, of generally short duration, requiring an alert infant and a rather attractive display. Given that young infants have a strong tendency to track moving contours, the pursuit of upward motions might produce a clumsy, uncontrolled, upward head movement. This would occasionally result in a loss of balance and a compensatory raising of the arms. At least, this seemed a reasonable interpretation of the behavior that we had observed in our earlier study and that Ball and Tronick reported.

Therefore, we set out to explore this hypothesis in an experiment in which head movements, blinking, and arm raising were scored from videotapes (Yonas, et al., 1977). The method was as close to Ball's as we could arrange. Twenty-four 3–6-week-old infants were presented with three trials of each of three optical shadow projections: (a) a symmetrically expanding diamond silhouette, providing information for collision; (b) an asymmetrically expanding contour, specifying an object approaching on a miss path; and (c) a nonexpanding rising contour. The rising contour display was created by masking the rear-projection screen so that only a narrow vertical column was visible to the infant when the collision display was generated. Although the collision display evoked more upward head rotation than the miss display (replicating Ball's results), it was the rising contour with no information for collision that produced the largest amount of upward head rotation. In contrast, the collision display evoked more blinking than the two control displays, but this difference was not significant, perhaps because of the small number of trials. A group of 4-month-old infants presented with the same three conditions showed the same pattern of results, with significantly more blinking to the symmetrical expansion display than to the miss or the rising contour conditions.

In a second experiment, 1–2-month-old infants were presented with a symmetrical optical expansion pattern, which specified impending collision, and an asymmetrical pattern specifying an object that misses the infant. The expanding object was a red, textured triangle with a vertex oriented downward. The upper edge of the triangle was at the same height as the infant's eyes so that, as magnification occurred, the display presented no upward-moving contour. The infants tracked the miss display off the screen as it expanded and followed the motion of various parts of the collision display. There was no difference in the amount of backward head movement in the two conditions. Thus, backward head movement may be the result of upward contour tracking, rather than an avoidance response.

In a third experiment, a real object approached 1–2-month-old infants on a collision or noncollision path. Perhaps because the object stopped too far (15 cm) from the infant's face in the collision condition, no reliable differences in backward head movements or blinking were observed.

Ball and Vurpillot (1976) studied the responses of 2-month-old infants to optical information for collision. Unfortunately, as in the Bower *et al.* (1971) study, Ball and Vurpillot confounded the effects of information for collision with the amount and location of upward-moving contours. They examined the backward head movements of 2-month-old infants presented with three types of expansion and contraction displays. In the first display, 800 small circles were projected with a constant density all over a large screen; in the second, 3 small circles formed a triangle in the center of the screen, with one vertex pointed downward; in the third, 1 small circle was located in the center of the screen. Motion pictures of the displays were filmed using a zoom lens to magnify and reduce the display. For all the displays, the zoom lens created a five-fold expansion so that the single circle expanded from about 2 to 10 deg. The distance between the circle in the 3-circle condition changed from 8 to about 40 deg. Ball and Vurpillot found that backward head movements occurred more frequently in the 800-circle condition than in the 3-circle or 1-circle conditions. These responses were infrequent in the contraction condition and did not differ for the three displays. Although they concluded that the observed head movements reflected a capacity to see movement in depth, the three conditions clearly vary in the amount and location of upward-moving contours on the screen. In the 800-circle condition, the upward moving dots fill the upper half of the visual field; in the other two displays, the upward motion is confined to a small area. It seems likely that the probability that upward-moving contours would be pursued and would evoke backward head movement may increase with the amount and location of upward-moving contours that are visible. In addition, it is unclear whether the zoom lens created an expansion pattern that would correspond to a collision event.

When the Yonas *et al.* (1977) study was published, Bower (1977) was asked by the journal's editor to comment on it. He argued that having a parent hold the infant from behind, about the waist, may have made the 1-month-old infants we tested less fearful than they might have been had they been supported by an experimenter, as the infants were in the Ball and Tronick study. Bower also pointed out that it is difficult for young infants to hold their heads upright, and that the infant's head must be supported for the response to be observed. However, Tronick (personal communication, 1971) has suggested that the head withdrawal response can be observed only if the infant's head is *not* supported.

The Yonas *et al.* (1977) study was, in part, a replication of the Ball and Tronick method, and the results were the same. That is, 3–6-week-old infants did rotate their heads upward to a greater degree in response to the symmetrically expanding display than to the asymmetrically expanding (noncollision) display. Although it is possible that this head movement was an attempt to avoid a looming object, it is also clear that simply the presence of a sector of the looming display (a nonexpanding rising contour in the visual field) is sufficient to evoke upward head rotation.

In his critique, Bower (1977) briefly reported a new study with Dunkeld that explored the hypothesis that the "head back" response to an approaching object may be attributed to tracking the rising upper contour of the expanding display. The experiment presented young infants with the silhouette of a rectangle with its upper edge falling downward toward the infant's eyes. The display contained no rising contours in the upper half of the field. Bower argued that the transformation from a rectangle through a series of trapezoids into a wide line would specify impending collision. The reverse of this transformation, corresponding to a surface rotated upward and away from the infant's eyes, was also presented, as were parallel projection (rather than polar) versions of the first two conditions. Bower reported that the downward-moving polar transformation produced backward head movement and that the other conditions, including the ones with upward-moving contours, did not.

The dependent variable that indexed backward head movement in Dunkeld and Bower's study was new: A sensitive pressure transducer was placed behind the infant's head on an infant seat, and the pressure the head exerted on the seat was sampled every 0.5 sec. No other responses were reported. Dunkeld and Bower's use of an objective measure of backward head movement, the pressure transducer, was a clear methodological advance. It is especially helpful in studying young infants who have difficulty holding their heads erect.

This measure was also employed in a study by Yonas, Pettersen, and Lockman (1979) of 20 3–5-week-old infants who were repeatedly presented with a real object that rapidly approached the eyes and a control condition in which the object was withdrawn. Pressure was sampled by a PDP–12 computer at 0.5 sec intervals. Because the measure reflected movements of the infant's head that were unrelated to the stimulus event, there was a great deal of noise in the recording of any individual trial. However, when 15–20 trials were averaged, a lawful pattern emerged, locked onto the stimulus event. Eighteen of the 20 infants showed more backward head movements to the approaching than to the receding object. There was more frequent blinking when the object approached than during the control trials, but the difference only approached significance. Although the study demonstrated the sensitivity of the pressure-sensing measure, it did not rule out the possibility that these young infants were not defending themselves against collision but were simply tracking the upward-rising texture of the approaching object. As the head was rotated upward, greater pressure was exerted against the back of the seat. To test this hypothesis, a shadow-casting device and a large rear-projection screen created two types of kinetic displays; both displays provided optical information for the imminent collision of an object with the infant. One display was a diamond-shaped object that was symmetrically magnified; the other was a triangle (the bottom half of the diamond). The upper contour of the triangle remained at the same height as the infant's eyes, while the triangle expanded downward and laterally on the screen.

Both the triangle and the diamond evoked more frequent blinking on approach than on withdrawal trials, but only the expansion of the diamond, with its upward-rising texture, evoked backward head movements. The study suggests that, although 1-month-olds have some sensitivity to information for impending collision, it is the frequently studied blinking response, rather than backward head movements, that may provide the more unambiguous indicator response.

A third experiment in this series also suggested that there are uncertainties in the interpretation of backward head movements. Because one of the consequences of expanding the dark shadow is the lowering of luminance, we wanted to see if a sudden change in luminance would elicit head movements. A large rear-projection screen was suddenly darkened or lightened in this experiment. Darkening the screen did evoke slightly more backward head movements than lightening it, suggesting that collision information is not necessary to evoke the response.

In the last study of this series, we explored Dunkeld and Bower's (Bower, 1977) finding that young infants push their heads back when presented with information for a surface that is rotating downward toward their eyes. In our study, 20 3–4-week-old infants were presented with a real rectangular object. In one condition, the rectangle was initially presented parallel to the infant's forehead and then rotated 90 deg, over 1 sec, moving the top of the rectangle close to the infant's eyes. In the second condition, the order was reversed; the rectangle was initially presented horizontally, with one edge close to the infant's eyes, and was then rotated 90 deg upward and away from the face. In contrast to the Dunkeld and Bower report, the downward rotation of the rectangle, with an optical transformation that indicates collision, brought about frequent eye closings but little backward head movement. Rotation upward, away from the face, evoked few blinks but it did produce backward head movement. The infants appeared to be tracking the rising and falling of the edge of the rectangle. Once again, the results are not consistent with the notion that the backward head movements have a defensive character in very young infants. Blinking, however, may be one of the few responses available to a neonate that would indicate the presence of depth sensitivity.

VI.   DEVELOPMENTAL CHANGES IN RESPONSIVENESS

Although infants under 2 months of age may be more likely to blink at the approach than the withdrawal of an object, the absolute probability of a blink is quite low, about 20%. Because early investigators presented relatively few trials and used no control conditions, they concluded that approach did not even evoke blinking in young infants. What they did observe was a substantial increase with age in the occurrence of this response. Similarly, Pettersen, Yonas, and Fisch (1979) found a consistent increase with age in the probability that the approach of a real object evokes blinking in full-term infants. The average response levels increased from a low of 16% at 6 weeks, to 45% at 8 weeks, to 75% at 10 weeks. How can we account for this rapid increase? Is it due to Pavlovian conditioning as Jones (1926) and Peiper (1963) have suggested, or to maturation; or are both factors involved? Schiff (1965) demonstrated that learning was not necessary for a precocial species of birds in that dark reared chicks behaved defensively when first presented with an optical looming display. Although dark rearing human infants is not possible, we can compare the performance of infants who have had gestational periods longer or shorter than the norm.

Pettersen, Yonas, and Fisch (1980) examined the probability that the rapid approach and withdrawal of a real object would evoke blinking in two groups of 6-week-old infants. One group was composed of 20 full-term infants born within 1 week of the expected delivery date; the other contained 20 post-term infants born at least three weeks after the expected delivery date. Both groups blinked on only 3% of the withdrawal trials. On the approach trials, the full-term infants blinked on 16% of the trials, and the post-term infants, on 37% of the trials. This finding was replicated in a second study in which sophisticated methods for judging gestational age were used and experimenters and scorers were not informed as to whether infants were post-term or full-term.

The finding that post-term infants blink more frequently at an approaching object than do full-term infants argues that maturation, rather than learning, underlies the substantial increase in responsiveness between the sixth and the tenth weeks. In addition, the discovery that approach evokes more blinking than withdrawal between 3 and 6 weeks of age suggests that some sensitivity to collision information is present at such an early age that the opportunity for learning to take place would be very limited. But to get a clear answer to this question, responsiveness in newborn infants ought to be assessed. At this point, we cannot rule out the possibility that greater maturation may make post-term infants superior at learning to blink to optical collision information.

VII. FURTHER SPECIFICATION OF THE EFFECTIVE STIMULUS

Much of the previous discussion has dealt with the question of whether the backward head movements of infants under 2 months of age, when produced by optical expansion patterns, would indicate that spatial perception is taking place. The same question can be raised regarding the blink response.

Bower (1974) argued that closing the eyelids is not an adaptive defensive response when an object rapidly approaches one's eyes. This is an arguable conclusion; but so simple and rapid a response as eye closure does not have the same power to compel the conclusion that spatial perception is functioning as do locomotion on a visual cliff and visually guided reaching. The complex, nonstereotyped quality of those actions and their inherently spatial nature leaves us with little doubt that, by 5 or 6 months of age, human infants are quite responsive to spatial information. The blink response, however, has often been described as a "reflex." It is entirely possible that the response can be activated by a perceptual process so primitive that it would be unwarranted to infer that spatial information is being picked up.

One approach to this question is to discover what aspects of the optical collision display are necessary to evoke the blink response in young infants. If the response is elicited by simple, low-level properties—such as an increase in the intensity of stimulation, or a rapid motion across the retina—this would not suggest spatial processes are necessarily present. However, if only the specific optical transformation that occurs when an object approaches an infant's eyes at a constant or increasing velocity evokes consistent blinking, this would argue that spatial information is being detected.

To discover what aspects of the optical collision display are necessary to evoke frequent blinking and backward head movement, Yonas, Pettersen, Lockman, & Eisenberg (1980) presented 14-week-old infants with displays that varied the visual angle of the display, the pattern of expansion, and the presence of motion. The study was based on Schiff's (1965) finding that the effective information for collision for several nonhuman species is carried in particular features of the display: Specifically, in the explosive last moments of the expansion pattern when a closed, dark contour rapidly fills more than 30 deg of the viewer's visual field. By varying the size of the shadow-casting object, its distance from the lamp, and its speed, two types of expansion patterns were created. The first specified an object approaching at a constant rate, by creating an optical magnification that accelerated geometrically (explosively). The second specified an object that slows as it approaches, by producing a nearly linear (nonexplosive), optical expansion pattern. Each of these expansion patterns was viewed from two distances, with final visual angles of either 30 or 100 deg, thus creating four conditions. A fifth condition assessed responses to a rapid change of luminance, with no motion on the screen, by presenting, in succession, a pair of color slides of the display at the beginning and at the end of a transformation.

The results were quite clear for the 100 3-month-old infants tested in the study. Consistent blinking (66% of the trials) occurred only in the condition in which explosive magnification filled a 100 deg visual field. Equally rapid minifications evoked a low level of responding (20%). Magnification and minification trials of the other four conditions also evoked a relatively low level of responding (20 to 36%).

In addition, this pattern of responses was also true for the backward head movement measure. Backward head movement was greater for approach trials than for withdrawal trials in only the 100 deg, explosive condition. One might argue from these results that 3-month-old infants are sensitive to the spatiotemporal transformation that specifies imminent collision. The backward head movements evoked by the collision event cannot be accounted for by the tracking hypothesis, because both explosive and nonexplosive displays contain an equal amount of rising texture and contour.

The next question we attempted to answer was whether 4-week-old infants would show the same degree of specificity in their stimulus processing as did 14-week-olds. This work is still in progress, but it is clear at this point that, unlike the older infants, the 4-week-olds blink more frequently to the expansion of both constant velocity approach (explosive expansion) and decelerating approach (nonexplosive expansion). That is, young infants do not appear to show the same degree of specificity in their pick-up of this type of stimulation as do older infants.

Perhaps there is increasing acuity in early infancy in the kinetic as well as in the spatial frequency realm; perhaps the detection of high velocity motion develops between the first and third months. It is also possible that, in 1-month-old infants, accelerating motion is not differentiated from a rapid, constant velocity motion.

A great deal of research is needed to explore the development of sensory processes involved in sensitivity to kinetic information. Even with our limited knowledge, however, it seems clear that before binocular depth information is effective (Fox, Aslin, Shea, & Dumais, 1980) and long before static monocular depth information is effective (Yonas, Cleaves, & Pettersen, 1978), kinetic information for an important event—collision—is effective in early infancy.

VIII. SUMMARY

Research on the issue of when infants first make defensive responses to optical information for imminent collision has a remarkably long history, beginning in the late nineteenth century. The early investigators found that, for the first 2 months, the infant generally stares at an object that approaches close to his or her eyes and rarely blinks or makes other defensive responses. They also found that the likelihood that approach will evoke blinking increases from the second to the fourth postnatal months. However, it now appears that they incorrectly concluded that sensitivity to collision information is absent in the first 2 months. Although infants at 3–6 weeks of age do not often blink at an approaching object, they do blink approximately 25% of the time; and given a sufficient number of trials, this level proves to be significantly above the level evoked by a receding object.

The finding that 6-week-old infants born after their due dates (3–4 weeks post-term) responded more reliably than full-term 6-week-old infants (Pettersen et al., 1980) leads us to believe that maturation plays an important role in the increase in responsiveness. In 1926, Jones suggested (see the closing comments of Section II) that the importance of associative learning and maturation ought to be explored through studies in which the possibility of conditioning is reduced to a minimum. These studies are still needed, and one obvious way to approach them would be to investigate sensitivity to optical collision information in newborn infants. Jones also suggested that research is needed to explore the effects of specific training on the development of defensive blinking; Little (cited in Lipsitt & Reese, 1979) began to study this topic, but more work is needed.

To fully understand what part maturation and experience play in the development of spatial sensitivity, we must explore the changing nature of the effective stimulus. Three-month-old infants only blink consistently at a collision display that expands explosively and fills the visual field, but 1-month-olds may blink at a higher rate at any expanding display. Collision and approach may not be differentiated by the 1-month-old infant, and the accelerating expansion may not even be detected. It is possible that motion outward on the retina alone will trigger a higher level of blinking responses in the newborn, and that over the next months a great deal of perceptual differentiation takes place.

As Eleanor Gibson (1969) has suggested, the development of spatial perception may not be the result of pure maturation or associative learning (i.e., classical conditioning of the blink response); instead, there may be increasing specificity of discrimination. With regard to sensitivity to collision information, there may be increasing specificity in the discrimination of spatiotemporal information for collision over the first months of life. Some spatial sensitivity may be present at birth, but experience in a visual world may be required for differentiation to occur. Although we have made some progress, we still know little about how sensitivity to spatial events develops.

REFERENCES

Ball, W. A. *Infant responses to looming objects and shadows.* Unpublished honors thesis, Harvard University, 1970.

Ball, W. A., & Tronick, E. Infant responses to impending collisions: Optical and real. *Science,* 1971, **171,** 818–820.

Ball, W., & Vurpillot, E. La perception du mouvement en profondur chez le nourrisson. *L'Annee Psychologique,* 1976, **67,** 393–400.

Bower, T. G. R. *Development in infancy.* San Francisco: W. H. Freeman, 1974.

Bower, T. G. R. Comment on Yonas *et al.,* "Development of sensitivity to information for impending collision." *Perception & Psychophysics,* 1977, **21**(3), 281–282.

Bower, T. G. R., Broughton, M. M., & Moore, M. K. Infant responses to approaching objects: An indicator of response to distal variables. *Perception & Psychophysics*, 1971, **9**, 193–196.

Campos, J. J., Hiatt, S., Ramsay, D., Henderson, C., & Svejda, M. The emergence of fear on the visual cliff. In M. Lewis & L. Rosenblum (Eds.), *The development of affect*. New York: Plenum, 1978.

Carel, W. L. *Visual factors in the contact analog*. General Electric Electronics Center Publication, Cornell University Press, no. R6ELC60, 1961.

Fox, R., Aslin, R. N., Shea, S. L., & Dumais, S. T. Stereopsis in human infants. *Science*, 1980, **207**, 323–324.

Gesell, A. *Mental growth of the preschool child*. New York: Macmillan, 1925.

Gibson, E. J. *Principles of perceptual learning and development*. Englewood Cliffs, N. J.: Prentice-Hall, 1969.

Gibson, J. J. *The perception of the visual world*. Boston: Houghton Mifflin, 1950.

Gibson, J. J. Visually controlled locomotion and visual orientation in animals. *British Journal of Psychology*, 1958, **49**(3), 182–194.

Gibson, J. J. *An ecological approach to visual perception*. Boston: Houghton Mifflin, 1979.

Greenberg, D., Uzgiris, I. C., & Hunt, J. McV. Hastening the development of the blink response with looking. *Journal of Genetic Psychology*, 1968, **113**, 167–176.

Hruska, D., & Yonas, A. *Developmental changes in cardiac responses to the optical stimulus of impending collision*. Paper presented at the meeting of the Society for Psychophysiological Research, St. Louis, October, 1971.

Johansson, G., von Hofsten, C., & Jansson, G. Event perception. In M. R. Rosenzweig & L. W. Porter (Eds.), *Annual review of psychology* (Vol. 31). Palo Alto: Annual Reviews, 1980.

Jones, M. C. The development of early behavior patterns in young children. *The Pedagogical Seminary and Journal of Genetic Psychology*, 1926, **33**, 537–585.

Kasahara, M., & Inamatsu, S. Der Blinzelreflex im Sauglingsalter. *Archiv fur Kinderheilkunde*, 1931, **92**, 302–304.

Kuhlmann, F. *A handbook of mental tests*. Baltimore: Warwick & York, 1922.

Lipsitt, L. P., & Reese, H. W. *Child Development*. Glenview, Ill.: Scott, Foresman, 1979.

Peiper, A. *Cerebral function in infancy and childhood*. New York: Consultants Bureau, 1963.

Pettersen, L., Yonas, A., & Fisch, R. O. The development of blinking in response to impending collision in preterm, full-term, and post-term infants. *Infant Behavior and Development*, 1980, **3**, 155–165.

Pfister, H. Über das Verhalten der Pupille und einiger Reflexe am Auge im sauglins- und fruhen Kindesalter. *Archiv fur Kinderheilkunde*, 1899, **26**, 11–44.

Preyer, W. *The senses and the will*. New York: Appleton, 1909.

Purdy, W. C. *The hypothesis of psychophysical correspondence in space perception*. General Electric Advanced Electronics Center Publication, Cornell University Press, no. R60ELC56, 1960.

Raehlmann, E. Physiologisch-psychologische studien uber die entwickelung der gesichtswahrnehmungen bei kindern und bei operierten blindegeborenen. *Zeitschrift fur Psychologie und Physiologie der Sinnesorgane*, 1891, **2**, 53–96.

Schiff, W. The perception of impending collision: A study of visually directed avoidant behavior. *Psychological Monographs*, 1965, **79**(11, Whole No. 604).

Schiff, W., Caviness, J. A., & Gibson, J. J. Persistent fear responses in rhesus monkeys to the optical stimulus of "looming." *Science*, 1962, **136**, 982–983.

Shinn, M. W. *The biography of a baby*. Boston: Houghton Mifflin, 1900.

Watson, J. B. *Behaviorism*. New York: Norton, 1930.

White, B. L. *Human infants: Experience and psychological development.* Englewood Cliffs, N.J.: Prentice-Hall, 1971.

Yonas, A., Bechtold, A. G., Frankel, D., Gordon, F. R., McRoberts, G., Norcia, A., & Sternfels, S. Development of sensitivity to information for impending collision. *Perception & Psychophysics,* 1977, **21**(2), 97–104.

Yonas, A., Cleaves, W., & Pettersen, L. Development of sensitivity to pictorial depth. *Science,* 1978, **200**(4337), 77–79.

Yonas, A., Pettersen, L., & Lockman, J. J. Sensitivity in 3- and 4-week-old infants to optical information for collision. *Canadian Journal of Psychology,* 1979, **33**(4), 268–276.

Yonas, A., Pettersen, L., Lockman, J. J., & Eisenberg, P. *The perception of impending collision in 3-month-old infants.* Paper presented at the meeting of the International Conference on Infant Studies, New Haven, Connecticut, April, 1980.

12

Stereopsis in Animals and Human Infants: A Review of Behavioral Investigations

ROBERT FOX
Vanderbilt University

I. INTRODUCTION

Stereopsis refers to the perception of the relative depth between objects in visual space based solely on the slightly disparate views provided by horizontally separated eyes. The first convincing evidence that the sufficient condition for stereopsis is the disparity in view between the eyes, so-called retinal disparity, was provided by Wheatstone (1838) in a justly celebrated investigation. Wheatstone presented to each eye, by a device (Wheatstone stereoscope) that kept accommodation, convergence, and viewing distance constant, two-dimensional drawings that mimicked the disparity that would occur under natural viewing

335

Copyright © 1981 by Academic Press, Inc.
All rights of reproduction in any form reserved.
ISBN 0-12-065302-8

conditions. He observed that the disparate portions of the drawings were seen as fused, or single, yet displaced in depth with respect to other elements of the drawing. The discovery that disparity alone could initiate seeing-in-solid or stereopsis immediately captured considerable interest. It at once provided a rationale for the elaborate machinery that seems to have evolved in mammals and particularly in primates for the promotion of binocular vision. It now seemed plausible to suppose that the anatomical structures and physiological mechanisms for binocularity evolved in response to the adaptive advantage conferred by the depth information provided by stereopsis, unique information unavailable to a single eye. Wheatstone's discovery also initiated a long series of technological developments directed toward exploiting stereopsis as an entertainment medium and as a technique for enhancing an observer's natural stereoscopic capacity. Finally, Wheatstone provided the starting point for a systematic and enduring psychophysical inquiry into the stimulus conditions governing stereopsis, an inquiry that continues with great vigor today. It is of interest to note that the quantitative descriptive formulations developed from this work are derived exclusively from a relatively small number of trained adult human observers. Only in very recent years has it been possible to expand the inquiry along phylogenetic and ontogenetic dimensions.

Indeed, the first demonstration of stereopsis in an animal other than an adult human did not take place until 1970 (Bough, 1970). The explicit purpose of this chapter is to review all the investigations of stereopsis in nonhumans and in human infants that have been performed at the behavioral or psychophysical level of analysis. Before turning directly to those investigations, it would be helpful to discuss briefly some of the terms and concepts attendant to stereopsis that have been developed over the years.

Many of these concepts can be illustrated with the aid of the geometrical arrangements given in Fig. 12.1. The horopter refers to those points in visual space that, when viewed binocularly, are seen as single and having a common visual direction. In Fig. 12.1, points X, Y, and Z are on the horopter and are said to stimulate corresponding retinal points. The horopter, of course, is really a surface whose shape will change as a function of viewing distance. The surface of the horopter can be predicted from geometrical considerations, and various empirical tests of the predicted theoretical horopter agree reasonably well, although some systematic deviations are found. The horopter depicted in Fig. 12.1 is actually a horizontal segment of the complete surface, and it is this dimension of the horopter that has received the greatest

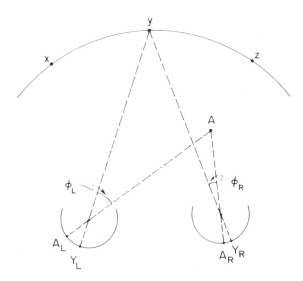

Fig. 12.1 The geometrical relationships that define retinal disparity. Point A is located in front of the horopter closer to the observer.

experimental attention.[1] Consider now point A in Fig. 12.1, which is closer to the eyes and horizontally separated from horopter point Y, to which the eyes are fixated. A is a disparate point that strikes slightly different retinal regions or points A(L) and A(R), as indicated by the difference in angle between Θ(L) and Θ(R). The difference between these angles defines the relative disparity between points Y and A and leads to the perception of A appearing to lie in depth relative to Y. Within certain disparity limits, disparate points such as A will appear as single or fused. The limiting values of disparity define a region known as Panum's fusional area. For small, discrete targets within central vision, the limit of the area is 10–15 min but increases to several degrees for more peripheral stimulation. Within Panum's area, the magnitude of perceived depth covaries with the magnitude of disparity. When stimuli exceed Panum's area, they are no longer fused but are diplopic, and continuous variation in disparity no longer produces concomitant variations in perceived depth. Nevertheless, diplopic stimuli

[1] Recently, however, following a conjecture by Helmholtz (1925), the vertical dimension of the horopter has been examined by Nakayama, Tyler, and Appleman (1977) and by Cogan (1979). They have found that, consistent with Helmholtz's hypothesis, the vertical horopter surface tilts away from the observer, with tilt magnitude increasing with increasing viewing distance.

can be localized correctly as lying in front of or behind the horopter (e.g., Mitchell & O'Hagan, 1972; Westheimer & Mitchell, 1969). Ogle (1959) has proposed the terms *patent* and *qualitative stereopsis* to distinguish between disparate stimuli falling inside and outside of Panum's area (i.e., between fused and diplopic depth percepts). Further refinements and elaborations of the distinction have been offered by Bishop and Henry (1971) and by Julesz (1978).

So far, only variations in the magnitude of disparity have been considered, and, in the case of Fig. 12.1, disparate point *A* is located in front of the horopter, closer to the observer. But the same geometrical considerations also apply to disparate points behind the horopter and, except for a reversal of the relative magnitudes of the disparity angles, the situation is symmetric. The location of the disparate objects relative to the horopter is referred to as the sign of the disparity, with ˙crossed disparities referring to objects in front and uncrossed disparity referring to objects behind the horopter. The origins of those terms are illustrated in Fig. 12.2. In Fig. 12.2a, the eyes are fixated at point *F*, whereas point *C* is disparate, and the angle of disparity is so great that it falls in the zone of qualitative stereopsis and stimulates the temporal retina of each eye, thus stimulating separate hemispheres. The observer will perceive a double image of *C*, and the position of each image with respect to its eye is indicated by the dotted projection lines passing through *C*. The left image will be seen by the right eye and the right image seen by the left eye. Hence the disparity is said to be crossed, in that the image and eye cross the midline. In Fig. 12.2b the fixation point is still at *F* but the disparate point *U–C* behind the horopter is as defined by *F*, and in effect is really *C*, which has been flopped over to *U–C*, with

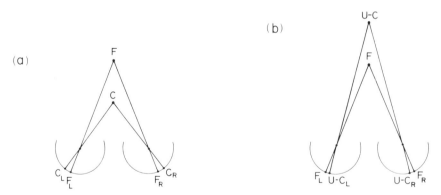

Fig. 12.2 (a) The geometrical relationship that defines crossed disparity. (b) The geometrical relationship that defines uncrossed disparity.

the geometry remaining symmetric. Point *U–C* is seen in qualitative stereopsis as lying behind the horopter plane and the diplopic images it produces are associated with eyes on the same side of the midline. That is, the right-eye diplopic image is seen by the right eye and similarly the left-eye image is seen by the left eye. In the sense of crossing the midline, the disparity is now uncrossed. Note also that *U–C* stimulates nasal portions of each retina rather than the temporal portions stimulated by the crossed disparity point *C*.

The definitions and concepts just reviewed, many of which were well established in the nineteenth century, are derived from stereopsis induced from quite simple stereograms consisting of fixation points and a small number of contours not unlike the drawings used by Wheatstone. The introduction of a new kind of stereogram, the random-element stereogram, by Julesz (1960, 1964), has forced reconsideration of a number of theoretical assumptions underlying research on stereopsis. A random-element stereogram, such as that illustrated in Fig. 12.3, consists of a large set of dots or other small elements randomly ordered in two matrices, one for each eye. Retinal disparity, defining the configuration of a particular form, can be introduced by laterally displacing a subset of elements in one matrix relative to corresponding elements in the other matrix. Under nonstereoscopic viewing conditions, the form defined by disparity cannot be seen, as can be observed in Fig. 12.3, which indeed does contain a disparate region. If an observer with stereopsis views the stereogram under stereoscopic conditions, the visual system detects the disparity and the observer will perceive the stereoscopic form. Because the form can be seen and responded to only if the observer possesses stereopsis, such stereograms offer a

Fig. 12.3 A random-element stereogram. Each matrix, which consists of 10,000 cells, is intended to stimulate a separate eye. A subset of dots that defines a square has been displaced laterally in one matrix. (After Julesz, 1971. Copyright 1971 by Bell Telephone Laboratories. Reprinted by permission.)

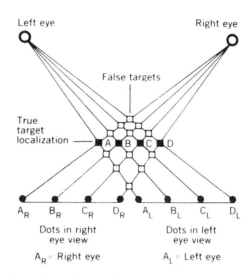

Fig. 12.4 An illustration of the problem of false localization of targets in binocular vision. Each of the four dots in each can give rise to 16 possible localizations, only 4 of which are correct. (From Julesz, 1971. Copyright 1971 by Bell Telephone Laboratories. Reprinted by permission.)

means of developing a conclusive test of stereopsis uncontaminated by monocular cues. This application, along with many others, has been discussed and examined by Julesz and colleagues (see Julesz, 1971, 1978, for reviews).

The presence of stereopsis induced by this kind of stereogram raises the problem of how the elements in one matrix are matched up with appropriate elements in the other matrix to yield a single clear-cut stereoscopic form at a perceived depth level consistent with the disparity value. As pointed out by Julesz (1971), the opportunity for inappropriate pairing of dots is very great, as illustrated in Fig. 12.4, which shows that four points can yield 16 possible pairings. Yet the ambiguous or false localizations are not seen. Rather, the visual system somehow resolves the ambiguity and arrives at the correct solution. The term "global stereopsis" has been used to refer to a stereoscopic situation that contains ambiguity about the appropriate pairing of elements in contrast to the so-called "local stereopsis" situation, in which the minimal number of elements in a stereogram, such as those of the Wheatstone type, do not yield ambiguity about element matching. Several groups of investigators are actively engaged in efforts to model formally global stereopsis—see, for example, Julesz and Chang (1976), Marr and Poggio (1979), and Mayhew and Frisby (1980). One reason for an interest in global stereopsis is that it is not simply a phenomenon unique to random-element stereograms generated by computer but rather corresponds to many natural world scenes involving textured surfaces and many disparate elements. Indeed, the investigation of texture perception has been one outgrowth of research on random-element stereograms (e.g., Caelli & Julesz, 1978). The problem of global stereopsis is just one of several research questions that have been triggered by the development of random-element stereograms. For instance, the production of stereopsis by differences in interocular stimulation other than the disparity provided by spatial separation has been investigated and several nonspatial "disparities" have been reported, including temporal delay (e.g., Burr & Ross, 1979), brightness (e.g., Kaufman, 1973), and color differences (e.g., deWeert, 1979).

Another concept derived from classic or local stereopsis now undergoing re-examination and elaboration is that of Panum's area. When two or three thin vertical lines seen in central vision constitute the stereoscopic display, Panum's area is small, on the order of 15 min, and there has been some tendency in the classic literature (e.g., Ogle, 1959), to regard it as a fixed quantity. However, with global stereopsis, the area becomes variable or elastic and can be altered by both temporal and spatial variables. For instance, Fender and Julesz (1967) and Burt and Julesz (1978) have shown that, once fusion of a random-element stereogram occurs, it can undergo a considerable increase in disparity before stereopsis is lost. This phenomenon has been called hysteresis by Julesz (1971) to characterize the time dependent nature of the process. Another temporal or memory process operating over a much longer time scale has also been reported (Julesz, 1971) in which extended exposure or experience increases the magnitude of disparity that observers perceive as fused. The magnitude of the maximum disparity is also determined by the size of the stereoscopic form, such that the disparity maximum increases with square root increases in area (Tyler & Julesz, 1980).

One topic, however, that has received relatively little attention is the constancy of the magnitude of the perceived depth produced by stereopsis as viewing distance varies. Recall that stereopsis refers to the relative depth perceived between the horopter and disparate points, and does not provide egocentric or absolute information about the distance between the observer and objects in space. Angular disparity, the physical substrate for the perceived magnitude of stereoscopic depth, is inversely proportional to the square of the physical distance between observer and stimuli in real space and inversely proportional to physical distance for stimuli presented as stereograms (see Graham, 1965, for derivation). This means that perceived depth should undergo great changes as physical distance is varied. The situation is analogous to the changes in the apparent size of objects that would occur if it were based solely on the size of the retinal image. But such changes do not occur because of the compensatory process known as size constancy. Is a similar constancy process operating for stereoscopic depth perception? A positive answer seems to have been provided by the small number of investigations of this question, the results of which have been summarized by Ono and Comerford (1977). The magnitude of perceived depth remains constant, primarily because information about perceived distance acts to calibrate disparity values in essentially the same way that perceived distance acts to modify apparent size. An interesting, but somewhat paradoxical observation that demonstrates the operation of depth constancy in a stereogram is the increase in perceived depth that occurs when viewing distance is increased. This is analogous to the increase in the size of an after image that occurs as projection distance increases (Emmert's law) and reflects the response of the visual system when the after image, fixed on the retina, remains constant and the constancy mechanism strives to maintain the balance between perceptual magnitude and perceived distance. Stereoscopic size constancy has not been incorporated within theoretical formulations of stereopsis, as Ono and Comerford point out. Kaufman (1973) agrees, and suggests that this is a major omission. Foley (1972) notes that models of stereopsis based upon disparity detection neurons cannot account for stereoscopic depth constancy and outlines a model by which neuronal disparity outputs would be modulated by the depth information derived from convergence eye movements. Perhaps depth constancy has not received greater theoretical attention because of a tendency on the part of some theorists to regard constancy as a higher order "cognitive process" and stereopsis as a simpler, more "sensory" phenomenon.

This very brief review cannot encompass the complete range of interests and topics embraced by current research on stereopsis. It may, however, convey some sense of the directions being taken in a field that, in the last 20 years, has become quite active. Perhaps it will serve to clarify the concepts attendant to the specific investigations of stereopsis dealt with in subsequent sections.

II. STEREOPSIS IN ANIMALS AND HUMAN INFANTS: METHODOLOGICAL CONSIDERATIONS

Although there has always been great interest in expanding the investigation of stereopsis beyond the domain of the adult human psychophysical observer to encompass nonhumans and developing humans, efforts have been thwarted by rather formidable methodological problems. But, recent advances on several fronts have overcome these difficulties. The purpose of this section is to examine the methodological issues and their resolution.

The two methodological requirements that have been difficult to fulfill are the need for a stereoscopic display that does not contain extraneous nonstereoscopic cues and the need for a sensitive training–response paradigm compatible with the capabilities of the subject. With respect to the stereoscopic display, the classic Wheatstone-type stereogram composed of discrete physical contours offers several potential sources of nonstereoscopic information that could be used to make successful discriminations in perceived depth. Because the contours in such stereograms can be seen monocularly, there are a number of ways that stimulus differences can be detected by a subject without stereopsis. One source of information is parallax, which can be provided by alternate eye closure, alternating interocular suppression, or by lateral head movements. The changes in visual angle of a contour as it advances or recedes can also be used as a cue. If contours are perceived diplopically, direction of lateral motion can serve to indicate direction of their motion in depth. To a great extent, these cues can be controlled or eliminated especially if the subjects are cooperative, trustworthy adults capable of complying with instructions. That kind of control, of course, is not possible with animals and infants.

The development of random-element stereograms represents a great advance because the monocular cues just described are not present. Because the stereoscopic form embedded within the stereogram cannot be seen monocularly, discriminations can be based on the presence or absence of the form or upon its configuration, rather than being limited to discriminations of its position in depth. In static versions of such stereograms, however, a subtle cue is still potentially available. This cue is the inevitable difference in dot pattern at the borders of the embedded stereoscopic form where disparity has been inserted that is not present in a stereogram without disparity. It is conceivable that a subject could, if given sufficient time, detect such local differences in detail. Furthermore, monocularly visible apparent motion will be introduced if an attempt is made to change some parameter of a stereoscopic form. The inability to change some parameter of the stereoscopic form without introducing a cue is a limitation, for such changes could be used to attract attention and enhance discriminability.

The dynamic random-element stereogram overcomes these limitations of static stereograms. In a dynamic stereogram, all elements are replaced randomly at a high rate, typically on the order of 30–60 per second. The continual replacement of dots produces random apparent motion similar to that seen on an untuned television received, yet the motion does not eliminate perceptibility of stereoscopic forms. This replacement does, however, eliminate the cue based on differences in dot position and the cue associated with changing parameters of the stereoscopic form. This makes it possible to continuously move stereoscopic forms in stereoscopic space (i.e., horizontal, vertical, and depth positions or x, y, and z coordinates).

The first dynamic stereogram was made by Julesz (1971), who used cinemagraphic methods to make films that demonstrate several characteristics of global stereopsis. Yet, film has the inherent restriction of being an expensive and inflexible method, particularly because it requires time-consuming animation techniques. A more flexible method of random-dot stereogram generation, made possible by advances in electronic technology, is the continuous generation of dot matrices directly on cathode ray tube (CRT) displays that, typically, are controlled by a hybrid system consisting of a minicomputer joined to an external hard-wired special-purpose electronic device. The device is used to execute high-speed repetitive tasks such as continuous generation of random dots, while the computer implements slower, more complex commands such as insertion of disparity at specific $X–Y$ points specified by the program.

Stereogram generation systems following this approach have been described by Bouldin (1975), Julesz, Breitmeyer, and Kropfl (1976), Ross and Hogben (1974), Uttal, Fitzgerald, and Eskin (1975), and Schumer and Ganz (1979). Although these systems generate dynamic random-element stereograms with many variable parameters, the applications are restricted by the need for a minicomputer and the sophistication of the programming personnel available at a specific installation. Furthermore, the computer cycle time often restricts the size of the matrices, dot density, and luminance levels.

An alternative approach that sidesteps these constraints has been described by Shetty, Brodersen, and Fox (1979). Stereograms are generated and controlled by a compact hard-wired digital logic unit that uses almost any commercial color television receiver as a display. The stereogram consists of large matrices of red and green dots, which, when viewed through appropriate chromatic filters, are each physically routed to a single eye, thus providing the conditions for stereoscopic presentation (i.e., the well-known anaglyphic method, Woodworth, 1938). Controls on the electronic unit permit rapid variation of many parameters of the stereoscopic form, including disparity magnitude and direction, $X-Y$ position, and exposure duration. In one version of the system, the configuration of the stereoscopic forms is controlled by an optical scanning device that translates any two-dimensional array of contours placed before it, static or moving, into its stereoscopic counterpart. This feature has made it possible to present stereoscopically an array of randomly selected alphabet letters to investigate iconic memory without inducing retinal afterimages (Fox, Lehmkuhle, & Shea, 1977). The same feature has also been used in an investigation of visual masking (Lehmkuhle & Fox, 1980). By presenting a set of vertically oriented stereoscopic contours that appear to move continuously in one direction, it has been possible to demonstrate that such contours are sufficient for generating optokinetic nystagmus (Fox, Lehmkuhle, & Leguire, 1978). Finally, as will be discussed in another section, the stereogram generation system has been used to investigate stereopsis in nonhumans and human infants.

In a great many ways dynamic random-element stereograms would seem to offer an ideal technique for testing stereopsis. One objection that could be raised is that some persons require a considerable amount of observation time before they can discern a stereoscopic form in a random-element stereogram. In a testing situation, such persons might be falsely classified as not possessing stereopsis. Indeed, casual observers who view representative stereograms printed in texts sometimes report an initial difficulty in perceiving a stereoscopic percept, but viewing conditions in that situation are not optimal. When the surface of a stereogram is clearly seen as a flat surface, it can serve as a strong perceptual anchor that impedes the perception of depth. In addition, the greater difficulty sometimes encountered in perceiving stereoforms with uncrossed disparity is due to a reluctance of the perceptual system to permit percepts that seemingly penetrate the flat surface. Furthermore, printed stereograms are often viewed by methods such as free stereoscopy, in which altered accommodation and convergence relationships can impede the emergence of stereopsis. The perceptibility of stereoscopic forms is also governed by the magnitude and number of disparity values contained within the stereogram; very large disparities can require considerable observation time before they are resolved.

Under more optimal viewing conditions, as would be provided by presenting a stereogram of a single form with a moderate disparity value in a display device that maintains proper accommodation and convergence relationships, perception time can be quite short. Julesz (1978) reports that detections of stereoscopic forms can be made at exposure durations on the order of 50 msec, a value well below the time required to execute an eye movement. The observers used by Lehmkuhle and Fox (1980) in their investigation of visual masking could make above-chance discriminations of the gap in a stereoscopic form configured as a Landolt C at durations of 60 to 80 msec and, at the same durations, could make correct discriminations of the depth position of the stimulus as a function of its disparity. A similar capacity for making graded depth discriminations at short exposure durations was also found by Mayhew and Frisby (1980). These authors note that their results contrast sharply with those reported by Richards (1977), who found that, at an exposure duration of 200 msec, observers could detect the presentation of a stereoscopic form but were unable to localize its correct depth position. They suggest that Richards' negative result might be unique to the conditions of his experiment. On that point, it is worth noting that the recycle time of Richards' CRT display was 15 Hz, a low value relative to the 30–60 Hz used by other investigators; the lower rate may have produced a disruptive apparent motion that impaired the processing of stereopsis information.

A comparison of the time required to resolve stereoscopic and physical monocularly visible forms was made by Staller, Lappin, and Fox (1980), who required observers to classify letter forms via reaction time in accord with the additive factors paradigm devised by Sternberg (1969). The reaction time analysis indicated that both stereoscopic and physical letter forms were processed in the same way, and that the time required to initially resolve the stereoscopic form was about 65 msec greater than the time required to resolve a comparable physical letter form.

Although much more research is required, a tentative conclusion about the perceptibility of stereoscopic forms produced by random-element stereograms is that, whereas their discriminability and resolvability are not equivalent to comparable physical stimuli, the difference is not great enough to pose a problem for the testing of stereoscopic capacity. This would not apply to the "complex" stereograms, that Julesz, in his explorations of global stereopsis, has deliberately devised. These are stereograms composed of large multiple disparities defining complex surfaces, and they do require considerable time to resolve. Although interesting in their own right, they would not be appropriate, of course, for basic testing purposes.

Granted that such developments as the dynamic random-element stereogram solves the stimulus problem, the next issue to consider is the response system required to indicate discrimination of the stimulus. The training of animals to make discriminations among stimuli has been a major concern of experimental psychologists since the beginning of this century, yet many of the procedures that have been devised do not lend themselves readily to discrimination of stereoscopic stimuli. A stereoscopic stimulus devoid of the companion physical stimuli that would normally accompany it in a natural world is not particularly salient. Its appreciation requires that an observer attend to a display with both eyes appropriately converged. Head movements should be minimal and viewing distance constant, at least until the response is initiated. These requirements do not always fit the natural response tendencies of many animals.

What is required are methods for transforming unruly animals into calm, attentive psychophysical observers. A major, perhaps unwitting, step toward meeting that goal has been Skinnerian behaviorism, whose emphasis upon the shaping of complex behavior by a judicious concatenation of simple responses and immediate reinforcement has promoted the development of procedures for teaching animals to engage in elaborate and, to some extent, unnatural activities. Many of these procedures lend themselves admirably to the transformation of animals into psychophysical observers. Some specific applications are discussed elsewhere in this chapter and a good overview of the field is provided by Stebbins (1970).

A major drawback of these experiments is that even the most powerful training techniques require considerable time, typically ordered on the scale of weeks and months. This is not a serious problem when the goal of the investigation is to determine the optimal perceptual capacity of an adult animal. It is unacceptable, however, if the goal of the investigation is to study ontogenetic development, as the time required for testing and training is completely confounded with the organism's developmental changes. What is needed are rapid methods of testing that do not require extensive pretraining. Methods for rapid testing are less advanced than those available for the steady-state testing of adult animals. Indeed, their invention is intrinsically more difficult because of the limited response repertoire and labile attention of immature animals.[2] Nevertheless, some improved methods of testing have appeared and are considered in following sections.

The forced-choice preferential looking technique (FPL) developed by Davida Teller and colleagues is a simple, yet effective method for testing

[2] There are many advantages in capitalizing upon the natural response proclivities of an organism whenever possible. A classic example is the testing of vision in rats by the jumping-stand technique developed by Lashley (1930). As will be described in a subsequent section, Mitchell, Giffin, Wilkerson, Anderson, and Smith (1976) and Mitchell, Giffin, and Timney (1977) devised a similar procedure for rapid testing of visual function in kittens.

the sensory capacities of both human infants and nonhumans (see e.g., Peeples & Teller, 1975; Teller, 1979). It capitalizes upon the well-established observation that human infants will be visually attracted to visual stimulation relative to zero stimulation. A method for systematically evaluating these visual preferences was first developed by Fantz (see Fantz, Fagen, & Miranda, 1975, for a general review). Pairs of stimuli that presumably vary in their attractiveness are presented on a trial-to-trial basis, and on each trial an observer judges which stimulus elicited the greater visual preference as defined by such variables as duration of looking or the initiator of the first look. Although a quite useful procedure, results depend heavily upon the judgmental criteria used by the observer. The FPL method eliminates the intrinsic subjectivity of the Fantz procedure by converting it into a forced-choice detection task analogous to the forced-choice methods of contemporary psychophysics (e.g., Blackwell, 1953; Green & Swets, 1966). On each trial, a stimulus pattern analogous to a signal is paired with a nonstimulus pattern analogous to noise. The lateral positions of the stimulus and nonstimulus are randomly alternated, and an observer who is unaware of the stimulus position is required to make a forced-choice judgment about the position based upon observations of the infant's behavior. The variation in the response criterion of the observer is minimized, and the presence of an external reference for defining performance in terms of hit rate or correct responses renders the method objective. If the observer succeeds in above chance localization of the stimulus, the infant must be engaged in some behavior, whether it be eye movements, head tilt, change of expression, or whatever, that is systematically correlated with the stimulus. Hence, the stimulus must have been detected or processed by the infant. In short, the logic is identical to that of the two-choice forced-choice method used in other contexts and of the "Class A" experiment described by Brindley (1960). Accordingly, a wide range of sophisticated mathematical and statistical techniques, as, for example, signal detection theory, are applicable. Although it has been applied principally to investigations of the visual capacities of human infants, the technique can also be applied to nonhumans. It is worth emphasizing that the method does not depend exclusively upon observing the eye movements of the organisms being tested; rather, any behavior that permits the observer to make correct detections can be exploited. In the case of infants, this can be a variety of rather subtle changes that the observer can use and, indeed, learns to use through the feedback received after each choice. Furthermore, the method is not limited to vision but could be applied in any situation where a stimulus naturally elicits an attention or orientation response. For example, one potential application might be the determination of which of a pair of auditory signals elicits the preference or attention in an animal such as a young bird. Finally, one virtue of the method is that it requires a relatively small amount of equipment and training to implement.

Optokinetic nystagmus, which refers to the reflexive induction of eye movements by repetitive moving contours, has been used to assess acuity in infants and in a variety of animals. The possibility that it could also be used to assess stereopsis has been suggested by Fox, Lehmkuhle, and Leguire (1978), who used a dynamic random-element stereogram display in which vertical stereoscopic contours appeared to move continuously in one direction and which induced in adult observers clear-cut nystagmus eye movements. Because stereopsis is required for the perception of such moving contours, the presence of nystagmus forces the conclusion that the observer possesses stereopsis. Although the method has not yet been applied to infants or to nonhumans, there is no reason why it would not be feasible. One qualification, however, is that the perception of steropsis is restricted to central vision; stimulation in the far periphery will not yield stereopsis. As a result, it is not possible to completely surround an organism with effective stereoscopic stimuli. Instead, the tested organism would have to direct its gaze to a particular visual display. This may mean that some kind of training or attention-attracting procedure is required before testing can begin but such pretraining is likely to be much less extensive and time consuming than traditional training procedures.

The use of visual cortical evoked potentials to measure visual function objectively is a well-established procedure. As will be described in a subsequent section, stereoscopic stimuli do elicit potentials and this method could be used for the objective assessment of stereopsis.

The procedures just described convey some sense of the range of techniques that have been devised and that are continuing to be developed in an effort to solve the difficult problem of quickly and validly assessing developing visual capacity.

III. STEREOPSIS IN THE CAT

The first investigation of stereopsis in the cat was made by Fox and Blake (1971), who used the technique known as shadow casting for presentation of the stereoscopic stimulus and the operant conditioning method known as conditioned suppression as the behavioral indicator of stereoscopic discrimination. Shadow casting (see Fig. 12.5) refers to

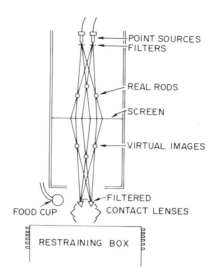

Fig. 12.5 A schema of the shadow-casting method of stereoscopic presentation. The shadows of the real rods on the screen are retinally disparate. For an observer with stereopsis, the shadows will fuse and appear in depth as indicated by the virtual images.

the projection of the shadows of physical contours on a ground glass screen by point sources placed behind the screen. If the contours, such as thin vertical lines, are presented dichoptically via polarizers or anaglyphic color filters, an observer with stereopsis will see single fused contours standing in depth in front of the screen. If the physical contours that cast the shadows are moved in the z-axis toward and away from the point sources, the stereoscopic images in front of the screen appear to move concomitantly along the z-axis. Stereoscopic shadow casting, which has been described in detail by Gregory (1964) and by Lee (1969), eliminates many of the monocular cues associated with stereograms made from conventional physical contours.

Conditioned suppression refers to a phenomenon discovered within the context of research on operant conditioning (Estes & Skinner, 1941), wherein an animal will suppress its ongoing operant activity, such as bar pressing, when it is presented with a stimulus that indicates that a noxious event, such as an electric shock, is soon to occur. Once the noxious event occurs, a well-trained animal will resume its former level of operant responding. This inhibition of response, known as the conditioned emotional response in the literature on operant conditioning, has received considerable attention within the domains of operant conditioning and animal discrimination learning. Independent of that interest, conditioned suppression has been exploited by investigators concerned with the assessment of sensory and perceptual thresholds in animals, as described, for example, by Smith (1970) and by Berkley (1970). In that application, the intensity of the suppression-inducing stimulus is varied, analogous to the variation of stimulus intensity attendant to the estimation of thresholds in psychophysical paradigms used with human observers. Suppression is used as an indicator of the detectability of the stimulus, with stimuli clearly above threshold inducing suppression, and those below threshold failing to elicit it.

In Fox and Blake's (1971) application of the paradigm, the operant response was continuous licking of a spout and the reinforcement was intermittent presentation of a food reward. By appropriate placement of the spout, animals were trained to keep their heads in one position to direct their gaze toward an enclosure containing the visual display. Once reliable baseline licking was established, a stimulus discrimination based upon conditioned suppression was introduced. Initially, the animal viewed three thin vertical contours in a frontoparallel plane; the center contour could be moved toward the animal or away from the animal at a controlled rate. Forward movements were followed some seconds later by a brief shock, while movements to the rear produced no shock. After sufficient training, forward movements or shock trials induced suppression of licking, and "safe" movements to the rear produced minimal suppression. Once discrimination had been mastered using the real movement of a physical contour, a shadow-casting display was introduced that projected three vertical shadows closely resembling the appearance of the physical contours. Apparent forward and backward movement of the center shadow immediately produced the same behavior elicited by movements of the physical contour. The immediate transfer from physical to stereoscopic contours suggests that the discrimination was based upon stereopsis. If it were not, the motion of the shadows would appear quite different and not discriminable between forward and backward motions. Fox and Blake noted that other perceptual monocular cues provided by head movement and systematic eye closure were not used, and they concluded that stereopsis was used to make the discrimination.

Packwood and Gordon (1975) have extended the investigation of stereopsis in the cat to include Siamese varieties and laboratory cats raised from birth through the critical period under conditions of alternating monocular vision. The Siamese, by virtue of an aberrant genetically determined geniculostriate pathway, are thought to have an inappropriate anatomical substrate for stereopsis, while animals raised under conditions of alternating monocular vision do not develop the appropriate binocular cortical neurons thought to be essential for stereopsis. Stereopsis was tested by means of a stereoscopic shadow-casting system similar to that used by Fox and Blake (1971). Animals were first taught to discriminate between the forward and backward motions of a physical contour, and after mastery were presented with the stereoscopic shadow-casting display that mimicked the appearance of the physical contour display. All three groups—normal cats, Siamese, and alternating monoculars—successfully learned to discriminate the position of the physical contour, but only the normal cats could master the stereoscopic discrimination. Several supplementary tests revealed that the failure of the cats with abnormal binocular visual systems could not be attributed to impaired visual acuity, memory deficit for the task, response bias, or an abnormal photopic sensitivity function. These data led Packwood and Gordon (1975) to conclude that the failure was due to the absence of stereopsis in these animals, a conclusion consistent with anatomical and electrophysiological findings. Using normal cats, estimates of the limit of fusion and of qualitative steropsis were also obtained. Fusional limits appear to be on the order of 50 min for crossed disparity and 30 min for uncrossed disparity. Qualitative stereopsis, presumably with diplopic images, occurred for disparities greater than 60 min. Although no attempt was made to reach a threshold, normal cats could discern or successfully discriminate disparities as small as 5 min. Finally, it was noted that both the Siamese and the alternating monocular cats exhibited a more convergent interocular alignment than did normals.

A comparison of the binocular performance of normal cats with cats raised under conditions of alternating monocular stimulation has also been carried out by Blake and Hirsch (1975), who used a real depth display similar to the one employed by Fox and Blake (1971). The ability of the cats to discriminate rod displacement was assessed under binocular and monocular conditions of view. For the normal cats, the threshold for detecting rod displacement under the binocular condition was much lower (4 min angular disparity) than under the monocular (40 min angular disparity). In contrast, the binocular thresholds in the alternating monocular cats did not differ from their monocular thresholds. The authors suggest that the superior binocular performance of the normal cats is probably attributable to stereopsis, while the performance of the alternating monocular cats would be attributable to its absence, a conclusion consistent with that of Packwood and Gordon.

The results considered so far support the hypothesis that stereopsis is present in adult non-Siamese cats raised under normal conditions. Nevertheless, the evidence is not conclusive, for one could maintain that discriminations presumably based on stereopsis were, in fact, based on the nonstereoscopic cues that are intrinsic to displays containing discrete contours. As noted earlier, these potential sources of nonstereoscopic information can never be eliminated with line or contour stimuli. A more compelling case for the presence of stereopsis can be made if the stereoscopic stimulus is a random-element stereogram, for it provides great intrinsic control over nonstereoscopic sources of information.

These considerations led Lehmkuhle and Fox (1977) to test stereopsis in the cat using the dynamic random-element stereogram generation system that produces a red–green anaglyph display on a color television receiver. The conditioned suppression paradigm was used with the presentation of a stereoscopic form in crossed disparity as the stimulus indicating an inescapable electric shock was forthcoming. Cats were initially trained to suppress to a physical stimulus display similar to the one used by Fox and Blake (1971) and Blake and Hirsch (1975). When the stereoscopic form was presented (the cats had already been habituated to wearing a helmet with red and green filters) the animals showed a rapid transfer of the suppression discrimination to this stimulus, a result implying that they possess stereopsis. Fig. 12.6 shows representative results for two animals. Included in the figure are the results of control conditions in which one eye was occluded—the failure of suppression under those conditions supports the conclusion that the animals have stereopsis. To determine if the cats were responding to the shape or orientation of the stereoscopic form rather than simply reacting to an undefined form in depth, the form was rotated so that it became a horizontal rectangle. This stimulus produced an appropriate change in performance, indicating that the altered rotation was detected. Because it is difficult to conceive of nonstereoscopic cues that would be operative in this situation, the successful discrimination by the cats provides conclusive evidence for the existence of stereopsis in these animals.

The behavioral methods for testing stereopsis considered so far, such as conditioned suppression, require that the animals receive considerable training, and even then, in the case where discrimination is difficult, not every animal is either temperamentally or intellectually suitable. This is not a serious problem when the experimental question involves testing the steady-state capacity of mature animals, but it is a very serious limitation for questions of ontogenetic development where a relatively large number of animals must be tested quickly to avoid confounding perceptual and developmental changes. In recognition of this problem, Mitchell, Giffin, and Timney (1977) and Mitchell, Giffin, Wilkerson, Anderson, and Smith (1976) have developed a jump-

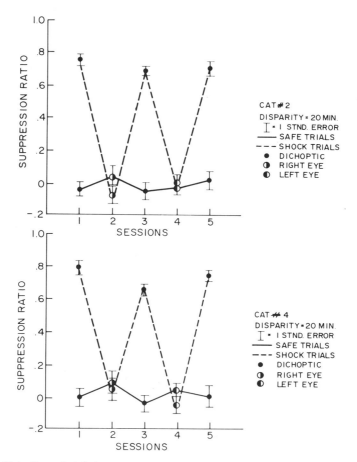

Fig. 12.6 Test of global stereopsis in the cat. The suppression is defined as a ratio of responses (licks) before and after presentation of the shock related stimulus. A ratio of 1.0 means complete suppression and 0 means no suppression. The high values under the dichoptic shock trials indicate the animals discriminating the stereoscopic form.

ing-stand technique for testing kittens in which kittens are placed on an elevated platform and encouraged to jump down to a pair of lower platforms upon which discriminable stimuli are imposed. On any given trial, the kitten views both platforms and is required to choose and descend to the platform that is "correct" for that trial. Descents to the correct platform are rewarded. Learning is quite rapid, probably because the technique exploits the cat's proclivities for climbing and leaping and for attending carefully to the object of its leap.

The jumping-stand technique has recently been applied to a comparison of binocular and monocular vision in kittens. The target platforms are set at unequal distances from the kitten and descent to the closest platform is rewarded. The question of interest is the smallest difference in platform distance that can be discriminated reliably. Kittens reared under normal laboratory conditions can discriminate much smaller differences in platform distance for binocular vision than for monocular, while kittens reared under special conditions designed to disrupt binocular mechanisms showed no difference between binocular and monocular performance. The authors acknowledge that their testing situation included a number of nonstereoscopic cues, such as relative size and parallax, and, indeed, after extended practice, performance under monocular viewing conditions improves substantially, presumably as a result of the animal's learning to capitalize upon such cues. Nevertheless, it is possible to at least consider the hypothesis that the initial superiority displayed by normal kittens under binocular viewing conditions is attributable to stereopsis. Given the assumption that stereopsis is operative, the smallest difference in platform distance that could be discriminated was 2 cm, which corresponds to an angular disparity of approximately 4 min. This value is consistent with those obtained in other experiments that exerted greater control over the presence of nonstereoscopic cues. Although the jumping-stand technique as presently applied does not provide unequivocal evidence for stereopsis, the substantial difference between binocular and monocular performance is noteworthy, especially as it has not been observed with other methods designed to assess depth perception in young developing animals, such as the visual cliff of Walk and Gibson (1961).

The relatively small number of behavioral investigations of stereopsis in the cat seem to support several conclusions.

1. There can be no doubt that cats with normal binocular visual systems possess stereopsis. The most compelling evidence on this point is provided by the work of Lehmkuhle and Fox (1977), who used dynamic random-element stereograms, although it seems quite likely that cats were using stereopsis in the experiments that employed physical contours.

2. Estimates of stereoacuity based upon contoured stimuli are in reasonably close agreement, from 5 min to 1 min, and these values are in approximate correspondence with the range of the smallest receptive field values obtained for disparity-tuned neurons in cat cortex (e.g., Pettigrew, Nikara, & Bishop, 1968).

3. Cats with impaired binocular systems, defined either anatomically or electrophysiologically, do not seem to possess stereopsis.

These conclusions are fundamental ones that pave the way for further inquiry, but they by no means embrace the full range of interesting questions that can be posed about the cat's stereoscopic capacities. Questions immediately arise about the existence of depth constancy, the form of the horopter, and asymmetry of sensitivity for crossed versus uncrossed disparities. Furthermore, it would be of great interest to establish the correlation between stereoscopic capacity and graded or refined reductions in binocular neurons produced by quantitatively controlled rearing conditions (e.g., Blasdel & Pettigrew, 1979).

IV. STEREOPSIS IN THE MONKEY

Because there are many similarities between the visual systems of monkeys and humans, as indicated by both psychophysical and neurophysiological data, it would be surprising if stereopsis were not present in monkeys. The first positive evidence was provided by Bough (1970), whose test for stereopsis was the discrimination of stereoscopic forms generated by photographs of random-element stereograms. Stump-tailed monkeys *(Macaca arcotoids)* viewed photographs of the stereograms dichoptically by means of a circular polarizing display system and were required to discriminate stereograms containing a square from stereograms without a square. The initial training began with monocular cues clearly available. These were gradually eliminated until the discrimination could be made only on the basis of stereopsis. In one test sequence, the stereoscopic square was presented with uncrossed disparity; in a second series, the square was presented with crossed disparity. To check on the possibility that the animals might, over a long series of trials, have capitalized upon differences in dot structure at the boundaries of the stereoscopic form, a second set of stereograms with a different dot structure was used. Immediate transfer of the discrimination to these new stereograms suggested that a cue based on dot structure was not being exploited. Rendering the animals monocular, either by occlusion or by induction of convergent strabismus, brought discrimination to chance values. These observations, taken together, led Bough to conclude that stereopsis was present in this species.

The question of the existence of stereopsis in rhesus monkeys *(Macaca mulatta)* was investigated by Cowey, Parkinson, and Warnick (1975). Their report is noteworthy in that, in addition to being ultimately successful, they describe in detail the many difficulties they encountered in eliminating nonstereoscopic cues. Their initial paradigm was conceptually similar to Bough's in that it involved discrimination of the stereoscopic form embedded in photographs of random-element stereograms presented dichoptically by polarizers. The animals quickly learned the discrimination, ostensibly on the basis of stereopsis, but various control procedures revealed that they were using nonstereoscopic cues. Considerable experimental effort was directed toward identifying and eliminating cues, and, on this, the report should be read in the original to gain some appreciation of the way resourceful animals can capitalize upon seemingly modest differences in stimulation. Several problems could be traced to the use of the dichoptic polarization system. The brightness of reflected polarized light varies as a function of the angle of initial polarization and of the angle of reflection, thus producing brightness differences between otherwise identical stimuli. Furthermore, when linear polarizers are worn by the subject, as they were in this case, tilt of the head changes the polarization angle and produces brightness differences. In a final experimental sequence, polarization was eliminated by the anaglyphic method of dichoptic presentation (chromatic filters of complementary wavelengths replaced the polarizers) and under these conditions of stimulus presentation, convincing evidence for stereopsis was obtained.

The threshold for resolving disparity in a stereogram (stereoacuity) was investigated in the monkey by Sarmiento (1975), who used a classic two-contour discrimination task and determined the smallest difference in depth between two rods that the animals could discriminate. The animals (three rhesus monkeys and two stump-tailed macaques) were trained to select the nearest rod to secure a food reward. The task proved quite difficult, however, perhaps because the positions of the stimuli, response level, and food dispenser were not optimal, and training of three monkeys was discontinued. A fourth died prior to completion of threshold measurements, but complete measurements were obtained from the surviving animal, who underwent training and testing for 550 consecutive days. The stereoacuity threshold for this animal was 2.4 sec of arc, a value equivalent to the smallest threshold found for human observers tested in the same apparatus. The animal also displayed the same relationship between luminance and stereoacuity found in humans. Performance was substantially impaired under repeated monocular viewing conditions, suggesting that performance was not based on a monocular cue, such as a change in the visual angle of the rods. Sarmiento concluded that performance was based on stereopsis, and that stereopsis in the monkey is comparable to stereopsis in humans.

The ability of monkeys to perceive stereopsis in dynamic random-element stereograms was described in an abstract by Julesz, Petrig, and Buttner (1976). Monkeys were trained, presumably by standard operant conditioning procedures, to react to the presence of a nonstereoscopic stimulus. When the stereoscopic equivalent of the stimulus was presented, discrimination was maintained. Further evidence for stereopsis was provided by control trials wherein the presentation of vertical disparity did not elicit discriminatory responses.

The most complete description of an operant training procedure used for testing stereopsis in monkeys is provided by Harwerth and Boltz (1979a). In a separate article, they (Harwerth & Boltz, 1979b) describe an investigation of the effect of exposure duration on stereopsis in rhesus monkeys in which the animals were required to discriminate between random-element stereograms (photographs projected as slides) containing either one or two vertically oriented rectangular stereoscopic forms. A prism stereoscope was used for dichoptic presentation, and each stereogram, containing either one or two forms, was presented successively. The independent variables were the direction of disparity (crossed or uncrossed), disparity magnitude, and exposure duration. Control conditions, which included stereograms with zero disparity and monocular viewing of stereograms, indicated that the discriminations were based on stereopsis. The main effect of exposure duration was impairment of performance as duration decreased, with smaller disparity values affected more than larger values.

For four of the six animals, performance with uncrossed disparities at smaller disparities and shorter exposure durations was poorer than for crossed disparities. The remaining two subjects exhibited no differences between disparity directions. The pattern of results obtained from the animals was at least in qualitative agreement with results from humans tested under the same conditions. The authors conclude that this commonality supports the view that stereopsis in the monkey is essentially the same as stereopsis in humans.

There seems to be no room for doubt about the existence of stereopsis in the monkey. All of the investigations provide positive evidence obtained by satisfactory methods. Furthermore, the quantitative characteristics of monkey stereopsis, although not examined extensively, seem to be similar to that of humans. This is not a surprising conclusion in view of other similarities in visual capacity that have been found between the two species and it increases confidence in the hypotheses about human vision that have been derived from research with monkeys. Apparently, no investigations have yet been made of the ontogenetic development of stereopsis in monkeys, or of stereopsis in monkeys with impaired binocular function—two lines of inquiry that appear to be promising.

V. STEREOPSIS IN NONMAMMALIANS

The visual systems of mammals, and especially that of primates, contain many features that seem designed to promote binocular vision and permit large scale interaction between the eyes. These include the frontal placement of the eyes, yoked eye movements, and the partial decussation of the optic tract which permits corresponding retinal areas to combine at the same cortical sites. However, the visual systems of most nonmammalians are characterized by more laterally placed eyes, which, in some species, can move independently of each other, and by complete decussation of the optic tract. As a result, the opportunity for interaction between the eyes in these animals is much more restricted. These differences between the mammalian and nonmammalian visual systems have led to the hypothesis, as enunciated by such workers as Ramon Y Cajal (1899) and LeGros Clark (1959), that the mammalian visual system evolved to gain the capacity for stereopsis. Accordingly, stereopsis would be a unique attribute of mammals and particularly of primates with frontal eyes. Until recently, this view has been the dominant one and has been termed the elite hypothesis by Fox (1977), as it confines stereopsis to relatively small numbers of the more recently evolved mammals. But there are special adaptations for binocularity seen in predatory nonmammalians that seem designed expressly to allow the animal to extract binocular information. Such adaptations include a second fovea in the temporal retina, convergence eye movements, and such specializations as sighting grooves—a paring away of the snout so that the eyes can look at a common segment of visual space. These adaptations offer support for an alternative view, called the proletarian hypothesis, which holds that all animals that have the capacity for binocular vision also possess stereopsis. Although favored by a few workers, for example, Polyak (1957), this hypothesis has not been widely accepted because evidence for a neural site for extensive interactions between the eyes in nonmammalians has been meager.

However, advances in neuroanatomical and electrophysiological methods have permitted a re-examination of the classic distinction between the visual systems of mammals and nonmammalians. The developing evidence suggests that both mammals and nonmammals possess two visual pathways—one from the retina to the tectum, and the second from the retina to the striate cortex by way of a thalamic relay nucleus. Evidence for the existence of two visual pathways or visual systems is accruing for a number of representative nonmammalians including the turtle (e.g., Granda & Hays, 1972; Hall, 1972), frog (e.g., Ingle, 1973), and shark (e.g., Duff & Ebbesson, 1973). Of particular interest is the extensive series of investigations of the avian visual system carried out by Karten and his colleagues (e.g., Karten, Hodos, Nauta, & Revzin, 1973) who have identified structures in the pigeon and in the owl that appear to be analogous to the lateral geniculate nucleus and to the visual striate cortex of mammals. The structure analogous to the striate cortex is the region on the dorsal surface of the avian cerebral hemispheres known as the visual Wulst. Input to the Wulst is by way of a pathway known as the superoptic decussation, which provides both ipsilateral and contralateral input from the retina, thereby providing a site for extensive binocular interaction within the Wulst.

Motivated by the anatomical evidence for binocular interaction in the pigeon and in the owl, Fox, Lehmkuhle, and Bush (1977) carried out a behavioral investigation of stereopsis in the sparrow hawk or American kestrel, a small unendangered bird, yet a true falcon, with all the attributes of its larger colleagues. A falcon was chosen because its extensive binocular overlap provided by well-developed temporal foveas, keen vision, and predatory lifestyle make it a likely candidate for stereopsis. A two-choice discrimination was required in which the animal had to fly to the display containing a dynamic random-element stereoscopic form to obtain a food reward. Control conditions included testing discrimination under monocular conditions and presentation of very large disparities that prevented clear perception of the stereoscopic form. The failure to discriminate under these control conditions indicated that discrimination was indeed based on stereopsis. In subsequent work, anatomical evidence for a biretinal projection to the Wulst has been obtained (Lehmkuhle, Casagrande, & Fox, 1977; Pettigrew, 1980). Furthermore, electrophysiological evidence for binocular neurons sensitive to disparity have been obtained in the owl (Pettigrew & Konishi, 1976) and in the kestrel (Pettigrew, 1977).

The behavioral, anatomical, and electrophysiological data are all consistent with the hypothesis that stereopsis is present in predatory birds. It is not known, however, if stereopsis is a general attribute of birds with binocular vision, or whether it is a specialization confined to predators. Pettigrew (1980) reports that several nonpredatory birds do not possess binocularly driven neurons in the visual Wulst, even though they do have considerable binocular overlap. Behavioral tests of stereopsis in these animals have not been conducted and that would be an important next step.

The only other nonmammalian that has been tested for stereopsis is the toad (Collett, 1977). Toads have a large binocular field and relatively immobile eyes. By placing prisms before their eyes, the convergence angle was altered and this change produced a systematic localization error when they attacked their prey. This result implies that both eyes are being used to judge distance. Under a monocular condition, however, depth accuracy was maintained, presumably based upon accommodation. A similar accommodative mechanism for judging depth has also been observed in monocular frogs (Ingle, 1972). It should be noted that the kind of binocular depth estimation found in the toad would not be considered stereopsis as conventionally defined, for it is really an absolute depth localization and not the relative depth perception of conventional stereopsis. The absolute estimation of depth has been called "stereopsis by triangulation" by Linksz (1952), and would reflect a simpler mechanism than the one considered essential for stereopsis.

It is simply too early to tell whether stereopsis is widespread among vertebrates with binocular vision. A variety of animals representing different lines of descent must be tested. Such tests are feasible but difficult because appropriate animals are not readily available and often pose special problems of training and testing. Eventually, however, these investigations will be implemented. These data will help clarify the longstanding and intriguing question of the evolutionary relationship between binocularity and stereoscopic depth perception. In addition, such data also promise to provide useful animal models for the investigation of the development of binocular vision. For example, if a common bird such as a pigeon or chicken could be used, many of the well-established embryological techniques could be applied to the investigation of visual development.

VI. EVALUATION OF STEREOPSIS BY THE EVOKED POTENTIAL METHOD

Although not strictly a behavioral method, the recording of averaged cortical evoked activity by the attachment of scalp electrodes is a noninvasive technique that can be used to test for stereopsis. Those investigations that have used the evoked potential method as a test are reviewed in this section.

The first investigation, by Regan and Spekreijas (1970), used static random-dot stereograms and a projection system that permitted the switching of stereograms from a no-disparity to a disparity mode. The stereoscopic square appeared to jump forward and backward in depth and elicited a potential that seemed to covary with disparity over values from 10 to 40 min. Fiorentini and Maffei (1970) used grating patterns which, when seen with disparity, appeared to be tilted in depth either toward or away from the observer. Changes in the apparent tilt of the fused grating pattern elicited a potential that could not be obtained under other conditions of stimulation, thereby suggesting that it was uniquely associated with a stereoscopic percept. However, it has been suggested (Julesz, 1971; Julesz, Kropfl, & Petrig, 1980) that responses seen in these studies could have been contaminated by eye movement potentials or by monocular cues present when rapid changes are made in static random-element stereograms or when monocular contours are present.

Such cues, of course, are eliminated by the use of dynamic random-element stereograms. Using a dynamic random-element stereogram generation system, Bouldin et al. (1975) investigated the origin of a central evoked potential known as the lambda wave, which is thought to reflect the operation of a saccadic suppression mechanism. Lambda waves can be elicited either by moving the eyes saccadically across a stationary contour or, with the eyes held immobile, by moving the contour quickly from one position to the other at velocities similar to those seen with saccadic eye movements. To determine if cortical stimulation was necessary for production of the lambda wave, Bouldin et al. used a stereoscopic form that appeared to jump abruptly from one side of a central viewing area to the other while the eyes were held immobile by fixation markers. Clear-cut potentials were elicited as long as the range of velocities employed produced good apparent movement. The latency of the potentials elicited by the apparent movement of the stereoscopic form was about 100 msec slower than the potentials elicited by the comparable movement of a physical form. Simultaneous recording of eye movements indicated that the stereoscopic potentials were not contaminated by eye movement potentials. The equipment generating the stereograms consisted of a hybrid system that joined a minicomputer and special electronic hardware to continuously generate random dots on CRTs. The CRTs, one for each eye, were brought into binocular coincidence using a haploscope. This system was used by Bouldin (1975) to investigate several parameters of potentials evoked by stereoscopic stimuli. It was found that the magnitude of the potential varied with disparity. There was an asymmetry in response between the onset and offset of the stereoscopic form with a larger potential associated with onset. Potentials were attenuated when the form moved from crossed to uncrossed disparity.

Rawlings and Yates (1979) obtained evoked potentials to a kind of checkerboard stimulus formed from a random-element stereogram wherein the checkerboards appeared to move in and out of depth in a counterphase motion. Potentials covaried with disparity magnitude, and blurring the stimulus by lenses reduced the magnitude of the potentials.

Lehmann and Julesz (1979) obtained potentials from dynamic random-element stereograms electronically generated on a CRT and found interesting differences in potential magnitude as a function of the cortical hemisphere stimulated.

Julesz et al., 1980, generated dynamic random-element stereograms on a colored projection television system and obtained potentials to a checkerboard configured stereogram, the squares of which appeared to move forward and backward in depth. They also report obtaining a potential to a stimulus called a correlogram, which consists of a dynamic random-noise display in which the dots in one eye's matrix are periodically complemented with respect to the matrix in the other eye. Complementation produces a kind of noise burst, or an instantaneous binocular rivalry that is perceptible and that induces a potential. The shape of the evoked potential produced by the correlogram, however, is unlike the typical peak function obtained by other kinds of stimulation. Rather, the correlogram potential takes on an almost horizontal or rectangular appearance similar to a very substantial change in the DC recording level. In a footnote, the authors state that an investigation with infants by Braddick and Atkinson (in Julesz et al., 1980) found that a majority of infants, 3–9 months of age, showed potentials produced by the correlogram stimulus. The authors go on to suggest that the correlogram technique might be used to assess stereopsis in infants and nonhumans and other uncooperative subjects. Although the correlogram does require participation of both eyes, it is, of course, not equivalent to stereopsis, and the question naturally arises whether observers who can either perceive the perceptual effect of the correlogram or yield an evoked potential would necessarily possess stereopsis.

There are other binocular phenomena that observers without stereopsis possess. A case in point is binocular rivalry. Westendorf, Langston, Chambers, and Allegretti (1978) note that there are stereoblind observers who do experience binocular rivalry. Furthermore, Levi, Harwerth, and Smith (1979) present evidence that stereodeficient persons retain inhibitory binocular interactions as defined by interocular adaptation procedures that elevate thresholds. Indeed, an interesting and unresolved question is the extent to which specific binocular functions are available to observers who are stereodeficient. It would be of interest to determine the development of these binocular functions in infants and in human children. Perhaps, the response to a correlogram might occur before manifestation of stereopsis, as the binocular inter-action represented by correlogram processing would be a necessary precondition for the subsequent development of stereopsis. The same considerations probably would also apply to the development of bi-nocular rivalry. In that regard, it is worth noting that objective methods for investigating rivalry using optokinetic nystagmus are available (En-oksson, 1964; Fox, Todd, & Bettinger, 1975), and these methods could be used to investigate the ontogenetic development in infants and young children.

Turning to the conclusions that can be drawn from the investigations of stereopsis using the evoked potential method, it seems clear that unique potentials can be elicited by stereoscopic forms particularly when those forms are presented under conditions that eliminate the possibility of nonstereoscopic cues. The potentials seem to have a longer latency than their physical counterparts as well as a somewhat reduced am-plitude. A comprehensive parametric investigation of the effect of such stereoscopic variables as disparity magnitude, direction, and stimulus area has not yet been performed, although sufficient information has accrued to warrant the use of the evoked potential method as an ob-jective indicator of stereopsis. The practicality of the method, however, is restricted by the intrinsic limitations and problems involved in ob-taining artifact-free cortically evoked potentials. For example, the am-plification and signal averaging equipment is expensive and requires placement in an electrically noise-free environment. The attachment of the electrodes requires special preparation of the scalp and pretesting to assess the integrity of the attachments. Also, special preparations must be taken to insure that potentials are not contaminated by en-dogenous potentials such as the alpha wave or potentials associated with eye movements or with cognitive events such as the contingent negative variation, a DC shift. Solutions exist to all of these problems, but their resolution requires a considerable intellectual and economic commitment.

VII. STEREOPSIS IN INFANTS AND YOUNG CHILDREN

A major source of interest in the development of stereopsis in infants and young children arises naturally from a general desire for a deeper understanding of the ontogenesis of perceptual capacity. An acute and poignant motive for such interest arises from the need for a method for assessing the integrity of binocular vision at an early age to detect binocular anomalies that can lead to serious visual impairment.

Indeed, the bulk of the evidence for stereopsis in young children derives from efforts to develop clinical tests. Reinecke and Simons (1974) and Walraven (1975) devised tests based on the random-element stereogram principle suitable for children old enough to respond to verbal instructions. Romano, Romano, and Puklin (1975) investigated the development of stereoacuity in over 300 children using a standard clinical test (Titmus test) and found a gradual improvement in stereoacuity extending from 2–9 years of age. Cooper and Feldman (1978) developed operant training procedures in an effort to circumvent the problems of verbal communication with young children. The general conclusion from all of these studies is that stereopsis is certainly present in the youngest children that are capable of understanding the task. All studies have found that an increasing proportion of children pass the test as they grow older; this is probably due to the greater facility in test taking and in ease of understanding instructions. Since children with clear-cut binocular anomalies fail these tests, the results suggest that stereopsis is a good indicator of normal binocular function.

Evidence that stereopsis may be present in infants as young as 7 days of age can be found in a series of widely cited studies by Bower and colleagues (Bower, 1966, 1971, 1972; Bower, Broughton, & Moore, 1970). However, that evidence is now regarded with considerable skepticism for several reasons. First, the response indicator for stereopsis relied on the infant making a reaching response to a stereoscopic image in space. As Aslin and Dumais (1980) point out, however, the norms for accurate reaching by infants indicate that such behavior does not develop until around 4 months of age. Furthermore, White, Castle, and Held (1964) could find no directed or intentional reaching toward real objects until 4 months of age. Second, the method and procedures are not detailed, and efforts to find directed reaching under conditions presumably identical to those reported by Bower have been unsuccessful (Dodwell, Muir, & DeFranco, 1976; Ruff & Hulton, 1977). Also, the published exchange between Bower, Dunkeld, and Wishart (1979) and Dodwell et al., 1979, is instructive. Finally, other investigators who have used reaching by infants as an indicator of stereopsis find that it first occurs several months after birth. Gordon and Yonas (1976) used a shadow-casting device to present a stereoscopic contour and found directed reaching in infants 5–6 months of age. In a replication, Bechtoldt and Hutz (1979) obtained essentially the same results. Yonas, Oberg, and Norcia (1978) used a shadow-casting display to present a stimulus that appeared to be on a collision course with the infant's face. Infants 20 weeks old showed more reactions, such as blinking, fixation, and head withdrawal on those trials when the stimulus appeared to approach. These studies would seem to offer presumptive evidence that the infants possess stereopsis, although some question might be raised as to the feasibility of eliminating all nonstereoscopic cues with the shadow-casting technique.

Appel and Campos (1977) used a habituation–dishabituation paradigm to test for stereopsis in infants 8 weeks of age. In that paradigm, stimuli are repeatedly presented so that reflexive responses become habituated, then a stimulus parameter is changed and detection of it is revealed by a dishabituation of responses. The stimulus was a picture of a toy rabbit that could be presented either with or without a fixed crossed disparity. The critical stimulus change was a shift from no-disparity to disparity or from disparity to no-disparity. The infants who observed the shift from no-disparity to disparity exhibited reliable changes on several measures of dishabituation, while those exposed to the complementary change, disparity to no-disparity, did not. The authors suggest that the difference might be attributable to a difference in salience of the stimulus change, with the shift from no-disparity to disparity being more salient. They also pointed out that, while the response to the shift from no-disparity to disparity might reflect the operation of stereopsis, that conclusion is not unequivocal, as other potential cues inherent in the situation, such as diplopia induced by the shift to disparity, could have produced the change in the habituation indicators.

To avoid the problem of monocular cues, Atkinson and Braddick (1976) used photographs of random-element stereograms to assess stereopsis in four 8-week-old infants by the methods of preferential looking and the habituation–dishabituation paradigm. For the preferential looking phase, a stereoscopic square was randomly placed to the left or to the right of central fixation. The three measures of preference were the infant's first fixation, the duration of looking, and the observer's forced judgment of the square location. A change from no-disparity to disparity was used as the habituation procedure. One infant showed evidence of stereopsis, as defined by two of the visual preference measures and by the habituation responses. A second infant showed evidence only on the habituation responses, and the remaining two infants gave no consistent pattern of results. The authors concluded that the ability to detect disparity may be present in some 2-month-old infants but note that they have no evidence to suggest that the stereoscopic forms were actually seen in depth.

A new approach to the testing of stereopsis in infants has been described by Fox et al., 1980. It combines the dynamic random-element stereogram generator described earlier and a modified form of the forced-choice preferential looking technique. The key feature of the approach involves presenting an infant with a moving stereoscopic form that can attract attention. As discussed earlier, the stereogram generation system permits stereoscopic forms to be moved about in x, y, and z coordinates without introducing monocular cues. Originally, Fox and colleagues had planned to test stereopsis by attempting to induce optokinetic nystagmus using the methods described by Fox *et al.* (1978) with nystagmus being recorded using the electro-oculogram method. They realized, though, that the same objectives could be reached by the technically simpler approach afforded by a modified version of the forced-choice preferential looking technique. The modification consists of having a single stereoscopic form located in the center of a display and then moving it to the left or to the right on a random basis. The task of the observer is to decide, on the basis of information gleaned from observing the infant, the direction, left or right, taken by the form on any given trial. The logic and attendant advantages of the conventional forced-choice preferential technique (see Section III) apply equally to this modification.

Many elements of the testing situation used by Fox *et al.* (1980) are illustrated in Figure 12.7. The stereogram is presented as an anaglyph on a projection television screen operating in the rear-screen projection mode. The infant is seated on the lap of the parent in front of the screen while the concealed observer views the infant from beneath the screen and makes judgments as to the position of the stereoscopic form. A complete description of the procedure can be found in Fox *et al.* (1980). In the first experiment, three groups of infants at $2\frac{1}{2}$, $3\frac{1}{2}$, and $4\frac{1}{2}$ months of age were tested. The performance of the youngest group did not differ from chance. Explanations of their performance on the grounds of poor acuity and labile attention were rejected as the dot size of the stereogram clearly exceeded the acuity threshold of 2-month-old infants and they could readily attend to and visually follow a physical form which was identical in configuration to the stereoscopic form. The performance of the two older groups was significantly better than chance. Because the dynamic random-element stereogram precludes the presence of nonstereoscopic cues, the significant performance was attributed to the emergence of stereopsis in these infants.

Yet, even though a dynamic random-element stereogram essentially eliminates nonstereoscopic cues, a skeptic might suggest that somehow the infants were reacting to the form but not perceiving it in depth. To test that conjecture, a group of older infants were tested with several disparities including two so great as to preclude stereopsis in adult observers. If the infants were reacting to a form independent of depth magnitude, their performance on these large disparities should be the same as their performance on smaller disparities. If they were perceiving the stimulus in depth, their performance on the largest disparities should decline. The latter result was obtained, suggesting that the infants were indeed perceiving the form in depth. An additional control for the operation of nonstereoscopic cues that was carried out but not reported in the Fox *et al.* paper, involved testing the ability of experienced psychophysical observers to detect the position of the stereoscopic form while wearing filters of the same color before both eyes under psychophysical conditions that would optimize detection (i.e., two-choice, forced-choice responding with feedback). Even after extended exposures, observers could perform no better than chance. This, of course, is consistent with the conclusion that the infants' performance was based upon stereopsis and nothing else.

In a second experiment, a group of nine infants initially ranging in age from $2\frac{1}{2}$–$3\frac{1}{2}$ months were tested weekly using two crossed disparity values and one uncrossed disparity value. The group performance did not become significantly different from chance until $5\frac{1}{2}$–6 months of age, although stereopsis was clearly present in four individual infants at earlier ages. There were no differences in performance across the three disparity conditions.

Shea and Fox (1980) undertook a longitudinal investigation of 19 infants starting at 3 months of age who were tested weekly. In addition to testing for stereopsis, the development of convergence was also assessed using the technique described by Aslin (1977). In that procedure, the ability of an infant to follow the forward and backward motions of a thin, vertical, self-luminous rod with convergence eye movements is assessed by an observer who makes a dichotomous judgment of convergence or its absence on each of a series of rod presentations. Stereopsis became evident at $3\frac{1}{2}$–4 months of age and convergence accuracy closely paralleled this development. Whereas both convergence and stereopsis were strongly correlated with age, the onset of one did not predict the onset of the other.

In several cross-sectional studies involving infants from 3 to 7 months of age, Shea (1980) measured sensitivity to crossed and uncrossed disparity at several disparity values. The collective result was that the onset of stereopsis occurs at $3\frac{1}{2}$–4 months of age, and the responses were equivalent for all disparity magnitudes and both directions (crossed and uncrossed).

The projection television system used by Fox *et al.* and shown in Figure 12.7 is a permanent installation that limits testing to the laboratory. To provide a portable testing system that could be used for field

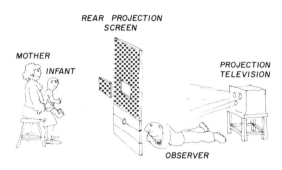

Fig. 12.7 The testing arrangement used by Fox *et al.*, 1980.

and clinical testing, Shea, Fox, Aslin, and Dumais (1980) described a system that uses a table model color television receiver as a display device. Several studies indicate that this system gives results comparable to the projection display system. Furthermore, it appears to offer some advantages; infants are easier to observe and the normal room illumination now possible maintains the infants' general arousal level.

At present, over 200 infants have been tested under several conditions with the two display systems. Approximately 142 infants of varying ages were administered a sufficient number of trials so that their individual performances could be tested for statistical significance. The percentage of infants yielding statistically significant performance as age increases is shown in Figure 12.8. The number of infants representing each age interval is unequal and, in large part, is responsible for the minor fluctuations in the generally increasing function. The median age of onset is 127 days. It now seems that the onset of stereopsis at $5\frac{1}{2}$ months as seen in the longitudinal study reported by Fox *et al.* (1980) is due to sampling variation. Overall, the data support the conclusion that steropsis does not become functional in the majority of infants until about 4 months of age.

Emergence at this age is consistent with the hypothesis that, whereas the basic structures for stereopsis may be present at birth, a postnatal period of maturation is required for the refined growth of intrinsic neural structures and for their calibration with other systems. The parallel development of convergence and stereopsis may reflect the need for these systems to join forces before stereopsis can become functional. On that point, the research on depth constancy (reviewed by Ono & Comerford, 1977) indicates that, at least for near distances, convergence provides the absolute distance information needed for the constancy that renders stereoscopic depth judgments veridical.

Further investigation of the development of stereopsis using the ap-

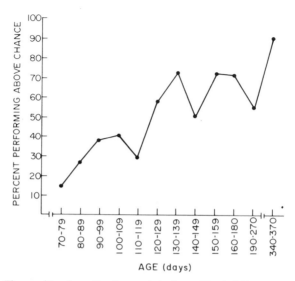

Fig. 12.8 The combined results of several studies at Vanderbilt on stereopsis in infants using the general approach of Fox *et al.*, 1980.

proach of Fox *at al.* may take two separate yet related lines of inquiry. One line would involve further refinement of the testing method to enhance its effectiveness as a screening and clinical assessment procedure. Although the time now required for testing is only about 5–15 minutes, further reductions could probably be made. It is apparent to observers of infants who are undergoing testing that a number of failures to discriminate are due to inattention to the stereoscopic form, but these trials are not deleted because of the conservative scoring procedures. Such trials could be minimized by increasing the salience of the stereoscopic stimulus. One tactic that appears promising along these lines is presentation of a "looming" stimulus that appears to jump forward in depth toward the infant while, at the same time, greatly expanding in size. Due to fusional limits, the looming stimulus can never appear so close that an avoidance or ducking response is elicited. Rather, informal observation suggests that the looming stimulus tends to elicit more attentive reactions. Further efforts to enhance the intrinsic salience of the stimuli could involve, for example, the presentation of the outline of a human face that appears to move and to continually change expression. Such stimuli may elicit responses so clear-cut that only a few exposures would be sufficient to confirm the presence of stereopsis.

The second line of inquiry would be concerned with tracing the development of stereoscopic capacities in infants and children. While it is now clear that infants can detect, and presumably perceive, a stereoscopic shape formed from a random-element stereogram, it is unlikely that they possess the full range of capacities present in adults, as, for example, the ability to resolve a complex stereogram containing several depth planes. The question that naturally arises is, what are the relevant dimensions that define developmental changes in the ability to process stereoscopic information? In the case of classic stereograms composed of two or three physical contours (local stereopsis), the obvious dimension to be investigated is the change in the minimal disparity threshold (i.e., stereoacuity). The exquisite sensitivity of adult observers to small disparities, for example, on the order of 2–10 arc sec, has always attracted considerable interest, but as Westheimer (1979) makes clear, this sensitivity or hyperacuity is not an exclusive property of stereopsis, but reflects a more fundamental capacity of the brain for resolving signals that have minute differences in space and time.

In random-element stereograms, stereoscopic thresholds on the order of seconds of arc have been obtained (Julesz, 1971; Schumer & Ganz, 1979). Yet stereoacuity has not been considered one of the more central issues in the research on global stereopsis. Efforts have centered on understanding how the combination of the patterns in each eye yields a stable stereoscopic form. It is known from work with adults that the perceptibility of the stereoscopic form depends on such variables as number of elements in the stereogram and their degree of binocular correlation. Furthermore, by varying the disparity and spatial frequency in stereoscopic grating patterns, a modulation transfer function for the "cyclopean" retina has been obtained, together with evidence that it is composed of several independent spatial frequency channels (e.g., Tyler, 1974, 1975; Schumer & Ganz, 1979).

These observations would appear to be promising lines to pursue in the investigation of the development of stereopsis. For instance, the tolerance for a reduction in binocular correlation may increase with age. Similarly, tuning of the stereoscopic spatial frequency channels may become sharper, not unlike the increase in visual resolution with age. Although these dimensions of stereopsis would seem to be ones likely to change with age, they by no means exhaust the domain of interesting questions that can be raised about the development of stereopsis and its relationship to other perceptual capacities.

The development of steroacuity in classic line stereograms has been examined by Held, Birch, and Gwiazda (1980), who tested 15 infants of about 10 weeks of age repeatedly for 10 weeks. The stereoscopic display consisted of three black bars seen against a white background. A polarizing system presented the bars dichoptically with varying amounts of disparity, so two of the bars appeared in depth. This display was paired with an identical three-bar display without disparity. Both displays were presented on every trial with their right–left positions randomly interchanged, and an observer, unaware of position, judged which elicited the greater visual preference. At 16 weeks of age, infants initially exhibited a preference for the largest tested disparity (58 min). After 4 weeks of testing using a staircase procedure to introduce smaller disparities and to determine thresholds, the threshold had decreased to 1 min, the smallest disparity available for testing. Three control conditions were run on subsets of the infants. One condition removed horizontal disparity by rotating the stereogram 90 deg. The other two tested for the salience of monocular cues due to incomplete polarization and irregular spacing of the contours. The results from all three conditions indicated that the infants were not attracted by these cues, leading the authors to conclude that the visual preference was attributable to stereopsis.

There were, of course, other potential nonstereoscopic cues present, but it is not clear why they would elicit a visual preference. For instance, because of the linear polarization system, head rotations of the infants would produce a variable change in the brightness of the stereogram. Whereas it is plain why the hungry monkeys used by Cowey *et al.* (1975) would use such a cue, it is not obvious why it would attract contented infants. The stereogram could have induced diplopia, perhaps intermittently, at least for some disparities, as Appel and Campos (1977) conjecture may have occurred in their experiments, but this would more likely elicit aversions rather than preference. Furthermore, the evidence that stereopsis first appears at 4 months is consistent with the results of Fox *et al.* (1980). Presumably, if a nonstereoscopic cue had been present, younger infants would have been attracted to it.

Rather than demonstrating the presence of stereopsis, the more remarkable feature of the Birch *et al.* results is the extremely rapid increase in stereoacuity shown by almost all of the infants—from 58 min to 1 min in 4 weeks. Comparable increases in visual acuity occur much more slowly over many months. Furthermore, the 1 min threshold at 5 months is artificially bounded because stimuli with smaller disparities were not available, so possibly the true threshold for the 5-month-old infants would be even lower.

The only other investigations of the development of stereoacuity are those using clinical tests for stereopsis, and those studies suggest a much more gradual increase in stereoacuity. For example, Romano *et al.* (1975) measured stereoacuity in 321 children from 1½–13 years of age using the Titmus stereo test and report a gradual improvement in

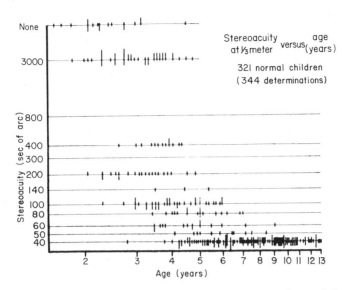

Fig. 12.9 The scatter plot obtained by Romano *et al.* (1975), who used the Titmus test to assess the development of stereopsis in children.

stereoacuity between the ages of 2 and 9 years. By age 9, almost all children could detect the smallest disparity (40 sec) in the test. In Fig. 12.9, the scatterplot from their study is given. However, as Cooper and Feldman (1978) point out, the gradual increase in stereoacuity as defined by passing the various clinical tests, is probably due in large part to nonperceptual factors such as an increase in communication skills and general test-taking abilities. In addition, clinical tests are generally scored on a dichotomous pass–fail basis to determine if stereopsis is present rather than attempting to reach a true threshold.

Nevertheless, some very young children seem to have quite keen stereoacuity. Note in Fig. 12.9 that one child, 2 years and 10 months of age, in the Romano *et al.* study reached the 40 sec disparity level. They report that, in the age range of 3–4½ years of age, 13 of 87 (15%) achieved 40 sec. In comparing their data with other developmental studies that used the Titmus test, Romano *et al.* note that in a study by Amigo (1973), only 2 of 100 children in the same age range (3½–5 years of age) reached the 40 sec disparity level, whereas an investigation by Tatsumi and Tahira (1972) found 11 of 78 (14%) children in the 3½–5-year range reached the 40 sec level. As 40 sec is the smallest disparity that can be assessed by the Titmus test, the true stereoacuity threshold of these children is probably lower. These data, together with those of Birch *et al.* (1980) suggest that at least some infants and young children may well have stereoacuity values comparable to those found in adults.

With respect to the time of onset of stereopsis, the evoked potential response to the correlogram stimulus described by Julesz *et al.* (1980) is relevant because they report a study by Atkinson and Braddick, where the correlogram produced a response in the majority of infants tested at ages 3–9 months. Although, as pointed out earlier, the correlogram response is not an indicator of stereopsis, but of binocular interaction that presumably is a precondition for the emergence of stereopsis, its appearance at 3 months is consistent with the psychophysical data obtained by Fox and colleagues as well as that of Birch *et al.*, all of which suggest that stereopsis is emerging within this time period.

The hypothesis that stereopsis appears postnatally in human infants at about 4 months of age rather than being present at birth now seems reasonably well supported. The onset at 4 months is not inconsistent (see Aslin & Dumais, 1980, for a review of the various lines of evidence) with the concept of a "sensitive period" (see Chapter 2 by Aslin in this volume) during which the human binocular system is extremely vulnerable to discordant stimulation that disrupts its normal harmony.

VIII. CONCLUSIONS

Viewed against the complete spectrum of research on stereopsis, the last 10 years can only be characterized as a period of explosive growth. The formidable obstacles to expanding the investigation beyond the domain of competent adult humans have been surmounted and methods are now available for investigating stereopsis in many classes of animals, as well as in infants and very young children. As with many issues in science, when there is general agreement about the question to be posed and on the form of a satisfactory answer, the solutions turn more upon technological advances than on radical omnibus theoretical reformulations. That is certainly the case here. To take but one example, the development of the random-element stereogram and its attendant advantages could not have been exploited without appropriate advances in computer technology.

Although satisfactory methods of testing are now available, their quite recent appearance has permitted only a small number of applications. However, it is now clear that there is satisfactory behavioral evidence for stereopsis in the adult monkey, cat, and falcon. It is also gratifying that, in all instances, the behavioral evidence is quite consistent with the anatomical and electrophysiological evidence, both of which imply that a behavioral capacity for stereopsis should be present in these animals. Whether such predictions from neurophysiological data will be invariably confirmed by the ultimate judgment that behavioral tests confer is an interesting question for the future. Its strongest test is likely to occur during the inquiry into the generality of stereopsis among vertebrates representing diverse lines of descent. The presence of a behavioral capacity for stereopsis in an animal that apparently lacks correlative neural mechanisms would be a discovery that could yield fundamental insight into the relationship between structure and function.

A second question that can now be pursued concerns the ontogenetic development of stereopsis in animals raised both in normal environments and in restricted ones known to induce anatomical and electrophysiological anomalies within the binocular visual system. The monkey and cat, for which elaborate paradigms for developmental investigation already exist, are prime candidates for inquiries into the development of stereopsis. In the rhesus monkey, it is known that, except for a rate parameter, visual acuity follows the same temporal pattern as in humans, and it would be interesting to know if stereopsis also fits that pattern (see Chapter 7 by Boothe in this volume). In the cat, it is known that animals reared in a normal environment possess stereopsis, whereas those reared under conditions of alternating monocular occlusion applied daily do not. Higher frequencies of alternation on a time scale of minutes or even seconds may result in more subtle behavioral deficits in stereopsis.

A similar inquiry into the ontogenesis of stereopsis in humans is now possible for infants with normal binocular visual systems and for those with binocular anomalies such as strabismus. Moreover, the effectiveness of treatment of those anomalies can be assessed. At the other end of the life span, the possible decline of binocular function during senescence can be examined by the same methods applicable to infants.

It seems reasonable to anticipate that information on all of these questions will accrue during the next 10 years. One outcome of research on stereopsis and related binocular phenomena, such as rivalry and fusion, is that it yields data that, at once, addresses several issues. It contributes directly, of course, to a deeper understanding of binocular phenomena, and, as the work on global stereopsis makes clear, more general perceptual processes involving the perception and classification of pattern and texture can also be explicated. At the same time, much of the information is directly relevant to the amelioration of visual disorders that produce severe impairment. Such immediate multiple benefits are not present in all research areas. Perhaps the realization of this explains why binocular vision has captured the research interest of workers from several disciplines.

ACKNOWLEDGMENTS

The writing of this chapter was aided by a grant from the National Eye Institute (EY-00590). The comments and suggestions offered by Richard Aslin, Randy Blake, A. B. Bonds, Robert Cormack, Maureen Powers, and Sandra Shea are gratefully acknowledged. Ellie Francis-Jaffe, Kathy Kymbal, and Cynthia McDaniel contributed much to the preparation of the final version.

REFERENCES

Amigo, G. Preschool vision study. *British Journal of Ophthalmology*, 1973, **57**, 125.

Appel, M. A., & Campos, J. J. Binocular disparity as a discriminable stimulus parameter for young infants. *Journal of Experimental Child Psychology*, 1977, **23**, 47–56.

Aslin, R. N. Development of binocular fixation in human infants. *Journal of Experimental Child Psychology*, 1977, **23**, 133–150.

Aslin, R. N., & Dumais, S. T. Binocular vision in infants: A review and a theoretical framework. *Advances in child development and behavior* (Vol. 15). New York: Academic Press, 1980.

Atkinson, J., & Braddick, O. Stereoscopic discrimination in infants. *Perception*, 1976, **5**, 29–38.

Becholdt, H. P., & Hutz, C. S. Stereopsis in young infants and stereopsis in an infant with congenital esotropia. *Journal of Pediatric Ophthalmology*, 1979, **16**, 49–54.

Berkley, M. A. Visual discrimination in the cat. In W. C. Stebbins (Ed.), *Animal psychophysics: the design and conduct of sensory experiments*. New York: Appleton-Century-Crofts, 1970.

Bishop, P. O., & Henry, G. H. Spatial vision. *Annual review of psychology*, 1971, **22**, 119–160.

Blackwell, H. R. Psychophysical thresholds: experimental studies of methods of measurement. *Engineering research bulletin 36*. Ann Arbor: University of Michigan, 1953.

Blake, R., & Hirsch, H. V. B. Deficits in binocular depth perception in cats after alternating monocular deprivation. *Science*, 1975, **190**, 114–116.

Blasdel, G. G., & Pettigrew, J. D. Degree of interocular synchrony required for maintenance of binocularity in kitten's visual cortex. *Journal of Neurophysiology*, 1979, **42**, 1692–1710.

Bough, E. W. Stereoscopic vision in macaque monkey: A behavioural demonstration. *Nature*, 1970, **225**, 42–44.

Bouldin, D. W. Visual evoked cortical potentials elicited by dynamic random-dot stereograms. (Doctoral dissertation, Vanderbilt University, 1975). *Dissertation Abstracts International*, 1976, **36**, 3516B. (University Microfilms No. 76–92, 172).

Bouldin, D. W., Bourne, J. R., & Fox, R. Lambda waves elicited by cyclopean contour movement. Paper presented at the Association for Research in Vision and Ophthalmology, Sarasota, Florida, May, 1975.

Bower, T.G.R. Slant perception and shape constancy in infants. *Science*, 1966, **151**, 832–834.

Bower, T.G.R. The object in the world of the infant. *Scientific American*, 1971, **225**, 30–38.

Bower, T.G.R. Object perception in infants. *Perception*, 1972, **1**, 15–30.

Bower, T.G.R., Broughton, J. M., & Moore, M. K. Demonstration of intention in the reaching behavior of neonate humans. *Nature*, 1970, **228**, 679–680.

Bower, T.G.R., Dunkeld, J., & Wishart, J. G. Infant perception of visually presented objects. *Science*, 1979, **203**, 1137–1138.

Brindley, G. S. *Physiology of the retina and the visual pathway*. London: Edward Arnold, 1960.

Burr, D. C., & Ross, J. How does binocular delay give information about depth? *Vision Research*, 1979, **19**, 523–532.

Burt, P., & Julesz, B. Extended Panum's area for dynamic random-dot stereograms. Paper presented at the Association for Research in Vision and Ophthalmology, Sarasota, Florida, May, 1979.

Caelli, T., & Julesz, B. On perceptual analyzers underlying visual texture discrimination: Part I. *Biological Cybernetics*, 1978, **28**, 167–175.

Cogan, A. I. The relationship between the apparent vertical and the vertical horopter. *Vision Research*, 1979, **19**, 655–666.

Collett, T. Stereopsis in toads. *Nature*, 1977, **267**, 349–351.

Cooper, J., & Feldman, J. Operant conditioning and assessment of stereopsis in young children. *American Journal of Optometry and Physiological optics*, 1978, **55**, 532–542.

Cowey, A., Parkinson, A. M., & Warnick, L. Global stereopsis in rhesus monkeys. *Quarterly Journal of Experimental Psychology*, 1975, **27**, 93–109.

deWeert, C.M.M. Colour contours and stereopsis. *Vision Research*, 1979, **19**, 555–564.

Dodwell, P. C., Muir, D., & DiFranco, D. Responses of infants to visually presented objects. *Science*, 1976, **194**, 209–211.

Dodwell, P. C., Muir, D., & DiFranco, D. Infant perception of visually presented objects. *Science*, 1979, **203**, 1138–1139.

Duff, T. A., & Ebbesson, S.O.E. Electrophysiological identification of a visual area in shark telencephalon. *Science*, 1973, **182**, 492–494.

Enoksson, P. *An optokinetic test of ocular dominance*. Goteborg, Sweden: Elanders Boktryckeri Aktiebolas, 1964.

Estes, W. K., and Skinner, B. F. Some quantitative properties of anxiety. *Journal of Experimental Psychology*, 1941, **29**, 390–400.

Fantz, R. L. Pattern discrimination and selective attention as determinants of perceptual development from birth. In A. H. Kidd & J. L. Rivoire (Eds.), *Perceptual development in children*. New York: International University Press, 1966.

Fantz, R. L., Fagen, J. F., & Miranda, S. B. Early visual selectivity as a function of pattern variables, previous exposure, age from birth and conception, and expected cognitive deficit. In L. B. Cohen & P. Salapatek (Eds.), *Infant perception: From sensation to cognition I. Basic visual processes*. New York: Academic Press, 1975.

Fender, D., Julesz, B. Extension of Panum's fusional area in binocularly stabilized vision. *Journal of the Optical Society of America*, 1967, **57**, 819–830.

Fiorentini, A., & Maffei, L. Electrophysiological evidence for binocular disparity detectors in the human visual system. *Science*, 1970, **169**, 208–209.

Foley, J. M. The size–distance relation and intrinsic geometry of visual space: Implications for processing. *Vision Research*, 1972, **12**, 323–332.

Fox, R. Binocularity and stereopsis in the evolution of vertebrate vision. In S. J. Cool & E. L. Smith, III (Eds.), *Frontiers in visual science*. New York: Springer-Verlag, 1977.

Fox, R., Aslin, R. N., Shea, S. L., & Dumais, S. T. Stereopsis in infants. *Science*, 1980, **207**, 323–324.

Fox, R., & Blake, R. R. Stereoscopic vision in the cat. *Nature*, 1971, **233**, 55–56.

Fox, R., Lehmkuhle, S. W., & Bush, R. C. Stereopsis in the falcon. *Science*, 1977, **197**, 79–81.

Fox, R., Lehmkuhle, S. W., & Leguire, L. E. Stereoscopic contours induce optokinetic nystagmus. *Vision Research*, 1978, **18**, 1189–1192.

Fox, R., Lehmkuhle, S. W., & Shea, S. L. Iconic memory in stereo space: Seeing without storing. Paper presented at the Psychonomic Society, Washington, D.C., November, 1977.

Fox, R., Todd, S., & Bettinger, L. A. Optokinetic nystagmus as an objective indicator of binocular rivalry. *Vision Research*, 1975, **15**, 849–853.

Ganz, L., & Schumer, R. A. Independent stereoscopic channels for the spatial frequency of disparity modulation. Paper presented at the Association for Research in Vision and Ophthalmology, Sarasota, Florida, May, 1979.

Gordon, F. R., & Yonas, A. Sensitivity to binocular depth information in infants. *Journal of Experimental Child Psychology*, 1976, **22**, 413–422.

Graham, C. H. (Ed.). *Vision and visual perception*. New York: Wiley, 1965.

Granda, A. M., & Hayes, W. N. (Eds.), Neural mechanisms in animal behavior I. Turtle. *Brain, Behavior and Evolution*, 1972, **5** (2–3), 89–272.

Green, D. M., & Swets, J. A. *Signal detection theory and psychophysics*. New York: Wiley, 1966.

Gregory, R. L. Stereoscopic shadow images. *Nature*, 1964, **203**, 1407–1408.

Hall, W. C. Visual pathways to the telencephalon in reptiles and mammals. *Brain, Behavior and Evolution*, 1972, **5**, 95–143.

Harwerth, R. S., & Boltz, R. L. Behavioral measures of stereopsis in monkeys using random-dot stereograms. *Physiology and Behavior*, 1979, **22**, 229–234. (a)

Harwerth, R. S., & Boltz, R. L. Stereopsis in monkeys using random-dot stereograms: The effect of viewing duration. *Vision Research*, 1979, **19**, 985–991. (b)

Helmholtz, H. Von. [Treatise on physiological optics (Vol. 3)] (J.P.C. Southall, Ed. and trans.). New York: Dover, 1962 (originally published, 1925).

Ingle, D. Two visual systems in the frog. *Science*, 1973, **181**, 1053–1055.

Julesz, B. Binocular depth perception of computer generated patterns. *Bell System Technical Journal*, 1960, **39**, 1125–1162.

Julesz, B. Binocular depth perception without familiarity cues. *Science*, 1964, **145**, 356–362.

Julesz, B. *Foundations of cyclopean perception*. Chicago: University of Chicago Press, 1971.

Julesz, B. Global stereopsis: Cooperative phenomena in stereoscopic depth perception. In R. Held, H. W. Leibowitz, & H. L. Teuber (Eds.), *Handbook of sensory physiology VIII. Perception*. New York: Springer-Verlag, 1978.

Julesz, B., Breitmeyer, B., & Kropfl, W. Binocular-disparity-dependent upper–lower hemifield anisotropy and left–right hemifield isotropy as revealed by dynamic random-dot stereograms. *Perception*, 1976, **5**, 129–141.

Julesz, B., & Chang, J. J. Interaction between pools of binocular disparity detectors tuned to different disparities. *Biological Cybernetics*, 1976, **22**, 107–119.

Julesz, B., Kropfl, W., & Petrig, B. Large evoked potentials to dynamic random-dot correlograms and stereograms permit quick determination of stereopsis. *Proceedings of the National Academy of Science*, 1980, **77**, 4, 2348–2351.

Julesz, B., Petrig, B., & Buttner, U. Fast determination of stereopsis in rhesus monkey using dynamic random-dot stereograms. *Journal of the Optical Society of America*, 1976, **66**, 1090.

Karten, H. J., Hodos, W., Nauta, W.J.H., & Revzin, A. M. Neural connections of the "visual Wulst" of the avian telencephalon. Experimental studies in the pigeon *(Columba livia)* and owl *(Speotyto cunicularia). Journal of Comparative Neurology,* 1973, **150,** 253–278.

Kaufman, L. A not entirely new theory of stereopsis. Paper presented at the United States–Japan Cooperative Science Program seminar on visual space and motion, Honolulu, 1973.

Lashley, K. F. The mechanism of vision I. A method for the rapid analysis of pattern vision in the rat. *Journal of Genetic Psychology,* 1930, **37,** 453–460.

Lee, D. N. Theory of the stereoscopic shadow caster: An instrument for the study of binocular kinetic space perception. *Vision Research,* 1969, **9,** 145–156.

LeGros Clark, W. E. *Antecedents of man.* Edinburgh: Edinburgh University Press, 1959.

Lehmann, D., & Julesz, B. Lateral cortical potentials evoked in humans by dynamic random-dot stereograms. *Vision Research,* 1978, **18,** 1265–1272.

Lehmkuhle, S., Casagrande, V. A., & Fox, R. Bilateral retino–Wulst projections in falcon revealed by transneuronal transport of 3-H proline. Paper presented at the Society for Neuroscience, Los Angeles, October, 1977.

Lehmkuhle, S., & Fox, R. Effect of depth separation on metacontrast masking. *Journal of Experimental Psychology: Human Perception and Performance,* 1980, **6,** 605–621.

Lehmkuhle, S. W., & Fox, R. Global stereopsis in the cat. Paper presented at the Association for Research in Vision and Ophthalmology, Sarasota, Florida, May, 1977.

Levi, D. M., Harwerth, R. S., & Smith, E. L. Humans deprived of normal binocular vision have binocular interactions tuned to size and orientation. *Science,* 1979, **206,** 852–854.

Linksz, A. *Physiology of the eye: Vision* (Vol. 2). New York: Grune & Stratton, 1952.

Marr, D., & Poggio, T. A computational theory of human stereo vision. *Proceedings of the Royal Society of London, Biology,* 1979, **204,** 301–328.

Mayhew, J.E.W., & Frisby, J. P. The computation of binocular edges. *Perception,* 1980, **9**(1), 69–86.

Mitchell, D. E., Giffen, F., & Timney, B. A behavioral technique for the rapid assessment of the visual capabilities of kittens. *Perception,* 1977, **6,** 181–193.

Mitchell, D. E., Giffen, F., Wilkerson, F., Anderson, P., & Smith, M. L. Visual resolution in young kittens. *Vision Research,* 1976, **16,** 363–366.

Mitchell, D. E., & O'Hagan, S. Accuracy of stereoscopic localization of small line segments that differ in size or orientation for the two eyes. *Vision Research,* 1972, **12,** 437–454.

Nakayama, K., Tyler, C. W., & Appleman, J. A new angle on the vertical horopter. Paper presented at the Association for Research in Vision and Ophthalmology, Sarasota, Florida, May, 1977.

Ogle, K. N. Theory of stereoscopic vision. In S. Koch (Ed.), *Psychology: A study of a science* (Vol. 1). New York: McGraw-Hill, 1959.

Ogle, K. N. The optical space sense. In H. Davson (Ed.), *The eye* (Vol. 4). New York: Academic Press, 1962.

Ono, H., & Comerford, J. Stereoscopic depth constancy. In W. Epstein (Ed.), *Stability and constancy in visual perception: Mechanisms and processes.* New York: Wiley, 1977.

Packwood, J., & Gordon, B. Stereopsis in normal domestic cat, Siamese cat, and cat raised with alternating monocular occlusion. *Journal of Neurophysiology,* 1975, **38,** 1485–1499.

Peeples, D. R., & Teller, D. Y. Color vision and brightness discrimination in 2-month-old infants. *Science,* 1975, **189,** 1102–1103.

Pettigrew, J. D. Coevolution of nocturnal vision and frontally placed eyes? Paper presented at the Meeting of the Optical Society of America, Sarasota, Florida, May, 1980.

Pettigrew, J. D., & Konishi, M. Neurons selective for orientation and binocular disparity in the visual Wulst of the barn owl (Tyto alba). Science, 1976, 193, 675–678.

Pettigrew, J. D., Nikara, T., & Bishop, P. O. Binocular interaction of single units in cat striate cortex: Simultaneous stimulation by single moving slits with receptive fields in correspondence. Experimental Brain Research, 1968, 6, 391–410.

Polyak, S. The vertebrate visual system. Chicago: University of Chicago Press, 1957.

Ramon Y Cajal, S. Die struktur des chiasma opticum oebst einer allgemenen theorie der kreuzung der nervenbabren. Leipzig. J. A. Barth, 1899.

Rawlings, S. C., & Yates, J. T. Visual evoked potentials from high-density checkerboard depth-reversal stereograms. Paper presented at the Association for Research in Vision and Ophthalmology, Sarasota, Florida, May, 1979.

Regan, D., & Spekreijse, H. Electrophysiological correlates of binocular depth perception in man. Nature, 1970, 225, 92–94.

Reinecke, R., & Simmons, K. A new stereoscopic test for amblyopia screening. American Journal of Ophthalmology, 1974, 78, 714–721.

Richards, W. Stereopsis with and without monocular contours. Vision Research, 1977, 17, 967–969.

Romano, P. E., Romano, J. A., & Puklin, J. E. Stereoacuity development in children with normal binocular single vision. American Journal of Ophthalmology, 1975, 79, 966–971.

Ross, J., & Hogben, J. H. Short-term memory in stereopsis. Vision Research, 1974, 14, 1195–1201.

Ruff, H. A., & Hulton, A. Is there directed reaching in the human neonate? Developmental Psychology, 1977, 14, 425–426.

Sarmiento, R. F. The stereoacuity of macaque monkey. Vision Research, 1975, 15, 493–498.

Schumer, R., & Ganz, L. Independent channels for different extents of spatial pooling. Vision Research, 1979, 19, 1303–1304.

Shea, S. L. Stereopsis in human infants: A developmental and clinical investigation. Unpublished doctoral dissertation, Vanderbilt University, 1980.

Shea, S. L., & Fox, R. Development of stereopsis in human infants. Paper presented at Meeting of Optical Society of America, Sarasota, Florida, May, 1980.

Shea, S. L., Fox, R., Aslin, R. N., & Dumais, S. T. Assessment of stereopsis in human infants. Investigative Ophthalmology, 1980, 19, 1400–1404.

Shetty, S. S., Brodersen, A. J., & Fox, R. Generation of random-element stereograms in real time. Behavior Research Methods and Instrumentation, 1979, 11, 485–490.

Smith, J. Conditioned suppression as an animal psychophysical technique. In W. C. Stebbins (Ed.), Animal psychophysics: The design and conduct of sensory experiments. New York: Appleton-Century-Crofts, 1970.

Staller, J. D., Lappin, J. S., & Fox, R. Stimulus uncertainty does not impair stereopsis. Perception & Psychophysics, 1980, 27, 361–367.

Stebbins, W. C. (Ed.). Animal psychophysics: The design and conduct of sensory experiments. New York: Appleton-Century-Crofts, 1970.

Sternberg, S. The discovery of processing stages: Extensions of Donders' method. In W. G. Koster (Ed.), Attention and performance II. Acta Psychologia, 1969, 30, 276–315.

Tatsumi, S., & Tahira, K. Study on the stereotest (Titmus). Eolia Ophthalmology of Japan, 1972, 23, 620.

Teller, D. Y. The forced-choice preferential looking procedure: A psychophysical technique for use with human infants. Infancy Behavior and Development, 1979, 2, 135–153.

Tyler, C. W. Depth perception in disparity gratings. *Nature,* 1974, **251,** 140–142.

Tyler, C. W. Stereoscopic tilt and size aftereffects. *Perception,* 1975, **4,** 187–192.

Tyler, C. W., & Julesz, B. On the depth of the cyclopean retina. *Experimental Brain Research,* 1980, **40,** 196–202.

Uttal, W. R., Fitzgerald, J., & Eskin, T. E. Parameters of tachistoscopic stereopsis. *Vision Research,* 1975, **15,** 705–712.

Walk, R. D., & Gibson, E. J. A comparative and analytical study of visual depth perception. *Psychological Monographs,* 1961, **75**(15, Whole no. 519).

Walraven, J. Amblyopia screening with random-dot stereograms. *American Journal of Ophthalmology,* 1975, **80,** 893–899.

Westendorf, D. H., Langston, A., Chambers, D., & Allegretti, C. Binocular detection by normal and stereoblind observers. *Perception & Psychophysics,* 1978, **24,** 209–214.

Westheimer, G. Spatial frequency and light-spread descriptions of visual acuity and hyperacuity. *Journal of the Optical Society of America,* 1977, **67,** 207–212.

Westheimer, G. The spatial sense of the eye. *Investigative Ophthalmology and Visual Science,* 1979, **18**(9), 893–912.

Westheimer, G., & Mitchell, D. E. The sensory stimulus disjunctive eye movements. *Vision Research,* 1969, **9,** 749–755.

Wheatstone, C. Contributions to the physiology of vision—part the first. On some remarkable and hitherto unobserved phenomena of binocular vision. *Philosophical Transactions of the Royal Society of London,* 1838, **128,** 371–394.

White, B. L., Castle, R., & Held, R. Observations on the development of visually directed reaching. *Child Development,* 1964, **35,** 349–365.

Woodworth, R. S. *Experimental psychology.* New York: Holt, 1938.

Yonas, A., Oberg, C., & Norcia, A. Development of sensitivity to binocular information for the approach of an object. *Developmental Psychology,* 1978, **14,** 147–152.

Index